ISBN 978-0-483-84580-0
PIBN 10243435

DISSERTATIONS,

John Ginty

CHRONOLOGICAL,

HISTORICAL, AND CRITICAL,

ON ALL THE BOOKS OF THE OLD TESTAMENT;

THROUGH WHICH ARE INTERSPERSED,

Meath County Ireland

REFLECTIONS,

THEOLOGICAL, AND MORAL,

ARISING FROM THE VARIOUS SUBJECTS.

By JOHN BAIRD, D.D.

VOL. I.

DUBLIN:

PRINTED BY R. STEWART, No. 200, ABBEY-STREET.

M,DCC,LXXVIII.

JAMES,

LORD BISHOP of DOWN and CONNOR.

MY LORD,

THE Order of Bishops, next to Kings and Sovereign Princes, unquestionably Claims the Patronage of all Writings, which Display and Vindicate the Power, the Justice, the Wisdom, and Grace of Almighty God. This, whatever my Success may have been, in the Execution of the Design, was my constant Aim, in the Performance now Offered to Public View. And, as the Desire of that Order has always Appeared no less Ready and Strong, than the Right was Evident, and the Duty Binding, to Encourage Works of this Sort; to whom shall I, an Unknown Author, Look up for Sanction to those Glorious Doctrines, but to a Truly Apostolic and Primitive PRELATE, who, *by Divine Permission*, hath been Raised up to be a FATHER of the Chriſtian Church, and an ORNAMENT to Religion?——Great and Solid Merit, always Abhorring Adulation, Forces its Way to the Beſt Affections, and never Fails, my Lord, to Draw a Tribute from Truth; or to Diſcern, and Accept, every filial Intention.

To your Lordſhip, therefore, with the Utmoſt Diffidence, I Aſſume the Privilege and Honor of DEDICATING the Following Diſſertations: And beg the Liberty of Declaring myſelf

Your Lordſhip's

Moſt Dutiful,

Moſt Obedient, and

Moſt Humble

Son and Servant,

Mary's-abbey,
Nov. 12th, 1777.

JOHN BAIRD.

PREFACE.

PREFACE.

THESE Diſſertations, following the orderly method of holy writ, begin with the ground-work of original or univerſal religion, particularly the creation of all nature, by one holy, and good, and wiſe being; the works of whoſe hands therein were, in truth, the ſeveral objects which the heathens worſhipped as divinities. They proceed to the introduction of ſin by the fall of our firſt parents, of which we experience the wretched effects. They go on to that amazing puniſhment of its increaſe, the general deluge, proved to be as certain, as it was wonderful, by the remaining traces of it throughout the globe. They then recite the ſecond peopling of the world, the relapſe of mankind into wickedneſs, through the groſſeſt idolatry; the origin of the patriarchal religion; and the choice of one family and people, to preſerve the knowledge of God, and to be *as a light ſhining in a dark place*, for the benefit of all about them, who were diſpoſed to receive direction for their ſteps. They lay before readers the moſt extraordinary providences and events, previous to the laws delivered to the Jewiſh people; and, finally, the glorious promulgation of *the ten commandments* on Mount Sinai,

by

by the Almighty himſelf. And, through the whole, human, or profane hiſtory is copiouſly interſperſed, chiefly reſpecting the moral and religious, the wiſe and magnanimous characters and actions of the moſt remarkable perſons, who ſupply the world with admirable patterns of all kinds of virtue.

CONSEQUENTLY, no more of the holy ſcriptures has been taken under conſideration, than from the beginning of Geneſis to the twentieth chapter of Exodus. This, indeed, is not agreeable to the original deſign; which was to comprehend within one volume, of this ſize, DISSERTATIONS on all the Five Books of Moſes; and which, by the propoſals for printing the work, ſubſcribers would expect. But, rather than purſue this plan, the author, afterward, reſolved to adopt another, convinced that his friends would be perfectly ſatisfied with the reaſons, of this reſolution, which he had to offer. Here he will be allowed to give ſome general account of the origin and progreſs of the work.

WITHOUT the leaſt view to a publication, many of theſe Diſcourſes were, at different periods, in the form of lectures, on Sunday evenings, delivered to a certain ſort of people, whoſe temper and behaviour, in general, muſt, neceſſarily, render it very uncomfortable and dangerous to preſide over them, in religious affairs. The author, however, perſevering in his labours, notwithſtanding their indifference about the revival of truths that had been long buried in oblivion among them, propoſed to himſelf, after ſome time, the pleaſure of preſenting the ſame diſcourſes to the world; and received the kindeſt encouragement

and

and aſſiſtance from many who had heard them. But, through the whole courſe, having adapted them to the weakeſt conceptions, that they might be the more uſeful, he found, that many other matters, with illuſtrations and proofs, might be pleaſing and neceſſary to the enlightened reader; and, accordingly, ſeveral whole DISSERTATIONS have been compoſed, and inſerted in their proper places, ſince the firſt ſheets of the manuſcript went to the preſs. By theſe additions, the work was ſo inſenſibly ſwelled, that, while heaps of papers, belonging to the ſubſequent parts of it, ſtill remained in the author's hands, the charge of upwards of ſixty pages, more than the price of the book would afford, has been incurred, to bring the ſacred hiſtory down to a diſtinguiſhed period. If ſuch additions had been left out, and the firſt ſcheme purſued, inſtead of the preſent title, *Select* Diſſertations would have better ſuited the performance; and ſubſcribers and purchaſers muſt have been diſappointed and injured. The author, therefore, begs the public may, at leaſt, excuſe his conduct, if they ſhould not applaud his juſtice.

HE hopes, alſo, that the extenſion of his plan, ſignified in the title-page, which is changed from Diſſertations, &c. *on the Five Books of Moſes*, to Diſſertations, &c. *on all the Books of the Old Teſtament*, will be ſo far from giving offence to any, that even ſuch as may think they have been injured, in the firſt inſtance, will conſider the laborious taſk, which the author has preſcribed to himſelf, as a ſufficient atonement for it; while others, who deſire farther information concerning the moſt important matters, will encourage his confident reliance on them, in an

undertaking

undertaking that depends entirely on their approbation, which, after a ſhort reſpite, they may be requeſted to give, by their ſubſcription for a ſecond volume.

THE benevolence and utility of ſuch a deſign will appear evident to every one who reflects, that though learned men have, with great piety and diligence, employed their various talents in making the holy ſcriptures plain and uſeful, yet many of their writings have been, neceſſarily, locked up in *dead* or *foreign* languages; that thoſe in our own tongue, which deſerve, and have gained, univerſal eſteem, are extremely voluminous and coſtly; and, as one cauſe of their bulk, have incorporated in them a vaſt mixture of ancient and ſcholaſtic erudition, which is equally unintereſting and perplexing to the moſt of ordinary readers.—Pure annals of religion, or of the periodical revelations of God's will and grace to mankind, in the ſeveral ages of the world, well digeſted, would obviate ſome difficulties apprehended to be in the ſcheme, and aſſiſt the ſerious enquirer in connecting the whole together, within a very narrow compaſs. To give this brief, but at the ſame time compleat and diſtinct hiſtory of religion, if the expreſſion may be uſed, was the intention of the author, in the preſent work. The omiſſion of ſome ſmall matters, was conſidered of no moment; as they appear to be only epiſodes in the ſacred writer's plan, which have no immediate connection with it: Though even from theſe, the pious reader of the ſcriptures will pleaſe to be informed, that, as *R. Maimonides* obſerves, on the affair of Judah and Tamar itſelf, in the xxxviii chapter of Geneſis, the moſt ſtriking

leſſons

lessons of modesty, justice, and ingenuity of mind, may be deduced.

Because those writings claim a divine origin, and the whole of this performance is considerably qualified with ingredients taken from them, surely none, even in this age, who have their taste, in the lowest degree, unvitiated, and have preserved any regard for the reputation of their understanding, will either inwardly entertain, or outwardly shew, any dislike to the subject. The most certain sign of a defective education, or of perversion and depravity of principle, is a neglect or contempt of writings tinctured with morality and religion. Rather than refuse instruction therein, a modest suspicion would be more becoming, that farther information and evidence are still wanting. The accumulated knowledge of mankind, and their uninterrupted and voluntary testimony, ought, certainly, to be respected.

With what pains the many authorities quoted through this work, as supplemental, elucidative, or probatory of the sacred writings, have been collected, the learned are best able to judge. It would, perhaps, be imprudent to reveal the difficulties attending the task. The author complained of none while he was engaged in it: The pleasure he had, in the laborious search, and in seeing, with his own eyes, the works of illustrious men, was felt to be a sufficient counterballance. His own private collection of books was far from supplying him with all the materials he has used. The truly noble and benevolent Earl of Charlemont, whose library is a

compleat

compleat *Encyclopedy*, gave him the freest admittance to it; and from thence he drew, what he could not easily find any where else. To some booksellers, and Librarians, he is, likewise, under obligations, which he here acknowledges, with the utmost gratitude.

Of the imperfections of the design, and the inaccuracies in the execution of what he has given of it, the author is highly sensible. Many were the reasons for these; more, perhaps, than ever concurred, when a work of this extent was concerted, and carried on. The death of a dear wife, whose memory he wishes he could render immortal, immediately preceded; and there followed, together with the utmost disrespect of her, the most virulent persecution of the author, already overwhelmed by afflictions, with two affectionate infants, by men who are enemies to every system of policy and religion;—to the latter, a disgrace and scandal.

But, leaving them in their own ways at present, or, rather, to their own consciences, if they may have any in future, the author sincerely prays, that they may receive benefit from what he has now done, before they stand at the righteous tribunal of God; and that all readers, overlooking errors, may derive instruction, direction, and comfort, equal to the dignity and importance of the subject.

P. S. The author following no authorities, and reckoning it perfectly indifferent, has spelled those words, which formerly imitated the French orthography, and, of late, the Latin, with and without an *u*, just as it occurred.

SUB-

SUBSCRIBERS NAMES.

A

MRS. Agnew
Doctor Achmet
Mr. Humphry Adams
Mr. Archibald Armſtrong
Mr. Peter Alley
Mr. Hugh Auchinleck
Mr. James Acheſon
Mr. William Andrews

B

Rev. Dean Bond
Mrs. Bunbury
Mrs. Catharine Brazill
Miſs Anne Bickerſtaff
Mr. Robert Black
Mr. Thomas Black
Richard Bolton, Eſq;
Mr. John Bones
Mr. Nugent Booker
Mr. Gilbert Bigger
Mr. Humphry Barber
Thomas Bayly, Eſq;
Mr. James Brown
Mr. James Ballentine
Rev. Mr. Blair
Mr. Thomas Bond, 2 books
Edward William Burton, Eſq;
Thomas Bond, of Bonds Glen, Eſq;
Mr. Alexander Boyd
Mr. Thomas Bond
Mr. Alexander Boyle
Henry Vaughan Brooke, Eſq;
Mr. Alexander Boyle
Mr. John Barclay
Mr. William Bond
Mr. George Burnet
Mr. Burrowes, Sen.
Mr Robert Burrowes, T. C. D. 2 Books
Mr. Thomas Brunker
Mr. Oliver Bond
Mr. John Batchelor

Right

C

Right Hon. Lady Clifden
Mrs. Elizabeth Clark
Mrs. Cowan
Right Hon. Earl of Charlemont
Rev. William Cradock, D. D. D. S. P. D.
Capt. Robert Clark
Thomas Cowan, Efq;
Mr. John Carey
Mr. James Clark
Mr. John Carleton
Mr. Thomas Craig
Mr. Hugh Combes
Mr. David Corbett
Mr. Hugh Cochrane
Mr. John Cowan
Rev. Henry Corbett
Mr. George Cole
Mr. John Crawford
John Chriftian, L. L. D.
Guy Moore Coote, Efq; M. P.
Rev. William Craig
Charles Croker, Efq;
Mr. Thomas Carpenter
Mr. Charles Curtis
Mr. William Crofbie
William Cleghorn, Efq;
George Cary, Efq;
Mr. Thomas Chambers
Richard Cowan, Efq;
John Cowan, Efq;
William Cowan, Efq;
Mr John Campbell
Mr. David Cowan
Peter Cantwell, Efq;
Anthony Coane, Efq;
Triftram Cary, Efq;
George Cary, of Caftle Cary, Efq;
Henry Cope, Efq;
Henry Boyle Carter, Efq;
Thomas Croker, Efq;
Henry Clarke, Efq;
Mr. James Cullen
Mr. James Carfan T. C. D.

D.

Mrs. Deane
Mrs. Efther Decluzeau
Mrs. Drew
Mifs Dodd
William Deane, Efq;
John Damer, Efq;
George Purdon Drew, Efq;
Mr. Chriftopher D'Arcy
Mr. Peter D'Arcy
James Dunkin, Efq;
Rev. Mr. Dunn
Mr. James Daniel
Mr. Arthur Dunn
Mr. Arthur Donellan
Mr. James Dickfon,

E.

Mrs. Ellis
Mr Pat. Ewing
Mr. Jofhua Dawfon

F.

Mifs Freind
John Farrell, M. D.
Mr. David Forreft
John Finlay, Efq;
Faithful Fortefcue, Efq;
Richard Fleming, Efq;
Mr. Zach. Foxall

Mr. Edward

Mr. Edward Fergusson

G.

Mr. James Given
Mr. James Given, Jun.
Mrs. Gough
Mr. Benjamin Gault
Mess. John and Charles Gault
Fortescue Gorman, Esq;
Rev. Edward Golding
Mr. Grundy
Mr. Robert Gibson
Mr. John Gillespie
Mr. Robert Given
Mr. John Gamble
Mr. Roger Gordon

H.

George Hale, F. T. C. D.
Mr. Joshua Houston, *the Author's Friend.*
Mr. John Houston
Mr. Henry Harping
Mr. Robert Henderson
Rev. Dean Handcock
John Stewart Hamilton, Esq; M. P.
William Hamilton, Esq;
Mr. Thomas Hamilton,
William Hudson, Esq;
Mr. John How
Mr. William Hunter
Col. Simon Hart, Esq;
Mr. James Haslett
Mr. Harper
Mr. Edward Hoey
Mr. William Hawthorn
Mr. Thomas Homan
Mr. James Hartley
Mr. Gilbert Hutchison
Mr. John Henderson
Mr. Samuel Hutchison
Mr. Simon Hazelton

J.

Rev. Thomas Jameson A. M.
Mr. Henry Jackson
Richard Jones, Esq;
Robert Johnston, Esq;
Rev. Jocelyn Ingram
Charles Johnson, Esq;
Mr. John Johnston
Mr. William Jordan
Mr. Wood Gibson Jones
Mr. James Jackson
Mr. John Jackson

K.

Mrs. Rachel Kilbee
Miss Margaret King
Sir Anthony King, Knt. and Alderman
William Knox, Esq;
Mr. Gilbert Kilbee
Mr. Edward Kilbee, jun.
Mr. William Kilbee
Mr. Luke Kelly
Mr. George Kerr
Samuel Croker King, Esq;
George Keys, Esq;
Charles King, Esq; M. P.
Mr. James King
William Knox, Esq;
Murray Kathrens, Esq;

Dennis

Dennis Kelly, Esq;
Mr. John King

L.

Rev. Dean Ledwich, D. D. Dean of Kildare
Rev. Robert Law, D. D.
Hugh Lyle, Esq;
Thomas Lee, Esq;
Mr. John Burjaud Lewis T. C. D.
Rev. Charles Cobbe Lyndon, A. B. 2 Books
James Lyndon, Esq;
Mr. Alexander Lawrence
George Lowther, Esq;
Mr. James Lowry
Michael Lewis, Esq;
Mr. James Lang
Mr. James Loyde, 2 Books

M.

Mrs. M'Farland, Luttrelstown
Mrs. Elizabeth Maffett
James M'Rea, Esq; Capt. 3d regt. of horse
David M'Bride, M. D.
Murdoch M'Kenzie, Esq; F. R. S.
Mr. James Miller, T. C. D.
Mr. William Makins
Mr. Thomas M'Minn
Mr. Charles Mulholen
Mr. Donald M'Naughton
Mr. George Murray
Mr. Thomas M'Gowan
Mr. Mullan
Mr. James M'Creery
Mr. Medlicott, 3 Books
Mr. John M'Connell
Joshua M'Geough, Esq;
William M'Geough, Esq;
Bryan Meheux, Esq;
Mr. George Melvin
Rev. Mr. Morgan
Rev. Alexander Marshal
Rev. Oliver Miller
Rev. Samuel Murphy
Mr. Charles M'Clenaghan
Mr. William M'Farland
Rev. John M'Caussland
Andrew Makilwaine, Esq;
Mr. Hamilton Moore
Rev. Ralph Mansfield
Rev. John M'Cleland, Coagh
Mr. B. O. Mitchell
Mr. Milbank
Mr. Robert Mercer
Malcolm M'Neill, Esq;
Mr. Thomas Millwood
Arthur M'Guyre, Esq;
Samuel M'Geough, Esq;
Mr. James Maxwell
Mr. Robert Mack
David Murray, Gent.
Mr. James Medlicott
Mr. Batholomew Madden
Mr. Peter Mazeire
Mr. John M'Cloure
Mr. Robert Moore
—— M'Cann, Merchant

N.

Archibald Nevins, Esq;

Mrs. Norton

Mrs. Norton
Mrs. Margaret Naſh
Mr. William Neill

O.

Mr. David Orom
Mr. George Overend
Mr. John Orr
Charles Oulton, Eſq;

P.

Miſs Palmer
Mr. John Pooler
Mr. Robert Percival, A. B. T. C. D.
Mr. Panniel
Mr. Thomas Porter
Henry Palmer, Eſq;
Mr. Samuel Prentice
Mr. Thomas Penroſe
Mr. James Peebles
Mr. James Prentice

R.

Mr. John Ruſſel
Mr. James Riky
George Robiſon, Eſq;
Mr. James Rouſſe
John Rea, Eſq;
Mr. William Roſs
Mrs. Catherine Rudd
Mr. Robert Roth
Mr. John Reid,
Mr. John Rambaut

S.

Sir Richard Steele, Bart.
Benjamin Shafton, M. D. *the Author's Friend*
Mark Sinnot, Eſq;
Walter Sinnot, Eſq;
Rev. Alexander Staples, A. M.
Mr. John Stewart
Mr. Thomas Shaw
Mr. Alexander Simpſon
Benjamin Span, Eſq;
Mr. Arthur Stanley
Rev. Abraham Seawright
Thomas Short, Eſq;
Mr. James Stevenſon
James Sheil, Eſq;
Mr. Robert Sproule
Rev. Nicholas Spence
Mr. James Sproule
Rev. Lewis John Scoffier
Mr. John Smith
John Spourling, Eſq;
Mr. William Speer
Mr. James Savage
Mr. Joſeph Slator
Mr. Richard Stewart

T.

Robert Thorpe, Eſq;
William John Talbot, Eſq;
John Traill, Eſq;
Mr. Francis Thome
Mrs. Travers
Mr. George Thompſon
Mr. John Thompſon
Rev. Mr. Thomas
Mrs. Elinor Tonge
Mr. Roſs Thompſon
Mr. Thomas Taylor

SUBSCRIBERS NAMES.

Mr. Thomas Travers
Mr. Peter Travers
Mr. John Taubman

V.

Mr. George Vernon, T. C. D.
Mr. Robert Vickers
Mr. James Vance.

U.

Mr. James Underwood.

W.

Mrs. Jane Wright
Mrs. Warren
John Jervis White, Esq;
Rev. Isaac Weld, D. D.
John White, Esq;
Mr. Stafford Wilson
Mr. George Wilson
Mr. Alexander Wallace
Mr. Woods
Mr. Francis Welsh
Mr. Robert Wallace
Rev. Brabazon Wye
James Whitelaw, Esq;
Mr. Lawrence Ward
Rev. William Weir
Rev. John White, Stewartstown
Mr. Charles Williams
Mr. Richard Williams
Mr. John Wright
Mr. Archibald Wright
Mr. Mathew Walsh
Mr. Richard Williamson
Mr. Thomas Woods
Mr. James Walmsley
Mr. Edward Williamson

Y

Alexander Young, Esq;

CONTENTS.

CONTENTS.

b XVIII. *Of*

XXXI. *Of*

DISSERTATION I.

OF THE CREATION OF THE WORLD.

GENESIS I.

IN the same order of holy writ, and as the matter itself requires, this work begins with the origin of things. The account given of it, by revelation, is very short, but comprehensive; and, independent of all other systems, calculated equally for people of every age and nation.

IN the beginning, says Moses, *God created the heavens and the earth.* To create, in strict language, is to bring things which were not, into a state of being, or out of nothing, into form and existence. Our conceptions of this amazing exertion of divine power and authority, may be assisted, if we suppose, that the original atoms, or first elements, were previously made, and next wrought up into very different shapes and sizes, in the substances which the all-wise Creator was pleased to compose. This operation implies no contradiction in itself; and, therefore, is possible. And that all things we see, or any way perceive with our senses, were, by some such process, produced and framed, the nature and aspect of things themselves testify, and the relation of the event before us declares.

 [WHEN

[WHEN the mind is fully affected with this great idea, and *clearly sees the invisible things of God, even his eternal power and god-head, in the creation of the world* *, the enquiry is unavoidable, *where is God my maker* †, and the maker of all these things? And the voice of reason, as well as the instruction of revelation, is still the same, *He goeth by us, though we see him not; he passeth on also, though we perceive him not* ‡.—Here then is the ground, and first principle of religious belief, and right practice---God is---the supreme uncaused cause---from whose will and act all other beings derive their existence, and upon whom they must continually depend for their support. Elohim, the potentate, and Jehovah, the Lord, who was, and is of himself, are the peculiar names given to him; and without something importing authority, immediately derived from him, or by way of derision to idols and false gods, never applied to any other, in the sacred tongue; thereby ascribing to him alone all power and perfection.]

INDEED, in what precise manner, out of the immense and inconceivable fulness of his own self-existence, he brought all things *in the beginning*, as by what settled laws, or direct agency, he still upholds them, we can neither explain nor comprehend. Several ancient authors, with the scattered fragments of tradition, have formed, not unpleasing hypotheses, concerning the generation and arrangement of matter; and many of the modern given the freest scope to their fancy. But of this most stupendous work of God, Moses is the only historian who speaks in a ra-

* Rom. i. 20. † Job. xxxv. ‡ Job. ix.

tional

tional and satisfactory manner; and from whom all other accounts of it, any way consistent, have been manifestly taken. To give all succeeding ages, just and affecting thoughts of that astonishing display of unoriginated excellence, so far as true religion was concerned, appears plainly to have been his design; and in such a way, that men's presumption should not be flattered, by the indulgence of a vain curiosity, about things which it is altogether unnecessary for them to know. And if the judgment of some should be supposed biased, in regard to his relation, by a kind of sacred reverence for his authority; it may be justly urged as an argument, of no inconsiderable weight, to establish the credit of the relation, that, so far as it proceeds, it does not in any degree, contradict the most accurate discoveries, which have been made in later ages, concerning the system of the universe, or any part of it.

THE heavens and the earth, mentioned by this inspired author, may be taken in a sense that comprehends all created nature, or all things visible and invisible. For, as a learned commentator observes *, if Maimonides † understood the matter aright, the Hebrew particle *eth*, put before both heaven and earth, signifies as

* Patrick, Gen. i. ver. 1.

† The words of this Rabbi, which his lordship hath not given, are in his More Nevochim, pa. ii. cap. 30. thus: "Quod autem hic te scire quoque refert, est et hoc, quod particula *eth*, quæ adhibetur, cum dicitur, et haschamajim veet haaretz (ut sapientes nostri in pluribus locis explicarunt) idem valeat quod *im* cum: ut sensus sit; Deum creâsse cum Cœlis, quæcunque sunt in Cœlis, et cum terra, quæcunque sunt in terra."

Vide edit. Basil. 1629. in Ling. Lat. conversus a Johan. Buxt. filio.

much as *with*; and makes the ſenſe to be this; "He created the heavens, with all things in the heavens; and the earth; with all things in the earth:" and likewiſe ſays, the famous Philo underſtood the firſt word of the chapter *, tranſlated *in the beginning*, to have a reſpect to the order wherein things were created; or that God began his creation with the heavens, and then proceeded to the earth.

And yet, in oppoſition to the Jewiſh interpreters, who have certainly ſometimes inſulted common ſenſe, with their traditions, and gloſſes upon words, it hath been thought, by others, no way conſequent from the deſcription Moſes gives, that he meant to ſay, the whole univerſe was created all together at once, or at the ſame period of time. *In the beginning*, ſay they, ſeems rather to imply, that when, at what time ſoever it might be, the world was created, it was by the wiſdom and power of the eternal God only. Nor is this fundamental truth in the leaſt affected, though the ſeveral parts of the univerſe may have been produced at different times; though God may ſtill be creating new worlds in the immenſe regions of ſpace, which is not at all improbable; or even have only changed the texture and qualities of the bodies within our ſphere, according to the opinion of a certain philoſopher †, who imagines that our earth, from its appearance, derived its laſt origin from fire; and that the greateſt part of the other terreſtrial matter was burnt, by that violent element, at the time Moſes ſays, *light was divided from darkneſs*; when the orbs,

* Heb. בראשית.

† Leibnitz, in the acta Leipſic. under the title of Protogæa, 1683.

composed

composed of it, had shined as fixed stars a long time before, and at length become opaque for want of combustibles. None of those notions invading the ground necessary to be maintained, in either way this truth may be established; that in the beginning of their existence, it is no matter when or how, God created, or does still create, and renew all things *. And the only doctrine Moses would inculcate, in his introduction to creation, most probably is this, that the whole universe had once, whether entire or separately, in the present, or any other state, a beginning; and not from necessity or chance, but from the sole power and agency of God †.

But instead of such excursions through the interminable fields of imagination; let us rather come closer to the subject, and observe, that the intention of revelation being only to instruct us concerning things within a certain limited compass of space and duration, it appears most reasonable to suppose this phrase, in the beginning, has a special reference to the time when our earth was created, and the bodies connected with it; seeing it's condition and appurtenances are so minutely described in this chapter ‡.

* This concession, being sufficiently large, may confound infidels, who have taken their advantage on every occasion; and triumphed, particularly, over a very extraordinary man, for having deduced ingeniously, though perhaps falsely, the knowledge of physics, and of the Christian mysteries, from Hebrew roots. Hutchinson.

† This was taught by Mercurius Trismegistus, by Zoroaster, Orpheus and Pindar, whom St. Aug. calls Summi Philosophi.

‡ Dr. Taylor's Scrip. Div.

Now,

Now, the matter produced by God's almighty word, whereof this earth was to be framed, was a chaos, *without form and void* *, that is, ſhapeleſs, waſte and uſeleſs; the conſtituent heterogeneous particles being all jumbled together, and eſſential *darkneſs covering the whole deep. Then the ſpirit of God moved upon the face of the waters*; exerted itſelf on this sevenfold gloom, and ſeparated and reduced the various parts of the confuſed maſs, to the beautiful order and harmony in which we now behold them.

Opinions about the ſpirit of God moving on the face of the waters, or the primary operations of the divine influence on the pulpy, uncompacted ſubſtance, of which the earth firſt appeared, have been variouſly ſupported and explained. That it could not be the influence of the ſun, when as yet there was none to warm the ground, is clear and manifeſt †. Incubation, or brooding over an egg, a figure, not very diſtant from the truth, aſcribed to the earth, was, in the earlieſt times, an idea very generally entertained ‡; by which ſeveral Jewiſh writers underſtood the deſcent of an elemental wind, called, on account of its vehemence, the wind, or the ſpirit of God; in the ſame manner as whatever is great and powerful is, in ſcripture language, aſcribed as proper and peculiar to him ‖: That the darkneſs which lay upon the faces of the deep, being now put in motion, is ſtiled ſpirit,

* Heb. תהו ובהו.

† The ſun did not appear till the fourth day after the work of creation began.

‡ Vide Patrick, under the article waters, and many others.

‖ Vide Synop. Critic. Poli in Loco.

that

that is, a moving air, or wind, is the exposition of the words by a late writer * before referred to. Nor can it be unobserved, that a celebrated commentator † rejects the notion of its being a wind; and yet makes no other distinction in the principle, than that it was a great wind, raised by the infinite wisdom and power of God, which made a vehement commotion, and mighty fermentation, *on the face of the waters*, or that fluid matter already mentioned, to separate the parts of it one from the another. While others have asserted that the active power of God, which now sustains and preserves the universe, did then form and distinguish matter, and communicate sprituality and natural motion, by giving heat, rarefaction, and subtilty to all its parts ‡.

SOME of these opinions, indeed, seem to have a foundation in nature; as an elemental, or even common wind itself, might produce mighty effects in this case; and serve the will of the creator, as an instrument, in the performance of his great design. A principle of this sort is found extremely efficacious, in reducing component parts to their proper places, and uncontroled operations; and in forming, at the

* Hutchinson's Moses's Principia, part I.

† Bishop Patrick in Loco.

‡ See Sir Walter Raleigh, B. 1st. page 6. fol. 1st edit. where, to support and illustrate his opinion, he quotes the words of Virgil:

> Principio cælum ac terras, camposque liquentes,
> Lucentemque globum Lunæ, titaniaque astra,
> Spiritus intus alit: totamque infusa par artus,
> Mens agitat molem, et magno se corpore miscet.
>
> Æneid. l. 8.

same

same time, the cement or bond of union, between the several constituent particles*.

But there are many, on the other hand, who have concluded that this energy, which gave vital influence to matter, of itself inert, was the self same spirit which now works on the minds of men for their sanctification†: an opinion no way contradictory to our holy faith, but rather perfectly consistent with it.

From revelation, nothing, with any degree of certainty, can be drawn, but this; that the word in the Hebrew tongue ‡ here translated wind, is the same as that used in the 1st verse of the 8th chapter, when things were to be restored to their former state after the flood. But whether this comparison of the texts, perhaps very seldom made, will assist us in the solution, either on philosophical or religious principles, must be left to every one's private judgment. If there should be an inclination to the side of piety, it cannot possibly do any harm.

However it was, Moses, pursuing the consequence, that some plastic enlivening power was actually impressed, proceeds, without farther explanation, to inform us, that on the first day, and the first thing, after the production of the chaos, the element of light was called forth. And the sublimity of his language, on this occasion, has not escaped the observation of a celebrated

* See the sagacious Doctor Macbride's Properties of fixed Air. Essay II. p. 20.

† Vide Synop Critic Poli in Loco.

‡ Heb. רוח.

celebrated critic *, in ancient times, who ſays, the legiſlator of the Jews, who was no ordinary man, having juſt and adequate notions of the greatneſs and power of the Deity, has at the beginning of his laws, expreſſed himſelf with all ſuitable dignity, in the following words; *God ſaid, let there be light, and there was light* †.

THE work of the ſecond day was the formation of air, called *the firmament*, or the widely expanded atmoſphere, where the feathered fowls fly, and which is ſpread above, and all around the earth, comprehending meteors and clouds; which, condenſed into liquid fountains, are the *waters* ſaid to be *above the firmament*, or air, in contradiſtinction to *the waters* of the ſea, and rivers, *which are under it* ‡."

ALMIGHTY power formed, on the third day, the element of water, by draining off the fluids of the chaos, and gathering them into reſervoirs and cavities to contain them; that the earth might become one firm, compact, and fertile ſurface, and be in a fit condition to *bring forth graſs, and herbs, and fruitful trees*, which he then commanded to ſpring.

ON the fourth day God collected the ſun, that glorious luminary, with the moon, and, probably, the

* Longinus, chap. vii.

† As a further argument that wind or air was the primary agent, after creation, it has been obſerved, that as ſoon as ever the air was put in motion, there was light, which is nothing, ſay ſome, but air rarefied by the colliſion of its concreted parts.

‡ Spectacle de la Nature, tom. iii.

other

other orbs within our ſyſtem, ſeeing they all influence one another; though, in this place, Moſes has not made mention of them, it being no way material to his purpoſe. But that the fixed ſtars, which ſeem altogether beyond our region, and probably are the centre of ſyſtems belonging to themſelves, as is the preſent faſhionable, and not very unlikely opinion, were all conſtructed out of the ſame elements, on this day, we are under no neceſſity to ſuppoſe. Moſt, if not all of them, as has been already admitted, might have been created before, and ſome of them ſince, our world was brought into being. For though the laſt clauſe, in the 16th verſe, in our tranſlation, reads, *He made the ſtars alſo*; the words *he made*, as has been judiciouſly obſerved *, are not in the Hebrew text; and, therefore, the ſenſe may be conſiſtently rendered, *And God made two great lights* †, *the greater light to rule the day, and the leſſer light to rule the night, with the ſtars*; that is, in the ſeaſon, when they are ſeen twinkling, let the moon alſo, as regent of the ſky, appear.

All fiſhes and fowls that inhabit the waters and the air were formed, on the fifth day, when animal life, with loco-motive powers began; and the divine bleſſing was beſtowed on them, in theſe terms, *Be fruitful, and multiply, and fill the waters in the ſeas, and let fowl multiply to fly above the earth in the open firmament of heaven, and it was ſo.*

* Dr. Taylor's Scrip. Div.

† Moſes, in this place, does not follow phyſical exactneſs, but the impreſſion made on our ſenſes, the ſun being larger than the moon, by many millions of times.

On

On the ſixth day, all cattle, creeping things, and beaſts of the earth, after their ſeveral kinds, were produced; and, laſt of all, when the world was framed and furniſhed, as a fit manſion to receive him, was Man made; and, as his maker's vicegerent and repreſentative, had *Dominion given to him, over the fiſh of the ſea, and over the fowl, and over the cattle, and over all the earth, and over every thing that creepeth upon the earth; and his head crowned with glory and honour.*— The ſame day, it is to be remarked, Eve was made, Moſes informing us that *God created man male and female.* And, accordingly in the ſecond chapter, where he is relating at greater length, what he had only ſketched in the firſt, the words *God made*, have been rendered *God had made*, by ſeveral commentators *.

Six days were thus employed in executing the great work of creation, though omnipotence could have performed it in a moment. But this time ſeems to have been employed, that natural means, and ſecond cauſes, which the Almighty had appointed, might be regularly exerted, and men made capable of tracing the proceſs, by a due application of thought and imagina-

* Voyez Saurin, de la creation, a Amſterdam, 1720.—Sanchoniatho, the Phenician, begins mankind from two mortals, called in Philo Byblius, who tranſlated him into Greek, Protogonus and Eon. This Sanchoniatho, inſtead of forming his account of the origin of mankind, as Diodorus Siculus hath done, from what he thought to be the ancient philoſophy, drew his hiſtory from regiſters, and hieroglyphical inſcriptions on the temples of Phenicia and Egypt; and had converſed with Jerombal, prieſt of the god Jao, whom Sam. Bochart hath conjectured to be Jerubaal, or Gideon. Vide Canaan ejus, lib. ii. cap. 17.

For the objections againſt this hiſtory, ſee H. Dodwel's Diſcourſe concerning it, printed at London 1681.

imagination, on the one hand; and, on the other, so limited a ſpace, for a deſign ſo vaſtly extenſive, demonſtrates the Creator's power, and forces our acknowledgments of wonder and admiration.

THE magnificent plan being now finiſhed, he who is bleſſed for ever, beheld, from the heaven of heavens, his high abode, this new addition to his empire, and pronounced *every thing which he had made very good.* And, the evening and the morning of that day, uſhering in ſabbath, we are not without intimation, that angels, called *morning ſtars*, who kept the firſt vigils, *ſhouted for joy* *, and ſung halleluias to their and the world's creator and Lord; in the ſame manner, though infinitely more glorious, as the prieſts did, in their apparel, with trumpets and cymbals, when the foundations of the ſecond temple were laid †.

OF the creation of thoſe purer ſpirits, and ſeemingly elder ſons of God, Moſes tells us nothing. Some imagining that they were created on one of the ſix foregoing days, have grounded their opinion on what is ſaid at the beginning of the ſecond chapter, *Thus the heaven and the earth were finiſhed, and all the hoſt of them.* In this ſenſe, indeed, the hoſt of heaven is ſometimes to be taken in ſcripture: for inſtance, where Micaiah ſays to the king of Iſrael, *Hear thou, therefore, the word of the Lord: I ſaw the Lord ſitting on his throne, and all the hoſt of heaven ſtanding by him, on his right hand and on his left* ‡. And from the notice given us, we are ſure they were witneſſes of crea-

* Job xxxviii. 7. † Ezra iii. 10. ‡ 1 Kings xxii. 19.

tion,

tion, and praised the Almighty for the wonders of his omnipotence and wisdom. But whether theirs immediately preceded that of the universe, or ought to be referred to more distant periods, no man has any right to determine; nor does any thing oblige us to believe that God alone had existed, till the period he brought this world into being. That there really are such beings as we call angels, that is, certain permanent substances, invisible, and imperceptible to our senses, endued with power and understanding superior to that of human nature, created by God, and subject to him, as the source and origin, the Lord and governor of all; ministring to his divine providence in the government of the world by his appointment, and more especially attending the affairs of mankind, is a truth fully attested by scripture; though we are not to give credit to every story about the apparitions of them.

A LEARNED Jew hath taken notice, at the close of the second day's work, that the words above cited, *God saw that it was good*, are not, as at the end of all the other days, pronounced. And his reason for the omission may be seen below *. From this expression, five times repeated, as well as from the wisdom and goodness of the Creator, and the universal fitness of things, a modern philosopher hath inferred, that all the parts of

* Silentio verò hîc minime prætereundum, quâmnam ob caussam in operibus secundi diei not sit dictum, quia bonum; nam de omnibus entibus innovatis, in ordinario, frequenti & constanti statu existentibus, dixit, quia bonum. Ratio hujus rei, meo judicio, manifesta est: hoc expansum, et res illa, quæ supra illud est (aqua appellatur) abdita est et occulta nimis, et omnino non Ens. Maim. cap. 30.

nature

nature," and the constitution of the moral world, are on the best plan, and in the best disposition, they could possibly be †. The thought is noble, and not to be altogether rejected. Though amidst all the possibilities, ever present to the divine mind, whether on another scale, the same plan might not have been constructed, with equal advantages, what mortal is able to determine?

How remote from the present time, the creation of this visible system happened, the learned of all religions, and in all quarters and ages of the world, to whom it would be endless to refer, have anxiously enquired; and their opinions have never come so near to each other, as when they have rested on the authority of the scriptures. And even on this ground it must be acknowledged, there has been a considerable difference, according as the Hebrew, Samaritan, or Greek texts have been received; which has inclined not a few to believe, that this Epocha is a gordian root, not to be unravelled by human art. But admitting the genuineness of the Hebrew text, disputes, in regard to this matter, will be very nearly calmed, and a correspondent chain of chronology easily drawn through all the books of the Old Testament. Tracing the periods there marked out, we reckon,

	Years.
From the beginning of the world to the deluge,	1656
From the deluge to the dispersion at Babel,	240
From the dispersion to the birth of Abraham, -	130
From his birth to his vocation, - - -	75
	2101

† Leibnitz.

Brought

	Years.
Brought forward - -	2101
From his vocation to Jacob's going down into Egypt, - - - - -	215
From that period to the exit of his posterity from Egypt, - - - -	215
From the exit to the death of Moses, - -	40
From the death of Moses to the building of the first temple, - - - -	440
From the building to its destruction by Nebuchadnezzar, - - - -	423
The captivity, leaving out twelve years, before it was destroyed, - - - -	58
An interpolation from Cyrus, who released the Jews, to the twentieth year of Artaxerxes, Longimanus, king of Pesia, depending on the monuments of profane history, when the commandment went forth to Nehemiah to restore and rebuild Jerusalem,	91
From thence to the final destruction of the second temple, by Titus, when the abomination of desolation, spoken of by Daniel the prophet, stood in the holy place,	490
Total	4073
But deducting the year of Christ, in which that event happened, - - - -	69
There will remain	4004

The difficulty indeed is great, between the creation and the birth of Abraham, to reconcile the three forementioned texts the one with the other. The Samaritan, from Adam to the flood, falls short of the Hebrew, three hundred and forty-nine years; and

and the septuagint exceeds the latter, five hundred and eighty-six. On the other hand, from the birth of Arphaxed, two years after the flood, to the time when Terah had Abraham born to him, the Samaritan rises above the Hebrew calculation, six hundred and fifty years, and is itself surpassed, one hundred and thirty years, by the septuagint. The whole difference from the beginning of the world, to the birth of Abraham, between the Greek and the Hebrew records, is one thousand three hundred and sixty-six years; while the Samaritan pentateuch is below the former, eight hundred and sixty-five years, and above the latter, five hundred and one *.

From any remains of ancient learning, with which we are furnished, at this distance of time, it may be freely declared impossible to ascertain, how these variations happened. The national antipathy which subsisted between the Hebrews and Samaritans; the presumption of the seventy interpreters, in departing from the text; the ignorance or oversight of transcribers, may have severally contributed to embarrass these calculations. But what does the whole difference amount to, in regard to the doctrine that is here to be established? Only about thirteen centuries; which cannot in the least shake the great truth that pervades the

* Usserii Armachani, Chronologia sacra, p. 46.

Note. Agreeable to the opinion of some learned men, who think the period in the Hebrew too short, on account of the youth of the postdiluvian patriarchs; I have taken the liberty to insert seventy-eight years, between the deluge and the birth of Abraham; which is not near an equivalent for one hundred and thirty years of Cainan's life, when the septuagint makes Salah to be born; and yet of whom the Hebrew takes no notice.

Mosaic

Mosaic history. And it is no small satisfaction, that the great differences between the several copies end here; that is to say, immediately at the birth of Abraham, when we enter on a more certain series of time, about which chronologers are more generally agreed, and the copies vary, not several ages, as they do in the foregoing periods, but only a few years.

To these years of the world till the birth of Christ, we are to add, agreeable to the Dionysian or vulgar Æra —1777, and the total will be, five thousand, seven hundred and eighty one, since the creation. And creation commencing in the seven-hundredth and tenth year of the Julian period, the birth of the Saviour of the world must have happened in the four thousand seven hundredth and fourteenth of that period, according to the best of our chronologers *.

Of this newness of the world, Moses hath made, so to speak, the foundation-stone, upon which he hath rested the whole system of religion delivered by himself to mankind. Nor, as was said before of his cosmogony, or creation and frame of the world, and the various parts of it, are there any appearances in nature to disprove this newness of it; but, on the contrary, every thing confirms it, when we consider the material phænomena, population, government, discoveries, and the progress of all the arts and sciences.

With regard to the question, from what season of the year, is the work of creation to be dated? a cer-

* Usserii armach: chron. sacra, pars altera, cap. xi. Strauch. brev. chron. l. 4.

tain Author * hath affirmed, that it cannot be resolved fully, and seems to imply some sort of contradiction; seeing it is impossible, in the space of six days, in which the world was formed, that it could either be spring or autumn, or any other season, over the whole earth, in so short a time; as the vernal equinox in one place must necessarily be the autumnal in another; and in like manner the other seasons; according to the climates, and the different parts of the world. But this difficulty has been removed by supposing, that the question itself can only refer to the place where Adam was created †. And yet, notwithstanding this sensible reply, to the above senseless quibble, the precise season still remains unascertained. Some have supposed the vernal equinox to have been the time; and others pitched on both the summer and the winter Solstices; while, by far, the greater number have ventured their opinion, that it was autumn ‡, which seems the more probable, that the year anciently began from that time. This indeed was afterwards altered by Moses, who ordered that the ecclesiastical year should commence from the vernal æquinox, or the month Nisan §: but the Jews, in civil affairs, still continued to compute from the former, or the month Tisri ||.

SOME difficulties of another nature, partly philosophical, and partly religious, which seem to clog this subject, come, after the account that has been given of it, to be considered. The first is; how it can be reconciled to the present system of the world, that our earth should be said to have been created

* Philo de opif. mundi. † Univ. hist. ‡ Jacob. capell. observ. in Gen. § Exod. xii. 2. || Stranchius chap. vi. of years.

four

four days before the sun; seeing the sun is supposed, and almost demonstrated, to be the centre of this, and of all the planetary orbs? The solution to be offered, and probably true, is, that perhaps our globe, and the other planets, were, by the Almighty power of God, for that space of time, suspended in the open air, in a state of rest. But when the sun, as a central point, was formed, and the earth reduced to firmness and solidity, they might, by certain physical laws impressed on them by the Divine wisdom, receive those rapid and regular motions about the sun, and their own centres, which, by the same wisdom and the co-operation of eternal power, continue to this day, producing the most agreeable and necessary variety of day and night, and seasons; and, therefore, the annual and diurnal motions may, on the fourth day, be reckoned to have commenced *.

The second difficulty of a similar nature, is, that light should be said to have been created previous to the sun; seeing the sun is alleged to be the fountain of light, by shedding luminous particles from his own body. Some interpreters are of opinion, that this part of the Mosaic history of creation, was adapted to the then present state and condition of the Hebrews, and calculated to serve, by way of precaution, to guard them against the idolatry of the Canaanites and Syrians, who worshipped Moloch, or the sun, as the Author of light †. But at the same time that he does strike at the root of this species of idolatry, by shewing that God alone is the Author of all that beauty which appears in the creation, and the sole giver

* Dr Taylor's scheme, &c.

† Abbé le Pluche.

of every good thing; and thereby confound those who admire *the creature more than the Creator*; he has not had recourse to a falsehood, to establish this important truth, nor advanced any thing in his history, which is repugnant to true philosophy. For light is visibly pre-existent to luminous bodies; if, in our notion of it, we distinguish between that sensation which we experience in ourselves on the presence of any illuminated body, and that inconceivably subtile matter, which makes the impression on the organs of sight, and paints on the optic nerve those objects, from the surfaces of which it was reflected to us. Light then, taken in this sense, is a body quite different from the sun, and independent on it, and might have existed before it, seeing it does now exist in it's absence, as well as when present; as electrical experiments abundantly shew, in midnight darkness. It is diffused from the one end of the creation to the other, traverses the whole universe, forms a communication between the most remote spheres, penetrates into the inmost recesses of the earth, and only waits to be put in a proper motion to make itself visible. In short, light is to the eye, what the air is to the ear; the body of light, as the other is of sound; and equally extended at all times from the most distant fixed stars to us, though it then only strikes our eyes, when impelled by the sun, or some other mass of fire *. Now, on this supposition, that light requires only to be excited, that element might well be created on the first day, and the Divine power alone might be the exciter, for the three first days of creation, till the sun, the instrumental, and stated exciter, was brought forth †.

* Spectacle de la nature, par le meme auteur. tom. 3.

† See Dr. Taylor's scheme, &c.

INDEED

Indeed as plants and trees ſprung on the third day, a thought, which has both ingenuity and probability in it, ought not to paſs unobſerved; that though the ſun had, for ſome time been obſcured, by the vapors and heterogeneous particles of the earth, we are not to imagine but his formation was going on with that of the earth, and even had all along a conſiderable influence on it, as light and heat gradually increaſed, and the air became, from time to time, more and more pure and defæcated, ſo as to aſſiſt the productions of the ground with greater power *. This energy in a certain degree ſeems to have been unavoidable, notwithſtanding the appearance of ſolar light cannot be admitted.

The third difficulty ariſes out of the profeſſion made by all chriſtians; namely, how God ſhould here be ſaid to perform all theſe things, while, in the new Teſtament, the formation of the world is aſcribed to the Son of God, who afterwards came perſonally among men for their redemption? This may be eaſily obviated, and rendered conſiſtent with our holy faith; either by conſidering our Lord to act by a derived power from his Father in creation, as the ſole agent of all things, as well as in our redemption; or as a perſon in the holy Trinity, by his own eternal might and authority, and as *God bleſſed for ever.* And, upon ſerious reflection, to many it will clearly appear, that nothing leſs than uncreated excellence, could be the author of this univerſe; and that He, whom we call our Saviour, muſt be acknowledged as *our Lord and our God* alſo.

* Univerſal Hiſtory.

THE

The last difficulty occurring is, that since, as has been already hinted, there may be, and it is almost certain there are, many other worlds of the same, or greater magnitude, with our own; is it reasonable to believe the account which the gospel gives us, of that God, who made them all, assuming mortal flesh, that he might suffer and die for sinners, to reclaim them from wickedness, and deliver them from misery. This indeed the gospel does declare *, and who is able to refute its assertions? What know we of the rank, or the condition of creatures in other regions? May not we be the only creatures, that either needed, or were indulged with, so expensive and glorious a remedy? *He took not on him*, we are told, *the nature of Angels, but the nature of the seed of Abraham*†. *Great is the mystery of godliness; God manifested in the flesh*‡. Instead of entertaining dangerous conceits, let us, therefore, correct our roving imagination, subject ourselves to the testimony of revelation, and *account this a faithful saying, and most worthy of our hearty acceptance that Christ Jesus*, the Creator came, *in the dispensation of the fulness of the times*, for the salvation of the world §.

And now in the end, reviewing this great subject, where the work of creation has been so minutely considered, who can with-hold the poet's beautiful exclamation?

These are thy glorious works, Parent of good!
Almighty thine this universal frame!
Thus wonderous fair! Thyself how wonderous then!

* St. John, 1st. and all the Gospels and Epistles. † Heb. 2. 16.
‡ 1 Tim. 3. 16. § 1 Tim. 1. 16.

How

How vaſt, and wonderous mighty the arm, *which ſtretched out the heavens, and laid the foundation of the earth!* How powerful was his command, who ſaid, *Let there be light, and there was light! Let there be a firmament! for he only ſpake and it was done, he commanded and it ſtood faſt! He formed Arcturus, Orion, Pleiades, and the chambers of the ſouth! Lift up your eyes on high eaſtward and weſtward, and ſouth and north, and behold who hath created all theſe things! And he* ſtill *bringeth out all the hoſt of heaven by number; he calleth them all by names, by the greatneſs of his might; for that he is ſtrong in power; not one of them faileth.* He ſuſpends thouſands and thouſands of worlds——of amazing bulk and weight——in diſtant regions of ſpace, and ſteadily guides their infinitely various, tremendouſly rapid, and moſt regular motions!——In ſuch lofty expreſſions do the holy ſcriptures celebrate the exertion of the divine omnipotence in the work of creation; and repreſent every thing as done inſtantaneouſly, and with as little difficulty as ſpeaking a bare word.

As for goodneſs, what can we ſay of it! when we go through all the works of creation, providence and redemption, it is a ſubject which the tongues of men and angels, ſhall never be able to exhauſt! For the goodneſs of God is boundleſs as his univerſal works, and endleſs as the ages of eternity. *Who can expreſs the noble acts of the Lord, or ſhew forth all his praiſe?* Not only by goodneſs was an incomprehenſible variety of creatures brought into exiſtence; but by the ſame goodneſs alſo, is ſuitable proviſion made for their preſervation and welfare. *The eyes of all things wait upon thee, O thou giver of all good, that thou mayeſt give them*

their

their meat in due ſeaſon; and thou openeſt thine hand liberally, and ſatisfieſt the deſire of every living thing. He maketh the graſs to grow upon the mountains, and giveth to the beaſt his food, and to the young ravens that cry unto him. The fowls of the air are fed by our heavenly father; and the lilies of the field are arrayed in colours far exceeding Solomon, in all his glory. Man, he has made only a little lower than the angels; and ſo loved the world as to give his only begotten ſon.——Not to ſpeak of myriads and myriads of other beings, which he is continually and plentifully ſupplying with all the neceſſaries of their natures, out of the plenitude of his own exiſtence! thus, *is he good, and does good, and his tender mercies are over all his works.*

THE wiſdom of God appears as illuſtrious in the variety, beauty, exactneſs, order, and harmony, in which he formed and fixed the whole univerſe. From the brighteſt ſtar in the firmament of heaven, to the ſmalleſt atom on the face of the earth, there is no part of matter, great or little, vile or precious, wherein the wiſdom of the Creator does not moſt clearly and undeniably appear. *But there are ſtill hid greater things than theſe, and we have ſeen but a few of his works.* And therefore in the devouteſt admiration, the language of the holy pſalmiſt is the fitteſt to be adopted by us: *O Lord, how manifold are thy works? In wiſdom haſt thou made them all! The world is full of thy riches!*

WITH ſuch reflections let us poſſeſs our minds, and our mouths muſt be filled with the higheſt praiſes. This God is our God, and will be our guide for ever. Let us in all things meekly and affectionately ſubmit

submit to the supreme ruler, in the most unreserved resignation to his Providence. Let us put our trust in God. We see his power, his understanding, and love. There can be nothing too hard for him to effect; and he is infinitely gracious and good. To this God, therefore, who made the heavens, and the earth, the eternal, and everlasting Father, let us ascribe unchangeable glory, dominion, and majesty, through ages and worlds without end.

DISSER-

DISSERTATION II.

OF THE CREATION OF MAN.

GENESIS I, 2.

HAVING before defcribed the inferior parts of nature, made and fafhioned for the reception and ufe of man, fome farther difcourfe concerning his formation, nature and ftate, may be neceffary and defirable.

HERE then obferve, the language of the Creator is changed, who, inftead of faying, *let there be men*, as he faid in regard to light, and all the other parts of the material univerfe, is reprefented as addreffing himfelf to the chief work here below, in this manner; now the earth is formed and finifhed, *let us make man*, the nobleft of all the fublunary productions, to inhabit, cultivate, and enjoy it. By which diftinguifhed manner of fpeaking, the fuperior excellence of human nature is manifeftly fignified.

AND Gods, for fo it is in the original reading, *faid*, *Let us make man*. Here, by a certain author, we are required to attend, that nouns appellative, afcribing dominion to God, according to the Hebrew idiom, are put in the plural number, inftead of the fingular; and

and that, in the genius of that language, it is only a magnificent way of expreſſing the majeſty of the moſt high. Of this ſuppoſed idiom ſeveral examples have been given; particularly, where, concerning the builders of the tower in the plains of Shinaar (a project hereafter to be conſidered) *the Lord God ſaid, go to, let us go down, and confound their language, and ſcatter them abroad;* * *and let Iſrael rejoice in his makers* †; *and thy makers is thy huſband* ‡.

But admitting that the phraſe, *and Gods ſaid let us make man*, and the other places adduced, is agreeable to the ſtructure of the Hebrew language; the queſtion, upon what idea is ſo ſingular an expreſſion founded, is ſtill pertinent. And the anſwer ſeems to be more than admiſſible; that when Moſes wrote the hiſtory of the

the Trinity, and couched their conceptions and belief of it, under this peculiar mode of ſpeech; as, moſt certainly, all languages derive their peculiarities from the nature of the knowledge which thoſe who ſpeak or write, deſign to communicate to one another.

The Jewiſh doctors, writing on this ſubject, have fancied ſtrange things, and had recourſe to many fictions, as one of themſelves teſtifies §. With whom does God here conſult? with the whole fabric of heaven and earth, ſays R. Levi. For in the ſame manner, as a king, though poſſeſſing ſupreme power and dominion, often refers his determinations to his ſubjects, as a proof of his tender regard to his

* Gen. xi. 7. † Pſalm cxlix. 2. Heb. בעשיו. ‡ Iſaiah liv. 5. עשיך § Vané differuerunt ſapientes noſtri, &c. R. Menaſſeh Ben. Iſrael Queſtio 6.

ſervants

servants and dependants; so did the king of kings convoke all the worlds, which he had created, when he was about to make this noblest of his creatures. The same opinion, R. Solomon also espouses, that God, in these words, proposes the example of his own humility to us, who, though the source of all power, is represented as taking counsel from inferior beings. Likewise R. Lemuel bar Nahman says, that God consulted with the work of each of the six days, by which he signified it to be his will, that every thing which he had made should, in some measure, concur in the creation of man. And the divine theologians of the Cabala (so R. Menasseh calls them) understanding the expression in a more refined sense, interpret thus, whereas we are to remark in all other places, that the sacred scriptures speak in the singular number, as, *let there be light*; *let there be a firmament*; the words, when man is to be made, are in the plural, thereby signifying, agreeable to the doctrine of Plato, that God conferred with second causes, about the constitution of a creature that was to participate of immortality. In this manner, do the most of them, too tedious to transcribe, speak; from their ignorance of that analogy, between the several parts of Revelation, which may very easily be traced.

Indeed this Rabbi, from whom these opinions are taken, at the same time he seems to be afraid of undermining the doctrine of God's Unity, by a literal interpretation of the words, *Let us make man*, relates a tradition among the Jews which deserves our notice, and passes unrefuted by himself. It is this; at the time Moses wrote his book by the command of God, and these words were dictated to him, he stopped,

and

and exclaimed, *O Lord, wouldst thou then drive men into error, and make them call in question the doctrine of thine own unity!* when the answer was given him, *I command thee to write; and if any one will err, let him err**. Another of the same denomination, likewise acknowledges difficulties in the passage where Moses says, *the spirit of God moved upon the waters*, by which some of our nation, says he, have understood *the spirit of the Messiah*†; as also in the words, *In the beginning Gods*, agreeable to the original, *created the heavens and the earth.* In short, the union of a plural with a singular, contrary to the construction of all languages, many of the Jewish doctors clearly perceived, could not be without design. And without attempting any other illustration, they freely confess, THIS IS THE MYSTERY OF THE WORD ELOHIM (GODS) THERE ARE THREE DEGREES, EACH DEGREE BY ITSELF IS ONE, AND YET THE THREE TOGETHER ARE BUT ONE; THEY ARE UNITED TO ONE, AND ARE NOT SEPERATE ‡."

WITH regard to the books of their law, which teach, *the Lord our God is one Lord*; *and thou shalt have no other Gods before me*§, it is to be carefully attended to, that nothing there is to be understood as descriptive of the divine nature, which is altogether incomprehensible; but only as a caution against idolatry, or the worship of the many false and imaginary deities, to which the folly and wickedness of mankind had, from the earliest ages, led them to pay supreme honors, through the vainest and most impious belief of their

* R. Menasseh, Ben Israel Quest. 6 p. 10.
† Hakspan Cabal, p. 342.
‡ R. Simeon Ben Jochai in zohar. Sect 6. in Levit.
§ Deut. 6. 4. Exod. 20. 3.

authority

authority and influence to protect and prosper them. And therefore a doctrine, no way repugnant to the unity of God, may be still insisted on as true; that there were at man's creation, and constantly are in the schemes of providence in relation to him, certain divine agents engaged, whom we reverently term the Trinity, without presuming to represent or explain, either their sacred essence or dependence, by any figure or reasoning whatever.

ANOTHER question, not less controverted than the former, hath arisen concerning the image of God. *And Gods said, let us make man in our image, after our likeness.* To reckon up all the opinions that have been entertained and urged, would be equally painful and unprofitable, and a perversion of the end here proposed. It hath been alledged by some interpreters, that it is the body of man which was made after the image of God;* that the divinity united itself to a body which was to serve as a model for Adam; and that this was no other than the body of the Messiah. The original and the copy, they even describe in the liveliest colours. How astonishing is it that men, who have had revelation for their guide, the words of which are so express and reasonable, though they still leave some room for a natural curiosity, should have followed such visions! They were much more pardonable in heathens who reasoned, from the suitableness of things, that the most excellent nature should be the most beautiful and perfect. Now what assemblage of members, what disposition of linea-

* Maimonides, more Nevochim. Pars. 1. Cap. 1. p. 1. where he expressly says, "Firmiter ipsi crediderunt, Deum eandem quam homines habere formam et figuram. Hoc tamen differe statuunt, quod ipsius (Dei sc.) corpus majus et splendidius.

ments

ments and features, what figure, what form, can be more elegant than that of man? So far does he excel all other living creatures, that if God be living, he hath, without doubt, the human form itself*.

THE opinion of some divines is, that this image consisted in holiness, or purity and moral perfection; which is certainly one of the principal attributes of the Creator, or perhaps only a summary term for compleat excellence. This, heathens themselves, who have said, that we cannot approach nearer the likeness of God, than by the exercise of righteousness, in the highest degree of which we are capable, have manifestly acknowledged†. And that Adam was created with such an inclination and power, unless we derogate from the divine justice and goodness, cannot be denied. Only we must take care, that the notion here suggested of his original innocence be such, as not to contradict that freedom of his will, which the event shews he had, in the forfeiture which he afterwards made of his happiness.

THERE are writers ‡, on the other hand, who are much disgusted with this opinion, that the expression under view, should mean that man was created either in righteousness or holiness, or even with any knowledge itself. For, say they, this is supposing, that Adam had actual righteousness concreated with him, or wrought into his nature, and belonging to him as a natural faculty and instinct; and needed not to make any acquisitions under trial, or by habitual practice. From the grossness of which misrepresentation the

* Cicero de natura deorum, lib. 1st. † Plato.

‡ See the whole tribe of the modernizers of divinity.

truth

truth will ſhew itſelf: That, in regard to knowledge, man had certainly impreſſed on his mind, ſuch principles of inſtruction, concerning his Maker, his duty and happineſs, as were neceſſary in his ſtate, and adapted to his chief end. While, by righteouſneſs, no other thing was ever underſtood, than perfection or rectitude of nature, ſuch as the wiſeſt and kindeſt of all Fathers thought fit to beſtow upon man, when he introduced him into exiſtence; and deſigned him, as the greateſt badge of his diſtinction, for moral ſervice and obedience. And the reſult of this knowledge unperverted, and of this diſpoſition preſerved, muſt neceſſarily be great holineſs, and ſerenity of heart, daily purified and refined, by the Divine favor, and ſubmiſſion to God's will.

If we will liſten, without prejudice, to the New Teſtament on this ſubject, we will hear St. Paul, in ſeveral of his epiſtles, ſpeaking of that ſtate into which the world had degenerated, and ſhewn the ſtrongeſt propenſity to love and abide in, ever ſince the firſt tranſgreſſion, under the notion of a nature that required to be made over again. *You have now put off the old man with his deeds; and put on the new man, which is renewed in knowlege after the image of him that created him.** *And the truth in Jeſus teacheth you, that ye put off concerning the former converſation, the old man which is corrupt, according to the deceitful luſts, and that ye put on the new man, which, after God, is created in righteouſneſs, and true holineſs* †.

These ſcriptures, it is true, have been ſuppoſed to relate only to the impure, idolatrous body of the hea-

* Coloſſ. iii. 9. 10. † Epheſ. iv. 21. 22. 24.

thens,

thens, and the Chriſtian church and community. But, by this explanation, what can be gained? *The Old Man* did repreſent the ſinful and miſerable condition of the world, in the Apoſtle's days; and for a long time before, even ſince the original apoſtacy; mankind from that time having had on them evident marks of infirmity and ſpiritual death, without the leaſt ſymptoms of a revival from the groſſeſt ignorance and wickedneſs, till, by another diſpenſation, the ſame in deſign as the firſt, they were reſtored from the ruins of the Fall, to the primitive univerſal religion of rational beings, or that *knowledge* of God and their duty, which the change of human circumſtances rendered neceſſary, by the peculiar doctrines of the Goſpel, in order to that *righteouſneſs* and *holineſs* in which Adam was created. So that, in the ſtricteſt, and moſt important moral ſenſe, *we are all God's workmanſhip created in Chriſt Jeſus unto good works*, to which *we were ordained*, when our firſt parents were *made after the image of God, in his likeneſs.*

But this is not all, nor yet the dominion over the creatures, which was granted to the firſt man, implied in the *image* of God: For, though either of theſe are frequently thus taken in ſcripture, there is a certain generality and comprehenſion in the words, which admit of a larger latitude, and not repugnant to any other paſſage. We may, therefore, underſtand by the *image* of God, a likeneſs of nature alſo, ſpirituality, a faculty of thinking, reflecting and loving, which exalts a man above all material beings, and brings him as near as his nature is capable, to that of God. This enlarged ſenſe, adopted by many modern interpreters, was likewise received by the ancients among both Jews and Christians *.

It only remains to be mentioned, as was hinted before, that the first pair were made *male* and *female*, in the manner described by Moses, who resolves the operation of making the *woman*, into the divine wisdom and power, by which all things, even out of nothing, can be made; that they might multiply, and supply a constant succession of their own kind, to inhabit the whole earth; and be a perpetual memorial of the conjugal union and affection in riches and poverty, in sickness and in health, till death part husband and wife, according to God's holy ordinance, which his blessing did, and does still, and will continue to accompany, till the consummation of the world.

And from this thrice venerable and most illustrious pair, have sprung the unnumbered millions, who, since their day, have stocked and overspread the face of the globe, and swayed the sceptre of power, conferred at creation, over all things on the ground, and in the air, in the seas, and in the caverns of darkness.

But to proceed: Lest man, dazzled with his own excellence, should regard himself as an independent creature, it was appointed by God, that his soul, which constituted the principal part of his being, should be joined to a portion of matter, to put him continually in mind of his maker; nothing suggest-

* R. Menasseh, Ben. Israel, Quæst. 7. Tertull. L. 11.

ing

ing to us more ſtrongly the ſupreme power God hath over our ſpirits, than the influence we feel the body to have over the ſoul: This is ſo great, that the faculty within us, capable of forming the greateſt deſigns, and of ſtretching its views almoſt over ſpace and eternity, is arreſted in the ſphere of its action by the external vehicle, vaſtly inferior to it in dignity. *The Lord God formed man of the duſt of the ground, and breathed into his noſtrils the breath of life; and man became a living ſoul.* To this man was given the deſignation of Adam, either to denote the beauty of his ſoul, or the baſeneſs of his body; as ſome of the learned have derived it from an Æthiopian word, which bears the former ſenſe, and others from the Hebrew, which ſignifies *earth* *. And for the ſuſtenance and nouriſhment of his mortal nature, the free uſe of all vegetable productions was allowed him: *Behold I have given you,* ſaid God, *every herb bearing ſeed, which is upon the face of all the earth, and every tree, in the which is the fruit of a tree, yielding ſeed; to you it ſhall be for meat.*

The particulars concerning the formation of man, and the ſtate he was made in, being thus collected, it cannot but be our intereſt and duty, to take a farther ſurvey of the *nature* which God has graciouſly beſtowed upon us. The body conſiſts of the meaneſt materials; but the mind is of heavenly extraction; an emanation from him who is the ſource and centre of intelligence. *The inſpiration of the Almighty gave Adam underſtanding*; and this nobleſt of our Maker's gifts, with all the other qualities that adorned

* Ludolphus, lib. 1. cap. xv.

the firſt man, may ſtill be our diſtinguiſhing portion, notwithſtanding our apoſtacy and fallen condition; with this difference, that they muſt be acquired by diſcipline and labour; and may lie uncultivated, or be ſet on wrong objects, having fatally received a contrary bias. But yet the force and excellence of the human underſtanding, weak and wavering as it is, through neglect and perverſion, ſhines forth in a ſurpriſing variety of inventions and diſcoveries. By this faculty we penetrate into the bowels of the earth; ſurvey and admire the contrivance and beauty of the vaſt fabric of the world about us; and trace the ſignatures of the moſt aſtoniſhing wiſdom and regularity, in the various adjuſtments and revolutions of the heavenly bodies. Generations and actions, characters and events, that exiſted long before we had a being, are brought under its powerful operations, on the one ſide; and on the other, futurity, even ſo far as to the final period of the world, with all its works, is raiſed up to view. Eternity itſelf is not covered; and the wretchedneſs and felicity of creatures, far beyond our ſtate, ſtrongly appear. In ſhort, we can ſtretch our thoughts to the utmoſt bounds, and contemplate the nature of God infinitely perfect.

Consider, O Man! this exerciſe of thought, by which thou art made able to improve thy nature, and this capacity of comfort and joy of which thou mayſt participate; and compare theſe powers and bleſſings thou poſſeſſeſt, with the allotment of the brutes that periſh, and the narrow limits within which they are confined; and ſay, if thou art not the chief of God's works here below, and in excel-

lence

lence and dignity only *a little lower than the angels* themſelves.

But the form and determination of our characters, in regard to good and evil, ſhew ſtill more remarkably wherein our ſingular honor and advantage lie. While mere inſtincts or accidents purely external and indifferent, fix the purſuits of inferior creatures; while they are utterly unable to judge of cauſes and events; to draw conſequences, or reaſon about the nature and tendencies of things; when to avoid, or when to embrace, unleſs it be by the information of ſome fallacious ſenſe; and are therefore rather impelled or actuated like a machine, than moved by a free and an enlightened choice; we *whom God has made wiſer*, can deliberate, compare paſt with preſent occurrences, examine and perceive what is before us; ſee this to be good, and therefore purſued, that to be evil, and therefore declined; this will improve and exalt our natures, and that ſink us into diſhonor and miſery. By a divine lamp, originally delivered to us, we can ſtudy and obſerve the precepts of divine wiſdom, and by an imitation of ſome of God's moral perfections, acquire farther lineaments of his *image*; converſe with the Father of all; and aſpire after, and long for the everlaſting enjoyment of his favour. In an higher degree, indeed, the moſt exalted ſpirits God has made may poſſeſs thoſe abilities; but they cannot have any of a nobler kind.

But the dignity of human nature will appear in a ſtill ſtronger light, when we conſider the improvement it has received by the grace of the goſpel. When

When the noble ſtructure of our body, diſtinguiſhed by its erect form, and majeſty of its appearance, from all the other orders of creatures upon the earth, was doomed to deſtruction, on account of tranſgreſſion, and to mingle with the duſt from whence it was originally reared; when the fineſt feelings of humanity were ſtifled, and the powers and abilities of the will and underſtanding impaired and perverted, by miſapplication and criminal indulgences; as Chriſtians we are aſſured of a glorious immortality reſtored, and the higheſt privileges conferred on us for our preſent improvement. To purchaſe all this, the Son of God vouchſafed to aſſume our nature; and by our relation to him as brethren, we are related to the father of all as his children. We are called to communion in the bleſſings of his kingdom, and the glory of his exalted ſtate. This high advancement and happineſs, is the fruit of a mighty apparatus in the divine adminiſtration; and of the moſt aſtoniſhing counſels. The Son of God muſt be incarnate. With all the characters of divine power about him, he muſt converſe ſome years in our world; ſubmit, notwithſtanding his high dignity, to all the ſinleſs infirmities of human nature; be perſecuted, ſuffer, and die; miraculouſly riſe again from the dead, aſcend on high; be inveſted with dominion over all worlds; and have the adminiſtration of all affairs given into his hands. Amazing counſel for the redemption of man, who had undone himſelf after the Creator had *made him perfect*, in his kind! It is the wonder of angels, and the ſubject of their loftieſt ſongs.

Having ſtill in us, indeed, principles of a very different quality from thoſe that originally belonged to us, while we are in this world we will be ſubject to perpetual attacks, and engaged in conſtant warfare. But *even hereunto are we called.* By the correction of our natures, and the removal of every thing that occaſions confuſion in them, the man of God muſt be reclaimed by diligent diſcipline, and brought back to his primitive excellence. *We are to grow in the knowledge of God, and of our Lord Jeſus Chriſt,* and in conformity of heart and life to the bleſſed will of Heaven. The objects of our ſtudy and care, are to be obedience to God, and *the recompence of reward.* Being enlightened after our darkneſs, by the bright truths of holineſs and ſalvation, we are obliged to learn and meditate on theſe things, *to hide them in our hearts,* that we may be thus fitting ourſelves for a much higher and more perfect degree of exiſtence and ſervice, in a better world.

DISSERTATION III.

Of PARADISE.

GENESIS II.

WHEN man was made, as if the whole earth, abounding with the richest productions, had not been sufficient for him, God, for his greater happiness, placed him in a part of it, distinguished from all the rest, by its delightful situation, and its extraordinary luxuriance and fertility. *The Lord God*, says Moses, *planted a garden eastward in Eden*; or *had planted*, probably on the third day; *and there he put the man whom he had formed*, perhaps in another place. *And out of the ground made the Lord God to grow every tree that is pleasant to the sight and good for food: The tree of life also in the midst of the garden, and the tree of the knowledge of good and evil. And a river went out of Eden to water the garden; and from thence it was parted, and became into four heads.*

IN the Vulgate version *, the puerile conceit, that *the Lord God had planted a paradise of pleasure from the*

* Plantaverat autem Dominus deus Paradisum voluptatis á principio. Vulg. Ed. Sixti V. Pont. Max. Jussu, 1592.

beginning,

beginning, is entirely grounded upon the transposition of the words *Eden* and *eastward*, from their local, to a strictly literal signification. That is to say, *Eden*, which is the name of a country, is there translated *pleasure*, and *eastward*, rendered *the beginning*.

INDEED this Hebrew word * itself is ambiguous; but the situation of the sacred writer; and the sense in other places, very plainly determine the meaning of it: and tho' *Eden*, interpreted sentimentally, is only another term for *pleasure*, the obvious intention of Moses was to describe a territory.

THE Septuagint † have only changed *garden* into *Paradise*, retaining the word *Eden*, and evidently understood it to have lain *eastward* from Egypt, or Midian, where this historian wrote.

A CERTAIN place, therefore, really existing, being designed by Moses, the situation of it, in respect either to the antediluvian or present state of the earth, comes very naturally to be inquired after. Though alas! the extreme heat, which have accompanied disputes concerning it, may convince us, that the spirit of meekness, which constituted the happiness of that blessed abode, is not always to be found among the learned themselves: While, perhaps, their utmost efforts to settle the point in question, will not be sufficient to reconcile them. The geography of Moses, it must be confessed, is sometimes so concise, that it is very difficult to establish critical doctrines on the short

* Heb. מקדם. † Vide LXX. in Loco.

hints

hints he has given us. And the very list of opinions arising from this difficulty, is enough to frighten any one from the slightest examination of them; seeing there is scarcely any part of the universe, which hath not been fixed on for the scite of Paradise. It hath been placed in the third heaven, in the fourth, in the heaven of the moon, in the moon itself, in the middle region of the air, above the earth, below, and beyond it, in a place concealed, and far from the knowledge of man. The regions under the Artick pole, Tartary, and the Caspian Sea, have alternately had this honor conferred on them. Terra del Fuego has been thought of; the Banks of the Ganges; the Isle of Ceylon, and the name of the Indies derived from *Eden*. The same privilege has been claimed for China; and even some country beyond it undiscovered. It has been placed in Armenia the Less; in Africa, under the equator; near the mountains of the moon, where the Nile is supposed to have its source; in Mesopotamia; in Assyria; in Persia; Babylonia; in Armenia the Greater; in Arabia, and Palestine. Europe itself has been esteemed a quarter of the globe not altogether unfit for the habitation of the fruit of man, and his happy consort *.

Yet, after all these sports of fancy, it is not denied, that the situation of this garden, by learning and industry, properly employed, may, in some measure be ascertained. In order to this investiga-

* Bochart, Phaleg. l. 1. cap. iv.

tion,

tion, the point muſt be firſt determined, whether Moſes is to be underſtood as deſcribing a country in its original ſtate, or as it appeared at the time when he himſelf lived. Adopting the former opinion, as ſome have done †, an inſuperable difficulty muſt be encountered; in regard to the preciſe ſpot where Paradiſe was ſituated, on account of the many changes which internal convulſions, and eſpecially the general deluge, may be well ſuppoſed to have produced on the ſurface of the earth, after a period of two or three thouſand years. Chuſing the latter, which ſeems perfectly reaſonable, as moſt of the names, uſed in the deſcription, are of modern impoſition, the difficulty will be avoided; and the only taſk remaining, will be to find out the place, by the characters given of it.

Out *of Eden*, or perhaps from the upper limits of it, we are told, *went a river to water the garden, and from thence*, which, in relation to the place, may either mean above or below it, *it was parted, and became into four heads*, or ſmaller rivers. *The name of the firſt is* Piſon, *which compaſſeth the whole land of* Havilah. *The name of the ſecond is* Gihon, *which compaſſeth the whole land of* Ethiopia,* as it is tranſlated for Cuſh, now Chuſiſtan. *The name of the third river is* Hiddekel, *which goeth towards the eaſt of* Aſſyria. *And the fourth river is* Euphrates. Of the names of two of theſe rivers, we are told, no traces have remained for a long time, viz. Piſon and Gihon; the Greek and Roman writers, calling them, after their parting, by the names they had before they met, Euphrates

† Saurin, Diſc. 11. P. 25. Imp. a Amſter. 1720.

and

and Tigris *. But notwithſtanding the abolition of names, the accidental variation of currents, and the new aſpects which the face of countries are well known to aſſume in a very ſhort time, conjectures not at all improbable, concerning the place of Paradiſe, have been formed on the above deſcription; of which the two following deſerve our notice.

FIRST, ſome † ſuppoſe Eden to have been near Cœlo-Syria; that the river mentioned aroſe ſomewhere between the mountains Libanus and Anti-Libanus, and from thence run to the place where Euphrates now divides Syria and Meſopotamia, or Diarbeck, where it was divided into two, namely, Euphrates, and a ſtream which paſſed through the ridge of mountains that run croſs the country, and joined itſelf to the Tigris, with which it run into the Perſian Gulf. This ſtream they call Hiddekel. Much about the ſame place where Hiddekel parted, they ſuppoſe the Euphrates to divide again into two other ſtreams, which ran through the land of the Iſhmaelites, and ſeparated the range of hills at the entrance of Arabia Felix, and, encloſing between their ſtreams, a part of that country, met again, and were afterwards divided, and ran, the one into the Indian; and the other into the Red Sea. Theſe they make Gihon and Piſon.

SSECONDLY, There are not a few, who all agree in the main, that Eden was in Chaldæa, and that the garden was ſomewhere near the rivers, among which Babylon was afterwards built: They prove the land

* Bp. Patrick in Loco. † Le Clerc.

of

of Havilah, by undeniable arguments, to be the country adjacent to the present Euphrates, all along and upon the banks of that river, and spreading thence towards the Deserts of Arabia. The land of Cush, which every one knows is falsely rendered Ethiopia in our translation, was that part of Chaldæa, where Cush the son of Ham settled after the flood.

Now, as to the *first* of these schemes, it is indeed true, there was a place in Syria called Eden, of which the prophet Amos speaks; '*I will break the bar of Damascus, and cut off the inhabitants from the plain of Aven, and him that holdeth the sceptre from the house of Eden* *; but this Eden was of much later date than that where Adam was placed. Besides Syria is not east to the place where Moses wrote, but rather, if not quite north. And none of the descriptions which Moses has given of Eden belong to any part of Syria. Nor are there any rivers in the world that run so fancifully as they are here represented, out of one another; and repeatedly reverting to the same tract; not to urge the extravagant assertion of the Indian and Red Sea, receiving them separately at their final *embouchure*; while the latter never could possibly be the outlet of any river, through the mountains and lands of Arabia, that had its source to the eastward of them. Even the reply, that the earth and course of rivers were altered by the flood, cannot be admitted. For, as was said before, Moses did not describe the situation of this place in antediluvian names, the denomination of rivers and lands about them, being all of later date than the

* Amos, i, 5.

flood;

flood; and it is certain Mofes intended, according to the known geography of the world, and his own notions of it, to give us hints of the place near which Eden in the former world, and the garden of Paradife was fituated.

The fecond fcheme feems to come much nearer the truth than this; and to have but fmall objections againft it. There is, indeed, no draught of the country which fhews the rivers exactly to anfwer Mofes's defcription of them; but it is eafy to fuppofe, that the rivers, about Babylon, have at feveral times been fo much altered by ftreams and canals, made by the fovereigns of that potent empire, that we never had a draught of them agreeable to what they were when Mofes wrote about them*.

It hath been vaguely faid, that the moft judicious among the learned, fuch as Patrick, Heylin, Huet, and Spanheim, are agreed that Paradife was feated in the fouth of Chaldæa, between the two rivers Tigris and Euphrates, *becaufe* thefe and feveral fmaller rivers effectually watering this land, render it always moft exceedingly fruitful †. But inftead of this, it is the Mofaic geography, not the amenity of the place, that guides thefe great men in their determinations; and they have the fuffrage of the moft eminent for learning and ingenuity, to fupport them in their opinion.

One of the above named commentators, hath fo diftinctly delineated the courfe of the river that wa-

* Shuckford, book 1, page 75.

† See Herm. Moll, under the article Diarbeck at large.

tered

tered Paradise, and the relative situation of the garden, in words †; that a late writer * hath been able to sketch it out in a draught, and inserted it in his work, to assist the understanding of his readers. But, alas! neither the one nor the other seem to have sufficiently attended, that in no chart ever exhibited, did the Tigris and Euphrates ever run so far in the same channel, as they represent them; nor, indeed, could they possibly, from their present distance from each other, and the nature of the country which lies between them.

This, therefore, may teach us the vanity of dogmatizing, in regard to the identical spot where our first parents had their happy residence during the period of their innocence; though it appears most probably to have been near the very place, where the first great monarchy of the world began, and its regal seat was erected.

And as most of the fabulous accounts, in old times, of things relating to the original state of man, were derived from the fountains of truth, and dressed up according to mens fancies, and the established theological opinions; so have the ancient Heathens evidently borrowed from the Mosaic description of Paradise, their accounts of the golden age of innocence and plenty; when man was perfectly happy, and the earth produced spontaneously every thing that was good and desirable. From this sacred tradition they multiplied their paradises, which they generally placed out of our continent;

† Patrick in Loco. * Dr. Taylor in his scheme.

in the ocean, or beyond it, or in another hemisphere; as the garden of the Hesperides, the Fortunate Islands, Ogygia, and the like; which being all characterized like so many paradises, were all romantically situated by their geography and descriptions of them *. The Christian fathers too, in their warm imaginations, followed, but too implicitly, the profane authors, and carried Paradise into the southern hemisphere, or beyond the equinoctial, where they believed the sun more *vivific*, and the soil more generous; and a late learned man has joined them in this notion; though he supposes the whole earth, before the fall, to be, in an eminent degree, paradisiacal †.

INTO *this garden*, the topography of which has been so amply discussed, *the Lord God put the man whom he had formed*. Having prepared a proper place of habitation for him, and furnished the garden of Eden with every tree that could delight the eye, or please the taste, the Almighty conducted man, the chief work of his creation, and lord of all inferior creatures, from the place where he made him, to this blissful dwelling; that he might *dress* and cultivate it, *keep* it, from the incursions of animals, and enjoy it as his own inheritance; and, no doubt revealed himself to him as his Creator and sovereign, to inform him of his state, his duty and dependence. Revealed himself to him he most evidently did, in the grant of the vegetable productions given to him, for his food, and in assuring him that he had the dominion over all animals; in regard to the law and state of

* Univ. Hist. B. 1. chap. 1. † Dr. Burnet, B. 11. chap. 7.

marriage

marriage, hereafter to be considered; in the communication of language, and such other necessary matters *. All these points are manifestly expressed in the Mosaic relation; excepting it may be thought divine instruction in the use and application of speech, is not so clearly inferable. But that God made man a social creature, needs not to be proved; and that when he made him such, he with-held nothing from him that was any way necessary to his well-being, in society, is a clear consequence from the wisdom and goodness of him who made him; and if he with-held nothing from him any way necessary to his well-being, much less would he withhold from him that which is the instrument of the greatest happiness, a reasonable creature is capable of in this world, the exercise of the tongue—the glory of man. If it was not good for Adam to be alone, neither certainly was it good for him to have a companion, to whom he could not readily communicate his thoughts; with whom he could neither ease his anxieties, nor divide, or double his joys, by a kind, a friendly, a reasonable, a religious conversation; and how could he do this in any degree of perfection, and to any height of rational happiness, is utterly inconceivable without the use of speech †.

One case in point, which strongly confirms all this reasoning, obviously presents itself. Moses tells us, that *the Lord God brought every beast of the field, and every fowl of the air unto Adam, to see what he would call them; and whatsoever Adam called every living crea-*

* Dean Delany's Rev. Exam. Diss. i, ii, iii, iv, v.

† Dean Delany's Rev. Exam. page 23.

ture, that was the name thereof. What is here said of Adam's language, must be applied to Eve also. And the passage is an express testimony that both of them were taught divinely the use of speech. As God instructed man in religion, says an ingenious, learned and masterly writer *, can we believe that he would not at the same time teach him to speak, so necessary to support the intercourse between him and his maker? Can we think that God would leave the man and the woman to themselves, to get out of the forlorn condition of brutality, mute and incommunicative, as they could? But, if I am not much mistaken, we have the clearest evidence from Moses, that God did indeed teach men language. It is where he tells us, that *God brought every beast of the field to Adam.* Here, by a common figure of speech, instead of directly relating the fact that God taught man language, the historian represents it by shewing God in the action of doing it, in a particular mode of information; the most apposite we can conceive, namely, elementary instruction, in giving names to substances, with which Adam was to be most conversant, and which, therefore, had need of being distinguished, each by its proper name. How familiar an image do these words convey of a learner of his rudiments? *And the Lord God brought every beast of the field, and every fowl of the air to Adam, to SEE what he would call them.* In short, the legislator's manner of relating this important fact, has, in my opinion, an uncommon elegance.

In this review of the creatures before Adam, as many wise and good ends might be designed and an-

* Warburt. Div. Leg. v. ii. p. 1.

swered

ſwered by it, ſuch as making him acquainted with their ſeveral natures, and giving him an early opportunity of exercíſing his dominion over them, by giving them names, which, we are informed, was the maſter's prerogative over his ſervants; ſo there appears neither difficulty nor abſurdity. For certainly it could be no hardſhip to him who created them, to cauſe every ſpecies of animals to paſs along as he pleaſed; nor is at all abſurd to ſuppoſe, that he would preſent theſe works of his hands to the view of that ſuperior creature, to whom he had given the dominion over them. If two of each ſpecies only were at firſt created, even in that caſe two were quite ſufficient to paſs before Adam, for the end deſigned. And if, by any means, the Lord God made Adam acquainted with the nature of the ſeveral creatures, he would doubtleſs give them names agreeable thereto, in that language, which was the primæval one; and with the power of ſpeaking which language, we muſt neceſſarily ſuppoſe him endued at the beginning. For, as being created in a ſtate of perfection, he muſt have been capable of converſing and communicating his ideas, which we can have no more difficulty in conceiving, than what we ſee every day, that the brute animals are born with their ſeveral diſtinct voices, and modes of expreſſing what they feel and deſire, how few or many ſoever their ſenſations may be. Man, therefore, may eaſily be imagined, as being endued with ſuperior faculties, to have been formed capable of expreſſing his ideas in regular language; a power wherewith God *can* endue his creatures inſtantaneouſly, as was abundantly proved on the day of Pentecoſt, when the diſciples of our Lord received the gift of tongues, and were enabled to ſpeak in languages to which before they were utter ſtrangers.*

But before we conclude this Diſſertation, what ſeveral commentators have well obſerved, muſt not be omitted; that the emblematical repreſentations of Heaven, in the new Teſtament, are borrowed, as from various other images of things, and ſcenes of happineſs on the earth, ſo chiefly from the deſcription of the primæval ſeat of innocence and felicity; hence Heaven is called Paradiſe in ſeveral paſſages, by our Lord and his Apoſtles. And in the deſcription of the new Jeruſalem, in the book of the Revelations †, *the holy city coming down from God* is repreſented as being *of pure gold, the foundation of the gates garniſhed with all manner of precious ſtones, and the twelve gates* themſelves *of twelve pearls*; plainly alluding to the gold, the bdellium, or pearl, and the onyx, or precious ſtones, in the deſcription of the earthly paradiſe in *Eden*. *In the midſt of the ſtreet of the city, and of either ſide of the river*, it is likewiſe ſaid, *was there the tree of life, which bare twelve manner of fruits, and yielded her fruit every month, and the leaves of the tree were for the healing of the nations.* Here all the figures fill our minds with the thoughts of that happineſs, only raiſed higher as this is heavenly, which our firſt parents enjoyed in perfect innocence, and the ſenſible favour of their maker. Moreover, *the water of life, proceeding out of the throne of God*, as plainly alludes to the *river* of Paradiſe, *that went out of Eden*, or came from the upper extremities of that country,

* See Dr. Dodd in Loco. † Rev. xxi, 22.

to

to water the garden below. And in like manner, from the ſame ſource, we find the prophets borrowing their ideas of happineſs. Thus, in the figurative deſcription of *Tyre*, in its once flouriſhing ſtate, moſt of the images are Paradiſiacal: *Thou haſt been in Eden, the garden of God; every precious ſtone was thy covering; the ſardius, topaz, and the diamond, the beryl, the onyx, and the jaſper, the ſapphire, the emerald, the carbuncle, and the gold.* *

THIS terreſtrial Paradiſe being forfeited by the original progenitors, for themſelves and all their poſterity, and the very traces of it, by time and various ſucceſſive devaſtations, obliterated from the earth, the only thing remaining for us the ſons of men, is to ſeek for another, which hath everlaſting foundations, and whoſe beauty, riches and happineſs, nothing in the univerſe can waſte or deſtroy. And where this place of divine pleaſure lies, it is not ſo difficult, though it be inviſible and remote, to explore, as is the ſituation of *Eden*, once a ſenſible object, and the ſeat of every temporal, as well as every moral delight. There is only a vail of fleſh between Saints and the true Paradiſe of God, *where the tabernacle of God ſhall be fixed among them* for ever; *and he ſhall dwell with them, and they ſhall be his people, and he ſhall be their God; and they ſhall ſee his face, and his name ſhall be on their forehead, and God ſhall wipe away all tears from their eyes, and there ſhall be no more death, neither ſorrow nor crying, neither ſhall there be any more pain; and they that ſerve him ſhall be before the throne of God, day and night in his temple* †.

* Ezek. xxviii, 13. † Rev. xxi. 3, 4.

DISSERTATION IV.

OF THE INSTITUTION OF MARRIAGE.

GENESIS II.

THE *bringing every beaſt of the field, and every fowl of the air to* Adam, *to ſee what he would call them*, ſeems to have been previous to the formation of the Woman; and the view of the Creator, in this act, beſides the reaſons already mentioned, probably was, that Adam, our firſt father, having ſurveyed all the animals, and obſerved that they were created in pairs, for the *increaſe of their ſeveral kinds, that the earth, the air, and the waters might be repleniſhed*, might be ſenſible of his own ſolitary, deſtitute condition, and of the importance of his being alſo provided with a mate ſuitable to his nature, which, by reaſon of its ſuperior excellence, could not be matched with any of the brutal race; in ſhort, that there was wanting to him, a companion in body and mind, fit to cohabit with him, for mutual converſe, delight, comfort, and aſſiſtance, eſpecially for propagating a reaſonable offspring, without which the world would have been ſtocked with irrational creatures only.

OF

Of each species of these, it has been said, there were created two, distinct from each other in their origin, and of different matter; intimating to us, it may be presumed, the natural incapacity of affection, which their wise Creator intended they should lie under, and the absolute dissoluteness, in point of social obligations, and animal sensations, in which they were to spend their existence. While, on the contrary, as being more fitting, perhaps more agreeable to the true nature of things, the formation of the Woman was accompanied with a circumstance expressive of the nearness of that relation, which was to be the fountain of the existence of all mankind, and of all the dear and intimate relations, so beneficial and comfortable to the life of man. *The Lord God caused a deep sleep to fall upon* Adam, *and he slept: And he took one of his ribs, and closed up the flesh*, where the opening was made: *And the rib which the Lord God had taken from Man, made he a Woman.* Thus, being taken out of a part of Adam's body, Eve became another self to him; and this was intended as a document to all posterity, that a wife should be regarded and treated under this delicate and just notion.— Hence St. Paul infers, as *no man ever yet hated his own flesh, but nourisheth and cherisheth it; so ought men to love their wives as their own bodies; he that loveth his wife, loveth himself* *.

In the words of this relation, particularly at the 23d verse, we are more than obscurely informed, that God intimated to Adam that he would create a companion meet for him. This, at least, is certain,

* Eph. v. 28. 29.

that

that Adam had afterwards communicated to him, the manner in which Eve derived her exiſtence from him. For, ſays he, *ſhe was taken out of man*.

THE notion that Adam had thirteen ribs on each ſide, and that God took away one pair, with the muſcular parts that adhered to them, and out of them made Eve, may be received or rejected at every one's pleaſure*. Though, if it was decent to indulge raillery on the occaſion, it might be aſked what became of the *vertebræ* to which thoſe ribs were joined; ſeeing if it remained there muſt needs have been a large ſpace of ſoft fleſh on either ſide, and if it was removed alſo, another miracle muſt have been wrought to preſerve Adam's life, as the ſpinal marrow muſt have been broken, which paſſes through that channel. This much we know, that he who created man out of the duſt of the ground, and can create all things out of nothing, as was obſerved in the firſt Diſſertation, could as eaſily have formed Eve from other materials, as from a rib out of Adam's ſide; but, by this method, not only perfect love and union are more effectually inculcated; but alſo the high wrought and delicate frame of woman is demonſtrated, ſeeing, if we may be allowed the expreſſion, the original clay of which ſhe was made, paſſed, as it were, twice through the great Creator's refining hands.

WHEN *the Lord God brought the Woman*, his wife, *to the man*, and told him how ſhe was produced, Adam, hitherto incompleat in his happineſs, without

* Bartholin. hiſt. anatom.

an

an help meet for him, ſaid, with great love and thankfulneſs towards his divine benefactor, *This is now bone of my bones, and fleſh of my fleſh*, the deareſt, the moſt neceſſary, and uſeful of all creatures to me; *she ſhall be called Woman, becauſe ſhe was taken out of Man.*

THIS may be either underſtood in a literal ſenſe, as referring to the manner of Eve's formation; or more generally, as expreſſing only nearneſs of relation, and proximity of blood; in the ſame manner as when Laban ſays to Jacob, *ſurely thou art my bone and my fleſh*, my near relation; and Abimelech addreſſed his mother's brethren, ſaying, *Remember, I pray you, that I am your bone and your fleſh*, your kinſman and brother.

SHE *ſhall be called Woman*; ſhe ſhall partake of my name, as ſhe does of my nature, being taken almoſt from my heart; and having both of us one common origin, one denomination ſhall be common to us both.

IT has been obſerved, that the agreement of the names of perſons, with the names of things from which they have been derived, is one of the main arguments offered in proof, that the Hebrew is the original, or at leaſt, a dialect of the original language. The inſtance before us is, the man was called Adam, from Admah, the ground from whence he was taken; the woman was called Aſhè, from Aiſh man, out of whoſe ſide ſhe was extracted; which analogy is loſt, if we take the names in other languages*.

* See Shuckford, vol. 1, page 121.

THESE

These two *Hebrew* words, at least shew us, that as a part belongs to any substance from whence it was taken; or as a member belongs to its proper body, so was the woman essentially the man's, and in whom he justly claimed a property. *And therefore said the Lord God*, as our blessed Saviour explains it, in the 19th chapter of St. Matthew, *shall a man leave his father and mother, and shall cleave unto his wife, and they two shall be one flesh.*

From this passage arises another evidence, according to a celebrated Divine †, that Adam was favoured with many revelations from God, especially in regard to the matters which it concerned him to know in his infant and primitive state. And indeed how could he possibly have any idea of father and mother, before there was any such thing as a father and mother in the world, unless God had instructed him, that though he and Eve had come into it miraculously, the rest of mankind were to be produced in another way, and a variety of relations formed agreeable to the will of God, for carrying on the great purposes of his providence to the end of time.

Here then is the institution of marriage; an ancient, sacred, and honorable ordinance, of high distinction, and very nearly connected with the dignity and happiness of the human race. It sprung not originally from libidinous desires, nor selfish worldly interests, but was the express law and appointment of the Creator. An *help meet* for Adam was necessary; he loved Eve as soon as he saw her, and maintained

† Dean Delany's Rev. Exam. page 20.

his affection, and Eve as quickly and constantly re-sented his tenderness. The labors of the day, and the homages of their great Lord, were willingly shared by the pleased, and the pleasing partners, and their nights spent in the softest dalliances. It is said, *they were both naked, the man and his wife, and were not ashamed. Shame,* says a profound writer*, *is an uneasiness of the mind, upon the thought of having done something which is indecent, or will lessen the valued esteem which others have for us; and even then is not always accompanied with blushing.* It was impossible, therefore, that our first parents, in their state of perfection, could have known or felt any thing of the passion of shame. "Wherefore should they blush? and if we have any difficulty in comprehending this circumstance of the sacred history, it is because the greatest part of men's judgments since the fall, is vitiated by sin; and we have equally lost the notions of true shame, and of true honor †.

THIS subject cannot be dismissed without various reflections, and unfolding the chief duties arising out of the close relation we have been speaking of.

NOW, it is plainly declared, by God's making one man and one woman only, that this relation was to subsist between no more than two parties at the same time. The prophet Malachi ‡ argues thus from it: *and did not he make one?* one man, and one woman, who is *his companion, and the wife of his covenant*; as a

* Locke, Vol. 1. Chap. 20. Sect. 17.
† M. Saurin, Dis. ii.
‡ Malachi, ii. 14, 15.

rule

rule to all mankind that ſhould deſcend from them: *Yet had he the reſidue of the ſpirit*, and could then have created more wives for Adam, or more men and women in general, if promiſcuous commerce had been for the greater happineſs of the world. *And wherefore*, the prophet adds, *did he make but one? That he might ſeek a godly ſeed*: that man and woman in holy wedlock, in ſincere and undivided affection, might propagate a pure race, for the honor and ſervice of God. *Therefore take heed to your ſpirits, and let none deal treacherouſly againſt the wife of his youth.*

It is true, indeed, in the earlieſt periods of the old diſpenſation, many of the patriarchs had, not only *two ſorts of wives*, but alſo ſeveral of thoſe ſorts at the ſame time, both of whom were reputed *lawful and true wives*, and their children accounted *legitimate*, in certain degrees. The one ſort was called by the Hebrews, *primary-wives*, married with the requiſite nuptial rites and ceremonies; the other *ſecondary*, or *half-wives*; in our Engliſh tranſlation *concubines*, and not unfitly from the Hebrew word *pillagſchim*, which ſometimes ſignifies *an infamous ſtrumpet, or common harlot.*

Between thoſe *concubines* and *primary-wives*, there were theſe differences; that whereas the *chief-wife* received from her huſband at the eſpouſals, certain *gifts* and *tokens*, as *pledges* of the *contract*; and *a bill of writing*, or *matrimonial letters*; and had full authority as *miſtreſs* in the houſhold government; *concubines* neither received *preſents*, nor any *obligation*, nor had the leaſt legal management in affairs; only *a right to the marriage bed*, and to have their children acknow-

ledged

ledged, who were yet excluded from the inheritance*; but capable of gifts and legacies, Gen. xxv. 5.

But, says one of the fathers of the church, the customs of mankind can never give a sanction to any thing not founded on divine authority †. Now such practices being contrary to the law of nature, if God ever positively permitted them, it was by a special dispensation, as in the case of sacrificing Isaac, and spoiling the Egyptians. Many have contended, that being inconsistent with the original institution of marriage, this was a liberty entirely usurped ‡.

Hence, from this subject, may fairly be deduced, an argument against *poligamy* and *concubinage*, publicly practised at this day in many nations of the world. The abettors of this custom, sometimes defend it, or at least apologize for it, by alleging that it is not a moral transgression, and that it tends to the multiplication of the human species; To whom the reply is obvious, that even admitting the last proposition, which is by no means clear, *we are never to do evil that good may come*; especially when the action evidently crosses the command of God, which, though published with regard to a positive institution itself, is always of sufficient authority to direct and govern us. And the question of morals, in this, as well as in many other matters, is not so much what may, or may not, be done, as what is prescribed by the law of God, and

* Godwyn's Aaron and Moses, p. 228.
† St. Aug.
‡ Synop. Critic. Poli, in Loco.

visibly hurtful and wicked, on account of its influence on society, and its vitiating effects on the minds of its individual members. And where God Almighty has consulted the interests or perfection of either, we ought to be so far from violating, or repining at his regulations, that we ought to thank him for his kindness, and gladly follow his will.

On the same principle is *divorce* as unwarrantable, except for the cause, on the part of the woman, of which our Lord has made mention, in the 'forecited 19th Chapter of St. Mathew; where, from the words of God to our first parents, and the nature of the matrimonial tie, he shews, notwithstanding the indulgence Moses gave, *because of the hardness of men's hearts*, in the iron age of the world, that *from the beginning it was not so*; nor till sinners had so *corrupted their way on the earth*, as to forget and disregard the divine statutes, which he declares to be one of the ends of his coming, to revive, enforce, and fulfil.

It is, indeed, allowed that there are cases, where a man may suffer as much injury and vexation, and, perhaps, more, through the length and irremediableness of other misfortunes, from his wife, as when she breaks the matrimonial faith, and violates her chastity; and yet a dissolution of the nuptial band is not permitted; because all the other miseries she may occasion in a family, are to be considered as so many trials and tribulations wherewith human life is full, for the discipline and improvement of her common partner, and to which, under this view, and to this end, he ought to submit. But a failure in the instance

inſtance of fidelity, in regard to the huſband's bed, breaking in on the eſtabliſhed order of human affairs, and rendering property, ſucceſſion, and every relation doubtful, the righteous governor has there interpoſed his authority, in relief of the immediate ſufferer, and for the general good permitted an entire and perpetual ſeparation.

Thus are mankind brought into the world with ſolemnity, if we may be allowed the phraſe, and have their procreation and birth ſettled by important preſcriptions, ſuitable to their peculiar excellence.

Were there no ſuch rules, we may eaſily imagine, conſidering the weakneſs and imperfection of infancy, in what a deep ignorance, and great diſſoluteneſs of manners, all of us would neceſſarily grow up to manhood. How important muſt good diſcipline and inſtruction be! Was the race of men produced in a vagrant, licentious manner, without well-known parents to own them, and, with tender care and affection, to give them an early education, this world, moſt certainly, would exhibit a ſcene, infinitely more wild and diſorderly, than hath ever been ſeen among the brutes, or we can poſſibly imagine. Surely the production of an intelligent being, in the moſt helpleſs and expoſed circumſtances, and in no otherwiſe than by the moſt painful culture, grows up to a due degree of underſtanding, ought to be tutored with every requiſite advantage in the propagators power. And, therefore, the procreation of the human ſpecies, according to the true nature of things, ought to be guarded and directed by the beſt exerciſe of reaſon, and is not to be the

the effect of a wanton thought, or the mere gratification of a ſenſual appetite. God, at the firſt, ſaid, *let us make man*, expreſſing a particular counſel and concern about his formation; and, conſequently, the ordinary generation of man, ſhould not be a matter of ſport, or of lawleſs paſſion. *This*, ſays a judicious and ſolid writer *, *is the rule of marriage; the purpoſe of the inſtitution, and true decency and ſobriety.*

One thing more reſpecting the parties in this conjugal covenant, is obſerveable, that Adam had no choice; from which the circumſtances of things then debarred him; and, therefore, being wholly dependent on his maker's Providence, there is much likelihood that Eve, was, in every reſpect, the moſt perfect of her kind, and, in the trueſt ſenſe, *an help meet for him.* But his poſterity, having the privilege of chooſing their conſorts, they are thereby called to the exerciſe of prudence and wiſdom, which there is great need to employ, in fixing a relation ſo important and laſting. After the cooleſt deliberations with themſelves, the advice and approbation of parents, are in this caſe, of great moment, as their judgments are generally riper, their views more extenſive, and their affectionate regards free from all youthful fervors. And beſides; as marriage leſſens the intereſt of parents in their children, it muſt be impious to alienate *that* from them, which they hold ſo dear, and give it to another without their knowledge and conſent. Of the fatal conſequences of this filial impiety we ſee the world full, and hoary locks ſinking into the earth under them; while a

* See Dr. Taylor's Scheme, on the Inſtitution of Marriage.

vagabond

vagabond life, and penury and disgrace prove the wages of the child's disobedience. Nor should parents, on the other hand, unreasonably oppose the inclinations of their children, through ambition, caprice, or covetousness, which may produce a multitude of sorrows to themselves, and great infelicity to their children, of which they will be the principal authors.

WHEN this sacred knot is tied, the husband owes the wife the most tender and affectionate love.— Not to repeat over again the comparison already used by St. Paul, which requires this, there is another to the same purpose in his writings, of extreme force, taken from the intimate communion of Christ with his church, and the ardent love which he hath testified towards it. *Even so,* saith that Apostle *, *ought men to love their wives, as Christ loved the church, and gave himself for it: and we are members of his body, of his flesh, and of his bones: This is a great mystery;* but not greater *concerning Christ and his church,* than that which is formed in consequence of the union between husband and wife. Therefore ought husbands to forbear every thing rude and shocking to their wives, which may injure their minds or bodies, and imbitter their lives; and cherish and comfort them, as the head of believers, and the saviour of the spiritual body of christians protects them, and restrains and conquers all things that are hurtful to them. Hence those husbands who tyrannize over their wives, and scarcely treat them as if they were their own species, ought to consider if they be christians, when they disregard

* Ephesians, v. 23, 32.

this precept of divine authority. Let them even consider if they be men, when the softness and innocence of female nature, have lost their power of charming them into mildness and compassion.

THE husband ought, next, to share with his wife all the good things wherewith God hath endued him; and neither, through avarice, deny her what is necessary, nor, through dissipation, so to impoverish her, that she shall not have wherewithal to subsist herself. And to this bodily provision of the wife, and other external accommodations, the husband must add her instruction, in matters especially which concern her salvation. St. Paul commands women to *learn from their husbands at home*, which supposes that their husbands ought to teach them. Indeed every head of a family is bound to communicate to every one under his care, such knowledge as is suitable to their capacities, of *the things pertaining to godliness*, and particularly to his wife, who is much nearer than all the rest. And this should make every man careful to be instructed himself, that he may be qualified to discharge his duty to another.

BUT as performances are not exacted on the one side only, let us view the duties of wives towards their husbands also. The wife then, first of all, owes obedience to her husband, as is declared in many passages of God's word; especially by the same Apostle, St. Paul, who saith, *wives obey your husbands in all things*; that is, in all things lawful, and consistent with the commandments of God; this being the rule of obedience, to *kings* themselves, *and all who are in authority*, and every superior whatever.

In

In all things not contrary to this rule, the precept will take place; and, therefore, condemn the obstinacy and imperiousness of many women, who disobey their husbands lawful commands, for no other reason, but because subjection is mortifying to them, though God has expresly enjoined it. If ever it should happen, as it often may, that the husband demands compliance in what may be even improper and inconvenient, the wife ought then meekly to submit, without noise or opposition; and, when a fit opportunity occurs, perhaps her expostulations may convince, and reform the husband of his mistake. And even when intreaties and friendship are unsuccessful, the wife is never to usurp government, nor refuse obedience to the man; seeing no case gives her a right to do it, but when the execution of her husband's order would be sinful.

Wives ought, moreover, to be faithful to their husbands, in regard to sobriety and pure manners, and the management of affairs entrusted to them. In this way chiefly, as well as in the other parts of their conversation, are they to testify their tender and cordial love. To comfort and assist them in all states and conditions, either of health or sickness, of opulence or poverty, which God's providence shall allot to them, is their indispensible duty: A conduct quite opposite to untowardness, turbulence, anger, peevishness, and other wicked humors, which render a woman insupportable, and a plague in a man's house, instead of an *help* and consolation to him. Nor let wives think of justifying their conduct by the faults of their husbands; for neither conscience nor sound policy can excuse them It is the abſolute command of God, that they obey—and refuſing to do this, how much do they often loſe. How many men, to avoid the clamor and inſolence of their wives, have had recourſe to companies, which have brought on an habit of intemperance, reduced them to poverty, and been the occaſion of innumerable misfortunes? Let every woman, therefore, be cautious of expoſing her huſband to ſuch temptations; and when any thing happens, which may call for her advice, let it be given, through the affection ſhe bears to her huſband, with all imaginable modeſty; let friendſhip appear in it, and nothing like authority, at which the ſpirit of every man muſt revolt, who is at all fit or worthy to govern himſelf.

Thus are huſbands and wives reciprocally bound, by the divine authority, to perform duties reſpectively becoming them; and which they are to diſcharge, with all readineſs and alacrity, being mutually benefited, and as they expect God's bleſſing upon them.

DISSERTATION V.

OF THE INSTITUTION OF THE SABBATH.

GENESIS II.

WHEN *the Heavens and the Earth were finished, and all the host of them, on the seventh day God ended his work which he had made, and rested from all his work which he had made: And God blessed the seventh day and sanctified it; because that in it he had rested from all his work, which God created and made.*

THE rest here mentioned has been made the subject of mirth and pleasantry by men of light and irreligious turns of mind, as if the God of Moses, after six days labour, had been tired and fatigued with his work, and stood in need of relaxation. But, all this banter apart, which deserves no serious reply, the words of the historian mean no more than this; that God having finished the great work of creation, agreeable to the plan laid in the divine mind, ceased to act; proceeded no farther in the production of more beings.

THIS

This *sanctifying the seventh day*, signifies the distinguishing it from the other six days, by setting it apart to the purposes of religion: in like manner as Jeremiah*, in after times, was sanctified from his mother's womb; that is, appointed and ordained by God to be a prophet in Israel. And this *sanctification*, or consecration of the sabbath to that holy use, was his *blessing* it, and commanding it to be observed, as a day of blessing and praising himself, for all his works of power and goodness, and his bestowing blessings on all his pious worshippers.

This then is one of the first and oldest of God's institutions, and so must needs have a real foundation in the nature of man, and an intimate connection with the great and the excellent ends of his creation. Those ends certainly are, to attain the knowledge, and to be confirmed in the love and obedience of God, in order to our being qualified for a more perfect state hereafter. But as a due and prevailing sense of these duties and rewards, cannot be preserved on our minds, without repeated and solemn application of thought; and as the affairs and necessities of the present life are so solicitous and importunate for our regards, as would engross our whole attention, were there no methods of employing ourselves otherwise; it is, therefore, necessary, in the nature of things, that some certain time should be specially and publicly appropriated to the exercises of religion, of instruction, prayer and praise, that our minds may be called off from temptations and sin,

* Jer. i. 5.

and

and seasoned with goodness and comfort. And, doubtless, he who made us for such improvements, and a blessed destination, hath wisdom and authority sufficient to fix that portion of time, which is most proper and competent for those several good purposes.

But that the subject may be treated at greater length, let us take a general view of the Institution of the sabbath, in regard to the observance of it in the several ages of the world, and the care that has been taken to preserve it. Now that our first parents, if they continued so long in innocence, kept the sabbath, as it periodically returned, in acts of lowly and grateful homage to their and the world's maker and Lord, conformable to his orders, we have not the smallest ground to doubt; nor need we question their practice, in regard to this, even after their fall, seeing their *repentance* appears to have been so deep and sincere, and perfectly recollecting the institution, *disobedience*, the effects of which they had lately so fatally experienced, would naturally fill them with horror. Nor is it unlikely, that it was on the weekly sabbaths, the sons of Adam presented *their offerings before the Lord:* For though in our english translation the words are, *and in process of time it came to pass*, the Hebrew is, *at the end of days* *, probably meaning that as time revolved, there were fixed and determinate portions of it, when Adam's family assembled to worship God, who, they knew positively, had given them life, and was daily blessing them with an increase of fruits and flocks, for their sustenance and happiness.

* Heb. ויהי מקץ ימים

It is true indeed, from the Mosaic records we receive no support to these conjectures, where there is not the least mention made of the sabbath, from the first institution of it, through the whole tract of the antediluvian and patriarchal ages, on which a direct proof of its observance can be founded. As little, however, can any one, on account of this omission, no way material to the history, assert, that the antediluvians and patriarchs, did not observe the sabbath; much less that the law concerning it, was not all that time well-known, and in full force. For we find not the least intimation of the sabbath in all the books of Joshua, Judges, Ruth, the two Samuels, and the first Kings; though those books were written after the Jewish monarchy was formed, at least the last of them, and when the law of the sabbath was in all its strength, and most scrupulously obeyed. But the book of Genesis itself, though containing but a very summary relation, and even admitting that the mention of the sabbath is not express in it, is yet not without some hints considerably clear, respecting its observance: Thrice Noah sent the dove out of the ark, after he had waited, every time, seven days: And we read of Jacob's fulfilling Leah's week; plainly shewing, that before the flood, and many generations after it, good men at least, reckoned by *seven days*, or *weeks*; who could derive their calculation from no other supposable original, than the institution of the sabbath at the creation.

There is no necessity to deny, and the case no doubt was so, that as mankind, from Cain the first murderer, degenerated daily, till *all flesh had corrupted their way on the earth*, at the deluge, this command of of God, like the reſt of his laws, would be greatly diſregarded, and generally violated; as alſo by the deſcendants of Noah, who ſoon fell into idolatry, and forgat the inſtitutions which their progenitors had tranſmitted to them. Accordingly we find the Iſraelites, during their continuance and ſervitude for 215 years, in Egypt, where the true God was not known, had loſt their reckoning of the ſabbath, having been conſtrained, by perpetual and moſt ſervile labour, to neglect the obſervance of it. Wherefore, when *God brought them up out of that land*, he ordered them to begin a new reckoning, and that the ſabbath ſhould be regulated by the falling of the manna. *And it ſhall come to paſs on the ſixth day, that they ſhall prepare the manna which they bring in; and it ſhall be twice as much as they gather daily; For to-morrow is the reſt of the holy ſabbath unto the Lord: Ye ſhall not then find it in the field; ſix days ſhall ye gather it, but on the ſeventh day, which is the ſabbath, there ſhall be none* *. This appointment, in regard to the manna, was wiſe and gracious, as it ſettled the day, which, otherwiſe, the Iſraelites, having loſt their computation, during their long captivity, might not have eaſily been engaged to agree upon. And a regulation ſo invariable for forty years together, till their eſtabliſhment in Canaan, would, of itſelf, diſtinguiſh the ſabbath, and ſecure reſpect to it; for having little more to do, the greateſt part of their time, but to gather and dreſs manna for their ſubſiſtence, and ſeeing no manna fall on the ſeventh day, they would, of courſe, be certified of the return of the ſabbath, and obliged to reſt from the ſmalleſt labour. Thus the firſt point of religion

* Exodus, 16.

that

that was settled, after the children of Israel came out of Egypt, was the restoring and ascertaining the sabbath, conformable to its original institution, as being of the greatest moment; for at this time they were only *in the wilderness of Zin*, on the borders of the red Sea, and did not march on to mount Sinai for three months afterwards.

Then, at that place, the ordinance of the sabbath was, with the greatest solemnity, made a part of the moral law of God, enforced with the same sanction, and the ancient reason for its observance expressly specified. *Remember the sabbath day to keep it holy; for in six days the Lord made heaven and earth, and rested the seventh day; wherefore the Lord blessed the sabbath day, and hallowed it.* And being thus placed among the other great articles of our duty, which are of unchangeable obligation, and always referred and appealed to by Christ, and his apostles, as binding upon us Christians, the sabbath must stand upon the same ground, and lay an obligation upon our consciences. For the same lawgiver, who said, *Thou shalt have no other Gods before me; thou shalt not bow down to any graven image; thou shalt not take the name of God in vain; honor thy father and thy mother; and do no murder;* said also, *Remember the sabbath day to keep it holy* *.

The other sabbaths celebrated by the Jewish nation, so called only as they were seasons for rest, which the word strictly signifies, our Lord, indeed, abolished, when the substance was come, of which they were no more than the shadows: And it is in re-

* Rom. xiii. 9.

spect

ſpect of theſe that St. Paul ſpeaks to the Coloſſians, when he ſays, *Let no man judge you in meat or in drink, or in reſpect of an holy-day, or of the new-moon, or of the ſabbath-days; which are a ſhadow of things to come; but the body is of Chriſt* †; that is to ſay, in matters that were local, temporary, and ceremonial, and to be ſet aſide by a more perfect and ſpiritual diſpenſation. But the ſabbath, properly ſo called, and the ſeventh portion of our time, being appropriated for the ſupport and encouragement of what is invariable, was before all the levitical inſtitutions, and therefore not to be abrogated with them. On the contrary, our Lord claimed dominion over the ſabbath, when he ſaid to the Phariſees, that *The Son of man was Lord of it*; intimating, that it belonged to his kingdom, the Chriſtian diſpenſation, together with other new ordinances, which he was to introduce into it.

In conſequence of this, our Lord, reforming the traditionary corruptions of ſeveral of the commandments of the moral law, corrected moſt ſignally, remarkably and conſtantly, at the peril of his life, the abuſes of the fourth commandment, ariſing out of the ceremonious ſanctity, and hypocritical ſuperſtition of the Jewiſh rulers; which he never would have done, if the ſabbath had been an ordinance, that was to expire in a little time with the reſt of *the commandments of men.* This amounts to a demonſtration that the ſanctification of the ſabbath was to be of perpetual obligation, and to have the greateſt influence on religion.

† Coloſſ ii. 16, 17.

THE

THE only difference he made in the institution was, the removal of the sabbath, from the seventh, to the first day of the week. For in the apostolic history we read, that the disciples met together on that day, as being a new festival, to break bread, or celebrate the holy supper, in commemoration of their Lord's triumph over the grave, which is the proper and distinguishing worship of Christians. This observance of the first professors of that name, originated, we may be assured, from an express injunction of the apostles; and the apostles could not possibly issue such an injunction without a commission from their master; though that commission be omitted in their writings; in the same manner as Moses makes no mention of the sabbath in the first ages of the world.

HERE it may not be improper to make a remark, in regard to the word sabbath itself. Be it therefore observed that sabbath, as it is always used, both in scripture and ecclesiastical writers, is constantly applied to the Jewish sabbath, or Saturday; and consequently there must be some absurdity in calling our Lord's day by that name. Indeed if any foreigner, from infidel nations, who had been instructed in the theory of the Mosaic œconomy, heard us express ourselves in this manner, he would verily believe that we meant Saturday, and not Sunday. But yet, notwithstanding this inaccuracy, seeing it is a custom among us to call the Lord's day by the name of sabbath, we need not quarrel about the use of the word, which signifies only a day of rest in general

general, on whatever day it falls; and the new sabbath plainly affords this to all Christians *.

But to return to the general view of this institution; there have been evidently three dates, from which the holy sabbath hath been reckoned; the *first*, by the the antediluvians and patriarchs, from the day after creation was finished; the *second*, by the Jews, from the the first day of the falling of the *manna*, when they were fed with bread from Heaven; and the *third*, by the christian Church, from the first day of the gospel dispensation. But still it is the seventh day which *God blessed*, and the day we now observe is as much, and as truly, the sabbath which *God sanctified*, as ever it was from the beginning of the world.

Nothing more needs to be advanced in proof of the antiquity, importance, and sacredness of this divine institution; than which there is none that can claim an higher origin, or produce better authority for its universal and perpetual obligation on all mankind: And, therefore, the guilt of that person, or nation, that violates it, must be equal to the dignity which the great commandment of the sabbath holds, among the laws of its author. How, indeed, can men possibly forget, or profane it, who profess any regard to the other precepts of the Almighty, is altogether unaccountable. Such open neglects and abuses of it, could not be believed, if they were not so common, and, by custom, almost established.

* Archbishop Sharp, vol. 3. Serm. 3. Dub. edit. 1744.

THE

The primary intention of the ſabbath was, that it might be a day of reſt, or ceſſation from all the ordinary buſineſs of life. And a moſt happy expedient it is, when men's minds are abſtracted from worldly cares and purſuits, for propagating the knowledge of religious truth; which could never have been ſo fatally corrupted or loſt, in any age of the world, as it is has ſo univerſally and repeatedly been, if the ſabbath had been duly obſerved, agreeably to it's firſt inſtitution. To the purpoſes of religion it has been conſtantly applied by the faithful, under all the diſpenſations of light and grace, and proved efficacious, in proportion as it has been thus employed. *The Lord hath given you the ſabbath* *, ſaid Moſes to the Iſraelites; *and ye ſhall keep my ſabbath, and reverence my ſanctuary; I am the Lord* †. Accordingly through the whole of the old teſtament, it is repreſented as *an holy convocation*, when that people aſſembled for divine worſhip. On this day they met together at the tabernacle firſt, and next at the temple, and in all the ſynagogues through the land, for the exerciſes deſcribed in many of the *pſalms*, particularly, in the *ninety-ſecond*; where the affairs of the ſtate, at that time, are ſolemnly repreſented before God, and a ſpecial dependance expreſſed on his providence. Theſe meetings our bleſſed Lord honored; and ſanctified the ſabbath-day by his preſence and inſtructions. And every denomination of chriſtians, that deſerve the name, for an ingenuous and undiſguiſed profeſſion of it, have, at at all times, and in all places, aſſembled on the ſabbath, to hear the word of God read to them, to

* Exod. 16. 29. † Levit. 19. 30.

offer

offer up their prayers and thanksgivings, and to celebrate the Lord's supper, perhaps two seldom celebrated by modern christians, in order to employ their thoughts in pious meditations, and furnish their minds with the best principles and dispositions. Services which cannot but require rest from ordinary business, and the whole of our minds and attention to be laid out on the spiritual concerns of the day.

It is indeed to be noticed in this place, that our Lord, in his instructions and example, concerning the sanctification of the sabbath, has distinctly taught us, not to introduce any thing superstitious into the observance of it, after the manner of the Jews; as if we conceived it to be such a scrupulous rest, that we may not do any thing fit and reasonable to be done, and which it is otherwise our duty to do. And, consistently with this doctrine, certain divines have very properly taught, that *the sabbath is to be sanctified by an holy resting all that day, even from such worldly employments and recreations as are lawful on other days, and spending the whole time in the public and private exercises of* God's *worship, except so much as is to be taken up in the works of necessity and mercy.* At the same time that *we worship* God, *give him thanks, call upon him, and honor his holy name and word,* on that day, whatever cannot be delayed till another, without loss or damage, may certainly be taken care of on the sabbath day. Our Saviour says, *the sabbath was made for man* *, that is, to be subservient to his improvement and happiness; and, therefore, the observance of it imposed on him, cannot be of so rigorous a nature, as to embarrass

* St. Mark, ii. 27.

and

and distress his life, or make him neglect any opportunity of doing good.

But of such an abuse of the sabbath as this, in an age of great licentiousness and impiety, there being very little danger, admonition to those who neglect and profane it will be much more necessary, than a caution against any such scruples. Now the obligation and duties of this day having been clearly set forth, must not men, on a comparison of them with the manner in which it is usually spent, be struck with astonishment, and filled with sorrow? The the sabbath ought to be an holy rest *, and yet do not multitudes make it a day of hard labour, at least of high living, great mirth, and public diversions? *It is a day for worshipping* God, in public and private; and, nevertheless, it is but too evident, that attendance in his house is infrequent and circumscribed by many, who make an outward profession the sum of their religion; and it is to be feared likewise, that all such persons, and, perhaps many others, through inattention, negligence, and the wilful want of knowledge and conviction in matters of the greatest moment, are entire strangers to the duties of the closet also. So prevailing, in short, are the evils of this kind, that men have grown so insensible of them, and are so far lost to all disposition to reclaim themselves, that every attempt to awaken and reform them, is thought to proceed from weakness and folly,

* Septima autem requievisse Deum (Moses facta esse dicit) et ab operibus cessavisse. Quamobrem etiam nos vacationem a laboribus per hanc Diem celebramus, appellantes eum Sabathum, quæ vox Requiem Hebræorum Lingua Significat. Joseph. Lib. 1. Cap. 2.

to

to be officious and ill-natured, and the common trade and business of *Ecclesiastics*. But will they only seriously consider with themselves, and candidly confess, that if confinement, through the week, and the want of recreation on the sabbath, would soon hurt and endanger the health of their bodies; what *that* of their souls must be, if they think they have any, without receiving the nourishment, from the exercises proper for them. Must they not, as certainly as the material frame, decay and finally perish? And, no doubt, the want of such nourishment is the cause of so much *leanness and barrenness*, even among those who profess the greatest strictness, and yet fall in exactly with the manners of the multitude, and *follow them to do evil*; and whose practices, universally giving the lie to their pretended principles, instead of encouraging, throw a damp on all improvements in religion.

The last thing to be suggested on the subject is this; that if the law of *nature*, of God, and of Christ, obliges us to pay tribute to whom tribute is due, and custom to whom custom; and yet hath not determined the measure of every man's ability and conscience in that matter; making it, however, criminal in him to refuse compliance with public authority; how much more may that man be said to sin against God, who hath, by the most immediate revelation, prescribed certain days, and the returns of them, if he defraud him of that portion of time, which he hath so solemnly consecrated and devoted to himself? No transgression against a canon, or an act of Parliament, can be so gross and penal; and the offence cannot possibly go unpunished, either in this world, or in the world to come. And that it may be so, LET ALL THE PEOPLE SAY, AMEN.

DISSERTATION VI.

Of a State of Trial, and the Fall of Man.

Genesis II.

Adam and Eve, placed in Paradise, did not long enjoy their honour and happiness. Efforts of malice were soon made to mar the original purpose, and proved too successful in their fatal mistake and overthrow. The hints of scripture concerning the great enemy of mankind, are but short, and seem to be reducible to these several heads of doctrine:

That he had been formed, like other celestial beings, perfect in his kind, and happy in his condition: That he was guilty of some crime, in his exalted sphere; which the learned, however, with their various conjectures, have not been able to define; tho', probably, ambition and insolence might be the principal ingredients of it: That the certain consequence was disgrace and misery; for the Almighty banished him and his accomplices, from their habitations of glory, into the middle regions of the air, as it is thought; where they are fixed in a manner inexplicable to men, who have no distinct idea how pure

 spirits

ſpirits diſengaged from matter, if any ſuch there be, except God himſelf, can poſſibly be confined: That this arch-traitor is *prince of the power of the air* *, and his companions *ſpiritual wickedneſſes in high places* †, *caſt down to hell, and delivered into chains of darkneſs* ‡; or, as many intepret the word, *Tartarus*, which celebrated critics underſtand to be, as has been already ſaid, the middle region of the air ‖: That in this abode, wherever it is, they wait for their decreed doom, which, probably, will not be declared till the laſt day: That this procraſtination of their final and permanent miſery, is the only happineſs which they at preſent enjoy; inferable from their alarm at the coming of the Son of God, when, dreading the period of their puniſhment was haſtened, they ſaid to him, at their expulſion from the bodies of men which they had poſſeſſed, *Art thou come to torment us before the time* § ? that is, before the period of our accumulated and eternal ruin: That, from the words of our Saviour, who ſpeaks of *a fire prepared for the devil and his angels* **, we are warranted to draw the concluſion, that their puniſhment, though ſuſpended in part, will be compleatly executed: That God *has*, actually, *reſerved them in everlaſting chains under darkneſs, unto the judgment of the great day* ††; and they were ſeen, in a viſion, *caſt into the lake of fire and brim-*

* Eph. ii. 2.
† Eph. vi. 12.
‡ 2 Pet. ii. 4.
‖ Voyez Suidas, Tom. 3. p. 432.
§ St. Matthew, viii. 29.
** St. Matthew, xxv. 41.
†† St. Jude, verſe 6.

ſtone,

stone, to be tormented day and night, for ever and ever *.

And if this be all which revelation affords us on the subject, it must be because it is less our concern to know the nature and destination of those evil spirits, than to be aware of the snares which they lay for our innocence, that we may exercise all our watchfulness to repulse and disappoint them. To *be sober and vigilant*, is the apostolic precept, *because our adversary the Devil, as a roaring lion, walketh about seeking whom he may devour* †.

Yet, instead of making this useful improvement of those divine and indulgent hints, the sense of them has been so criticised and controverted, that their most important meaning has been greatly enervated, and, indeed, totally explained away, by men who have endeavoured to apply all this language to the *Roman Emperors*, and their *servants*, as they were the rulers and governors of unenlightened and idolatrous nations, in the days of the apostles. But, besides the concurrent testimony of *antiquity*, which is plainly on the side of the commonly received opinion, the words of St. Paul, in the first of the passages under view, may be adduced as a full confutation of all such new-fangled doctrines; there being in these words an obvious distinction between *flesh and blood*, or men who are merely compounded of those materials, and *principalities and powers*, or those evil spirits which have their stations in the regions of the air, preside, peculiarly, and in an eminent degree,

* Rev. xx. 10. † 1 Pet. v. 8.

over the nations which are yet under *heathenism*, and *work* inwardly *in the children of disobedience.*

CONCERNING their origin, their functions in heaven, their apostacy and fall, no other sentiments are to be entertained than what the divine oracles suggest to us; which seem to represent them as very ancient beings *, and literally tell us that they *kept not their first estate, but left their own habitation* †, and are condemned to the severe displeasure of the Almighty.

OF the chief of those evil spirits, who could not behold the felicity of others without envy, and, as if misery was more tolerable when shared by many, wished to seduce them into rebellion similar to his own, that they might partake with him in the same punishment; of this head, I say, of the evil spirits, our first parents soon experienced the subtile and destructive malice. To Eve, who he, possibly, well knew possessed more levity, and a stronger inclination to vain glory, than her husband, his first addresses were made: And as there can be no conversation with spiritual beings without material organs, he borrowed the body and voice of that particular animal, which of all others hath the most vivacity and alertness, that she might be the less surprized at hearing it speak with understanding. The animal meant was a serpent; and the pretext used appeared the most plausible to make Eve withhold, in one instance at least, the obedience which she owed to her Creator, and wise and most benign lawgiver.

* See Dissertation first. † Jude, verse 6.

IN

In that garden where the first pair were placed, of all sorts of fruit there was the greatest plenty; and they were permitted to make the freest use of them all, for their sustenance and pleasure, and as a reward for their labour, except *of the tree of the knowledge of good and evil; for*, said God, *in the day that thou eatest thereof, thou shalt surely die.* There was another tree, besides this, in the midst of the garden, or, as the eastern phrase signifies, distinguished remarkably from the rest, and called *the tree of life.* Those two trees were, probably, uncommon in their appearance and situation as well as in their use; having been appointed, it is very likely, for instruction and religious meditation, to preserve in Adam's mind a sense of his dependence on the divine bounty, and of the consequences of obedience and transgression; and may be considered, in regard to him, as revelation, or the written word, is to us, from whence, in his infant state, he was to draw maxims, or general principles, by which he was to direct his conduct.

Here we are to excite our attention, and pay the strictest regard to this important truth, that the first of the human race, immediately on their creation, were denied a certain thing which was daily within their reach, as an evidence to them that they were in a state of probation. Though they had been *made in the image of him that created them*, and were, like the angels of God, pure and perfect in their nature, suitable to his excellence and goodness from whose hands they came, and the constant and willing service which he required of them; yet being without the confirmed *habits* of holiness, they were put under this instance of discipline, and obliged to perform voluntary

voluntary acts of respect and submission to their Creator, in order to the acquisition of those habits. While they continued obedient, they were allowed to eat of the tree of life, as a pledge, and perhaps, a principle, of their living for ever, or being immortal. The other tree, on the contrary, was designed to give them the knowledge, the sense, or apprehension of good and evil, or of carnal good enduring for a moment, connected with complicated and lasting evil; in short, of pernicious pleasure, which cannot be enjoyed without transgressing the law of God. This tree, it is presumable, entirely indifferent in itself, being yet strongly emblematical of all criminal pursuits, the fruit of it, tho' it was *pleasant to the eye, and to be desired*, our original progenitors were forbidden to eat, upon the pain of death; to make them understand, that unlawful enjoyments of any kind would be their destruction. A lesson still forced upon ourselves by experience, and even ever present in our understandings, which ought to guard us against all such presumption, that we may escape the misery of it.

Availing himself of this restraint, and with a direct view to detach her from a dutiful submission to it, *the great dragon* *, *the old serpent*, *the devil*, or *Satan* †, accosted Eve in the most flattering terms. No room is left in these characters, to doubt what adversary she had to encounter on this occasion. He is here stiled the Serpent for no other reason, but because he had joined himself to that animal, as the Son of God is called Man, because he assumed

* Rev. xii, 19. † Rev. xx. 2.

his

his nature. His words were these: *Yea! hath God said, ye shall not eat of every tree of the garden?* unreasonable, selfish, prohibition! to hinder you of a more extensive happiness! *For God doth know, that in the day ye eat thereof, then your eyes shall be opened:* your minds shall be so enlarged by this simple experiment, that *ye shall be as gods* yourselves, *knowing good and evil*; and taste pleasures at present denied you without danger; *ye shall not surely die. And when the woman saw*, or believed the deceiver, that *the* forbidden *tree* had the power of making her *wise, she took of the fruit thereof, and did eat, and gave also unto her husband with her, and he did eat.* This was their trial, and failing under it; here ended their innocence and felicity.

About the duration of that state, authors of great name have been much divided. Some assert that our first parents fell on the very first day of their creation, and continued only six or seven, or at the longest, ten hours in paradise; others extend the period of their happiness to as many days: For instance, the great primate of Ireland, who says, that it seems to have been the *tenth* day of the world's age, when Adam was cast out of Paradise; in memory of which calamity, the solemn *day of expiation*, and the great *fast* was instituted in after times, whereon all were to afflict their souls *; but he had no other authority for it than the Jewish doctrines grounded on the 16th chapter of Leviticus: while even thirty-four years have been the computation of some learned men †. The opinions of the greatest number rest upon a sup-

* Vide, Usserii annal. † Salian: annal. Tom 1.

posed resemblance between Adam and Jesus Christ: As the latter fasted forty days in the wilderness, and lived upon earth thirty-four years; so it is to be analogically inferred, say they, that the former was either of those spaces in Paradise. Here revelation is totally silent; and wherever it is, or any way obscure, disputes arise without end. To the opinion of those who limit the state of innocence to a few hours, there are very strong objections; and stronger still to that which lengthens it out to years. Some circumstances of the story, make *years* improbable, on the one hand; and, on the other, a few *hours* appear insufficient for transactions that may very reasonably be supposed to have occurred: And, therefore, *a medium* between parties may be the truest account; and a few weeks or months have been the period of Adam's primæval honor.

That an *apple* should be the object in question, Infidels have greatly wondered; and given full vent to their blasphemous ridicule. But was not some instance of human obedience necessary? Was not one test, of whatever sort, as sufficient for that purpose as another? And from whence could any be chosen, but from among the few things with which our first parents were most conversant, in their peculiar circumstances? And the apparent *trivialness* of that which the wisdom of God pitched on, is a plain aggravation of their offence, who unboundedly enjoyed the possession of every thing else; though it may wantonly be the sport of fools. By appointing this trial, a slight abridgment only was intended of their natural liberty, in the uncontrolled exercise of which

which, it is unfit that any created intelligence should be indulged.

To this reasonable representation the reply usually made, that the temptation must have been too strong, when diabolical artifices, and desperate designs, were opposed to the innocence and unguardedness of our first parents, almost immediately on their coming into the world, is destitute of all solidity, when calmly considered. For no possible temptation could of itself be strong enough, to shake their allegiance, unless the grand adversary had been suffered to personate God himself, which we see he never had power to do. Adam and Eve had lately received a command, in the most express terms, from their almighty maker; which it was, therefore, their duty to obey. If they were ignorant *who* it was that tempted them, they were not ignorant *what* he was tempting them to do; and they knew that if the highest arch-angel from heaven, speaking in his own name, and without any commission from God, endeavoured to persuade them contrary to that command received, they ought to resist his solicitations; because nothing less than the same divine authority which gave the law, could either annul or dispense with it. But no such stumbling-block was laid before them; the trial was moderate. God considered their nature, their inexperience, and situation; and only proved them by the sophistry and pretences of *a beast of the field*, whose figure could by no means be subservient to his rhetorick or authority.

Respecting *the tree* itself, which produced this apple, though, as has been already declared, it may be be considered as perfectly indifferent in itself, and void of any extraordinary quality *, yet the variety of opinions concerning it, which have furnished much amusement and speculation to *the unlearned and unstable* †, may make a few words necessary. It is called by Moses, *the tree of the knowledge of good and evil.* Josephus thinks that it had the physical virtue of producing knowledge and light in the mind of those who eat of it ‡. But perhaps this name was only given it by way of anticipation; or not till after the event had shewn man the difference between *good and evil*; between obeying God and rebelling against him. Whether it was a common apple-tree or a fig-tree, there have been the warmest disputes, without affording the smallest information. The truth is, a determination concerning the nature of that tree, and the reasons of the name it bears, is as difficult, as it is perhaps unimportant.

The account given of the *tempter* has, likewise, been freely examined by *unbelievers*; and strangely enlarged both by Jewish and Christian commentators. One of the former hath said, that this account, like the other relations in the Mosaic history, hath neither truth nor goodness in it, and is a wretched invention of superstition and blindness, contrary to all reason and common sense ||. Such is the boldness of those who refuse to follow every guide, but their own imaginations, disordered and inflamed by corrupted hearts. Another of them says that Cicero laughed at

* Vide F. Turret. Loc. oct. Quest. iv. p. 637.
† St. Pet. 3. 16.
‡ Arbori enim acuminis & cogitandi vis inerat. Jos. L. 1. C2.
|| Dr. Morgan.

the

the story of Alexander's dreaming, that a serpent spoke; but, how would he have laughed, says he, at the literal story of a serpent not only speaking actually, but reasoning too *. Many of the last classes have entertained the world with the most insupportable opinions; that all beasts at the beginning had the faculty of speech †; that *the serpent* possessed it like the rest ‡; that the devil in this form had carnal commerce with Eve ||, or was only riding on this animal, as on a camel §, when he presented himself to the mother of mankind; that the serpent perched upon *the tree of the knowledge of good and evil*, and eating of the fruit, Eve was struck with the sight, and tasted of it in imitation ¶; that the language of beasts, becoming only unintelligible to men by their studying one of their own, was perfectly understood by Eve, and that the relation of Moses regarding the conversation of the devil with her, contains no mystery **. There have been authors, who have turned the whole relation into figure and allegory; making the *serpent* represent irregular desire; the *man*, whom he was afraid to assault at first, an image of reason, and the *woman*, who was easily overcome, the emblem of sense, and in the same manner all the rest of the things that are there said ††.

* See Letter to Dr. Waterland, p 17. &c.

† Philo de Confus. Ling. St. Basil, de Paradiso.

‡ Joseph. Antiq. l 1. c. 2.

|| R. Jarchi in Gen. 2.

§ Spectatum admissi risum teneatis, amici? Hor. art. poet.

¶ Abarbanel in Gen. cap. 3.

** Joseph Mead, discourse 40.

†† Philo de opif. Mundi. Maimonides, More Nevochim, Pars. 2. cap. 30.

To

To the moſt of theſe reveries, not the leaſt attention is due; they are only the productions of idle men, and mere lumber in the works of the learned. Borrowed meanings, it muſt be confeſſed, would be a compendious way of reſolving many difficulties that occur in the ſacred records; but would open up the wideſt ſource of novelties, in giving a liberty to convert into allegory the moſt circumſtantial hiſtories, when events are related that baffle our comprehenſion.

A PRELATE, whoſe merit raiſed him to the firſt rank in the church of England, hath ſuggeſted an ingenious overture in this matter, which being but little known, pardon for publiſhing it here will be the more eaſily procured. There are, ſays he, in the eaſt and the ſouth, winged ſerpents which appear like fire: The inſpired writers ſpeak of them in a variety of paſſages. The *mercy of the* LORD having been promiſed to *the houſe of Jacob*, Iſaiah, to guard a part of them againſt a fatal miſtake, ſays, *rejoice not thou whole* Paleſtina, *becauſe the rod of him that ſmote thee is broken: For out of the ſerpent's root ſhall come forth a cockatrice, and his fruit ſhall be a fiery flying ſerpent* *. The doctrine conveyed to them is ſtrongly figurative; but the figures are lively, and were undoubtedly taken from nature.

THE ſerpents which God ſent *among his people* of old, to puniſh them for their murmurings, were of this kind. *The Lord*, ſays *Moſes*, *ſent fiery ſerpents* † *among the people, and they bit the people, and much people*

* Iſaiah, 14. 29.   † הנחשים השרפים

of

of Israel died. And, upon their confession, *the Lord said unto* Moses, *make thee a fiery serpent, and set it upon a pole; and it shall come to pass, that every one that is bitten, when he looketh upon it, shall live* *. The activity and splendor of those animals, intimated in this relation, have been used as an emblem of the zeal and purity of divine beings, who are set forth to us in scripture, as surrounding the throne of God, and *filling the places* which they visit with the most striking tokens of their desire to please him, and of their readiness to execute his sovereign command †. Hence the learned have been of opinion, that the visible form which those celestial spirits assumed, when they were employed as ambassadors to men, was that of those serpents; and that from this appearance the name of seraphim was derived, which signifies *burning*. By such a resemblance, therefore, it may be supposed Eve was deceived; and that the dignity of the personage with which she thought she conversed, gave the utmost weight to the words he used §.

Although this illustrious author hath placed this point in a light entirely new, he hath yet the modesty, not to suspect any other passion or affection of the mind, to declare, that, many ages before him, the same doctrine had been taught by others: He hath even referred to a learned Jew, who said,

* Numb. xxi. † Isaiah, vi. 2. Rev. iv. 8.

§ Archbishop Tennison, in his Discourse of Idolatry. The author of these Dissertations hath taken the liberty to quote the passages of scripture at large, and to comment upon them. But his Grace's sense is faithfully given.

that

that as the angels of God, of one of the orders, were called *Seraphim* *, the ſerpent had the ſame name from the likeneſs he bore to them.

GIVING the credit due to the Arch-biſhop's authority, this notion might be the origin of the romantic ſentiments of ſome ancient heretics, who believed that the ſerpent which tempted Eve, was the ſon of God himſelf, and that, thinking he was preſent, ſhe had ſinned out of reſpect to him †.

SUCH fancies might be eaſily checked by aſking, what idea Eve could poſſibly have of the Meſſiah, in a perfect and innocent ſtate, and before he was actually revealed?

BUT, whatever idea ſhe might have of the ſecret nature of many of the miniſters of her maker, yielding to the ſolicitations of ſuch a creature as a ſerpent, for no other, we may preſume, its outward form indicated it to be, and expecting the accompliſhment of the moſt fulſome promiſes, muſt render her, in the judgment of every diſpaſſionate perſon, highly culpable, with all her reaſon and underſtanding about her, and in direct oppoſition to the expreſs law of God. How extremely negligent were our firſt parents of their own natural reaſon? How preſumptuous in doing what was poſitively forbidden?

WHY God ſhould permit ſuch a danger and cataſtrophe to befal the very firſt of mankind, is quite another queſtion, and beyond the ſphere of our un-

* Heb. שרפים

† Vide Tertul. de preſ. Hæret. Cap. 4 & 7. ſecundum Saur.

derſtand-

derſtandings. This, however, we plainly perceive, that every rational creature requires to be put upon trial. The angels themſelves were laid under the ſame rule; and from heedleſs and voluntary tranſgreſſion reſults all the miſery in the univerſe. Farther than this, we have no principles at preſent, to go upon; the counſels and ways of God being unſearchable by us, and all the ſubjects of his kingdom; and therefore, the government of his whole accountable family, in a way ſuitable to their liberty, and his own moſt perfect wiſdom, holineſs and purity, being one of the moſt delicate and myſterious parts of the Almighty's conduct, under this preliminary diſpenſation, may, moſt probably, be the ſtudy and admiration of angels and men to all eternity.

THIS alſo is plain, and here all our enquiries may be ſatisfied, that he who made all his own ſervants knows perfectly what is in them; and how neceſſary and ſeaſonable it is that they ſhould undergo ſuitable diſcipline. *And this confidence we have in his faithfulneſs, that he will never ſuffer any of* his creatures *to be tempted*, either by their ſtation, by wicked ſpirits, or men, *above what they are able to bear*; *but will with the temptation alſo make a way to eſcape*, if they be dutiful, *that they may bear it* *. This is natural and immutable juſtice, from which juſtice infinite and eternal cannot ſwerve. And this ſingle poſition, abſtract from the foregoing reaſoning, aſſures us, that our firſt parents were not overcome by violence, which they were not able to reſiſt, and could not but fall before; but by an abuſe of their own liberty and

* 1. Cor. x. 13.

free will, and the want of exerting the natural ſtrength they had, ſufficient to withſtand the temptation.

THE atrocioufneſs of their guilt will clearly appear, by the extent of their puniſhment, in the following Diſſertation.

DISSERTATION VII.

OF THE CONSEQUENCES OF THE FALL.

GENESIS III.

THE original ſin having been fully deſcribed, the conſequences of it require to be as amply unfolded. That a repetition of crimes, can only form the wretched habit of committing them without remorſe, is evident, at firſt ſight, from this introductory circumſtance; that the conſcience of Adam and Eve ſtill remained tender after one very groſs violation of it, and inſtantly reproached them for the firſt tranſgreſſion. Their repentance indeed is very briefly characterized; but, from the general account of it, we may fairly conclude, that if the Holy Spirit had been pleaſed to inform us fully of all the painful effects, which a ſenſe of diſobedience immediately produced in the guilty pair, the relation would have been extremely affecting. The ſacred hiſtory begins that account with ſimply telling us, that *the eyes of them were both opened*; that is, they had a perception, directly, of the conſequences of diſobedience, and knew they were degraded and expoſed by it; juſt as ſinners, in general, under the influence of a moral blindneſs, are totally inſenſible of the miſerable fruits of vice; till they have committed ſome flagrant act of it; when, the very firſt moment of reflection, they ſee the deep traces of their folly, and feel the galling ſcourges of a ſelf-condemning heart.

THE words following will bear a literal interpretation; *they knew that they were naked.* Their bodies, which had been entirely under the government of their will, became rebellious, as ſoon as pollution was contracted; and, by the inordinate motions of ſenſe, diſturbed that purity of their minds which they had lately poſſeſſed. The conſciouſneſs of ſuch an alteration within themſelves, would unavoidably be productive of confuſion.

SOME, indeed, have thought, that a figurative explanation, by which the knowledge of their *nakedneſs*, is made an image of their conviction, upon the loſs of their innocence, would be no way repugnant to the ſpirit of the expreſſion. In ſupport of this opinion, another ſimilar paſſage has been produced, where we read, that Moſes, after the idolatry of the golden calf, *ſaw that the people were naked; for Aaron had made them naked unto their ſhame amongſt their enemies* *: Intimating, that the divine protection was withdrawn; for the glory of the Lord in the cloud, it is likely, had departed: And Aaron had laid them open, by this ſin, to the ſcorn of the hoſtile nations, who ſhould hear of ſuch a ſcandalous revolt from their God †.

* Exod. 32. 25. † Bp. Patrick on the place.

THE

THE exposition of these words is certainly very just; but the application of them *, to illustrate the other, is much to be suspected; and the first gloss seems more naturally to claim our regard; as Adam and Eve, on the knowledge of their *nakedness*, were immediately engaged in *sewing fig leaves together*; which, by their magnitude and texture, were proper for the use of *making themselves aprons*.

To the pungent sensations of their own minds, the great avenger of wickedness, soon added his awful voice. *In the cool of the day*, or, agreeable to the original, *the wind* †; and, in the oriental phrase, the decline of the day; when their refreshing winds rushed from the Indian ocean; the presence of the Lord was perceived in Paradise.

THIS is a farther evidence that Jehovah had indulged our first parents, in their innocent state, with intercourse and revelations, in his own person, some way gloriously manifested; and that they were well acquainted with them. But the tokens which signified the divine presence, before the appearance of the Messiah in the flesh, will be hereafter given in their proper place.

LIKE all their descendants, the first criminals confessed their guilt as reluctantly, as they had been eager in the commission of it. When *God called unto* Adam, *and said unto him, where art thou?* the fugitive, in the best manner he could, converted the fault, which forced him to retreat, into a virtue. By

* M. Sautin, Discours. 4. † Heb. לרוח היום

way

way of impoſition, after he had rebelled againſt him, Adam endeavoured to perſuade the Almighty, if poſſible, that it was reverence for his heavenly maſter which prevented his immediate attendance. *I heard thy voice*, ſaid he, *in the garden; and I was afraid, becauſe I was naked; and I hid myſelf.* His underſtanding being diſordered, and his whole mind confuſed, the weak imagination prevailed, that if he could not conceal himſelf from the eye of his judge, he might at leaſt palliate the offence, for which he ſtood ſecretly condemned. Accordingly, when preſſed farther by the queſtion, *Who told thee that thou waſt naked?* he proceeded from one extravagance to another, and threw the blame in part upon God himſelf, by charging with the temptation *the woman whom God had given to be with him*; as if that *gift* had been fatal in itſelf, and drawn him forcibly and irreſiſtibly into tranſgreſſion. And as he had thus excuſed himſelf by the ſeduction of his wife, Eve imitated his example, and accuſed the ſerpent of the original temptation. But excuſes of this ſort rather aggravate guilt, and generally bring on a ſpeedy retribution.

HAVING been the primary agent, condemnation was firſt pronounced on the devil; and that every participant in the horrid wickedneſs, might likewiſe be involved in the puniſhment, *the Lord ſaid unto the ſerpent*, which had been viſibly ſubſervient in the execution of it, *Becauſe thou haſt done this, thou art curſed above all cattle, and above every beaſt of the field: upon thy belly ſhall thou go, and duſt ſhall thou eat all the days of thy life*. By this act God declared his deteſtation of every creature which he had made, concerned in moral tranſgreſſion; as he did ſtill more expreſsly, in the

law

law afterwards given to the *Israelites*, where it is enacted; *If a man lie with a beast, he shall surely be put to death: and ye shall slay the beast. And if a woman approach unto any beast, and lie down thereto, thou shall kill the woman and the beast: they shall surely be put to death: their blood shall be upon them* *: Thus making accessaries in guilt, destitute of understanding, partners with the intelligent principals, in the chastisements inflicted on them.

Some commentators have softened this part of the sentence, which relates to *the serpent's eating dust all the days of his life*, by supposing the meaning of it only to be, that he should be always under the necessity of eating his food on the ground, and so swallowing dust with it, from the creeping form to which his body was reduced †. But this, not sufficiently distinguishing the curse of the serpent, from the natural condition of other creatures, more diligent enquiries shew to be a mistake, and evince that he actually eats the dry, dusty earth ‡. Indeed in those sandy deserts to which God has, in a great measure, condemned him, no otherwise could he possibly subsist. So strangely is the divine sentence executed in every sense, and in every part, to a tittle!

And as the expression of *eating the dust*, denotes the lowest state of humiliation to which an enemy can be reduced; as in the Book of Psalms §, where it is prophesied of God's anointed, that *his enemies should*

* Levit. xx. 15, 16. † Saurin Discourse iv.

‡ See Pliny and Bochart of Serpents.

§ Psal. lxxii. 9.

lick

lick the dust; so was the serpent moreover sunk into the abject condition of *going upon his belly*; from a flying *Seraph**, changed into a foul creeping creature, to afford Adam a significant emblem of that utter prostration and subjection, to which he himself deserved to be brought; and the evil spirit, who had seduced him, should, without remedy, be finally doomed, when the great conqueror *shall tread upon the adder, and trample the dragon under his feet* †.

For the words immediately following shew us, that a sentence, reaching much farther than that under which the serpent had instantly fallen, was denounced against the devil himself. *I will put enmity between thee and the woman, and between thy seed and her seed: It shall bruise thy head, and thou shall bruise his heel.* In the most literal sense, indeed, this is true of the serpent, between which and mankind there is such an antipathy, that it discovers itself both in the *natural* and *sensitive* faculties of them both; the humours of the one being poison to the other; and as man is frightened at the sight of a serpent, in like manner is a serpent terrified at the sight of a man ‡.

But these natural circumstances, like the foregoing, being only adumbrations of something more secret and hidden, we are, therefore, to seek for a sense of the above words, that is more compleat, and pregnant with instruction. The celebrated *Arabian Jew*, who wrote his *Elucidations* of the *obscurer parts of Scripture*, above six hundred years ago, hath freely confessed, that *this is one of the passages of scripture the most* PERPLEXING, *and altogether unintelligible, if we stick to*

* Heb. שרפ † Psal. lxi. 13. ‡ Pat. in Loco.

the

the letter, and do not penetrate the profound wiſdom which it contains *. The diſtinction of *the ſeed of the woman* without the intervention of the man, has engaged his attention, by its ſingularity; and ſome have thought that he found in it the whole myſtery of the incarnation †; but without any foundation, in his application of it. Though on very good authority it may be aſſerted, that the two *Targums*; the one of Jeruſalem, and the other by Jonathan, underſtood by *the ſeed of the woman* the Meſſiah.

BUT while ſuch interpreting may, very properly, ſerve to aſſiſt our underſtandings, and are very illuſtrious teſtimonies to the truth of the ſacred ſcriptures, we have far ſurer ground to go upon, in the explication of the dark, and diſtant hints thoſe ſcriptures give us, than any that the moſt ingenious Jews have afforded. He who pronounced theſe words at firſt, hath unfolded their meaning by holy men whom he inſpired, and, by their miniſtry, drawn aſide the vail which covered them, before the full accompliſhment of the promiſes which they conveyed, in this preſent ſtate of truth. The writers of the *new Teſtament*, by their acquaintance with *the old* doctrine, *which* they had *heard from the beginning* ‡, and the infallible influence which directed them, have made plain all myſte-

* Odium perfectum manet inter ſerpentem et Evam, inter ſemen illius et inter ſemen hujus; neque dubium eſt, quin ſemen illius ſit ſemen adami. Sed mirandus magis eſt,—quod illa vincat ipſum in capite, et ille vincat ipſam in calcaneo.———Secundum literam paradoxis ac abſurdis.——Sed ſi ſolide intellexeris, admiraberis, quanta ſapienta in illo libro lateat, &c.

† M. Saurin, Diſcours. 4.

‡ 1. John, ii, 7.

ries,

ries, if we do not *love darkneſs rather than light* *. And that this curſe, pronounced againſt the ſerpent, agreeable to what has been ſaid, was only an emblem of that pronounced againſt the devil himſelf, is abundantly clear from their words. St. Matthew informs us that *Jeſus was led up of the ſpirit into the wilderneſs, to be tempted of the devil* †; when attacks on his *power*, and the cruſhing of his kingdom, were juſt commencing. And the author to the Hebrews, hath repreſented *the Son of God*, on the other hand, as *deſtroying him that had the power of death, that is, the devil, through* his own *death* ‡; which the *God of this world* effected by his malice, *blinding the minds of them who believed not* §.

These divine authorities ſufficiently inſtruct us, that by *the ſeed of the woman*, we are to underſtand the *Meſſiah*; and by *the head of the ſerpent*, the dominion of *ſatan*, by which he had immerſed the human race in idolatry and wickedneſs, and ſubjected them to innumerable miſeries of life, and to the pains of death at laſt. *It ſhall bruiſe thy head*, expreſſes the triumphs which our redeemer gained by his miniſtry, obedience and croſs. *Bruiſing the head*, in profane authors, ſignifies ſhaking off the yoke of tyranny. Thus a Theban general encouraged his countrymen to attack a body of the Lacedemonians, by ſhewing them a ſerpent's head, which he had compreſſed, and ſaying, *See, the ſerpent's head is cruſhed, his body can never do us any harm* ‖. Now the ſon of God, in this ſenſe, and by the apteſt means, effectually deprived

* John iii. 19. † St. Matthew iv. 1.
‡ Heb. 2. 14. § 2 Cor. 4. 4.
‖ Polyæni Strat Epaminon. Lib. ii. Cap. 3.

his

his enemy of all his destructive influence. And what is most remarkable in his conquests is, that the very wounds which he received in the conflict were the cause of his victory. By these indeed *his heel was bruised*, that is to say, his flesh was crucified, but by submission to that very indignity, and *despising* it, *he spoiled* evil *principalities and powers, and made a shew of them openly, triumphing over them in his cross* *; and chiefly over him who had solicited his death, and imbittered his sufferings.

The sentence pronounced upon the woman comes, next, to be considered. *Unto her the Lord God said, I will greatly multiply thy sorrow, and thy conception: in sorrow shall thou bring forth children; and thy desire shall be to thy husband, and he shall rule over thee.* On the last part of this sentence, which, it must be owned, merits some regard, it hath been observed, that nothing could be more mortifying to a creature affecting independence, than a positive subjection to another; which every one of her sex, entering into the state of marriage, is required to acknowledge †. And, notwithstanding another sense which an ancient author puts upon the words, that Moses only inserted this, *to preserve the Jews from the infection of the Theology in Egypt, where, impressed with the idea of* Isis, *the people thought* Queens *more honourable than* Kings, *and* Women *than their* Husbands ‡; whoever consults facts, and the laws of God, already cited, in relation to marriage, will find the above doctrine sufficiently confirmed.

* Coloss. ii. 15. † M. Saurin Discours. 4.
‡ Diod. Sicul. Lib. i. p. 23.

ANOTHER

Another remark, very worthy of our notice, ought not to be passed over in this place; that lest the mutual grievances of Adam and Eve, the former having been seduced, and the latter degraded from her original equality, should have occasioned jealousies, contention, and even a rupture, between them, the wisdom and goodness of God are here most conspicuous, in making the gracious promise of a redeemer, related above, who should repair all their losses, to depend upon the strict preservation of the matrimonial union.

But the severest part, perhaps, of the woman's sentence, is still behind: *I will greatly multiply thy sorrow and conception*, in the Hebrew idiom; signifying thy sorrow in thy conception; which includes all the time of pregnancy, when women generally nauseate all their food, have the most troublesome longings, and endure other things very grievous to them; especially when they are in danger of miscarriages, very frequently happening.

Beginning regularly with *the suppression of the menstrual discharges*, we see the lively colour of the lovely sex, changed into a greenish, pale, and wan complexion; when the vessels *peculiarly* appropriated to the nutritious fluid, are employed in a new office. Then what head-achs, vertigos, mists before the eyes, qualms, languors, and aguish fits, indicate that a man is begun. And as the load increases, so doth the loss of strength, till parturient pangs issue in delivery. Nor even when this is procured are women always out of danger, especially while the after-birth

stays

ſtays behind, occaſioning ſore anguiſh, and expoſing the life to the greateſt peril.

These ſufferings may now ſeem no way ſtrange to us, who every day ſee all, or ſome part of them endured: And yet on reflection they are truly aſtoniſhing. Brute creatures are obſerved to conceive, and bring forth their young, with much leſs difficulty, pain and hazard, than women, who are the only beings under heaven, ſo far as we know, that have any trouble at conception. This a nice inveſtigator of nature affirms to be the caſe, except in the inſtance of a mare conceiving by an aſs, and, in general, where there is any thing monſtrous, injured, or diſtorted in the fœtus.

If it ſhould be aſked, how we can be certain, that other creatures have no ſickneſs on the occaſion, it may be confidently replied, that we can judge of the ſickneſs and health of brute animals, by as ſure marks, as of our own; though not always ſo clearly, in what particular part their diſtempers lie. And, to put the matter beyond all doubt, it is evident, that, whereas women are, all of them, diſordered by conception, other creatures are in more perfect health, and have more ſtrength, and a better habit of body, after it, than before.

Besides, *the woman's conceptions are greatly multiplied*, as ſhe is remarkably ſubject to abortions, and falſe conceptions, above all other animals in the world; as are alſo *her ſorrows*, by the mortality of her iſſue; fruſtrating, as it were, the ends of providence

dence and society; and by her pangs and dangers, just now mentioned, at the instant of production, contrary to what might be expected, from several circumstances in her form, which naturally promise more ease to her, than that of any brute to it, in this case, that we are acquainted with *. So singularly and emphatically true also is this other part of the woman's punishment.

Nor is the truth of what still remains to be examined less demonstrable: *Thy desire shall be to thy husband.* That is to say, not only she should be henceforth dependent on the will of her husband, as she had early indulged her own in a most criminal act, without his advice or consent; but likewise, after all the miseries, which she and her daughters, from generation to generation, should suffer, as a general consequence of the mysterious rite, *the appetite* for gratification should still subsist, and be the most predominant.

Adam, being last in the transgression, has sentence last pronounced upon him. *Unto him God said, because thou hast hearkened unto the voice of thy wife,* more than unto me, *and hast eaten of the tree of which I commanded thee, saying, thou shalt not eat of it; cursed is the ground for thy sake; in sorrow shalt thou eat of it all the days of thy life. Thorns also and thistles shall it bring forth unto thee: And thou shalt eat the herb of the field. In the sweat of thy face shalt thou eat bread; till thou return unto the ground: For out of it wast thou taken: Dust thou art, and unto dust shalt thou return.* This sentence re-

* Dean Delany's Revel. Exam. page 74.

quires little explanation; the import of it is obvious; and the fulfillment clearly verified: Toil and drudgery was to be the consequence of departing from an easy and reasonable obedience; hard labour was to subdue, and keep within certain bounds, those appetites and passions which had now broken loose from the restraints imposed upon them; and, notwithstanding man's utmost industry, to cultivate and improve it, the earth was to be less desirable to him, when his guilt had reduced him to the necessity of leaving it: *For dust thou art*, and into the very same state from which thou wast taken, *shalt thou* assuredly *return*.

And as it was no longer convenient that guilty man should remain in the abode of innocence and pleasure, *God drove* him *out* from it for ever; and even with the keenest irony; *Behold the man is become as one of us, to know good and evil.* Whether such a mode of speech, implies a plurality of persons in the divine nature, partaking of the same essence, we have examined in another place. And to prevent our surprise, when irony is attributed to the majesty of God, we may turn our attention to the various and repeated strains of it, introduced into the scriptures, after the manner of men.

Where the place of exile appointed for our first parents was, Moses hath not informed us; only by heavenly guardians being *placed at the east of the garden of Eden*, it is probable that it was toward that quarter of the earth, in relation to paradise. The vagueness of the expression, laying no foundation upon which opinions can be grounded with any certainty, both Jews and Mahometans, have presumptuously

tuously determined the place, and told ridiculous ſtories concerning its productions *. What the ſacred recital teſtifies is ſufficient for us to know, that they were baniſhed from the garden of God; and, to prevent creatures, who were no longer to be immortal on the earth, from *putting forth their hands, and taking of the tree of life*, which was the ſymbol, and, as has been ſaid, perhaps the principle of immortality, that he placed at the entry of paradiſe, neareſt to them, *Cherubims, and a flaming ſword which turned every way.*

Upon the words, *ſo the Lord God drove out the man*, it hath been likewiſe obſerved, that ignominy and violence attended the expulſion, in the ſame manner as an huſband repudiates his wife; and that God, who is ſaid by many of the prophets, to be married to his people, put away Adam and Eve, for ever, from his ſpecial favor, as a man does a woman, whom he rejects, and furniſhes with a bill of divorce †; or as a prince baniſhes a ſubject, rebelling againſt him, whom he ſends into exile, out of his own country ‡.

In the explanation of the word *Cherubim*, much learning hath been employed. A reſpectable Jew § hath ſaid, that the word, in general, ſignifies any form or figure of a creature; but that here, on account of the article ¶, it denotes *choſen Cherubims*. Others are for deriving the ſecond letter || from the *Arabic*, and thereby would have the appearance of a boy ſub-

* Selden de Synedr. Lib. i. Cap. 2.
† Vide Synop. Critic. Poli, in Loco.
‡ Bp. Patrick in Loco. § Aben Ezra.
¶ Heb. הכרבים || Heb. כ Polus, in Loco.

ſtituted

stituted. But all these conjectures are foolish, and have no foundation in the analogy of grammar.— Of this only we can be certain, that *Cherubims* are heavenly messengers; supposed to be *destroying angels* *; *excelling in strength*; different from *the* other hosts *of the Lord, and the* swift *ministers of his that do his pleasure* †; and that those, as well as these, appeared of old, as attendants on the divine majesty, in extraordinary dispensations, supporting the Almighty's throne: A scene gloriously described by Ezekiel, in the first chapter of his prophecies, where he presents to our imagination *a great cloud, a fire infolding itself, and a brightness about it, out of which proceeded a colour like that of amber.* Herein were *four living creatures*, always reckoned *Cherubims*, *every one of whom had four faces, and four wings, and feet sparkling like the colour of burnished brass.* The distinction of their faces, and the disposition of their members, are delineated with great accuracy. *Over their heads was a firmament, and above that firmament a throne, as the appearance of a sapphire-stone, and upon the likeness of the throne, was the likeness as the appearance of a man above upon it. And he had the brightness of fire round about him; as the appearance of the bow that is in the cloud in the day of rain, so was the appearance of the brightness round about. This was the appearance of the likeness of the* GLORY *of the* LORD, *when I heard the voice of one that spake to me.*

* The author of these Dissertations regrets the want of Archdeacon Sharp's Discourse upon this word, in refutation of the *Hutchinsonian Scheme*, which he hath formerly perused with pleasure. But it is not to be found in *Dublin*.

† Psal. 103, 20, 21.

The passage into the garden of *Eden*, one, or more of those *Cherubic* watches, (the word being plural, has been variously interpreted) guarded with *a flaming sword which turned every way*. By this *flaming sword*, one of the fathers of the church, agreeably to the loose fancies of his age and country, understood the *Torrid zone*; his vicinity to which, perhaps, sometimes incommoded him *. A learned Rabbi †, giving a signification to the text different from what it offers at first view, hath believed this *flaming sword* to be no other thing than the angel mentioned in conjunction with it; and supported his opinion with that place in the *Psalms*, where it is said, that *God maketh his angels spirits, and his ministers a flaming fire* ‡. That one of the *Seraphim*, or a flaming angel, in the form of a fiery flying *Seraph*, or serpent, whose body, moving in the air, resembled the vibrations of a sword, was appointed, with the *Cherubim*, to keep the entrance of the garden, has been the doctrine of a most judicious divine §. A sense, extremely forced, hath been put upon our Saviour's words, who, in the *tenth* of St. Mathew, says, *he came not to send peace upon the earth, but a sword*, and in the *eleventh* of St. Luke, instead of *sword*, uses *division*; from whence the conclusion is drawn, that by the *flaming sword*, in this place, we are to understand, an insurmountable barrier, or

* Tertullian apologet. Cap. 47.

† Locus illa, *Labet* flammam gladii versatilis, vel vertentis se, intelligendus est juxta illud; ministros suos ignem *lobet* flammantem——quia angeli instar prothei in varias formas se convertunt. Maim. Mor. Nevo. Pars 1. Cap. 49.

‡ Psalm 104, 4. § Bp. Patrick, in Loco.

an

an impervious fire, obstructing, or cutting off the way to Paradise *. There have been a few, who have amused themselves with the fancy that *Naphtha*, with which the province of *Babylon* abounded, and where Paradise is supposed to have been situated, was the *flaming* appearance, which deterred Adam and Eve from re-entering their late habitation. This *Naphtha*, we are told, in other respects resembles Bitumen, and is so inflammable that before it touches the flame, it will take fire at the very light of it, and often kindle the intermediate air. In the country about *Ecbatana*, Alexander saw streams of it so copious as to spread into large lakes, and fire bursting out of the clifts of the earth; which is so heated and relaxed by this porous substance, that often the grains of barley leap up, as if the violent inflammation had given a pulsation to the ground †. But instead of turning over more volumes, which only multiply fancies about this matter, our enquiries may be more usefully closed, with a plain acknowledgment, that Revelation affords us no other information here, but that our first parents were driven out of Paradise as a punishment for their transgression, and totally deprived of all hopes, by visible and the most awful demonstrations of the divine displeasure, that ever they should return.

By this *ejectment* and *exclusion* from the blooming and opulent inheritance their bountiful father had gi-

* Polus.

† Plutarch's Life of Alexander. The anecdote immediately follows his taking Susa.

Caverna ibi est, ex qua fons ingentem vim bituminis effundit, adeo ut satis constet Babylonicos muros ingentis operis hujus fontis bitumine interlitos esse. Quint. Curt. L. v. C. 1.

 ven

ven them, they lost the benefit of *the tree of life*, which, as has been repeatedly said, was either ordained, by its physical virtue, to invigorate and renew human nature, that man, by eating of it, might *live for ever*; an opinion very justly rejected by many divines*; or, as the *Rabbi*, frequently referred to, thinks, should, by the thickness of its trunk, and enormous strength, be allegorical to them; perhaps, he means, give them the assurance of their coœvality with it. And this tree, proceeds he, our sages say, God never discovered to any man, nor ever will he discover it †.

To draw the line of truth through this work, the opinion of those in regard to the tree of life, who make it purely *sacramental* and symbolical of the immortality, which Adam had conferred on him, ought to be recommended. The venerable Bishop of *Hippo* says, that the other trees in the garden had nourishment in them for Adam's food, and the tree of life was

* Meritò à Scoto, Thoma, et aliis hæc sententia rejicitur, quia potentia finita, not potuit habere efficaciam infinitam vitam in infinitum tempus extendendi: Adde quòd cum fructus ejus non minus ac succus corruptioni obnoxius esset, absolute non potuisset ab interitu hominem vindicare, nisi alia causa intercessisset. F. Turret. Loc. Oct. Quæst. v. p. 639.

† Dicunt sapientes nostri; non finis ramorum, sed Crassities Trabis vel Trunci ipsius, iter est quingentorum annorum, stantis in terra. Atque hæc metaphora vel allegoria quoque ab ipsis ad perfectiorem rei alicujus explicationem allata est.——Et arborem vitæ non revelavit Deus ulli homini, neque etiam unquam revelabit. Maim. Mor. Nev. P. ii. C. 30.

his

his sacrament †; or a pledge that he should enjoy them. And might be, moreover, an illustrious type of that eternal felicity, to which he should be translated in due time, and possess for ever in his maker's immediate presence; in the same manner as Christ, who purchased it back again for all of us, is called, in two passages of the Revelations, *the tree of life in the midst of the paradise of God.*

HAVING thus given an explication of this most important event in the annals of mankind, some difficulties that lie against it come, now, to be considered. And *first*, some unbelievers, to whom the *history of the fall* would have been altogether as *incredible*, though perhaps not quite so *entertaining*, if even every thing had been *simple* and *clear* in it, seem to declare they can as easily believe, that a *serpent* tempted Eve, as that any *evil spirit* could ever be permitted to do it. This kind of unbelief having no right to an argument, where a resolution appears to reject the most reasonable principles; it may be sufficient here to refer those who entertain it, ever so obstinately, to the beginning and close of the dissertation immediately going before.

OTHERS, indeed, who are not unbelievers in general, in matters respecting religion, yet stagger at some of the circumstances of the fall above related, are requested to consider, that the *speculations* arising from that event, upon which the *Supralapsarians* and the *Sublapsarians* have built the most absurd and indigestible *systems*; and even the most *philosophical di-*

† St. August. de gen. ad lit. lib. 8. cap. 4.

vines

vines introduced the distinction crudely, between *natural* and *moral* evil into the world *, are of all others the most abstruse, and the farthest removed from the reach of our understandings †. This difficulty led men in the *earliest* time to form, in their imagination, two *independent* principles of *good* and *evil*; the one called *Oromasdes*, and the other *Arimanius*; a notion entirely destructive of the sovereignty of God; the maintenance of which is the principle end and design of the Mosaic history. If this history, it is true, had, gravely and authoritatively, introduced an *invisible evil being*, to confound the works of God, by the fall of his noblest creature here below, and to be the author of *iniquity*, great countenance might have been given to this error, of two principles: Or, to colour it properly over, without any regard to the extent of his commission, Moses must have written the history of *the fallen angels* likewise, from which, perhaps, we might have derived no useful instruction: But nothing of this appearing in these holy pages, and the contrary being the prevailing principle through the whole of the *old scriptures*, the conclusion is evident; that, under the mixed government of the Almighty, so to speak, malice and wickedness, in a superior being might be *permitted*, though not *ordained*, much less supposing that being *co-ordinate* with God in power or existence, to effect all this mischief through the equality of the *poize* in the critical trial; for the greater aggravation of *his* guilt and sufferings, and of his *wicked associates*; while the frail victims, of his

* Dr. John Clarke, in his lectures, is the most intelligible

† See Dissert. 6, near the end.

envy

envy and wrath, were to be *ransomed* from all the *natural*, and never-ending consequences.

A SECOND objection often urged is, why God punished the evil spirit, under the figure of the serpent? The answer offers itself to our minds at once: It was necessary, in the wisdom of God, to punish the author of evil immediately; and in the presence of Adam and Eve; otherwise they might have been led into the most dangerous and destructive error, that there was some principle of evil in the world; some powerful malignant spirit independent of God, capable of controling his will, and destroying his creatures; and, therefore, such an exertion of the power of Jehovah over this apostate was necessary, in the very presence of those whom he had betrayed, as might convince them in the style of the prophet, that *he was God, and that there was none else*;—*that he was God, and there was none like him*;—that he formed *the light, and* created *darkness*; made *peace and* created *evil*;—that *the Lord*, in short did *these* and *all* other *things*, consistent with his wisdom and goodness, and the rectitude of his moral government *.

FOR a corroboration of this doctrine, let it be farther considered, that a spirit cannot be punished to human eyes, otherwise than under some sensible appearance; and what other sensible appearance could have so mnch resemblance to the *Devil* and his *crimes*, as a *serpent*, an *insidious* and *artful* animal? And, besides, what could be a more proper humiliation of his pride, than to punish him under the brutal form,

* Isaiah, x. lv, 5, 6, 7.

in

in which he perpetrated the guilt? A supposition will illustrate how the case really appears to have been; that a prince surprised a rancorous subject, of the first quality, plotting rebellion against him, in the most obscure and disguised garb; and to the circumstances of the mortification, attending his condemnation and execution, all the infamy of that character he had taken upon him, is added. Apply only this, though more might be annexed, to the proudest spirit in heaven, and tell us how it could be relished by him, when sunk below the vilest condition of brutality *?

A PART of the sentence pronounced upon the woman, has, in the third place, been thought, by some, very doubtful, and the question seriously urged, if it be really imaginable, that the race of females would have suffered less pain, and been exposed to less danger, on the supposition that Eve had never transgressed, than at present. Now, in reply, we must either admit the infelicity of women, at the time of child-bearing, to be the effect of a just punishment, or of very hard treatment from their maker: There is no alternative. He who made other creatures perfect in their kind, could have formed the fairest of his works proportionably perfect. But the infinite goodness of the divine nature will not suffer us to suspect any partiality on this occasion. All this misery must, therefore, demonstrably be the effect of a curse pronounced on the original mother, and by her entailed upon all her daughters; and

* Let the Dean of Down's 5th dissertation be read throughout, and a part of the 6th on this subject. And likewise Dean Sherlock's Discourses on Prophecy.

acknowledged

acknowledged as such by all, who take a just view of the matter.

It has been objected, fourthly, that the threatening, annexed to the charge that Adam should *not eat of the tree of the knowledge of good and evil; for the day that thou eatest thereof, thou shalt surely die*, was not executed. That he did die, and that every generation of his descendants, except the present, has died since, is allowed by all. But, say Infidels, consistently with the words of the sentence, he should have died immediately after the act of disobedience; whereas he *lived nine hundred and thirty years*.—Those who make such objections ought to have their understandings enlightened, and be informed, that it is no where said, nor to be understood, that Adam should die on that very day he eat the forbidden fruit. For the Hebrew words *, which, when literally translated, are, *dying, thou shalt die*, signify only the certainty of the event, not the time of it: They import that he should, that instant, lose the privilege with which he was invested of *living for ever*; and become *mortal*; that is, not liable to *death* only, against which there was to be no remedy, but to the *corruption of it* also; as all of us should likewise have been, after many sicknesses, pains and diseases, the direful fore-runners of dissolution, if the *second* Adam had not obtained for us a happy resurrection.—An entire deprivation of existence, a total extinction of being, after Adam's leaving this world, seems to be the extent of the

* Heb. מות תמות

divine

divine threatening; though others have conceived eternal pains included in it *.

How long the first scene of things might have continued, and man remained on the earth, if obedience had preserved him from death, has been likewise made a question, and difficulties insuperable are apprehended to arise out of the opinion that the human race, would have perpetually multiplied, without any diminution; and there are equal difficulties about the translation to any other state. This is the utmost force objectors can give to their scruples, on this part of the subject. To whom, it would be infinitely more easy to give a variety of answers, than to fix upon one that may be fully satisfactory to them. *Known unto God from the beginning are all his works*,—and his *counsel* concerning them *shall stand, and* he *will do all his pleasure* †: For they *are done in judgment; from the time he made them, he disposes the parts thereof*. But for us, his kingdom is vastly too universal and permanent for contemplation; and the plan upon which he has laid all the parts of it altogether inscrutable; and, for very wise reasons, communications of light may be denied us, which we would be very glad to have. A conjecture, however, about the removal of mankind from this, to another place of residence, after a certain period of probation, may be modestly offered. Though St. Paul says, *Flesh and blood cannot inherit the kingdom of God; neither doth corruption inherit incorrup-*

* Comminatis mortis, quæ denunciatur transgressori, complectitur et temporariam et eternam mortem in inferis subeundam F. Turret. Loc. Oct. Quæst 6.

† Isajah, lxvi, 9. 10. Eccles. xvi, 26.

kingdom

tion *; and Adam was plainly *corruptible*, by the meat and the drink that nourished him, and as many bodily necessities, such as sleep and rest, testified; and, therefore, could not enter upon a celestial life, without being changed from his animal state; yet the divine power, that fashioned him at first, could, with the same ease, transform his nature, and fit him for immortality in heaven, when the length and fidelity of his services had, in a certain degree, qualified his soul for it.

NOR is this conjecture destitute of all ground in revelation. In the covenant made with Adam, indeed, no mention is made of a life in heaven conferred on him; but, notwithstanding the brevity of the relation, the doctrine may be collected, by the most legitimate consequence, from the commination opposed, and from the *sacramental seal* of the promise, *the tree of life*. The silence, or rather obscurity of Moses, who delivers many things, concerning this covenant, only under shadows, making but a few of them now and then easy, by a gentle ray of light let in upon them, does not hinder us to conclude even positively, that a point of such great moment, to support him in obedience, was actually revealed to the first man.—The translation of *Enoch, the seventh from Adam* †. and of Elijah, in later times, *in a chariot of fire*, confirms the foregoing reasoning; in which we plainly see the mutability of matter, by the divine operation; not to insist on that of our blessed Saviour immediately into the presence of God, to be a priest for ever, as divines

* 1 Cor. xv. 50. † St. Jude, verse 14.

are

are not agreed, whether the celestial body was assumed at his resurrection or ascension.

After all this, it has still been objected to the Mosaic account of the consequences of the fall, that there is great harshness and cruelty in the conduct ascribed to the Almighty, who is represented as *fierce* and *enraged*, *driving out* his own creatures *in anger*—and, in *a kind of fury*, *cursing the very earth* for their sakes. Now if this were true, the objection would have irresistible force upon our minds, whether we considered the all-perfect nature of the parent of all, or his own declaration, that *fury is not in* him †. But where does Moses make use of all these expressions, to set forth the vehemence and excess of the divine anger on this occasion? There is no other foundation for all this calumny, than the delusion of a vain and blasphemous imagination, except in the single expression of *cursing the earth*;—not a single word appears of *anger*, *rage*, *fury*, through the whole relation. On the contrary, we see the strongest signs of compassion and mercy to the guilty: *unto Adam and to his wife, did the Lord God make coats of skins, and clothed them:* That is, of the skins of those beasts, which they were to offer in sacrifice to him, to be discoursed of hereafter, the Lord God gave direction that they should make themselves warmer cloathing, and fitter to defend them from the injuries of the weather, than the *fig-leaves they* had *sewed together*, upon the first sight of their *nakedness*.—In this he was not cruel to his poor creatures, nor regardless of their welfare; but, like an affectionate father, who feels the suffer-

† Isaiah, xxvii, 4.

ings

ings he inflicts upon the most beloved children, for their disobedience, made instant provision for their comfort and happiness.——Even in *cursing the earth*, there was clemency, when those guilty creatures had entailed death and misery upon themselves, and all their posterity, stood in need of having their minds detached from it, by every method of discipline, and set on the things of another life.

ADAM himself grounded his hopes clearly on these, and the like intimations of his maker's goodness, after his claim to it was lost, and he had none to expect. *He called his wife's name Eve, because she was the mother of all living*. Before, it was *Ashe*, woman, as she had been taken out of *Aish*, man; now it is changed into Eve, in belief that God wonld not inflict death on them soon; nor leave the world uninhabited after their death, but make her the mother of many generations; and particularly of the promised *seed*, by whom he might even hope to be raised from the dead again, and restored to immortal life.——If he saw this day, even afar off, his heart could not but rejoice! Here then was another plentiful source of comfort to our first parents, and a fresh evidence of the divine bounty.

OF their expectations from this promised *seed*, unbelievers, besides all the foregoing scruples, have suggested the strongest doubt. What unreasonable liberty of interpretation, say they, has been taken by Christian Divines? Let them tell us, by what rules of language, *the seed of the woman*, so much insisted on by them, is made to denote *one* particular *person*; and by what art the mystery of *Christ's* miraculous conception

conception can be diſcovered, in this common expreſſion? Let them tell us, farther, how the bruiſing the ſerpent's head, can poſſibly ſignify the deſtroying the power of ſin, and the redemption of mankind by a general ſaviour? The words of the ſentence pronounced upon the deceiver are only theſe: *I will put enmity between thee and the woman, and between thy ſeed and her ſeed; it ſhall bruiſe thy head, and thou ſhalt bruiſe his heel.* Whence they argue, that Adam, and his poſterity, ſhould now and then knock a ſerpent upon the head, and ſuffer the ſmart and danger of a bite on the heel, by that agile and revengeful animal.

It is true, Chriſtian Divines apply this part of the ſentence to our bleſſed Saviour, as a prophecy of him, who is, no doubt, called here *the ſeed of the woman* emphatically, and who came, *in the fullneſs of time*, to bruiſe the ſerpent's head, by *deſtroying the works of the devil*, and reſtoring to *the liberty of the ſons of God*, thoſe who were held under the bondage and captivity of ſin. And it is no wonder that ſuch queſtions are ſtarted by thoſe who look no where elſe, for the ground of the chriſtian application, and the unfolding this promiſe, than to this third chapter of *Geneſis*. As the promiſe, or the prophecy ſtands *there*, nothing may appear to point out this particular meaning; or to confine the words to it. But ſearching the whole diſpenſations of providence and grace, we will find this application of the paſſage, by chriſtian divines, fully juſtified; and that the various events, under thoſe diſpenſations, which mere hiſtorians, without a belief in religion, will acknowledge to be well authenticated,

ticated, confirm, with the greateſt ſtrength, the uſe that has been made of it.

THE very ſtate itſelf in which Adam was, at the time their ſentence was pronounced, explains the words, by the faireſt conſtruction. He was in a ſtate of ſin, ſtanding before God to receive condemnation for his diſobedience. He had, when the firſt inſtructions were delivered to him, heard the penalty, *on the day thou eateſt thereof thou ſhalt ſurely die*; the full execution of which he had reaſon to expect immediately, and without mitigation; and, at the end of the judgment, heard theſe awful words, the laſt that were to be ſpoken, and therefore irreverſible, *Duſt thou art, and unto duſt ſhalt thou return.* Now, to preſerve him and his wife, as objects of mercy, from final deſpair, it was abſolutely neceſſary to communicate *ſo much* hope to them, as might be *a rational foundation* for their future endeavours, to reconcile themſelves to their maker, by a better obedience. And what could ſo powerfully inſpire them with this hope, as the proſpect of a deliverer, however dark and indeterminate that proſpect might be, who ſhould repair their loſſes, and reſtore them to their primitive rights? After informing Adam that his days ſhould be ſhort, and full of miſery, any other comfort would have been inadequate to his caſe; and, conſequently, the interpretation given, by chriſtian divines, in a very qualified ſenſe, muſt be acknowledged fully reaſonable, nay altogether juſt, upon the moſt critical examination of the hiſtory itſelf.

BUT this claſs of objections to the conſequences of the fall being removed, another opens upon us, of divines,

divines themselves, who ask, What has all this to do with the whole race of mankind, with the corruption of the moral world, and the ruin of all the glory and happiness of the rational creation? Here, as was said on another occasion, is *labour* and *work* indeed, where matters of the last moment in religion, are brought into question.

A certain writer represents the sentiments of divines, both popish and protestant, in this manner, and says they have been generally, and for a long tract of time, such as are here collected; namely, that the guilt of Adam's first sin is imputed to, or charged upon, all his prosperity—that there is a total defect of that righteousness, wherein he is supposed to have been created; and that the corruption of human nature, whereby all mankind are utterly indisposed, disabled, and made opposite to all that is spiritually good, and wholly inclined to all evil, and that continually, is the source of all the wickedness committed in the world—further, by Adam's transgression all mankind were deprived of communion with God—and that all, as soon as ever they come into the world, are under his wrath and curse; by nature the children of wrath, bond-slaves to satan, justly liable to all the punishments in this world; and, in the world to come, an everlasting separation from the comfortable presence of God, and the most grievous torments in soul and body, without intermission, in hell for ever.

This, in the same writer's words, is, no doubt, an affair of the most dreadful importance, and requires to be examined with all possible care and impartiality. For an error in this point will affect the whole scheme of of christianity, and enervate the great design. Let us, therefore, examine the affair, with all possible care and impartiality; and remember that it is with Pelagians and Socinians we are arguing these points.

First, it is made an objection that the guilt of Adam's first sin should be imputed to, or charged upon, all his posterity. But the objection being too general, and, in this form, having staggered some that would otherwise have admitted the doctrine, when explained, things ought to be fairly discriminated; and the state of the question given. It is plainly this; 'Adam being the root of all mankind, must not the punishment, in all its consequences, except personal remorse for having incurred them, equally affect them, as those consequences did himself? In his sentence, there were included diseases, sickness, pains, and dissolution; and could he transmit to his posterity, any other kind of nature, than that to which he was now reduced? In the sweat of his face he was to eat his bread, till he returned to the ground, and what right could his offspring claim to a better condition? As he had been taken from the dust, by the divine omnipotence, and when fashioned for immortality, had forfeited his life and existence, and was actually condemned to die; could any of his children, begotten during the suspension of the sentence, or of his more remote descendants, issuing from them, expect any other lot than that of mortality, under which the original progenitor had manifestly fallen?

The reasoning is not less conclusive, when we view it in a legal, than in a natural light. Adam being clearly a fæderal head, or common representative, his

his personal sin was very different from that which is now frequently committed, the guilt and punishment of which rests with a man's self. His extended to those who were to derive from him. Nor are we without examples in the policy of nations, which is fixed by God himself, upon the natural course of things, of one, of many suffering for the crimes of another.—There are few countries in the world, where high treason is not punished with the forfeiture of estates and titles, to the transgressor, and all his posterity.—And if this sentence is changed, as it sometimes is, into a milder form, in imitation of the divine goodness, have not those whose privileges are restored to them, under certain restrictions, the strongest reasons to be thankful?

This doctrine is not false, when applied to the great governor of the world. That he will not punish vice, in the most awful and exemplary manner, is a false notion, and has the most dangerous tendency; though all the Pelagians and Socinians, the Free-thinkers and Philosophers that ever lived, should join in defending it.

But, secondly, what has all this to do, say they, with a total defect of that righteousness in his posterity, wherein Adam is supposed to have been created? The nature and extent of that righteousness has already been examined and set forth, as they result from the evidence of scripture *. And if that evidence be admitted, in regard to the knowledge, righteousness and holiness, in which it evidently appears, and must, from the nature and government of

* See Dissertation ii.

God,

God, and the firſt man, be concluded, Adam was made, or endued with; can we, conſiſtently with the cleareſt teſtimonies, deny that all his children, ever ſince his tranſgreſſion, have loſt thoſe original qualities, ſeeing ignorance, injuſtice and impiety have been the univerſal characteriſtics of mankind, except, where powerful remedies, under gracious diſpenſations, have been adminiſtered, and ſubmiſſively applied. Even theſe, powerful in themſelves as they have been, have too ſeldom been ſufficient to draw the world out of the abyſs of depravity and wickedneſs. Notwithſtanding all that education and correction can do for us when we are young, and all the influence that religion, and the laws of our country, have over us, when we are grown up, thoſe, of our fellow-creatures who make themſelves tolerably acquainted with their duty, and keep themſelves in the paths of it, are but few, in compariſon of ſuch as are deplorably defective in knowledge, and lead very diſorderly and ſinful lives; and even the beſt of men are ſo very often, and ſometimes ſo extremely, wanting to themſelves, in point of duty, intereſt and honour, that experience ſufficiently proves the univerſal change of our nature from light to darkneſs, and from rectitude to corruption. The cauſe and effect here are ſo combined, that it is altogether impoſſible, in a reaſonable imagination, to ſeparate them. A deprivation of righteouſneſs muſt be moral corruption, ſpiritual death, and the ſcource of all the wickedneſs committed in the world.

THE third objection is, that by Adam's tranſgreſſion all mankind were deprived of communion with God. This communion muſt imply a maintenance of that relation in which God was pleaſed to place his rational offspring; his favour, ſecured by obedience, would largely reward all the labours of it, by imparting unſpeakable comfort to the human heart; and experience of its paſt indulgence and liberality inſpire the moſt delightful confidence in the ſame, for all times to come. But violate that relation, and immediately all this happineſs is forfeited, and neceſſarily deſtroyed by the very conſciouſneſs of demerit. Beſides, as God *loveth righteouſneſs, and hateth iniquity, holds the way of the wicked as an abomination, and is of purer eyes than to behold evil*, his grace and approving regards are withdrawn from the ungrateful and rebellious; of which claſs, without new methods of amendment and reſtoration, all the ſons of Adam would at this day have been; bond-ſlaves to ſatan and their own luſts. And how the final conſequence, ſo much objected to, could have been avoided, of wrath and diſpleaſure, of an everlaſting ſeparation from the preſence of God, and of the moſt grievous torments, to the utmoſt extent of our nature and capacity, without intermiſſion for ever, let thoſe who are of a contrary opinion, condeſcend to explain.

In ſhort, on theſe doctrines briefly ſketched, the doctrines of the goſpel ultimately depend. They are addreſſed indeed to particular ſinners; but manifeſtly ſuppoſe that *there is none righteous, no not one.*—— Through Chriſt alone the tidings of life and favour are announced to mankind, who, by nature, have no other claim to them than Adam had after his tranſgreſſion. As a token of his wretched condition, he was ſhut out from acceſſion to the tree of life, which was cloſely guarded by *a flaming ſword* in the hand

of

of a *cherub*: And in allusion to this pledge and evidence of God's love, our Lord, in the book of the revelations, is designed by *the tree of life, which grows in the midst of the paradise of God, and whose leaves are for the healing of the nations.*

DISSERTATION VIII.

Of the Murder of Abel; and Cain's Curse.

GENESIS IV.

THE first ſin, with its dreadful univerſal effects, we have long had under our conſideration; and here we have another, ſpringing, undoubtedly, from the polluted fountain, of the blackeſt die, and introducing deſolation, horror and infamy into the common family of mankind. The tragical act of one brother towards another, very ſoon gave fatal evidence of the fallen ſtate of man. On the birth of the firſt ſon, *the ſoul of Eve*, to borrow Mary's words, *magnified the Lord, and her ſpirit rejoiced in God*; when ſhe could not poſſibly know that the tranſports of joy, uſual on ſuch occaſions, would, in a few years, be turned into ſorrow and mourning. *I have gotten a man from the Lord*, ſays ſhe; for this is the ſignification of the name Cain, which was given him. Some divines, on the ambiguity of the Hebrew *, have tranſlated the words, *I have gotten a man which is the Lord*; and

* Heb. קניתי איש את יהוה.

imagined

imagined that Eve believed this new-born infant to be the Messiah.' But, perhaps, this may be only a fond imagination of some good Christians, whose views of the general scheme of Redemption must have been much larger, than those the original mother of mankind had, who only saw the beginning of that scheme.

For the name of the second son, which was Abel, divers reasons have been given, according as the word has been deduced from different roots. It has been thought to import mourning; and that Abel was so called, either by a particular appointment of providence, prefiguring to his parents, their grief on his death; or that he was only called by this name, after the event had explained the meaning of it. Others, again, derive it from a word that signifies *vanity*, and think that Eve either confessed the vain hopes she had entertained at Cain's birth, and that she could not reasonably form the same upon that of a second son; or that he was called *vanity*, because all that was in the world, into which he was entering, was *vanity, and vanity of vanities.*

When those minute criticisms, of little moment, are dismissed, from the plain history it obviously appears, that the two brothers ought to have been united in the closest bands of friendship and love. Every field, with its vegetable productions, and living stock, nay, the whole earth, and all its riches belonged to them, as joint-heirs and lords paramount. None of those vexatious claims could possibly subsist, which, in after ages, have so much disturbed society, and been the occasion of bloody wars and fightings, between

tween sovereign and subject, and children of the same family, about property and dominion. And yet Cain murdered Abel, for the following reason; that *the Lord had respect unto Abel, and his offering: But unto Cain, amd to his offering, he had not respect.*

Here it may be enquired, whether their own consciences, dictating guilt to them, directed them to offer sacrifices as a proper method of appeasing the divine anger; or were they prescribed by revelation, not transmitted to us? Was it natural reason which declared the duty indispensible of offering a part of their wealth to him, of whom they held the whole? Were those sacrifices to be offered in a place of their own chusing, or of Adam's, or rather God's, where sensible marks of his presence were to be seen? Were those offerings always to be made by the ministry of Adam, or was every father of a family, the head of his own house, to make them? These points it may be equally difficult to determine, to the satisfaction of those who insist upon demonstration, or would be contented with probability. In another place, we shall enter on a larger discussion of them. The only thing, with certainty, affirmed here is, that Cain, being an husband-man, *brought of the fruit of the ground an offering unto the Lord*; and Abel, who was a shepherd, *brought also of the firstlings of his flock, and of the fat thereof.*—The notion of milk, instead of the beasts themselves, is totally to be rejected.

How deceitful is the judgment formed on outward appearances! Who would have imagined, that between two of the first inhabitants of the new world, sons of the same family, acknowledging the same

same true object of divine worship, and seemingly animated with the same desire of doing him homage, there should have been made so great a difference by their maker? *The Lord had respect unto Abel, and to his offering; but unto Cain, and to his offering, he had not respect. For the Lord seeth not as man seeth; for man looketh on the outward appearance, but the Lord looketh on the heart* *; and in its dispositions, under every dispensation of religion, we are to seek for the rules of acceptance and disapprobation.—Of these the great searcher of hearts can alone be the proper judge.

If we read the whole relation given by Moses, we will plainly see that Abel *did well*, that is, acted righteously in offering his sacrifice, and that Cain *did not well*, that is, unrighteously, in offering his sacrifice; and, as a consequence, *sin lay at his door*. The apostle to the Hebrews points out the particular defect, when he says, *By faith Abel offered unto God a more excellent sacrifice than Cain, by which he obtained witness, that he was righteous, God testifying of his gifts* †. By some eminent divines the interpretation of these words, of the greatest importance in the œconomy of religion, is, that though *animal* sacrifices had been appointed upon the fall, as an atonement for sin, yet Cain, for want of due conviction of guilt, and of reverence for the supreme command, presented only *the fruits of the earth*; which were no more than *eucharistical*, or a tithe, so to speak, for the divine blessing on the ground; and neither an acknowledgment of his corruption, nor of the necessity of appeasing God for it; and much less any way expressive, or typical, of that *seed of the woman*, which was to come into the world, to

* 1 Sam. xvi, 7. † Heb. xi. 4.

suffer

suffer death, and *shed his blood for the remission of sins*: and therefore could not be accepted, because it was not performed in contemplation of the great propitiation.—But this matter, when the subject of sacrifices comes expressly under our consideration, shall be more particularly examined.

The holy scripture is more express, in regard to the *respect* that was paid to Abel's sacrifice, than the reasons which occasioned it. *Respect*, in the sacred language, often signifies to give approbation, both in the new, and the old testament, as every one will remember, without a reference to the places. But the external sign which the Almighty gave of his approbation of the sacrifice of the younger brother, is, in a great measure, unknown to us; though we shall likewise, enquire what the divine *appearances* and tokens were, in the sequel. If we may judge here, from the procedure of God in following ages, what this *testimony* was, *fire*, probably, descended from above, and consumed Abel's offerings, as a mark of the preference given to his sacrifices. Thus an old commentator * hath translated the passage, that *God consumed Abel's offerings by fire*; and heathens pretended that their Gods often signified their pleasure at fæderal rites, much after the same manner †.

* Theodot.

† ———— Sequitur sic deinde Latinus,
Suspiciens cælum, tenditque ad sidera dextram:
Hæc eadem, Ænea, terram, mare, sidera, Juro,
Latonæque genus duplex, janumque bifrontem,
Vimque deum infernam, et diri sacraria ditis.
Audiat hæc genitor, qui *fœdera fulmine sancit*.
Æneid, Lib. 12. ver. 196.

It

It is no uncommon thing, as the discerning see, and the quick and sensitive part of mankind feel, that the innocence and goodness of the purest and most benevolent men, shall be the only reason for drawing upon them the hatred and resentment of a villain; and the virtues and excellencies of our neighbours, be considered as the condemnation of our vices and defects. The application to Cain fills us with conviction, that this reflection was very early just: He bore, impatiently, the distinction between him and his brother. Perhaps he imagined that Abel would also invade his birth right, which might then, as it afterwards did, give a certain dominion over the rest of the family; of the greater importance to Cain that no other division of power was ye made. This suspicion God repressed, and condescended to assure him, that his prerogative should be preserved; that to become as acceptable to him as his brother was, nothing was wanting but his *faith* and *righteousness*; and that there could be no political cause of bearing hatred to Abel, who should always be inferior to him, as he was the first-born.

But for this very reason that the Almighty was Abel's advocate, Cain's wrath was kindled the more against him. The defence made by the Being who was supreme over all, redoubled that jealousy, which it ought to have destroyed. Seeking, accordingly, an opportunity of betraying a man, whom he hated, because he was better than himself, and acknowledged to be so, Cain, it is not unlikely, proposed to go to the *fields*. The innocent man, unsuspicious of perfidious designs, followed the murderer, who created a quarrel, as a pretext to kill him. Of the nature of the

the dispute no notice is taken in the history; where it is only said that *Cain rose up against Abel his brother, and slew him.* Some of the Jews thought Abel not only *a saint*, but *a martyr* also; and that he was killed by his brother for no other reason, but maintaining some orthodox point of religion *. A conjecture which, though it hath nothing in it opposite to the analogy of faith, hath yet no foundation in the words themselves, nor in the circumstances of the story.

By way of reproach, and to give Cain an opportunity of confessing this murder, that he might obtain pardon for it, *the Lord said unto him, Where is Abel thy brother?* But instead of recommending himself to the mercy of his judge, he scornfully rejected it, by another question; *am I my brother's keeper?*

The divine justice never borrows such formidable arms as from an abuse of goodness. God, accordingly, replied to Cain, *What hast thou done? The voice of thy brother's blood crieth unto me from the ground*; and to that voice I grant the vengeance which it solicits; that very earth, which hath received his blood, shall execute it. The soil shall refuse germination to the seed which thou shalt deposite in it, and to answer thy expectations in cultivating it. Thou shalt also seek a place of refuge in barren and uninhabited lands, far from the habitation which I had assigned to thy family, in the same manner as thy father was driven from Eden for his transgression; and in what country soever thou shalt settle, it shall prove a place of exile, where thou shalt spend a life as wretched as it has been criminal.—An early instance of God's severity in the pu-

* Targum of Jonathan, in Loco.

nishment

nishment of enormous wickedness; given literally in these awful words, *And now art thou cursed from the earth*.*; *when thou tillest the ground, it shall not henceforth yield unto thee her strength. A fugitive and a vagabond shalt thou be in the earth.*

A FEW verses after, where the execution of this sentence is related, it is said, that *Cain went out from the presence of the Lord.* This expression, by many interpreters, is supposed to signify the Schechinah, or glorious appearance of God, by which the divine presence was made known to pious worshippers. After the establishment of the Mosaic dispensation, it is evident, that those who went up to the tabernacle in Shiloh, and to the temple at Jerusalem, for religious services, were said to appear before God, because there the shining light resided: That, in the very same manner, such a visible token of the presence of the Almighty appeared to the church, in their solemn assemblies, in its primitive state, spake and conversed with men, and approved and disapproved of their actions, is likewise certain; from the frequency and familiarity of the divine appearances to Adam, and the conferences we have seen held with Cain; neither of whom seem in the least alarmed at them; which plainly shews, that such appearances were no extraordinary things. And in the Book of Job, *when the sons, or children, of God came together to present themselves before the Lord*, the Lord is represented as discoursing with satan, about the character and circumstances of that holy man †. This scene, though an allegory, is clearly grounded on an allusion to the divine manifestations, so common in ancient times.

* Heb. הארמה

† Job. i. 8.

EVERY

Every one of Adam's family, so long as their number permitted them to assemble for sacrifice, in one place, would, as the sabbath returned, have this glorious vision before their face. It is not improbable, but that it was on the sabbath, when Abel's place was empty in the assembly, that the Lord said to him, *where is Abel thy brother?* And let us conceive, if we can, his dread and fear, when charged, by a divine witness, before a worshipping assembly, with the most flagitious crime, and exposed to the resentment of his almighty maker, whose prerogative of life and death he had sacrilegiously usurped! All would wait in silence, and foreboding expectation, when the sentence, mercifully mitigated, came forth.

From this shining light, which denoted the divine presence, it has been imagined, that the first inhabitants of the world were led to pay the honour of adoration to the sun; that orb, of all the other phœnomena of nature, having the strongest resemblance of that glory which then appeared; and to place fire, in later times, among the objects of idolatry. But while we relate these things, it is rather to give the thoughts of some commentators, than the true history of the first ages of mankind.

A reflection a great deal more important, is, that the same principle of baseness which prompts some men to wickedness, when they expect to escape, plunges them into despair the moment punishment is denounced. Cain testified his fear of sinking under the weight of the sufferings which awaited him, and that they would certainly prove greater than his strength to support them. He imagined that his misfortunes would exceed the words of his sentence, and that ex-

ile

ile was the least of the evils which he had to apprehend; in short, *that whoever found him would slay him*, as a strolling brute, dangerous to the human species; and against their hatred and resentment he had no security from the providential care and inspection, now withdrawn, like his presence. But God, who remembered compassion, in the midst of his anger, removed this terror, in a great measure, from his mind. *He set a mark upon him*, which should distinguish him from all others, and thereby obviate every pretext for killing him out of mistake; and declared besides, *whosoever slayeth Cain, vengeance shall be taken on him sevenfold*. The lives of the very wickedest are often protected and prolonged, for wise and holy ends; and Cain was to live to a great age, either that he might have time to repent; or, being impenitent, remain a monument of divine justice.

INTERPRETERS have contended, with great warmth, about the nature of the mark which God set upon Cain. The passion for conjecture must be very powerful, when, with some Rabbins *, a dog is supposed to have always gone before Cain, and intimated to every one that this is the man whom it is dangerous to approach. Those, to whose authority the learned pay great respect, have been of opinion, that God ordered him to wear a particular garb, to make him remarkable from the rest of men, who were cloathed with skins; in order to prevent his being killed in place of a wild beast of the field †. A very diligent compiler hath said, that the ridiculous conjectures

* Vide Cornel. a Lapide, Tom. i. Gen. 4.

† M. Le Clerc, Gen. 4.

upon

upon this point, have been almoſt without number. Some imagine that God impreſſed a letter on his forehead. And others have been ſo curious in their enquiries, as to pretend to tell what the letter was. A letter of the word Abel, ſay ſome; the tetragrammaton, or four letters of Jehovah, ſay others; or a letter expreſſing his repentance, ſay a third ſort of writers. There have been other writers, who rather think his face and forehead were leprous; others that his mark was a wild aſpect and terrible rolling eyes; others ſay, he was ſubject to a terrible trembling, ſo as to be ſcarce able to get his food to his mouth; a notion taken from the words uſed by the Septuagint for *fugitive and vagabond* *. And there are ſome writers that have improved this conceit, by adding that wherever he went the earth ſhook and trembled round about him. But there is another notion of Cain's mark, as good as any of the reſt, namely, that he had an horn fixed on his forehead, to warn all men to avoid him †. Among all theſe *marks* which have been enumerated, who ſhall determine *that* which was really ſet upon him. And where the field of fancy is ſo wide, and the event capable of being diverſified by a thouſand circumſtances, to ſuggeſt one, accompanied with probability, is altogether ſufficient. The Hebrew word ‡ ſtrictly ſignifies a ſign or token. It is uſed in the ninth chapter, when the bow was ſet in the cloud, as a ſign or token that the earth ſhould be no more deſtroyed by water. So that there is no better reaſon for ſaying there was any *mark* ſet on Cain, than that Noah had the bow delineated on his body. God gave Cain a ſign or token,

* Septuagint στένων καὶ τρέμων

† Shuckford's Con. Vol. i. p. 8.

‡ Heb. אות

to

to assure him that none should kill him; and the guesses about his mark testify how egregiously writers will trifle. They cannot avail themselves, by having recourse to the Septuagint itself*, where the word used by the interpreters, signifies the same thing as in the original text.

The goodness of God, in itself infinite, and, in the exercise of it, to his creatures, vastly beyond the limits of ours, to one another, was yet regulated by Cain's repentance, in the sentence that was passed upon him. He had, in a very little time, a full conviction of his folly and wickedness. He repeats over God's sentence against himself, as acknowledging the justice of it, and condemned himself so much as to imagine *his sin was too great to be forgiven.* For the translation we have, *My punishment is greater than I can bear*, rests on the ambiguity of the words in the Hebrew †; which may be rendered either positively, *My iniquity is too great to be forgiven*, or, as the Rabbinical expositors take it, by way of interrogation, *Is my iniquity too great to be forgiven* ‡? Can I find no mercy? No alleviation of the punishment I have brought upon myself?—The very language of a self-convicted and condemned wretch, who knows not the extent of the judgment incurred, for the mischief he has done.

After these observations on the text, we have still to deplore, on this occasion, that the enemies of religion have taken every audacious and subtile method to undermine it. Because a great number of

* Sept. σημεῖον τῷ Κάϊν

† Heb. גדול עוני מנשא

† Vide Fag. in loco.

 inhabitants

inhabitants appear to have been on the earth, at the time Cain killed his brother, and there are traces of various arts in this first age of the world, some of that sort have boldly maintained, that the earth was inhabited before Adam himself. Because it is said by Cain, *every one that findeth me shall slay me*; and that he *went out from the presence of the Lord, and dwelt in the land of* Nod, *on the east of* Eden, the argument has been thought conclusive, that there were pre-adamites *. To make it still stronger, they alledge, that even Moses makes mention of two distinct creations, one of mankind in general, and the other of Adam and Eve; and, in the progress of his history, gives strong intimations that there were several more men in the world when they were created; else it is not easy to conceive how all the circumstances, related above, could possibly happen: and would from hence infer, that Moses intended only to give an account of the origin of the Jews, and not of the primitive parents of the whole human race.

But these deistical, or rather altogether infidel objections, are easily answered; for the passage, wherein the creation of man is mentioned the second time, is plainly no more, as has been said already, than a recapitulation of what had been said before of the creation of the world in general, with a more particular detail of our first parents. And as to the numbers of mankind, about the time Abel was murdered, and of whom Cain was so much afraid, it is by no means improbable, that these should be all descended from Adam and Eve, whose posterity might well have multiplied to many thousands, by a fair calcu-

* Saurin, Discours. v.

lation,

lation, conſidering the original fœcundity, and that none are ſuppoſed to have died ſince the reſpective births. For, in one hundred and thirty years, when Seth was born in the place of Abel, the number ſuppoſed might clearly have been produced.

The moſt plauſible objection to the Moſaic account, on the pretence of *pre-adamites*, remains indeed to be conſidered; and is this,—that if Adam and Eve be allowed to be the progenitors of all mankind, there can be no tolerable cauſe aſſigned of the difference of the colour between the *whites* and the *blacks*; while two ſources, if admitted, would reſolve the whole difficulty.

To this it may be anſwered, that the variety of complexions in the world, may be eaſily accounted for another way. We know how the hair and colour of men's bodies differ according to the climate they inhabit, and their greater or leſſer diſtance from the ſun; though they are all confeſſedly from the ſame ſtock, and of the ſame deſcent. And beſides many of the cauſes which we evidently ſee producing this difference, there may be a great many more, with which we are unacquainted, perfectly natural, as well as appointed peculiarly by the wiſdom of God. Hence we may conclude, that the firſt colony, which ſettled in a very hot country, received a great change in their complexion, proportionable to the heat of the climate, and became very tawny, gradually inclining to blackneſs, as the ſun was more intenſe upon them, till in a generation or two, that high degree of tawnineſs might become natural, and at length the pride of the natives. And this tint, once given, would be communicated to children, who, on every birth, would approach nearer to an abſolute blackneſs; and as their tender bodies came to be expoſed naked (as the manner of ſuch countries is) to the violent heat of the ſun, their ſkin muſt neceſſarily have been ſcorched to an extraordinary degree, and, perhaps, its very texture altered, and by that means contract a blackneſs far ſuperior to that of their parents. By ſuch a progreſs, it is not improbable, that people of the faireſt complexion, when removed into a very hot climate, may, in a few centuries, become perfect negroes *.

"After all, wherein does the difference really conſiſt? The moſt induſtrious and penetrating anatomiſts tell us, in nothing more than in the lymph depoſited in the fatty membrane, or reticular work that lies under the ſkin. The colour of the blood, the muſcles, the thoracic, the abdominal viſcera, and the bones, are found to be the ſame in blacks, as in the whiteſt men. So that the celebrated judge †, who has ſtrained hard, to induce the readers of his book to have faith in providence, as he expreſſes himſelf, may, perhaps, on reflection ſee, that there are not ſo many races of men upon the earth, as he once thought to be neceſſary to fit them for the different climates: He may remember that there have been wonderful emigrations to the moſt diſtant parts of the globe, from north to ſouth, as well as from the eaſt to the weſt, and that the ſettlers have not only lived, but ſoon become ſo adapted to their circumſtances, as to be in all reſpects like the natives, if they followed their manners,

* Univerſal Hiſtory, p. 99.
† Lord Kaim's Hiſtory of Man, p. 10.

To

To resume the thread of the history; we are certain that in about one hundred and forty years after the creation, the human race was greatly multiplied. For we are told that Cain *builded a city in the land of* Nod, *on the east of* Eden, about ten years after the murder of Abel; that his own family, by this time considerably increased, and others who ventured to join a man and his house, who were so infamous, might live together in society, preferable to wandering up and down, as formerly; and be more secure, as some think Adam's family was still seeking an opportunity to revenge an unnatural crime, which they could not possibly forget. This city he called *Enoch, after the name of his son*; in the same manner as Nimrod called his city *Nineveh*, in honour of his son Ninus; proofs sufficient of the antiquity of this custom. Several writers * have mentioned the *Enochii* in old times, who have been imagined to be the descendants of this son of Cain †. But this is extremely conjectural, as those *Enochii* inhabited some countries on the borders of *India* long after the flood, when all the tribes of the earth were deducible from Noah and his sons. And in the Mosaic history, it is very remarkable, the line of Cain's genealogy ends in this chapter, with the children of Lamech, as if it was unworthy of farther notice; while that of Seth begins, and is traced down to the days of the great legislator.

It cannot be unobserved, that no woman has been hitherto mentioned in the world except Eve, nor any that Cain had, or could have taken for a wife. This point has been attended with some difficulties, and variously managed according to men's fancies. A

* Pliny, Mela, Lucan. † Sir Walter Raleigh.

wife,

wife. however, he most certainly had, though we are not informed whether he took her before the murder of his brother, or after. It is more probable, if we may supply the defect of the history, that it was previous to the fatal event, as most women, especially a sister, would naturally abhor an impious murderer. That his wife was his sister, we have no room to doubt, there being no other in the world, but his own family. But, according to the tradition, Eve, at her two first births, had twins, a son and a daughter; and Cain married Abel's sister, and Abel Cain's; which was absolutely necessary, and, for this reason, lawful: But, when that necessity ceased, the practice was prohibited by God, and hath ever since been held in abhorrence by men*.

From this example of distress and misery, introduced into a family, by the wickedness of some of its members, and many other warnings and admonitions of holy scripture, let every one learn their duty, and avoid those calamities which transgression brings upon themselves and others.

* Selden, Lib. v.

DISSERTA-

DISSERTATION IX.

OF THE INSTITUTION OF SACRIFICES.

GENESIS, IV.

IN the Diſſertation going before, we viewed Cain and Abel performing an act of religious devotion, by way of oblation or ſacrifice to the Almighty; and ſuggeſted ſome of the reaſons, why Abel's might be accepted, and Cain's condemned. And now a queſtion, of great conſequence to be reſolved, comes, in this place, to be conſidered; namely, whether this kind of worſhip was of divine or human inſtitution. If it was divine, ſacrificing abounds with inſtruction; if humane, it is arbitrary, and of diſputable authority. Some object, that we read of no command from God, in this early account of the world, for offering ſacrifices; and therefore, conclude that men offered them of their own accord, from a grateful inclination to return to God ſome of his own bleſſings, and to acknowledge him to be the abſolute proprietor of all their enjoyments; without any poſitive directions about them.

THIS

This objection, however, seems to have no force, and the conclusion to be false, when we rationally reflect; that, in the infancy of time, men wanted instruction more than at any time since; and consequently, were directed in every thing relating to religion, agreeable to the principles of God's justice and goodness, and to his proceedings in every age, under the respective dispensations. Besides, an apostle says, in a passage quoted before, that *Abel offered his sacrifice in faith*. In faith of what? certainly of God's acceptance, in the first instance. But how could he do this, if his faith had no other ground than his own fancy? For mere opinion never was, nor can possibly be, the solid foundation of faith. And it is, at the same time, said by Moses himself, that *God had respect to*, or, in other words, shewed his approbation of *Abel, and his offering*; in the language of the apostle, *he obtained witness that he was righteous, God testifying of his gifts*, that they were proper, and offered in the prescribed manner. While, on the other hand, Cain's were not pleasing to God, because they were presented contrary to the rule; which plainly supposes a previous institution, of which he was, or might have been well informed. For if no such rule had been given, it is impossible that any censure could have been passed upon him, for not having observed it.

This reasoning is not, in the least, affected by what was before said of the disposition, which is principally regarded by God, in every service that is performed; seeing the externals, as well as the intention with which it is done, must be right. Nor is it to be urged, that the institution of sacrifices, in so concise

cise a history, is not mentioned, when other things, of considerable moment, are also omitted: Such as religious assemblies, Noah's preaching, and the exact increase and number of Adam's family. Things which were well known, or generally believed, when Moses wrote, required no particular description, but might be taken for granted.

That men, so early, had no communication with the Almighty, nor revelations from him, is far from being true, on the clearest evidence; God, in some visible form, having actually appeared, and made his will frequently known to Adam, and to all the succeeding patriarchs, whose names are recorded in this book, for upwards of two thousand years. When, therefore, Adam, and all the other patriarchs, had the fullest opportunity of knowing from God himself, what kind of worship was most acceptable to him, there was no necessity, nor room left for human inventions; nor is it to be supposed that Cain was excluded from a privilege which all the rest enjoyed; especially while he remained in a state of innocence. In fact, we find that God condescended to converse with him also, and to give him instructions for his conduct.

We have, moreover, another source of auxiliary testimonies from scripture itself, that the institution of sacrifices was divine. Those beasts, with the skins of which our first parents were clothed immediately after the fall, were certainly slain, as sacrifices, by divine appointment. For till the flood, no such thing appears, as eating flesh of any kind, for food. And this rite of slaying beasts, seems highly suitable to the

circum-

circumſtances, into which mankind were brought, by tranſgreſſion. Eating the tree of life became a ſtate of innocence, and aſſured immortality to a faithful continuance in duty. But the killing a living animal was more correſpondent to a guilty condition, as it expreſſed the deadly nature of ſin, and the demands of a broken law.

A FARTHER argument, upon which an inference may be fairly founded that ſacrifices were of divine inſtitution, is, that the death of an innocent creature cannot be, in itſelf, an action acceptable to God; and, conſequently, nothing could make it ſo, but ſome ſpecial propriety in the inſtitution; we may rather ſay ſome neceſſity in the divine wiſdom, for the inſtruction of mankind. It is even evident, that Moſes, merely as an Hiſtorian, would never have given ſuch an abſurd relation, if the fact had not been fully aſcertained, and reſted upon the beſt authority.

THE proof here purſued reſults, indiſputably, from the account connected with Abel's ſacrifice, that he *offered it to God by faith*, which is declared to be the very thing that rendered it more *excellent* than Cain's; in the ſame manner as Noah built the ark by the expreſs command of God; Abraham left his country and kindred, and Sarah believed that ſhe ſhould have a ſon in her old age; and for that faith, and firm truſt and confidence in the Almighty, had the fulfilment of the promiſes made to them, in their ſeveral circumſtances. For what other faith could poſſibly conſtitute the excellence of Abel's offering, than that it was acceptable to God, and an act of obedience

ence to his will? though, otherwise, an act most unlikely to be pleasing to him, or *righteous* in itself; because it was the destruction of an innocent creature. Nothing, indeed, but such a faith, as prompted Abel to that obedience, could ever make the blood of any being, *which is its life**, praise-worthy in any man, since the foundation of the world.

If this account given by Moses, of sacrifices and the manner of accepting them, be thought too short, it may be remembered, that the Jews, to whom he wrote, needed no more information; a clear and uninterrupted tradition from their ancestors, who lived long before Moses, having made them perfectly familiar to them: For it would be ridiculous to imagine, that he communicated to that nation all the knowledge, which the divine providence, by the preservation of his writings, hath, with equal grace and wisdom, transmitted to our own times. They were, likewise, soon to know, by miraculous fire from the divine presence, which fell on the first oblation, after the solemn consecration of Aaron and his sons†, that their own sacrifices were of divine institution, and pleasing to God, by this manifestation of acceptance; and therefore could have no reason to doubt from the shortest relation, that they had been instituted, and accepted, in this manner, from the beginning. Besides, a short relation, there is reason to believe, was necessary, at least very prudent; as this rite, in all probability, was loaded with many additional circumstances, at its revival under Moses; that the Jews, in this point, might be guarded from the infec-

* Gen. ix. 4. Levit. iii. 17.
† Levit. ix. Chapter.

tion

tion of the heathens; and it might not be proper to explain the matter more fully, to an untractable and rebellious people.

But without insisting farther on the original hints of revelation, or the uncontroverted history of the Jewish church, from the first formation of the priesthood, till its final dissolution; an argument, of the greatest force, may be deduced from the universal practice of sacrificing beasts, and other animals, in all ages and nations, prior to the present dispensation of religion on the earth. Concerning objects of the mind's immediate intuition, and of sense, there can be no dispute: But in points of speculation, an uniform agreement seems to proceed from the voice of nature, or God himself speaking intelligibly to every nation by his works, or his words *.

Now that sacrifices obtained universally, for two thousand years at least, if not four, over all the regions of the known world, none can deny who has the least knowledge of antiquity †. And, that the practice did not take its rise, or prevail, from any dictate of reason, it is to be presumed, every one will readily own, who consults his natural understanding, and observes the aversion most men have to gratify their appetites, by wantonly shedding the blood of an harmless being of any sort whatever. For there could be no other temptation, in those ages, when the blood was actually spilt on the ground, and the body burnt on an altar, by all the religious part of men, we have the strongest reasons to believe, for

* Grot. de Verit. Ch. Relig. Abernethy, Serm. 1.
† Homer. Hesiod. Thucydides. Horace. Virgil.

the

the first sixteen hundred years after the creation.— And though, under some distant succeeding periods, parts of the offerings were dedicated to the priests who served at the altar; yet priest-craft cannot be charged with beginning the practice of sacrifices; seeing the duty of sacrificing belonged, for some centuries, to the father of the family, who was more affected than any other, by the addition of an unnecessary expence. And when fathers became princes, by the increase of their dependants, royalty and the priesthood were united in one person, and sacrifices were provided at the sacrificer's own cost.

What then can the ingenuity, or infidelity, of men possibly suggest, in order to invalidate or refute those accumulated arguments, that the institution of sacrifices, which we are here considering, is divine? The evidences adduced, to prove this, unprejudiced reason must judge to be clearly conclusive. *This was a statute for Israel, and a law of the God of Jacob*; and to our first parents was an appointment of infinite wisdom, for their humiliation and comfort; and for the peace, prosperity, and confidence of the succeeding generations.

Adam, condemned to death, was daily to be reminded of it. And what a striking emblem of mortality, must the carcases of those animals exhibit, which, a very little time before, could exercise their members and organs, in a wonderful manner, and were so beautiful and lively? When, in Holocausts, they were consumed to ashes, and reduced to a handful of dust, the first pair could not avoid the indulgence of meditations on their own sad condition, on account

account of sin, and the fullest assurance, that they themselves must, in process of time, no great matter when, follow the same humilitating steps to destruction.

And, at the same time, that their hearts were to be pierced, by sacrifices, with the detestation of guilt, and the dread of misery; those very sacrifices were the seals of a covenant of mercy, into which God had entered with our first parents, immediately after their fall. From hence, comfort would necessarily arise, when they saw, that though death was the wages of sin, yet God, in great compassion, would accept of the life of another in the room of the offender's.

That sacrifices were really intended as a token of mercy, who can doubt, when the divine solicitude for an hardened murderer, for so vile a wretch as Cain, is ever so little considered. Would God fail to intimate to Adam, the exercise of that attribute, at a time when it was more wanted, than ever it was since the world began? Would he take care of the health of Adam and Eve, after the grossest instance of disobedience, and make no provision for the peace of their minds? Nor lay any foundation for the hopes of the whole race of mankind, which was to spring from them?

On this very presumption, that sacrifices were instituted by the Almighty at the beginning, and, therefore, acceptable to him, as a method of propitiation for sin, all nations, for a long series of time, rested their expectations of pardon and forgiveness. The chosen people had recourse to this method, under all

their

their calamities, to atone for guilt, and avert deserved judgments, as evidently appears through the whole volume of their history. And along with this act of devotion, they were taught, not only that God was propitious and indulgent, but also the reformation and improvement of their own nature and actions. The divine majesty, on his own account, derived, from this mode of worship, no other advantage than a testimony of penitence and duty, on the part of his offending and dependant creatures.

He who is the creator, upholder, disposer, and everlasting proprietor of all things in the universe, neither needs, designs, nor gains any thing to himself, from ought within the whole compass of it. His laws, therefore, are not like those of earthly superiors, calculated for the common benefit of lord and servant, but framed and delivered for the sole advantage of the latter. *For if thou sinnest, what dost thou against him? or if thy transgressions be multiplied, what dost thou unto him? If thou be righteous, what givest thou him, or what receiveth he of thine hand? Thy wickedness may hurt a man as thou art, and thy righteousness may profit the son of man* *. Whatever, accordingly, he hath appointed, by any revelation of his will, to be offered or done in his service, was and is merely for the emolument of the agent and giver. For it is not to be imagined, that any oblation, worship, or praise, contributes in any other sense to the glory of God, than as it includes the perception of his goodness, and serves to render it the more diffusive and effectual.

* Job, xxxv. 6, 7, 8.

WHEN,

When, therefore, such appointments, are, by immorality or false opinions, perverted from their end, become misunderstood, or insufficient to quicken and fix men in their obedience to the everlasting laws of piety and justice; then he who made those appointments, with the greatest solemnity declares them, not only vain, but abominable, and an aggravation of other transgressions, instead of an atonement for them. This, by the mouth of many prophets, particularly Amos and Isaiah *; God distinctly and copiously pronounces: *I hate, I despise your feast-days, and I will not smell in your solemn assemblies. Though ye offer me burnt-offerings, and your meat-offerings, I will not accept them; neither will I regard the peace-offerings of your fat beasts. Take thou away from me the noise of thy songs; for I will not hear the melody of thy viols. But let justice run down as water, and righteousness as a mighty stream.*——*To what purpose is the multitude of your sacrifices to me? saith the Lord: I am full of the burnt-offerings of rams, and the fat of fed beasts; and I delight not in the blood of bullocks, or of lambs, or of he-goats. When ye come to appear before me, who hath required this at your hand to tread my courts? Bring no more vain oblations: Incense is an abomination unto me; the new moons and sabbaths, the calling of assemblies, I cannot away with; it is iniquity, even the solemn meeting. Your new moons, and your appointed feasts, my soul hateth. They are a trouble unto me; I am weary to bear them. And when ye spread forth your hands, I will hide mine eyes from you; yea, when ye make many prayers, I will not hear. Your hands are full of blood: Wash ye, make you clean, put away the evil of your doings from before*

* Amos v. 21, Isaiah i. 10, &c.

mine eyes: Cease to do evil, learn to do well: Seek judgment, relieve the oppressed, judge the fatherless, plead for the widow.

ACCORDINGLY, when the Jews had prostituted this ordinance to the purposes of wickedness, God, who had anciently appointed it, provided for its suppression. *Without repentance*, on the great day of atonement, when the guilt of the whole nation had the promise of oblivion, there could be no efficacious *remission** granted to individuals. For their general guilt and impenitence, the daily sacrifice finally ceased at the destruction of the temple by Titus; and, notwithstanding the most vigorous attempts, hath never since been restored. There are the strongest reasons in the world to believe, that the rite is for ever abolished †.

THE Gentiles likewise had, so to speak, lost the Almighty, and all sense of duty and devout obligation, amidst those rivers of blood which they incessantly shed at the altars of Idols, and the shrines of dead men. Cruelty, at length, aided superstition; captives taken in war were slain, for the honour of departed heroes, and imaginary deitie: And, in seasons of danger and distress, the most innocent and lovely of our own species were offered up. This horrid abuse, of a design originally beneficial, called for redress: A divine interposition was necessary to enlighten and mollify the world. Accordingly, whatever barbari-

* Heb. ימי התשובכם

† The daily sacrifice, called by the Jews תמיד consisted of two lambs, the one of which was offered in the morning towards sun-rising, after the burning the sacred incense, and the other in the evening.

ties may be practiſed in reſentment, or by the cuſtom of ſavage nations, the civilization of the human race, advancing for ſome ages paſt by a happy progreſſion, has aboliſhed through the earth, ſo far as accounts have been ſufficiently authenticated, the immolation of our fellow-creatures, to any god or dæmon, in the heavens, or the deep. Animal ſacrifices alſo have been diſcontinued; and new modes of worſhip adopted, under the influence of a general diſpenſation, in all countries, and by the various tribes of mankind.

The truth is, all former ſacrifices ſeem altogether inadequate, in their own nature, and by the ordination of God, to reach the ultimate end, to be accompliſhed only by one ſacrifice, of infinite value, *in the fulneſs of time*. Believers, in the firſt ages, might not, through a long train of ceremonies, and bloody ſacrifices, ſee *the lamb ſlain from the foundation of the world*; but we, *upon whom the ends of the world are come* *, can compare the ſeveral parts of the divine plan which are paſt, with one another, and plainly perceive to what concluſion they lead every contemplative mind. The object to them was, in many reſpects, evidently indeterminate, and, conſequently, a weaker degree of faith, all that was required; but to us it is fixed, and certified by the cleareſt revelation, and, therefore, nothing but the greateſt ingratitude, guilt, and miſery, can follow our rejection of the ſon of God, who is our propiation with the father. *There* can *remain no more ſacrifice for* our *ſin* †.

* 1 Cor. x. ii. † Heb. x. 26.

IN

In regard to the *design* of some of the ancient sacrifices, and the advantage of christians, St. Paul's argument is this; *if the blood of bulls, and of goats, and the ashes of an heifer sprinkling the unclean, sanctifieth to the purifying of the flesh; how much more shall the blood of Christ, who, through the eternal spirit, offered himself without spot to God, purge your conscience from dead works to serve the living God?* * And in regard to their *insufficiency* for the taking away sin, he gives this representation of the matter, in support of the gospel: *the law having a shadow of good things to come, and not the very image of the things, can never with those sacrifices which they offered year by year continually, make the comers thereunto perfect. For then would they not have ceased to be offered? because that the worshippers once purged, should have had no more conscience of sins. But in those sacrifices there is a remembrance again made of sins every year. It is not indeed possible that the blood of bulls and of goats should take away sins. Wherefore when the son cometh into the world, he saith, sacrifice and offering thou wouldst not, but a body hast thou prepared me. In burnt-offerings and sacrifices for sin thou hast had no pleasure! Then said I, lo, I come (in the volume of the book it is written of me) to do thy will, O God. By the which will we are sanctified, through the offering of the body of Jesus Christ once for all* †.

Therefore, *when he said, sacrifice, and offering, and burnt-offerings, and offerings for sin thou wouldst not, neither hadst pleasure therein (which are offered by the law) and, lo, I come to do thy will, O God; the first* was taken *away, that the second* might be established ‡.

* Heb. ix, 13, 14. † Heb. x, i. &c. ‡ Heb. x. 8, 9.

AND by the dignity of his person, and finishing the *work which* was given him *to do* *, our blessed Lord hath, for ever, excluded all impostures from troubling the thoughtful ages, nations, or individuals of mankind, seeing *the sacrifice of himself* †, which he freely offered as a ransom for all ‡, hath, at all times, effectually answered the doubts, and satisfied the desires of every sinner, upon the face of the whole earth.

HENCE let every sinner, upon the face of the whole earth, say, with the *Seraphims* in heaven, *Holy, Holy, Holy Lord God Almighty, who was, and is, and is to come* §; and again, with *the ten thousand times ten thousand, and thousand of thousands, worthy is the lamb that was slain, to receive power, and riches, and wisdom, and strength, and honour, and glory, and blessing* ‖. *Amen. Hallelujah.*

* St. John xvii. 4. † Heb. ix. 26. ‡ 1 Tim. ii. 6.
§ Isaiah vi. 2, 3. Revel. iv. 8. ‖ Revel. v. ii. 12.

DISSERTA-

DISSERTATION X.

Of the Translation of ENOCH.

GENESIS V.

MOST of the events, it has been well obferved, which fucceeded the fall of our firft parents, till the period at which we are now arrived, nine hundred and eighty-feven years after the creation, appear to have been ftriking confequences of the fentence then pronounced againft them. Juftice only feems to have been exhibited to mankind; and believers themfelves could not but find it difficult, to extract the promifes of grace and immortality, from the obfcure meaning of this prediction; *the feed of the woman fhall bruife the head of the ferpent*. Hence religion could furnifh but imperfectly the moft powerful of all motives, to engage men in the fervice of God, which is, that *he is the* rewarder of them who diligently feek him *. God was, therefore, pleafed, at this time, to give an illuftrious evidence of this truth, and hold forth to his church an image, anticipating the conquefts which the Meffi-

* Heb. xi. 6.

ah

ah ſhould, in the *fulneſs of time*, obtain over all the enemies of our ſalvation; namely, *the Tranſlation of Enoch.*

It muſt be confeſſed, that we have but few circumſtances related concerning this man ſo highly privileged by heaven; and yet what we have, raiſe our thoughts of him very high.

First of all, it is clear that he was famous, not only in the church of God, but alſo among idolaters themſelves; who have ſaid that *Iconium* is a city of *Hanac*, who lived three hundred years; that the inhabitants of the place, having enquired of their oracle, how long the prince ſhould live, received for anſwer, that when he died they ſhould all periſh; which when the *Phrygians* heard, they made great mournings; and from thence came the proverb, to weep for Hanac*. See a remark on this, in an author quoted below†. Another, more directly ſpeaking of this patriarch, ſays, that the Babylonians regarded Enoch as the founder of aſtrology among them; that the *Atlas* of the Greeks is Enoch, who had learned all things from angels; and had afterwards diffuſed knowledge among the Phrygians‡. But though theſe teſtimonies ſupport the argument, that Enoch, who was tranſlated, was celebrated in after ages; they have no more ſolidity in them, than the ſtory of the *Enochii*, the ſuppoſed deſcendants of the ſon of Cain, related before; who exiſted long before the flood, when the genealogies of mankind were changed, and all earthly traces of them loſt.

* Stephanus Byſantinus, in voce ἰκονιον.

† Bochart. Phal. L. 2.

‡ Euſeb. Præpar. Lib. 9. Cap. 17.

THE

The next thing we know, more certainly, is, that Enoch was a prophet; not altogether unknown by pagan nations. St. Jude gives him this character, and repeats ſome of his words: *Behold, the Lord cometh with ten thouſand of his ſaints, to execute judgment upon all; and to convince all that are ungodly among them, of all their ungodly deeds, which they have ungodly committed, and of all their hard ſpeeches, which ungodly ſinners have ſpoken againſt him* *. From whence St. Jude had this fragment, it is not eaſy, if at all poſſible, to determine. There was, in the firſt ages of chriſtianity, a book, known by the Jews, which bore the title of *the Prophecies of Enoch*; but the extracts which the fathers have given, convey no high idea of it. They have quoted it with contempt. When Celſus urged a paſſage in it againſt Origen, that father replied that the book had little authority with the Hebrews †. Tertullian, indeed, not only defends it with great warmth, and laments that every one is not as zealous to aſſert its authenticity as himſelf; but alſo pretends that it had been preſerved with Noah in the ark; paſſed from his hands to the whole church; and that the Jews of his time only rejected it, becauſe it was too favourable to the cauſe of chriſtianity ‡. This father was too ſanguine, and very ſingular, in many of the opinions which he eſpouſed. But ſtill this work, notwithſtanding it carried on it many marks of fable, might yet contain many noble truths; and the gift of inſpiration enable St. Jude to *diſcern* thoſe truths from falſhood.

* St. Jude, 14, 15.

† Origen. contr. Cels. Lib. 5.

‡ Tertull. de cultu Fœmin.

THE

The desire of possessing so precious a relick, cost a celebrated person of the last age, immense pains and expence *; and after all, he was deceived by an impostor, who gave him the work of one Bahaila Michael, for the prophecy of Enoch. The author who writes the history of Ethiopia, searched that country, where the true copy was alledged to be, with the greatest care; and at last finding the pretended prophecy of Enoch, immediately discovered on it evident marks of fraud †. The exordium of the suppositious piece is this; *In the name of the Father, of the Son, and of the Holy Ghost. This is the book of the mysteries of heaven, and earth. It contains the secret of the first and the last tabernacle, and of all creatures. Abba Bahaila Michael learned it of Tamhana Samai. The angel who was sent to him said, hear: The Father is not before the Son: The Son is not before the Father: nor the Holy Ghost before the Father and the Son, &c.*

Returning to the history, it shews us, that Enoch possessed greater qualities, than those that have been yet mentioned; he was a good man and singularly righteous ‡. Moses gives him this compleat character, when he says, *Enoch walked with God.* The expression being utterly insusceptible of any than a good sense, there are but few rabbins who have ventured to attribute any other to it; and yet one, in

* Peiresc, ou Nicolas Claude Fabri, Sieur de Peiresc; qui se rendit si habile en toute sorte de sciences, & principalement dans la connoisance de l'antiquité, qu'elle n'avoit rien eu de curieux qui fut caché à lui. Grand Dict. de Moreri.

† Ludolph. Comment. in Hist. Ethiop. Lib. 3, Voyez aussi Le pere Cavazzi, traduite par J. B. Labat.

‡ For the distinction, see Rom. v. vii.

Buxtorf's

Buxtorf's Bible *, is ſaid to underſtand by *walking with God*, inconſtancy in principles, as if Enoch had only a ſlight and tranſient piety, the ſhadow and outſide garb of virtue. But St. Paul, if we give any credit to his authority, ſays, that *he pleaſed God*, which expreſſes more, in few words, than the moſt elaborate elogiums. And what can we poſſibly think of men of learning, who indulge ſuch fancies, in all religions, both in ancient and modern times!

We ſee, likewiſe, in the cleareſt manner, that a piety ſo eminent was crowned with the higheſt privilege that God had ever granted to the ſons of men, ſince the fall; which was, to be exempted from that law, which condemns all Adam's poſterity to death. Reading the relation Moſes gives us of this important event, it is impoſſible not to wiſh, with ſome Chriſtians themſelves, that he had enlarged his account of it. *God took him*, is, however, all that is ſaid, leſt ſome, who are over-curious, ſhould have required every circumſtance. Some interpreters who profeſſed chriſtianity, and whoſe judgment was certainly very good, have aſſerted that Enoch died like the reſt of men. But if they had admitted the authority of the epiſtle to the Hebrews, where it is literally declared, that *by faith Enoch was tranſlated, that he ſhould not ſee death* †, it is impoſſible any doubt could have remained of the event. Thoſe who reject all other teſtimonies, except what this book contains, may likewiſe ſee the ſtrongeſt preſumptions of this fact. Moſes at the end of every patriarchal life, both before and after Enoch, adds, *and he died:* This

* Tom 1. † Heb. xi. v.

ſtile,

stile, as if it had been purposely chosen, distinguishes every relation. And is it to be supposed that he would have changed it for Enoch alone, if the lot of that holy man had been exactly the same as others? Besides, the manner in which the translation is described, represents it as a favour granted to the efforts which he made *to please God: Enoch walked with God, and he was not; for God took him.* For though death conducts good men to a blessed life, and God, by shortening their days, abridges thereby the period of their sufferings on earth; yet, in the first ages of the world, it clearly appears, that long life, for the most part, was the temporal recompense of virtue. In short, if there was nothing extraordinary in Enoch's exit from this world, that man, so distinguished by his piety, might complain that he lived only 365 years, while most of the antediluvian patriarchs reached near a thousand. This argument, which has lost all its force under the gospel, was of great weight in preceding periods, when commonly it fell out that the wicked alone did *not live out half their days* *. It made such an impression upon the Jewish commentator †, who understood what is here said concerning Enoch to signify an ordinary death, that he rather chose to sully the memory of that patriarch, than allow himself, or others, to imagine, that God would snatch away a good man in the midst of his course. *Enoch walked with God*, says he, *that is, was a just man, but his righteousness was so inconstant and fleeting, that he quickly passed from virtue to vice: and this was the reason that God hastened his death.*

* Psal. lv. 23.

† R. Jarchi, alias Raschi, alias Isaaki in Genes. v. 24.

But if some of the Jewish Doctors have reversed the idea which Moses plainly gives of the life of this patriarch, others of them have formed juster notions, and spoken of his departure from this world, as a consequence of his piety *. And among Christian interpreters there is scarcely one of any name, who has not followed the same thought †.

In what manner God disposed of this holy man, after his translation from the earth, writers different from one another, in a variety of respects, have much more contested. Mahometans place him in the fourth sphere of the sun. In the Koran the words are, remember Edris, who is Enoch, a just person, and a prophet: And we exalted him to a high place ‡. The impostor feigned that he found him there; when, in the twelfth year of his devotion, he was carried, in one night, from Mecca to Jerusalem, under the form of a mule, and from Jerusalem was raised to heaven, where he received all the mysteries of his religion §.

Ancient interpreters, both Jewish and Christian, assign the terrestrial paradise, of which we discoursed already, for the place of his residence. The most of our people, even of our learned men, says one of the Rabbins ||, think that Elijah entered into a body in paradise, where he lives, in the same state our first parents were before the fall; and Enoch also, in the same manner.

* R. Abarbanel in Genes. v. 24. Philo de nominum mutatione.
† Saurin. ‡ Al Koran, chap. xix. page 134. Sale.
§ M. Saur. Disc. vi; vol. 1, p. 70. Octav. Amster.
|| R. Kimchi in ii Kings, ii, 1.

Of the primitive fathers, the greatest part has adopted this opinion *. It has been said by some, that both of them should, at a certain time, return to the earth, and confute Anti-christ; that they should re-build the walls of Jerusalem; that their dead bodies should be in the streets of that city, which had been always the murderess of the prophets; that they are the *two witnesses* mentioned in the revelations. But these fancies are set forth here, for no other purpose but to expose them: Even they who have advanced such predictions, have given us no other motive to believe them, than the liberty they have taken in publishing them, without alleging one single solid proof in their support, or so much as plausibility itself.

In regard to the real place of Enoch's happy abode, it may be sufficient to say, that, as Christians, we henceforth know no other paradise, than that which is represented to us in the holy scriptures, as a place where God gives the most illustrious proofs of his presence, and displays his glory and grace with the greatest majesty. To that happy mansion, our Lord prayed to his father that he might be restored; and said to the converted thief on the cross, *this day shalt thou be with me in paradise* †. St. Paul calls the same place, *the third heaven* ‡, and simply, by way of excellence,

* Placens deo, cum Enoch esset homo, Dei legatione ad angelos fungebatur, et translatus est——quoniam angeli quidem transgressi deciderunt in Judicium; homo autem placens, translatus est in salutem.——Nunc dicunt presbyteri, qui sunt apostolorum Discipuli, eos qui translati sunt, translatos esse in paradisum in Eden. Irenæi L. iv. Cap. 30.—L. v. Cap. 5.

† St. Luke, xxiii, 43. ‡ ii. Cor. xii, 2.

cellence, *heaven* *, in a multitude of passages. Thither Elijah was carried by *a whirlwind* †: And there we believe Enoch was translated.

Thus, in each of the three great periods of the church, there hath been one, taken up, soul and body, into heaven, that the hope which believers had conceived of their own future happiness, might be properly supported. Enoch was the first example, before the law, when it was peculiarly necessary; Elijah under the legal œconomy, at a time when universal corruption prevailed; and our Lord Jesus Christ, who opened the Kingdom of God upon earth, which the wisdom and goodness of God had determined to establish, from the beginning of the ages.

In this manner, the divine providence hath so dispensed light in each of those three periods, that it hath appeared by degrees, till it shined in full splendor. It was a circumstance, highly favourable to the faithful of the old world, to see a good man disappear, and disposed of, after his sojourning on the earth, in another place than the grave. Those who lived under the second period, had the strongest presumption in their favour, when heaven was opened to receive one of their prophets, *in a chariot of fire* ‡. But to Christians, it is a demonstration, and like an anticipation of what they expect, to see *the finisher of their faith* §, go through all the intermediate spaces between human life and mortality, time and eternal existence. If the text may be so interpreted, hear the

* Heb. ix, 24.
† ii Kings, ii, 1.
‡ ii Kings, ii, 1.
§ Heb. xii. 2.

church

church triumphant addressing the portals of paradise, to open for his reception, and prepare themselves for his entrance, into the blessed habitations appointed for him. *Lift up your heads, O ye gates, and be ye lifted up, ye everlasting doors, and the king of glory shall come in. Who is this king of glory? The Lord strong and mighty, the Lord strong and mighty in battle. Lift up your heads, O ye gates, even lift them up, ye everlasting doors, and the king of glory shall come in. Who is this king of glory? The Lord of hosts, he is the king of glory**.

THE words of a poet, famous for his descriptions, might be borrowed here; but falling far short of the language of inspired authors, they are omitted, out of the profoundest respect for his talents and design †.

HAVING finished this subject, it is almost impossible not to reflect on the strange infatuation of some men, who say they believe the sacred writings; and yet deny that there are any traces of doctrines or examples, in the writings of Moses, indeed in the old Testament, from whence we can clearly infer that the people of God, in those ages, expected a future state. Here we see Enoch taken away from among men, at a very early period of the world; and it is perfectly reasonable to suppose, that his co-temporaries, would believe him to be taken to another state of life. If, through increasing corruption, they had, for some time, lost the original principle, this event would necessarily revive it; and was designed and calculated to have this very effect. It is very certain, that the better sort of heathens were not without some strong

* Psalm xxiv. 7. † Milton.

presages

presages of another state after this; and several of the philosophers spake great and excellent things concerning it: And can we imagine that the whole Jewish nation, the whole earth before the death of Moses, was entirely ignorant of this comfortable truth? There can be no doubt but the earliest men, the old patriarchs, and all the pious Jews who lived to our Saviour's time, did expect and hope for an *heavenly country*. Would they be less attentive to the nature of their own souls and faculties, than other men; to the strong appetites and desires of life in the human constitution; to the fears and presages of the wicked; and the necessity of rewards and punishments for vindicating God's providence? It is not to be imagined.

INDEED the gospel of Christ, hath made a much clearer revelation, and his own resurrection from the dead, given a much stronger demonstration of life and immortality, than ever the world had before.

DISSERTA-

DISSERTATION XI.

Of the GENEALOGY from ADAM to NOAH.

GENESIS V.

THOUGH the ſubject of this Diſſertation is, in part, antecedent in time, to that of the foregoing, yet the genealogy from Adam to Noah is placed here on account of the families inſerted, in the Moſaic hiſtory, between Enoch, whoſe character and diſtinguiſhing privilege we have juſt now conſidered, and the latter of thoſe patriarchs: And the age of the world, between the creation and the deluge will, very properly, be given.

IN this chapter Moſes deſcribes the names and lives of the patriarchs, within that ſpace of time; with the age of every father, when every ſon was born. Now, if we add that of Noah, when the flood happened, to thoſe aggregate periods, we ſhall form chronological tables, of the beſt authority, from the beginning of things, to their diſſolution by water. Nor, in this calculation, and biographical view, ſhall we we be altogether without the instruction and improvement, which we ought constantly to seek in all our researches, in the holy annals of truth and salvation.

At the first verse, we are told, *this is the book of the generations of Adam*; that is to say, this is the pedigree, or the genealogy of his descendants; as, in the first chapter of St. Matthew, it is said, *this is the book of the generation of Jesus Christ*, where his extraction is drawn from Abraham, to his own manifestation in the flesh. In the catalogue here presented, there is one thing, in the third verse, which may deserve a remark; namely, that Seth appears first in the list, when we know that before him Adam had both Cain and Abel born to him, whose names are both omited. The reason of this seems to be, that as Abel died childless, and Cain was struck out of the line, as an atrociously wicked man, the progeny of Adam was reckoned from Seth, Abel's successor in his father's family, whom Cain had killed.

This circumstance, it has been thought, may give room to infer, that Cain and Abel themselves might not, perhaps, be Adam's first sons; and that both he, and the other patriarchs, might have several children, before those that are here set down; the design of Moses, in all probability, being only to give the names of such persons as would preserve the genealogy entire from Adam to Noah, through genuine ancestors, whether they were the eldest of the family or not *. But while no objection needs to

* Dr. Taylor's Scheme, &c. p. 173.

be made to this thought, on account of its repugnancy to any important principle in the Mosaic history, if it be wisely and reasonably applied; what others have imagined cannot yet be perceived, how it can, in the least, obviate any fancied difficulties, that critics and unbelievers have been perpetually raising, in regard to the connections first formed among the children of Adam's family. For it is evident that the first of them, whoever they were, must have married the nearest relations, by the permission of God, and as the necessity of the case then required.

To the suggestion, that Moses, like all other historians, only meant to give the pedigree of his own nation; and that no certain conclusions can be drawn from his history concerning the common origin of mankind, or whether they are at all to be derived from one root; to this suggestion, I say, it may be replied, that if any credit be due to the other parts of his writings, we may stretch our faith a little farther, and believe what he says of Cain and Abel also; that they were the first of Adam's sons, and Seth, in the line delineated, the successor of the latter; Adam the fountain of all.

ANOTHER thing, in this account, which strikes us with equal curiosity and astonishment, is the enormous space of time during which those antediluvians lived; Adam, Seth, Enos, and Cainan, nine hundred years and odds. Mahalaleel, eight hundred and ninety-five; Jared, nine hundred and sixty-two; and Methuselah, nine hundred and sixty-nine years. This last named person, though the eighth generation from Adam, lived co-temporary with him two hundred

dred and forty-three years, and, no doubt, conversed with him the greatest part of that time; and would have opportunities, abundantly sufficient, to receive from Adam a distinct account of what he knew concerning the creation, and all the transactions and events in the four first chapters of Genesis. Methuselah, therefore, dying only in the year in which the flood happened, would serve as a living chronicle of all the knowledge in the world, for the space of sixteen hundred and fifty-six years; of which Noah had lived six hundred, and so had time enough to receive all that knowledge from him, and may be well supposed to have carried it with him entire into the ark, from whence he communicated it to the new world. For his sons being only young, and all the patriarchs, who stand in this genealogy, dead, when he entered into the ark, things, as they were at that period, must afterwards be traced from him *.

ONE reason for the long lives of the antediluvians may have been, that knowledge, without writing and archives, might be safely preserved, and incorruptly transmitted to future ages. It is allowed that the air and food, of which those wonderful men had the advantage, and the manner of life they pursued, might, in some measure, contribute to sound health, and lengthen out their days beyond the ordinary bounds. Among ourselves, in these latter ages, we have some very extraordinary instances of life, and alertness, being prolonged, almost two generations †. But all na-

 tural

* That men lived so long in ancient times, we have the testimony of Manetho, Berosus, &c. Patrick on Gen. v.

† The illustrious Archbishop of Armagh, after giving many instances of longævity in former times, says, atque ut ad nostra tempora

tural causes being now found inadequate to such an effect, as to preserve life for nine hundred years and more, the phenomenon must be resolved into the will of the Creator only, and can be accounted for in no other way. The first men lived so long, that they might be the records, and conveyers to posterity, of religious affairs, at a time when those records could not otherwise be treasured up; and the knowledge of them must either have been totally lost, or miserably depraved, if men had lived no longer than seventy or eighty years, as they now do. Besides, their great age and strength, were the most effectual means to people the world speedily *, and bring all the necessary arts, in tillage, building, and cloathing, to greater perfection.

BUT, to return to the matter; we see, at the twenty-first verse of the chapter, that Methuselah was the son

tempora propius accedamus: Thomas Ravennas in 5° capite libri, *De vita hominis ultra* cxx *annos protrahenda*, ad Julium iii. pont. scripti, inter alia, An. Christi, 1536. Zaconum quendam ex Lacedæmone, annis fere cxxx. et alium ex eadem urbe ultra annos cxxx. supervixisse; et in ægeo mari viros duos cxxx.—— Dux anglus Jacobus Weston, A D. 1600. annos cxxxi. natus vitam finiit. In Hibernia Desmoniæ Comitissa, circa annum vitæ cxl. defuncta. Laurentius quidam Scotus anno ætatis cxl. mortus est. Unus etiam Senex Lutetiæ cxl. Et ut tandem concludamus, Thomas Parrus fuit clii. Ex his igitur satis apparet, ad nostra usque tempora, nonnullus ultra annos cl. vitam produxisse. Chr. Sa. p 203.

* There are several authors, who have formed calculations of the increase of mankind in the first world, and suppose, upon the moderate scale, that they had no children till they were one hundred years old, and none after five hundred, that there were in this world about two millions of millions of souls, which they think is a number far exceeding that of the inhabitants of the present earth. Shuckford's Con. Vol. i. p. 36.

of

of Enoch: And some very ingenious men have conjectured that his father gave him this name, from two Hebrew words *, which literally signify, *when he dieth, there shall be a shedding forth, or an inundation of water.* Allowing this conjecture to have a reasonable foundation, we may here see, as well as in many other instances, how facts have been changed, by nations ignorant of the sacred writings; and that both smaller and greater errors, in point of time, lie open to detection. For it is not at all improbable, that the Phrygian oracle, mentioned in the foregoing Dissertation, referred to the son of Enoch, and not to himself, when it pronounced, *that when he died, they should all perish* †. And admitting the criticism above to be just, Enoch must be supposed to have predicted the deluge, nine hundred and sixty-nine years, before it happened; with this circumstantial token of the event, that it should fall out in the year in which his son should die; as it certainly did. This some may think too refined and fanciful: And yet we have the authority of an apostle for asserting, that Enoch was a prophet,—perhaps, not inferior to any in after days, notwithstanding the shortness of his history; and might, therefore, foresee and foretel the deluge to that generation of men.

But, his distinguishing character having been considered already ‡, we proceed to Lamech, Enoch's grandson by Methuselah, the next patriarch in this list. Concerning him nothing remarkable occurs, except the name which he gave the first mentioned of his sons, Noah ||, derived from a Hebrew root, signifying

* Heb. מת כשלח

† Page 166.

‡ See Dissertation x.

|| Heb. כוח

to

to reſt, or to take reſt, or to take repoſe; ſaying at the ſame time, *this ſame ſhall comfort us concerning our work and toil of our hands, becauſe of the ground which the Lord hath curſed.* Of this text many explanations have been given: Some think Lamech might give his ſon this name, when he found that he had an extraordinary genius for agriculture, and was likely, by his uſeful inventions, to diminiſh the vaſt toil which had hitherto attended the tillage of the earth *: Others imagine that Lamech, being a good man, and believing his grandfather's prophecy, called his ſon Noah, becauſe in his days mankind being ſwept away, there would be an entire ceſſation of all worldly buſineſs, the chief of which then was to plow and fertilize the earth, rendered ſterile and unfruitful by Adam's tranſgreſſion: And certain illuſtrious interpreters apply this prophecy to the enriching manure which was thrown over the face of the habitable globe, at the time of the deluge; as marle, ſea-ſhells, and ſea-ſand; by whoſe ſaline and nutritious qualities, the ſtubborn and barren ſoil was mellowed and fructified, and hence mankind were *comforted, concerning their work, and the toil of their hand, with regard to the ground which the Lord had curſed:* The ſame prophecy has, likewiſe, been referred to the practice of employing beaſts in tilling the ground, which before had been managed by men's hands; and to the grant made to Noah of eating fleſh, till then, it is thought by many, totally prohibited †.

ADMITTING ſome of theſe expoſitions to be juſt, what cauſe of thankfulneſs have we, and to rejoice, that God, who alone can bring good out of evil, hath, among other advantages which we derive from the ſins

* Biſhop Patrick in Loco. † Synop. Critic Poli in Loco.

ſins

ſins of the antediluvians, changed the earth from a wilderneſs of briers and thorns into a fruitful field, *even the garden of God*; and, aſſiſting men in the cultivation of their genius, brought arts to the greateſt perfection; by which we now enjoy comparatively what Noah's name ſignified, *reſt and conſolation.* But this belonging properly to another ſubject, we ſhall proceed to conſider the moral cauſes which contributed to bring on that amazing and tremendous ſcene, *the flood.*

DISSERTATION XII.

Of the general Corruption of Mankind.

GENESIS VI.

AT the laſt verſe of the fourth chapter we read, *then began men to call upon the name of the Lord*; that is, in the days of Enos, ſo called perhaps, by Seth his father, to denote the weak and miſerable condition of mankind, ſince the original apoſtacy. Whatever ſenſe we put upon theſe words, they cannot, in the leaſt, import that men did not call upon the name of the Lord, before this time, which was between two and three hundred years after the creation. The meaning may rather be, that, by the conſideration of their miſeries, they became awakened to be more ſerious and frequent in religious ſervices, or began to hold more public aſſemblies. For families, to which religion was before confined, being now multiplied, mankind joined together, and met in larger ſocieties and communion, for the more ſolemn ſervice of God by ſacrifices, and other religious offices; and *to call upon God*, comprehends all religion, private and public.

INDEED

INDEED many of the Jewiſh interpreters, with whom a very learned antiquary ſeems to agree, would have the words expounded thus; *then men began to neglect the worſhip of God; or were guilty of profanation, by invoking the name of the Lord* *. The Arabic interpreter, publiſhed by another great man †, gives the text this gloſs, *then began men to apoſtatize from the worſhip of God.* But all ſuch notions ariſing out of the ambiguity of the word *began*, which in one place ſignifies *to profane* ‡, other very learned and judicious men have oppoſed this interpretation; eſpecially as Moſes is here ſpeaking of the pious family of Seth only, and nothing of Cain's wicked race. They, therefore, think the meaning is, that public forms of worſhip were now appointed, at ſet hours, or ſome other conſiderable improvements made in religious offices. And the Arabian Chriſtians repreſent this Enos as an excellent governor, who, while he lived, preſerved good order in his family, and when he died, called them all together, and gave them a charge to keep God's commandments, and not to aſſociate themſelves with the children of Cain §.

IT has been, likewiſe, ingeniouſly conjectured from theſe words, that thoſe who adhered to God, and his worſhip, began to give themſelves a denomination expreſſive of their relation and regard to God;

* Apud Onkelum legitur *tunc incepiſſe homines non orare in nomine domini*—Aut *tunc inceperunt homines deficere a cultu dei*—*profanari autem in invocando nomine Jehovæ*, idem eſt, ac ſi dixiſſet Moſes ſacroſanctum illud nomen, quod totius univerſi creatorem et dominum deſignat, rebus creatis impié tributum. Selden. de diis Syris, Proleg. Cap. iii. pag. 28, 29.

† Erpenius. ‡ Levit. xix 12. § Biſhop Patrick in Loco.

in

in other words, they began to assume the title of *the sons*, or children, *of God*; to distinguish and separate themselves from the profane and irreligious, who neither feared nor served him *.

THIS, at least, appears certain, that the descendants of Cain and Seth formed two different societies, each of which followed the example of their ancestors. Moses says *Cain dwelt in the land of Nod*, which either signifies *fugitive*, or describes a country bearing that name. The friends of the first opinion insist that Cain wandered during his whole life; while others contend that Moses, by the land of Nod expresses no more than simply the place where this unnatural brother lived in exile. That place some have thought to be *the fields of Nyseus*, mentioned, many times, by profane historians †. He still went eastward, we know, from that country, where Adam had settled when he was thrust out of Paradise. In his short notes, a celebrated translator hath offered his opinion, that Nod was in that tract of ground where the *Nomades* afterwards dwelt, bordering upon *Susiana* ‡.

IT is sufficient for us to know, that the posterities of Seth and Cain, possessed different regions, and formed separate societies. But after the prodigious multiplication of the human race, which God ordained in the first ages, they had occupied the whole

* Taylor's Scheme, &c. page 176. † Saurin, Disc. vii.

‡ *Terra Nodi*: id est, agitationis & vexationis: hanc Nomadum esse puto in deserta Arabia, Babyloniæ contermina, quæ regio, respectu Cenahanææ, sita est ab oriente Hedenem versus. Junius in Loco.

intermediate

intermediate ſpace; they began, like two diſtant colonies, extending their ſettlements, to unite. The children of the former, whom the ſcripture calls *the ſons of God*, probably becauſe they were attached to his worſhip and laws, were ſtruck with the beauty they beheld in the daughters of the latter. They inſtantly attempted to remove the bars which ſeparated them from creatures ſo full of charms.... They contracted marriages with them, in which they observed no other laws, but thoſe of their own luſts; and ſurrendering to thoſe enchantreſſes their heart and their freedom, they ſurrendered at the ſame time their virtue and religion. For from this union proceeded what we ſee has always been the caſe, in the courſe of ages ſince, when a pure ſociety has been mixed with a profane; that the good has been tainted by the corrupt manners of the bad, and a degenerate nation has never imitated the virtues of the more pious and juſt.

THIS is the ſimpleſt and moſt rational conſtruction that can be put upon the words of the hiſtorian in the holy text: *And it came to paſs, when men began to multiply on the face of the earth, and daughters were born unto them, that the ſons of God ſaw the daughters of men, that they were fair; and they took them wives of all which they choſe.* But notwithſtanding the reaſonableneſs of this comment, interpreters have raiſed on theſe words, and ſome that follow, the greateſt difficulties.

SOME of the ancients have grounded an opinion upon a paſſage in the Pſalms, where, of governors and magiſtrates, the character is, *I have ſaid that ye are*

are Gods *, that by *the ſons of God*, in this place, we are to underſtand the phraſe, of the great ones of the earth, who violently carried away *the daughters of men* of inferior rank and fortune, and made attempts upon their modeſty.

AMONG the extravagancies of the imagination, we may rank the opinion of thoſe, whom a great father of the church refutes †, who believed that, by *the ſons of God*, either good or bad angels were intended. Whether the old verſion of the Septuagint might encourage this notion, it is not eaſy to determine ‡. Among both Jewiſh and Chriſtian interpreters, ancient and modern, this fancy, however ſtrange, hath had, it cannot be denied, many to ſupport it. Even a wilder than this has been entertained, concerning *Incubes*, ſo called, like the nightmare, on account of their carnal commerce with women, by whom they had a monſtrous iſſue; as many *deities*, in fable, are ſaid to have had, by the unguarded *nymphs* of intermediate ages.

BUT to collect all that has been ſaid, by writers on this ſubject, would be a taſk equally tireſome and unedifying. Thoſe who delight in curious relations of this ſort, may conſult a variety of authors, who have not been ſparing of their labours, to amuſe others, and diſplay their own learning ||.

THE meaning of the ſacred hiſtorian, when he ſpeaks of the children, who ſprung from thoſe mar-

* Pſalm lxxxii, 6. † St. Chryſoſt. Homil. xx, in Genes. v. ‡ Saurin, Diſc. vii. || Voyez Le même Auteur, ibid.

riages,

riages, hath occasioned, on the other hand, as many disputes, as the quality of the parties in the marriages themselves. His words, at the fourth verse, are these; *There were giants in the earth in those days; and also after that, when the sons of God came in unto the daughters of men, and they bare children to them; the same became mighty men, which were of old, men of renown.* It is here asked, who is the interpreter that dares decisively to pronounce what is the meaning of these expressions *? It is said, that Moses certainly intended from the beginning of his history, to make mankind stumble in a thousand curious questions, by difficulties which he seems purposely to throw in their way; and that it is almost impossible to derive any determinate knowledge from the original word which he employs here, and is translated *giants* †.

To this it may be answered, that no historian, tried by the rules of false criticism, could possibly stand the test, in a single page or sentence of his writings. But if descriptions of facts are to be taken in the plain and simple meaning in which they are given, no words can be clearer than these under our consideration. Moses asserts, *there were giants in the earth in those days:* Men of enormous statures and strength, which tempted them, as has always happened, through an abuse of power, to oppress others by violence; before the time when the sons of God married with the daughters of men: Probably produced at first by those who went down, and mixed with the posterity of Cain in the days of Jared. And the word

* M Saurin, Disc. vii, page 78.
† Heb. נפלים

children not being in the Hebrew, the text may be read thus; *Also after that, when the sons of God came in unto the daughters of men, and they bare* giants *to them*, there was a new race of robust and unrighteous men added, to those of the same nature and principles who were before; and possessed themselves of great power by the same practices.

It has also been enquired, whether the word is to be applied to the body or the mind; as signifying the height of their stature, or their extraordinary courage. Here, in the same manner, as on all other parts of the holy scriptures of the like nature, commentators of the first rank, appear on both sides, equally formidable. *The Rephaims, the Emims, the Hanakims, and the Zamzummims* *, have presented the same difficulties on this subject, which we shall slightly consider, as the passages occur. The clearest question is, if the relation of the spies, who were sent into the land of promise, in much later times than those we are writing of, is to be taken in a figurative or proper sense †? *There we saw the giants, the sons of Anak, which come of the giants: And we were in our own sight as grasshoppers, and so we were in their sight. Whither*, therefore, *shall we go up?* said the Israelites: *Our brethren have discouraged our heart, saying, the people is greater and taller than we, the cities are great and walled up to heaven; and, moreover, we have seen the sons of the Anakims there* ‡.

On the side of the latter party, we are still asked, what the height of those giants really was? On this,

* Deut. ii. † Saurin. ‡ Numb. xxxiii. 33. Deut. i. 28.

Jewish

Jewish Doctors *, and others more safely to be followed, have advanced the most absurd traditions, contrary to common sense, and the very nature of things; and given the most improbable of all dimensions, on the two extremes. So critically, in short, has this matter been canvassed, that while some authors pretend, there are monuments in the bones and teeth of corps, of a monstrous size, which demonstrate the magnitude of those extraordinary men; there are others who maintain that those are no more than sports of nature, which, by a coagulation of different matter, are collected, and formed into an hard substance, assume the figure of an human body. The opinion of the first is founded on the testimony of travellers; and the second, alledging that they have too strong an itch for the marvellous, refer them to the stature of Goliath, of Og, King of Bashan, and some others.

The plain meaning of the passage is this; the families of Seth and Cain, placed at first at some distance from one another, afterwards joined. And the consequence of this junction was, a scene of impiety, lewdness and injustice. The issue of the aforesaid marriages, growing up without any sense of religion and goodness, soon turned the scale; engaged themselves wholly in sensual ambitious pursuits, and imitating and assisting a flagitious race of giants, or strong, adventurous, and rapacious men, who were then on the earth; they affected to be men of renown for great and valorous exploits, by every method of oppression and violence. It appears, that they every

* Pirké Eliez. cap. xxiii. pag. 285.

where

where subjected others to their will and power, and extinguished a sense of God, both *by their wicked ungodly deeds, and their hard speeches against him**, and his holy laws. They despised his goodness, and the restraints of his government, till *all the earth was corrupt before God, and filled with violence, and every imagination of their hearts become only evil continually:* Which, in process of time, cut off all hopes of their amendment, when their minds were wholly intent upon gratifying ambition and concupiscence.

This was the effect of that criminal union, which *the sons of God*, as the scripture calls them, made with *the daughters of men.* The world changed its face, and presented nothing to the eye of the Almighty, but falsehood, lewdness, and injustice; the proper fruit of Idolatry. It might then be said, that not only giants, but the whole human race had plotted against heaven, and concerted to violate God's laws and worship. If credit may be given to an ancient tradition, preserved by an Arabian author †, the children of Seth, by marrying the daughters of Cain, broke the solemn vow they had taken to avenge the blood of Abel, and never to mingle with the blood of him who

* St. Jude, verse 15.

† Pervetustus codex arabicus M. in Bibliotheca Cottoniana, narrat Sethi familias posterosque montis occupasse cacumen in quo Adam sepultus est; Caini, Vallem in qua Abel ab eo occisus. Posteros item Sethi, ob easdem rationes, filios Dei dictos; et ob Abelem adeo Caino infensos ejusque nepotibus, ut solemni se juramento obstringerent, *per sanguinem Abelis*, in Vallem se nequaquam, seu *a monte sacro* descensuros. Seld. de diis Syris. Prolegom. Cap. III. pag. 46.—Autor Libri est Sain Aben-Batrick qui historica in eo quamplurima de festis, Æris, patriarchis, aliis rebus, congessit.

had

had ſlain their brother. However this may be, the terms, here uſed, denote a general corruption: For, ſays Moſes, *God looked upon the earth, and, behold, it was corrupt: For all fleſh had corrupted his way upon the earth.* And this ſenſe of them being natural, why ſhould the meaning of the words be reſtrained to a particular idea, as ſome interpreters have, ſeeing they comprehend the whole earth?

It is very pertinent to this ſubject to remark, that the ſixth in deſcent from Cain, introduced the corruption of polygamy into the world, which could not fail to produce anarchy and unnatural luſt. Lamech, we are told, *took unto him two wives; the name of the one was Adah, and the name of the other Zillah.* By a ſmall tranſpoſition of letters, Lamech being the ſame with Melech, which ſignifies a *King*, ſome of the Jews have imagined that he was a great man: Such only, ſay they, had two wives in thoſe ancient times; though they maintain it was lawful for any one that could ſupport them, to have had more. But, notwithſtanding the proneneſs of that nation to palliate practices of this ſort, out of complaiſance to thoſe of their forefathers, and from their own inclinations, it is a great deal more probable that Lamech was the firſt, who ventured to tranſgreſs the original inſtitution, which evidently appears to have been obſerved by the Cainites themſelves till this time. His deſire, perhaps, of ſeeing that *bleſſed ſeed* which was promiſed to Eve, might induce him to take more wives than one, that by the extraordinary multiplication of his poſterity, ſome of them might prove ſo happy as to be the progenitors and parents. And this hope might be ſtrengthened, by the notion that the right, which was in Cain the firſt born, was now revived in himſelf; who being the *ſeventh* ſon from Cain, might have ſome reaſon to imagine, that the curſe laid upon him, of being puniſhed *ſeven-fold*, or, as he might underſtand it, for *ſeven generations*, was then removed; and his poſterity reſtored to the privilege of fulfilling the promiſe *.

It has been thought highly probable, that Lamech made his way to that crime of plurality, by the murder of the huſband of one of his wives. This has been collected from his bitter exclamation to them on a certain occaſion: *Hear my voice, ye wives of Lamech, hearken unto my ſpeech; for I have ſlain a man to my wounding, and a young man to my hurt.* For, ſays the ingenious writer, there could have been no other cauſe ſo probable for his committing murder, as the gratification of his luſt; eſpecially in an age of the world when there ſeems to have been little occaſion for contention about any property, except that of women; the earth not being yet peopled, and the beaſts in great plenty †.

But though the words be thus rendered affirmatively in our tranſlation, they have been read, by ſome, with an interrogation: *Have I ſlain a man? Or, ſo much as a boy?* that you ſhould be thus afraid of my life ‡. On what account it may not be eaſy to conjecture. A ſuppoſition may be grounded on them, as likely as any, that at this period of time, family diſturbances and quarrels prevailed, and the nuptial tie was grown uneaſy and troubleſome; as we ſee

* Patrick in Loco. † Delany, page 113.
‡ Lud. de Dieu. Vide Patrick.

Lamech calls with great vehemence to his wives, and complains to them under that particular character, either for having ſeduced him to ſome wicked deed, or treated him with perfidy and ingratitude.

Thus, notwithſtanding the divine manifeſtations which mankind then enjoyed, and the preaching of Enoch and Noah, and probably of other good men, the contagion of wickedneſs, by degrees, entirely infected them. Concerning the world, in this ſad condition, the Almighty at length declared, probably from the *Schechinah*, in the ſmall aſſembly of his worſhippers, *My ſpirit ſhall not always ſtrive with man, for that he alſo is fleſh:* I will ceaſe to addreſs men, as I have done in former times, by vain exhortations to repentance; I will no longer ſpeak to them by my prophets, ſuch as Enoch was, and Noah now is, nor work inwardly in their hearts; for beſides the extent and degree of their wickedneſs, they are grown wholly ſenſual in their inclinations and affections.

Of theſe words, this interpretation has, indeed, been given; *My breath, the life which I have given to men, ſhall ſoon be taken away from them, and I will deſtroy all of them in an hundred and twenty years, by a violent death.* But, notwithſtanding the approbation of an eminent man *, this ſenſe appears extremely forced, when it is compared with the conſiſtency of the former. It is much more probable, that by *ſpirit* here is to be underſtood, that ſelf-ſame *ſpirit, by which*, St. Peter ſays, *our Lord went and preached*, not perſonally, but by the miniſtry of the aforementioned prophets, *unto the ſpirits*, which are *now*, that is, at the time when

* M. Saurin, Diſc. vii. p. 81.

the apostle wrote, *in prison*, or confined in the state of the dead, and reserved in safe custody to the day of judgment. This gloss appears evidently natural, from what follows in the same passage; *which spirits were disobedient in the days of Noah, while the ark was in preparing* *.

HENCE it was, that God, speaking after the manner of men, is said *to repent, and to be grieved that he had made man on the earth*; and, accordingly, formed the resolution to destroy that whole generation. The execution of this decree, however, would have been prevented, if the men of that age had turned to God by repentance and amendment: Noah was a preacher of righteousness to them, to try if they would hear his voice and live; in the same manner as Jonah was sent to *Nineveh*, to cry aloud in it, *yet forty days, and Nineveh shall be overthrown* †. And, if, by their humiliations, *God had seen the works of the former, that they turned from their evil ways*, they would have been pardoned and saved, as well as the latter. For when repentance intervenes, the judgments threatened are never inflicted. But incorrigible rebellion and wickedness, for the dignity and holiness of the divine government, and the safety of the world, must inevitably be punished.

AND yet, amidst this universal depravation and impiety, how indulgent was the goodness of the supreme ruler! *The days of man shall yet be an hundred and twenty years.* So long, as if God had said, will I wait on

* 1 Pet. iii. 19, 20.
† Jonah. iii. 4.

sinners,

sinners, under this dispensation, and no longer; then shall a flood of waters be brought in upon them.

THOSE hundred and twenty years, it is presumed, must respect the time of God's forbearance with that guilty race, and not the limits which were then prescribed to the life of men, in the following ages. It cannot, with truth, be asserted that an hundred and twenty years bounded human life, even for many long periods subsequent to the flood. According to the doctrine of the most celebrated Chronologers *, from the flood till the time the tower of Babel was built, men continued to live four or five centuries: From that period till the age of Abraham, they sometimes lived almost three: After that till Moses, an hundred and twenty, and an hundred and thirty: And in the reign of King David, human life appears to have been nearly of the same measure that it is now. The hundred and twenty years here mentioned, must therefore, refer to the time which was to elapse between the threatening denounced against the old world, and the final execution of it †.

THIS account of the corruption of mankind, may be closed with the reflection, that luxury, at the same time that it polishes life, and softens the mind, is al-

* Usserius, ætas mundi i.

† Opinio multorum nostrorum sapientum est, Deum illis verbis, *Dies hominis*, &c. nequequam hoc spatium ponere vitæ humanæ, quippe postea fuisse qui multo longius vixerint, sed tantum indicare Noacho, prophetæ illius sæculi, dare se hominibus spatium cxx. annorum ad pænitentiam peccatorum: cujus rei cunctos admonitos voluisse, ut nisi intra illud tempus pœnitentia ducerentur, scirent diluvio sibi pereundum. R. Menasseh Ben Israel Conciliator, Quæst. xxii. p. 30. Per omnes partes,

so

so the source of innumerable evils: It begets a disposition to injure others in their property; and such a disposition, armed with offensive weapons, naturally excites all kinds of insolence and outrage to our fellow-creatures. The process is extremely evident in the historical sketches here given of the first ages of the world. Jabal seems to have been the first in Cain's family, who brought the art of tent-making, folding flocks, and all other parts of pasturage, to perfection; and taught men, when the grass was all eaten up in one place, to remove their cattle, and fix their habitations in another. His brother Jubal invented many *stringed* and *wind* instruments of music *, and instructed men to play upon them, in the same manner as Apollo afterwards did among the Greeks. These were the sons of Lamech by Adah. By Zillah he had Tubal-cain, who began to melt metals, and make all sorts of weapons, and warlike arms, of *brass and iron*, and is probably the very same with the Vulcan of ancient times. His sister's name was Naamah, which signifies fair, or one of a sweet aspect. She may have been the heathen Minerva; it is said that she mixed *colours* and *painted*. Here we see the symbols of improved and elegant societies appearing, and have seen corruption, nevertheless, in a superior proportion, for which the displeasure of the Almighty was just ready to be manifested.

We may, therefore, conclude that religion and righteousness alone are the soul and support of the universe; and when they are destroyed, no worlds, nor men in them, can possibly exist; because their existence would be to no purpose; nay, in direct opposi-

* Heb. נכור ועוגב

tion

tion to the perfections and designs of the great governor of all. And while the holy scriptures not only assure us, that the wages of sin is death, and constantly affirm that the impenitent workers of iniquity shall be cut off, they give us, likewise, a true and just account of past events, and of the dreadful judgments of God upon the guilty. *Now all these things that were written before, were written for our instruction; and happened unto* former ages *for examples unto us, upon whom the ends of the world are come**. To those writings let us give the most watchful attention, as *unto lights shining in a dark place; knowing this, that no prophecy*, or practical inference from *the scripture is of any private*, temporary or national *interpretation* †: all are to hear and fear.

* 1 Corinth. x 11. † 2 Pet. i 19, 20,

DISSERTATION XIII.

Of the Flood.

GENESIS VI, VII.

THIS dreadful overthrow of the world, for which the growing wickedneſs of former ages had been making gradual preparation, now preſents itſelf in the courſe of theſe holy pages. But, *in the midſt of wrath, God, remembering his mercies* *, *which have been of old, even for ever* †, choſe Noah, and *hid him in the day of his anger* ‡, that he might be the reſtorer of Adam's poſterity, which was about to be ſwept off the earth by the Deluge. His piety, through the divine condeſcenſion, obtained this diſtinction for him. *Noah was a juſt man and perfect in his generations*, ſays Moſes, *and Noah*, like Enoch, *walked with God*. Some authors have ſupplied, by their imagination, a deſcription, wanting in the ſacred books, of the virtues which theſe words may be ſuppoſed to expreſs. This is not leſs vain than the fancy which

* Habak. III. 2. † Pſalm xxv. 6. ‡ Zephan. II. 3.

others

others have entertained, that it was by the assistance of judiciary astrology, that this patriarch foresaw the calamity which was soon to fall on the human race. No words can more expressly affirm, that he was *warned* of it by an immediate revelation from God, than those we have in the relation of Moses, and in St. Paul's account of the fact to the Hebrews *. And besides the revelation of the catastrophe, he was afterwards instructed by what means he was to preserve himself from it. God commanded him to build *a vessel*, or an *ark*, of which himself prescribed to him the materials, the form, and the dimensions. Noah, without delay, expressed his humble and entire faith, in the divine monition, by applying himself, according to the instructions he had received, to the building of that sanctuary, for the safety of his own person, of his family, of creeping things, of birds, and of four-footed beasts.

10 THAT Noah was an hundred and twenty years in building the ark, seems to be a notion which the inattention of many interpreters may have contributed to encourage. It has been said, that the sight of such a structure, advancing in size and compleatness, before their eyes, and every stroke that was given to it, rendered the inhabitants of the old world utterly inexcusable, if they did not repent of their evil ways, and earnestly seek for pardon. The patience of God has been thought concerned in this circumstance; the exhortations which Noah would address to the men of that time; and the fervent prayers he would prefer to heaven on their behalf. These,

* Heb. xi. 7.

indeed,

indeed, are fine reflections; but yet we are not warranted to judge by them of an historical fact. The world had otherwise sufficient notice of the impending destruction: God had made it publicly known to that whole generation, by the ministry of his prophet; and the time allowed them for reformation, was a striking proof of his forbearance. Noah might piously embrace every opportunity of calling sinners to repentance, and beseech the mercy of heaven to bestow that grace upon them.

In regard to things even of this nature, the want of discussion may raise in the mind many perplexing mistakes. Supposing the ark to have been *an hundred and twenty years* in building, there must have been a concurrence of miracles, to prevent those parts of it from rotting which had been first constructed, till the other parts were finished; and to keep the whole fabric in a condition to answer the end for which it was designed, during a long space of time before it was employed.

But Moses says nothing from whence we can conclude, what time precisely Noah was in constructing the ark. There are in his words sufficient evidence, however, to refute the opinion, that is generally entertained. It is demonstrable that Noah was five hundred years old when Shem, Ham, and Japhet were born to him. It is also clear, that when he received the command to build the ark, those very sons were married. *Make thee an ark; for, behold I, even I, do bring a flood of waters upon the earth, to destroy all flesh; and every thing that is in the earth shall die. But with*

with thee will I establish my covenant*: *and thou shalt come into the ark; thou, and thy sons, and thy wife, and thy sons wives with thee. For the end of all flesh is come before me.* After this, no command appears for building the ark, into which Noah entered in the six-hundredth year of his age; and, therefore, no certain conclusion can be drawn concerning the time that was spent in preparing it. This account of the matter is farther confirmed, by the tenth verse of the eleventh chapter, where we read, that *Shem was an hundred years, and begat Arphaxad two years after the flood*; which corresponds with the reckoning going before; that at his birth, Noah was in the fifth hundred year of his age; and he himself, according to the course of things in those times, must have been married only a little before that event. Consequently the foundation of the ark could not be laid so long before the flood as some have imagined.

BUT while this stricture is made on the one side, the other must not pass uncorrected. There have been divines of certain nations, whose warm fancies †, and talents for controversy, have exceeded proper bounds: And it plainly appears, that they have mistaken the manifestation of the divine patience, and the incorrigibleness of the antediluvian transgressors, in the case now before us. The words, *My spirit shall not always strive with man: yet his days shall be an hundred and twenty years*, those commentators think, were not spoken to Noah, an *hundred and twenty years* before the flood, but express a resolution to destroy

* Heb ברית † Athan. Kircher. M. Saurin, Disc. viii. p. 85.

the

the earth, which the Almighty had formed within himself: And that it was not till a long time after, that the patriarch was honored with this particular revelation, *the end of all flesh is come before me.* But establishing the concession which has been already made, that the ark was not an *hundred and twenty years* in building, it will, nevertheless, be impossible to admit that the period of God's forbearance was a secret known only to the divine mind; *For who hath known the mind of the Lord,* without positive declarations concerning it? *Or who hath been his counseller* *? Besides, *if he had not spoken to them,* the wicked and sensual men of that age, *would have had a cloak for their sins* †. It must, therefore, on every principle, be believed, that they had timely and the most inequivocal intimations of their ruin, if they delayed their repentance: And Noah himself might remain ignorant of the method, by which *the grace he had found in the eyes of the Lord,* was to be shewn till a few years before *the measure of iniquity was full* ‡.

The form of the ark has been as much contested, among interpreters, as the time of its construction. Moses says, it was made of *Gopher wood* ||; a term not to be found in any other part of the sacred writings; and, therefore, cannot be explained by those writings themselves. The greater part of commentators, however, have determined that it was of *Cypress*: A wood, as travellers tell us, very plentiful, in those parts of *Assyria*, where the ark is supposed to have been made. The sacred historian farther informs us, that there

* Rom. xi. 34. † St. John, xv. 22.
‡ St. Mathew, xxiii. 32. || Heb. גפר

were

were *rooms* in it; and that the whole was pitched *within and without with pitch:* That *the length of the ark* was *three hundred cubits, the breadth of it fifty cubits, and the heighth of it thirty cubits.* It was, therefore, like a large cheſt; and, in our meaſure, four hundred and fifty feet in length, ſeventy-five in breadth, and forty-five in heighth. The *three ſtories*, or diviſions, that were in it, whether they were by the heighth, the length, or the breadth of it, we know not. *The door of the ark* was *ſet in the ſide thereof.* And, as the Hebrew word * literally ſignifies, it had a *window*, which may be a collective term for many windows; as it is very unlikely that ſuch a vaſt building had but one. Indeed ſome of the Jewiſh commentators have been of opinion, that it was lighted by a precious ſtone †. *Credat Judæus:*

Here then, in the kind command and inſtructions given to Noah, we have another illuſtrious inſtance of the Almighty's regard and condeſcenſion towards integrity and innocence. Him, and his family, becauſe *he was a juſt man, and perfect in his generation*, God was graciouſly pleaſed to diſtinguiſh by a miraculous preſervation; that from ſo good a ſtock, when the flood ſhould be over, the human race might be again propagated, and religion reſtored in the world. With him God purpoſed *to eſtabliſh his covenant*; and through him, and his faithful family, were the grace and bleſſings of the governor of the whole earth, eſpecially the gradual ſchemes of redemption, to have their full effect.

* Heb. צהר † R. Jarchi, in Gen. vi. 16.

MOSES

Moses saying no more on this subject, it may be left to architects to enter deeper into it: Nothing should have made us touch upon it, unless it had been a part of the sacred relation, to which many odious objections have been raised.

A learned and ingenious prelate hath gone a great length towards obviating all of them *, in his compleat and precise idea of the ark, and it's capacity to hold every thing that Moses says it contained. And others †, to whom we refer, have followed him in the same tract, and found sufficient provision for all the creatures that could be in it.

When the ark was finished, Noah, *the eight persons*, according to the expression of St. Peter, namely, his wife, his three sons, and their wives, entered into it. There went also with him, seven pair of every species of *clean* animals, and of *unclean* one pair. The historian, whose very words these are, in regard to clean and unclean beasts, gives us no information, whether this distinction was established before that time, or was then ordained, or is only mentioned, by way of accommodation to the notions of the Jews at the period when he wrote. It is, however, probable, from the circumstance of taking only one pair of unclean animals into the ark, and seven pair of the other, with a view to his own subsistence and that of his family, if other provision was spent, during the flood, and to offer some of them in sacrifice when the desolation should be over; it is probable, I say, that

* Wilkins, Bishop of Chester. † Peletier, Cumberland, Grave, *Jour. de Paris.*

this

this distinction was not altogether unknown to Noah in those early times. We have translated the word by *seven pair*, and not seven *animals*, as some interpreters have done. The text, indeed, seems to have no ambiguity in it: *Of every clean beast thou shalt take to thee by sevens* *, *the male and his female.*

On this part of the subject, many a witty caviller has enquired, how it was possible for Noah to collect such a number of all kinds of *beasts, and birds, and creeping things*, as it is said were lodged in the ark with him; seeing many of them are immensely large, many fierce and wild, and to be found only in sequestered and uninhabited corners: And seven days were only given him to complete his embarkation. With this apparent difficulty, many a stout infidel has affected to be hard set.

But absurd as this matter may appear to men of this class, very remote tradition has preserved the memory of the fact. An ancient author, describing the deluge, says, that all creatures went *pair and pair* into the ark †. The supposition of an interpreter, who asserts that they flocked to Noah naturally, through fear of the increasing waters, appears not sufficient to explain what the sacred history relates on this occasion ‡. Some Jewish doctors have taught that God appointed an angel to every species of animals, and served himself of the ministry of those spirits at this conjuncture §. The truth seems to be, that those beasts reptiles and fowls, were not brought together by the

* Heb. שבעה שבעה

† Lucian de Dea Syra.

‡ Voy. Buteo de l'Arche de Noe.

‡ Pirké Eliez. C. xxiii.

care

care and assiduity of Noah and his family, but were either rendered docile and obsequious to his voice, or sent in to him after a miraculous manner, by the direction or wonderful power of God. *For it was said to him, two of every sort shall come unto thee, to keep them alive.* And all that Noah had to do was to make provision for this heterogeneous houshold; agreeable to the following command: *Take thou unto thee of all food that it is eaten, and thou shalt gather it unto thee; and it shall be for food for thee, and for them.*

When the work of this week was finished, and Noah and his family, with the beasts, the fowls, and the creeping things, had entered into the ark, God no longer saw any thing on the earth, which could determine him to suspend the design which he had formed of drowning it with water. Moses says it was *in the six hundredth year of* Noah's age that the fatal purpose was executed; *in the second month, the seventeenth day of the month*: That is of the civil year, and in the month which we call *October*: Consequently in the year of the world, one thousand six hundred and fifty-six; four hundred and forty-five years before the calling of Abraham; eight hundred and seventy-five before the departure of his posterity from Egypt; one thousand seven hundred and seventy-eight before the destruction of the first temple by the Chaldeans; and two thousand three hundred and forty-eight years before the *Dionysian* æra of Jesus Christ *.

Another calculation, falling short of this, fifty-six years, between the flood and the birth of the savi-

* See the table in the first Dissertation.

our

our of the world, has been made by an author of great erudition; who attempts to prove his hypothesis by Chaldaic and Egyptian fables, with which he presents us, and confirms them with the Macedonian and Roman *. But whether we are to pay more respect to the sacred chronology, assisted by well known records, or to *characters* very obscure, and of uncertain interpretation, let every one deliberately judge.

Moses, in his manner of describing this dreadful overthrow of nature, has hardly left any difficulties about the two principal questions which have been so much agitated, by men of all countries and professions. It is, first, asked, if the deluge was so universal, as to inclose in its bosom the whole terrestrial globe; or if the divine vengeance was confined to the habitable part of it, which alone being guilty, appears alone to have deserved extermination? And, next, from whence was drawn the prodigious quantity of water necessary for such an inundation?

In regard to the first question, the historian says, *the waters prevailed exceedingly upon the earth, and all the high* hills, *that were under the whole heaven were covered. Fifteen cubits upwards did the waters prevail; and the* mountains *were covered. And all flesh died that moved upon the earth, both of fowl, and of cattle, and of beasts, and of every creeping thing that creepeth upon the earth, and every man:* Noah *only remained alive, and they that were with him in the ark.* No expressions can suggest to the mind a stronger idea of an universal desolation.

* Guill. Bonjour, Selectæ Differt.

P On

On the ſecond queſtion, Moſes ſays, *the ſame day in which the Lord ſhut Noah in, were all the fountains of the great deep broken up, and the windows of heaven were opened.* By *the fountains of the great deep,* interpreters, for the moſt part, underſtand thoſe vaſt and innumerable cavities, which are in the bowels of the earth, and through which lakes, and rivers, and ſeas have communications with one another, as through ſo many ſubterraneous pipes. Certain ſolid bodies, and collections of water, ſhut up in the clouds, by their own gravity being drawn down to the earth, the Jews called the apertures, which they were ſuppoſed to make in falling, *the windows of heaven.* In this ſenſe it is ſaid, that *God commanded the clouds from above, and opened the doors,* or the windows *of heaven, and rained down manna upon his people to eat* *. Thus Moſes' ſyſtem concerning the flood ſeems to be this; that the Almighty, having called forth all the waters which were under the earth, and condenſed the clouds exceedingly, in order to form more, employed them in drowning the world. Yet, notwithſtanding this intelligible repreſentation, other writers, on theſe points, have given their fancies the greateſt liberty. And, therefore, departing from the text, for a little, we ſhall relate, with the utmoſt hiſtorical brevity, ſome of the difficulties that have been raiſed on the Moſaic hiſtory, in this place.

Those who confine the deluge to a part of the world, alledge, that the deſign of it being to puniſh tranſgreſſors, the ſcourge could hardly be univerſal; when, in the courſe of ſixteen centuries, the world

* Pſalm lxxviii. 23, 23.

could

could not be compleatly peopled, ſeeing it is not all inhabited at this very day. And it is incredible that God ſhould extend his judgments farther than there were delinquents and malefactors.

To this objection, it is oppoſed that the inhabitants of the world were then very numerous; and that the waters which overſpread ſuch extenſive parts of the globe as their ſettlements muſt neceſſarily occupy, would by the ordinary laws of nature, cover others alſo, unleſs a miracle ſhould obſtruct and ſuſpend them in the air. It is argued beſides, that concluſions drawn from God's deſigns, are rarely juſt, becauſe he hath often more views than one, while only one is attended to by men, and that what may be uſeleſs to one purpoſe with which we are acquainted, may ſerve another of which we are ignorant. If, for inſtance, the univerſality of the deluge was not neceſſary for puniſhing ſinners who lived at that time, it might be appointed to convey greater ideas of God's power to the guilty in after ages; and to make the religious part of the world admire his mercy, which kept cloſely locked up, deſolating floods ſufficient to deſtroy the whole earth, from breaking forth on the rebellious, when they have been impiouſly leagued againſt him. God might, likewiſe, propoſe by the univerſal deluge, that men ſhould every where find, by its ravages, marks of his hatred to iniquity, and motives to avoid it; in the ſame manner as the curſe pronounced upon the ground where Adam and Eve dwelt, affected every other part of it poſſeſſed by their deſcendants. A certain author is of opinion that the earth at firſt bore a reſemblance to the human body in innocence; and that it was neceſſary to give a constitution to the one; suitable to the other, in a state of guilt *.

It is said by those who limit the flood to a part of the habitable world, that the universality of it implies a contradiction, except there should have been a new creation of waters, which is so far from being notified in the sacred history, that it seems to contradict it, seeing Moses expressly says that they came from *the windows of heaven*, and from *the fountains of the great deep*. Though the Almighty should have collected all the waters which are dispersed through the world, in the air, in the caverns of the earth, and in the vast cavities of the ocean, they would not have been sufficient, according to them, to have raised the flood *fifteen cubits above the highest mountains* of the earth. It is farther said, though God should have condensed the whole atmosphere which surrounds our globe, and turned it into water, it would still have been insufficient for an universal inundation; seeing it has been demonstrated by undoubted experiments, that the gross air which we breathe is eighty times more rare than water; so that to make any given quantity of water out of condensed air, there must be a volume of the latter eighty times larger than that of the former †. The argument is yet strengthened by the consideration, that there is no gross air above a certain height of our hemisphere, where matter becomes more subtile and less condensed. The objection, in short, drawn from the exorbitant quantity of water necessary for a general deluge, has been carried so far, that some have asserted, that twenty times more water

* M. Bernard, Nouv. de la Repub. des Lettres.
† Edm. Halley, in act. Philosop.

than

than there is in the ocean, would not cover the terrestrial globe *. It was this difficulty, no doubt, which induced a celebrated writer to contrive, that a comet, flying off at the extremity of its ellipsis, should enter a section of the earth's orbit, and so crush its arch, and envelope it in watry vapors, with all its productions †.

THE answer is, that no experiments, nor even the whole accumulated knowledge of man, can possibly ascertain, with precision, to what height the waters supposed to have been collected, or formed by the condensation of the air, would exactly rise. A certain author affirms that the *Wolga* furnishes every year the *Caspian Sea* with as much water as is necessary to cover the whole earth ‡. If this be thought an extravagance, what would we think if the contents of the *Orellana*, of *Rio de la plata*, and the *Oronoque* were added? not to mention *St. Lawrence*, the *Ganges*, *Niger* and the *Nile*: which are all supplied by copious subterranean springs, and some of the rains that fall on the adjacent countries, without the smallest diminution of the ocean. All these, with this vast reservoir, would furnish a quantity of water, almost immense. And besides these sources, to effect the flood, God might modify other parts of matter the most subtile, and convert them into the same element. As to the mountains, they say, that though some of them appear extremely high, there are none of them of an extraordinary perpendicular elevation. *Olympus*, so extolled by the Poets, is only, in that direction, one mile and an half, and about seventy paces. The same

* Ray, on the Deluge.

† Buffon, Hist. nat. ‡ Ray.

heig

height is aſcribed to *Pelion*. Mount *Athos*, which is ſaid to throw its ſhadow as far as the Iſle of *Lemnos*, notwithſtanding the enormous height it was thought to be of, by an ancient author *, has, in late times, been found to meaſure no more than two miles perpendicular †. Another writer hath fully exhauſted this ſubject ‡.

By thoſe, who reſtrain the deluge to the part of the world that was inhabited only, it has, laſt of all, been ſuggeſted, that the living creatures, which went with Noah into the ark. could not poſſibly travel ſo far, in ſo ſhort a time, as to arrive at the place where it was built; nor could they, on account of the ſlowneſs of ſome of them in moving, return to their former habitations, in leſs than twenty thouſand years; conſequently, that they could not have been found at this day, if the countries where they have been diſcovered, had not been preſerved from the waters of the flood §.

To this final effort of ingenuity, it has been anſwered, that the terreſtrial globe has undergone innumerable changes ſince the days of Noah: That the flood, ſuppoſing it to have been univerſal; even local inundations, and violent earthquakes, muſt have changed *dry ground into watry-ſprings, and turned rivers into a wilderneſs* ‖: That three quarters of the earth are evidently contiguous, and it is not yet plain that the fourth is not alſo. A miraculous providence may likewiſe be urged on this occaſion. One thing

* Pliny. † Stillingfleet orig. ſacr.
‡ Voſſius Pomp. Mel. § Voſſius.
‖ Pſalm cvii. 23, &c.

is

is certain that animals of the slowest motion are, at this day, at a prodigious distance from the place, where, the very objector will allow, Adam gave them names in the beginning. And if twenty thousand years were necessary for them to go thither, how could they have yet arrived? The very answer which this learned man must give to the objection, will refute the reason he alledges against the universality of the deluge.

It has been said, that though the words of the historian concerning this event, be seemingly express, they should yet be qualified according to the subject to which they are applied: That the waters fell with such rapidity, and in such abundance, that the retreat of the wicked, to the smallest distance, was impossible: That several of the productions of the earth, which are taken for wrecks of the flood, are nothing more than *sports of nature*, which has given a certain form often fanciful, to some parts of matter: That the concurrence of several natural causes, such as winds, and an extraordinary compression of the air by vapors, has often raised liquid masses, and prevented them, for some time, from diffusing themselves, according to the settled laws of material substances.

On the other hand, it is urged, that the words of Moses must be taken literally, and in their full extent; *the waters prevailed exceedingly upon the earth; and all the high hills, that were under the whole heaven, were covered; fifteen cubits upward did the waters prevail; and all flesh died that moveth upon the earth:* That Noah, his family, and the animals staid in the ark, *till the face of the ground was dry:* That if the flood had not been

been univerſal, God would have conducted them to a place of refuge, and ſome of the guilty might have eſcaped with them: That nature manifeſtly bears on it traces of that event, which can never be eraſed, from mountains, vallies, and the midſt of rocks: That waters run to their level, and cannot be ſuſpended without a miracle, not to be ſuppoſed, in this caſe, where none is mentioned: And that by the concuſſion, or agitation of the waters, they might riſe *fifteen cubits* above the higheſt mountains, ſo long as to ſweep the human race, and beaſts from thence, though they did not continue at that ſtanding depth. Theſe ſpeculations grounded on the holy text, in a great meaſure, and the authority of the ſacred writer, plainly induce us to conclude in favour of an univerſal deluge.

THIS ſubject a very ingenious writer hath treated with great erudition, and a force of genius deſerving the admiration of the learned; but his *theory* * is deſtitute of facts and obſervations. He repreſents the earth, before the flood, as a globe, whoſe ſurface was equal and uniform, without mountain, ſteep, cavern, lakes, pools, ſeas or rivers. He encloſes all the waters in nature, in the bowels of the earth, as in a thick and poliſhed ſhell. This ſhell, he ſuppoſes, was broken and cruſhed, by a divine vindictive power, for the extermination of mankind: And that by this act, all theſe waters guſhed out with great impetuoſity, and drowned the world. This ſcheme has

* T. Burnet, Theor. Sacr. Telluris.

had

had but few followers, and has been refuted at great length *.

An opinion more generally followed, in regard to this subject, we have in an *essay towards a natural history of the earth* †. The author, with the most of philosophers, imagines that there are subterraneous caverns full of water; that by these Moses understands *the great deep*, and the heathens *Erebus*; that between these, and the waters of the ocean, there is a continual communication through certain fissures which join one another; and that there is even a perpetual circulation of the waters in our atmosphere. He thinks, likewise, that near this abyss there is a constant and uniform heat diffused through all the interior parts of the earth; that earthquakes and volcanoes proceed from this heat in the centre, which not being always equally distributed on every side, is collected in one place, and there rarifies, to an extreme degree, the waters of *the great deep*, and makes violent efforts on those parts of the earth, by which it is confined; in the same manner, perhaps, as a redundancy or stagnation of the nervous influence in the human body, often bring on palsies. By the mediation of this heat, he alleges, the waters of the ocean were raised above the earth at the deluge; and that those of the *great deep* immediately followed them. This system the author left unfinished.

* Keil's Theory of the earth. † Woodward.

A Great

A GREAT mathematician enlarged and arranged thoſe ſchemes; but, very different from the rules of his profeſſion, he proved nothing *.

ANOTHER theory, in the form of a philoſophical dream, has been ſuggeſted. If, ſays the author, we whirl upon its centre a round veſſel half full of water, till the water hath fully caught the ſwiftneſs of the veſſel, and then ſtopping it ſuddenly, the water will continue to move, and even with ſo much force, that it will overflow the edges of the veſſel: In like manner, if God ſtopt the rotation of the earth upon it's axis, the waters of the ſea would be thrown from all parts with violence on the land †. The author offers this only as a philoſophical dream, and thereby prevents all objections.

As the fine elaſtic air, which is diffuſed all round the globe, cannot be totally excluded from any part of nature, even the bowels of the earth, ſome have thought that the eruption of the ſubterraneous waters would be naturally produced, by the efforts ſuch quantities of that air, as had been collected and pent up, would violently make, to recover their freedom, and mix again with their kindred element, when many perforations, and large holes were made, by the divine power, in the outward ſurface. In this way, indeed, the waters entangled and propelled, might, probably guſh forth, not in ſmall ſpouts, but tremendous torrents, like thoſe which are ſeen to

* Whiſton. † Scheuchzer's Diſſertation, addreſſed to the Academy of Sciences 1708. Voy. Journal des Savans, Octobre 1713.

fall

fall from the clouds in the Indies. Among all thoſe theories one thing is very obſervable, namely, that the authors of them, however much they may differ, in reſpect to the application of natural cauſes for the deſtruction of the old world, do all agree in this, that the work was evidently miraculous, in regard to the direction. And they, who have attempted to account for it any other way, are found to have departed juſt ſo far from philoſophy and experiments, as they departed from revelation.

A MEMORIAL, deſerving high encomiums, was drawn up on the ſame ſubject, of ſtill a latter date; but death carried the author from the waves of human life, before he had completed his deſign *.

OTHER ſyſtems might be produced, but there is too much co-incidence in them with thoſe which have been already ſketched; and perhaps they do not come nearer the truth. Whatever means the Almighty employed to collect the waters of the deluge, *it rained upon the earth forty days and forty nights*, and the waters remained on it *an hundred and fifty days* before they *were abated*; which makes it evident that cataracts had not ceaſed all that time. An inundation ſo violent and ſo general would, indeed, occaſion great changes over the whole terreſtrial globe. But it is carrying the matter to exceſs, to aſſert that the axis of the earth was originally perpendicular to the plain of the *ecliptic*, that is to ſay, to the plain which paſſes through the line, in which the earth is moved round the ſun; that every country

* M. Bourguet. printed at Amſt. 1729.

enjoyed

enjoyed a perpetual ſpring; and that the flood changed this ſituation, and inclined the axis of the earth to the plain of the *ecliptic*, which now cauſes the diverſity of ſeaſons *.

But remote as we may be from ſuch a flight of fancy, for which there is as little ground in nature as in revelation, every one muſt be obliged to acknowledge that the flood produced great changes on our globe. Leſt we ſhould contradict a theory, hereafter to be conſidered, we ſhall not pronounce what effect the flood might have upon the atmoſphere itſelf, unleſs it may be ſuppoſed to have made it more moiſt and watry, by more copious exhalations, from the increaſed volume of the ſeas below. But torrents, ruſhing forth from all parts could not fail to ſhake and diſmember various countries, to change the whole ſurface of the earth, and to render it ſuſceptible of the many alterations which have likely happened in it ſince that fatal period. Plato introduces Solon relating that he had learned from the prieſts of the city of *Sais*, that there was formerly towards the mouth of the ſtreights of *Gibralter* an iſland called *Atlantis*, larger than Aſia and Africa joined together †. Sicily, ſome have thought, was a portion of land broken off from Italy. The ſituation of *the low countries* hath made others believe that they were once a bed for the ocean. The authors are numerous that handle this ſubject, at great length ‡.

The imagination of man cannot be ſtruck with a more dreadful ſpectacle, than that of the whole world,

* Th. Sa. C. 1. † *In Timæo.* ‡ Ovid Metamorp. Plin. Hiſt. Nat. Strabo. Ray's Conſeq. of the Deluge.

and

and all the human race, buried under waves. The object presents to the mind still more gloomy thoughts, when we judge of the event at the tribunal of conscience and religion. *Fruitful land was turned into barrenness*, and chaos brought back upon the earth *for the wickedness of them that dwelt therein.* The chastisement proceeded from a most righteous judge incensed.

Eating *and drinking, marrying, and giving in marriage* *, thinking of nothing but sensual enjoyments, in contempt of every serious admonition, how would the careless and impenitent unbelievers be surprised, when all on a sudden the most terrible rains and inundations threatened their inevitable destruction. How would they be terrified! How would they condemn their own unbelief, and be compelled to own that there was a just and righteous God, who executed vengeance on all the incurable workers of iniquity! when there were such violent eruptions of the subterraneous waters, and such streams and spouts, with wrathful sounds, coming down from the sky, and meeting together so *prevailed over the earth*, as to put it beyond the wisdom of the wise, and the power of the mighty, to relieve either themselves or their friends! And *the flood came, and took them all away* †.

But let us pause, and reflect on this wonderful dispensation! Like all the rest of God's ways, it had a direct tendency to reduce the enormous degree of corruption, and to preserve and advance true religion

* St. Matthew xxiv, 38. † Ibid. 39.

in the earth, the great end for which man had it given to him in poſſeſſion. If the whole tainted body, ſo to ſpeak, had not been cut off, the ſingle family that remained ſound, would ſoon have been infected, or deſtroyed by violent and bloody hands; and then the whole creation muſt have been ruined, and the ſchemes and purpoſes of God, from the beginning of the world, had been defeated. But when a total infection was prevented, the reſervation of a ſelect family for propagating their own kind, gave full ſcope to the divine counſels, and laid a foundation for the eſtabliſhment of truth and righteouſneſs in the new world; eſpecially as Noah, a good man, would neither fail to communicate all he knew of the divine works to his poſterity, nor to inculcate a ſtrong ſenſe of them upon their hearts.

But why do we ſpeak of him only? His *commands* would not be needful *to his children to keep the ways of the Lord* *; his family would aſſiſt him in the ſervice of religion. They, as well as he, had been eye-witneſſes of the overthrow of ſinners. They knew it was not an unfortunate accident, but occaſioned by the depravation of the world. All the terrors of the deluge, muſt, therefore, give them the moſt ſenſible perception of the malignant nature of wickedneſs, that it is infinitely odious to God, and dreadfully pernicious to the offender. They muſt, for the ſpace of twelve months reſidence in the ark, have been much affected with their ſingularly awful ſituation, convinced of the almighty power and univerſal dominion of the moſt high, the impoſſibility of eſcaping

* Gen. xviii. 19.

his

his resentment, what *a fearful thing it is to fall into his hands* *, and how much interest and duty, gratitude and fear, obliged them to reverence and obey him.

Leaving the ark, what dismal appearances would present themselves—a desolate world—the ruins of palaces, towns, and cities—and the sadly changed faces of countries, once cultivated, fair, and flourishing, *where the spring was blessed, the pastures clothed with flocks, the vallies also covered over with corn, and the year crowned with goodness* †. Never did *Tyre*, *Alexandria*, or *Jerusalem*, in their desolations, exhibit such a scene; nor the most cruelly ransacked and plundered kingdom since time began. This also would revive in Noah and his family, the good impressions they had received on the mighty waters, and fix them in their hearts for ever. And the admonitions of this patriarch, who lived three hundred and forty-nine years after the flood, and was the instructor, and, for some time at least, the governor of the new world, would have the greatest weight and authority.

From the whole, therefore, it appears, that this was a very just and proper dispensation for the reforming mankind, and restoring religion in the earth, and had the intended effect, by suppressing violence and rapine, which universally prevailed, and hath never since, degenerate as the world has been in subsequent ages, arrived at such a monstrous pitch. And to the remotest generations, the flood is an awful warning to all who, like those who lived before it came, remain deaf to the instructions of repentance

* Heb. x. 31. † Psalm lxv. 10, 11, 13.

and righteousness. As such it is represented in the holy scriptures; especially by St. Peter, where he says, *And God spared not the old world, but saved Noah, a preacher of righteousness, bringing in the flood upon the world of the ungodly* *. It bears also a comparison with *the coming of the son of man* †, when the final destruction of the universe shall be by fire at the last day, *which God hath revealed by Jesus Christ* ‡. *Then let us not harden our hearts* ‖, as the ungodly did of old, but believe and prepare! *For behold! he cometh; and every eye shall see him! and they also who pierced him* §.

* 2 Pet. xi, 5. † St. Matthew, xxiv, 37. ‡ St. Matthew, xxv, 31. ‖ Psal. xcv, 8. § Revel. 1, 7.

DISSERTA-

DISSERTATION XIV.

Of NOAH's coming out of the ARK, and offering SACRIFICE, &c.

GENESIS VIII. IX.

THE rain, as has been said, continued incessantly *forty days*; the waters covered the whole earth *an hundred and fifty days*; and then began to *assuage*, by *a wind which God made* to dissipate one part of them in vapor, and to drive the rest back into the caverns from whence they had been brought. The original word translated *wind*, signifies also *spirit* *, and some interpreters have been of opinion that Moses speaks here of the third person of the blessed Trinity. *The ark rested in the seventh month, on the seventeenth day of the month, upon the mountains of Ararat: And the waters decreased continually, until the first day of the tenth month*, when *the tops of the mountains were seen.*

* See the first Dissertation, page 6. Consider likewise *Col-pi-jah.*

It is to be deplored that the enemies of religion ſeize every opportunity to embarraſs it, not only with difficulties in the phraſeology, but alſo with whatever has the appearance of them, in places of the ſacred text where there are really none. They have ſaid, that ſuch a building as the ark would require more than fifteen cubits water; that the higheſt mountains, according to Moſes, had not more; that the ark might have reſted on *Ararat*, when the waters were at their height; and, therefore, the hiſtorian is not to be underſtood as giving a token of their *decreaſe*, when he ſays that it reſted on that mountain. It has alſo been objected that every large veſſel would be broken to pieces by its own weight, if it was to reſt on dry land, and muſt have its lading ſupported by water.

These, and the like objections, one would naturally think, ſhould ariſe from great ſkill in the arts, upon which ſome men fondly pretend to ground them. And yet when the expert are conſulted on theſe matters, ſuch objections are found to be, either the fruit of ignorance, or plauſible fancies forced into the ſervice of infidelity.

It is much leſs by the burthen of a ſhip, than by the conſtruction, that we are to judge how much water it will draw. Now, though the figure of Noah's ark, be not circumſtantially given in this ſhort deſcription, it evidently appears that it was not deſigned to ſail faſt but to float, which is ſufficient to prove that it took much leſs water, than thoſe whom we are now refuting would inſinuate. And in regard to a ſhip breaking, by the weight of its cargo, when it takes ground; experience shews the contrary; especially when the winds are not tempestuous; and there is a smooth and sandy bottom, such as we may suppose the mountains of *Ararat* were after the flood. And what would follow if the hulk was bulged?

Whether those mountains be the highest on earth, as some geographers and travellers say they are; or whether the ark rested precisely on one of their most elevated summits, is not insisted on: But interpreters have exercised themselves greatly on the question respecting the situation of the mountain itself. Many are the opinions which have been given; and nice criticisms employed to very little purpose. One thing is clear that by the word *Ararat*, frequently occurring in scripture, is meant the country of *Armenia*. In this sense the *Septuagint* * understood it, the author of the *vulgate* †, and several others. A very learned man hath not only proved that *Ararat* and *Armenia* are synonymous, but likewise that the *Gordian* mountain, so called in modern times, is that upon which the ark first touched ground, after the waters had subsided ‡.

A much larger account might be given of this mountain, if it was consistent with the present work: But this being sufficient for ordinary readers, the curious may be farther satisfied by looking into the authors below §.

* Sept. 2 Kings xix, 37. καὶ αὐτοι ἐσωθησαν εἰς γῆν 'Αραράδ: in our translation, Armenia.

† Vulg. Gen. viii, 4. Requievitque arca mense septimo, vigesimo-septimo die mensis, super montes Armeniæ.

‡ Bochart.

§ La Boulaye, Voyages. Tavernier, Voyages de perse.

IF ſome unbelievers have vainly attempted to invalidate the teſtimony of Moſes, the *Armenians*, to confirm it, produce evidences, which they have received with too much credulity. On the ſuppoſition that it may be credited the ark will never decay, they ſell pieces of it at a great price. In Muſcovy a black croſs is ſhewn, which is ſaid to be made of the ark, and eſteemed a moſt precious relick *.

TAVERNIER ſays, the city of *Nakſivan*, the oldeſt in the world, is three leagues diſtant from the mountain *Ararat*; that Noah ſettled there after he left the ark; and that the word is derived from *Nak*, which ſignifies *ſhip*, and *ſivan*, *to ſtop*. The application is eaſily ſeen.

LA BOULAYE ſays, there is an *Armenian* tradition, that Noah's ark reſted on the top of that mountain, but they cannot aſcend it; that one of their pilgrims, a man of a moſt holy life, made the attempt, and reached the middle of it; that falling ſhort of water, he prayed to God, who made a fountain ſpring to preſerve his life; but told him with an audible voice, that none ſhould be ſo raſh as to proceed farther towards the ſummit of that mountain. Here we have one inſtance, among many, of the diſagreement of hiſtorians, who, as too plainly appears, take their accounts, from the accidental acquaintances they form in the ſeveral countries through which they paſs.

BUT to reſume the Moſaic hiſtory; two months and ſome days after the ark had reſted, on one of

* Olearius.

mountains of Ararat, the tops of others were discovered. *At the end of forty days more, Noah opened the window of the ark which he had made*: probably in the roof of it, a circumstance which would facilitate and extend his view. *And sent forth a raven, which went to and fro, until the waters were dried up from off the earth.* This phrase in our translation might be purposely adopted, on account of the equivocality of the Hebrew text, which renders what Moses says, concerning the *raven*, equally susceptible of another interpretation, than is here given *. The most of commentators, indeed, understand the words, as they are in the margin of our bibles, *going forth and returning*. But the *Septuagint*, on the contrary, and the *vulgate*, render them, *it went, and returned not again, until the waters were dried up from off the earth* †. This variation, among the several editions of the ancient scriptures, inclined a great man to think, for which he raised up many enemies against himself, that the seventy interpreters had other copies of the sacred books, from which they drew their translation, than those of which we are now possessed, and that they were more correct. The subject of the controversy is too trifling, to enter upon a serious discussion of it, in this performance, which is designed for instruction and edification, and *not for doubtful disputations* ‖; nor strife *about words to no profit* §.

* Heb. את הערב ויצא יצוא ושוב

† Sep. Καὶ ἐξελθὼν οὐκ ἀν, ἐςρέψεν ἕως τῦ ξηρανθηναι τὸ ὕδωρ ἀπὸ τῆς γῆς. Vulg. Qui (scil corvus) egrediebatur, & non revertebatur donec siccarentur aquæ super terram.

‡ Louis Capel, Critic. Sacr.

‖ Rom. xiv. i.

§ ii Tim. ii. 14.

NOAH

NOAH *also sent forth a dove from him, to see if the waters were abated from off the face of the ground.* Here interpreters have again enquired, whether the *raven* and the *dove* were sent out at the same time. It is a happy circumstance, that few chronological questions can be less interesting than this. For though matters of the greatest moment depended on the period, many authors would insist on it as absolutely certain. It has been thought the interval was forty days; that it was only seven; that there was no interval at all*. A learned and solid commentator is of opinion, that the tenth verse of the chapter, where we read, *and* Noah *staid yet other seven days*, relates to seven days preceding, which seem to have passed between the going forth of the *raven* and the *dove* †.

SEVEN *days* after *the dove* returned, Noah *sent her out of the ark again.* The second time, she brought *in her mouth an olive leaf pluckt off.* A weaker argument against the universality of the deluge, than that which has been grounded on this circumstance, can hardly be conceived. The text imports, that the dove had *in its mouth an olive branch pluckt off*; to which some have been pleased to add, that it was *green*. This, they say, could no where be found but in such places as the flood had not reached, the leaves every where else being withered and dry. But as is well known, the leaves of the olive continuing for a long time *green*, under water, this is sufficient to refute such a weak objection, without having recourse to some interpreters, who have advanced that the dove had taken this leaf from the garden of *Eden* ‡.

* Heideg. de vit. Patr. Exércit. *passim*,

† Bishop Patrick, in loco. ‡ R. Bibi.

UPON

Upon the prince of commentators we are sorry to criticise *. He has said that the word translated *leaf* signifies equally *a branch*; and to obviate the difficulty, how a dove could break off a branch from a tree, he has suggested that it was summer-time, when new shoots out of trees are easily cropt. But the learned will see in the Hebrew bible and concordance, that the words for *branch* and *leaf* are very different, and that the latter in this place is plainly expressed.

Other *seven days* having elapsed, Noah *sent forth the dove* the third time, *which returned not again unto him any more:* notifying to the patriarch, not only that the tops of the mountains were dry, which he beheld standing up out of the waters, and also the lower grounds, but likewise that there was wanting neither food, nor a nest where she might repose herself, and expect a mate for the propagation of the kind; in short, that the earth was not only drained, but fit to be inhabited, and afforded food for the creatures he had with him.

The reasons given for the choice of those fowls, in preference to all others, on this occasion, are these; that the *raven*, being a carnivorous animal, would soon discover, by its smell, if any putrid carcases had infected the air, and would not return to the ark if it found any dead bodies to prey upon; and the *dove*, possessing a strong wing, and loving to feed on the ground, and pick up seeds, was a very fit creature to make farther discoveries.

* Bishop Patrick, in loco.

We

We must not omit to remark, in the relation of these circumstances, the interval of *seven days*, which seems to have been observed for some particular reason: Perhaps on this day Noah expected a blessing, rather than on any other: Being devoted from the beginning to religious services, he might entertain the hope of receiving good tidings on it: If not a compleat demonstration, this, at least, furnishes a presumption, in favour of those who think the sabbath was celebrated before the giving of the law on *Sinai* *.

Though Noah knew that the waters of the flood were withdrawn, it was not till the end of fifty days after he had sent out the dove the last time, that he made his debarkation. Perhaps he thought that time necessary for drying the earth compleatly, or rather, as he had entered into the ark at a precise time, by the special command of God, he might wait for the same command to leave it. This conjecture Moses seems to encourage, when he says, at the expiration of that time, *God spake unto Noah, saying, Go forth of the ark, thou, and thy wife, and thy sons wives with thee. Bring forth with thee every living thing that is with thee, of all flesh, both of fowl, and of cattle, and of every creeping thing that creepeth upon the ground; that that they may breed abundantly on the earth, and be fruitful, and mulriply upon the earth.*

The good patriarch entered on the possession of the restored world with a solemn act of divine worship, in testimony of his thankfulness for his preservation, and that of his family, and in obedience, it

* See Dissertation v. page 72.

is

is probable to some previous command. If ever a sense of gratitude and fear, could produce a sincere homage, it might certainly be expected on this occasion. Could Noah render any other to God, amidst so many objects, which, at once, presented in so lively a manner, both his resentment and his mercy? The patriarch was surrounded, on the one hand, with the dead bodies of his own species, and the wrecks of a ruinous world; and, on the other, he saw himself, with his family about him, who would naturally have been involved in the universal desolation, and could not have been preserved, but by the concurrence of multiplied and continued miracles. *He*, accordingly, *builded an altar unto the Lord, and took of every clean beast, and of every clean fowl, and offered burnt offerings on the altar.* That is to say, he sacrificed all those kinds of animals, which Moses calls *clean*, even before the publication of *his* law *.

Of the acceptableness of this act of devotion, there is a signification in the verse following, in figurative or hieroglyphical language: *And the Lord smelled a sweet savour.* Bodily sensations, and external representations, were, in the first ages of the world, and are at this day, where men are entirely in a state of nature, employed to express abstract notions, or the first and most genuine sentiments of the mind. In like manner the divine approbation, or the pleasure the Almighty took, in the exercise of Noah's piety, is set forth by an odour, or fragrance grateful to the smell; in other words, the relish of the body, is transferred to the relish and taste of the mind. This

* See the foregoing Dissertation.

mode

mode of ſpeech is very frequent in the levitical law, where it is often ſaid, *when any one will offer a meat-offering unto the Lord, he ſhall bring it to the prieſts, who ſhall burn it on the altar, with frankincenſe, to be an offering made by fire, of a ſweet ſavour, unto the Lord* *. A deſire is, hereby, required in the worſhipper, of purity and grace, and that his ſacrifice might be accepted. Hence David ſays, *O Lord, let my prayer come before thee like incenſe, and the lifting up of my hands as the evening ſacrifice* †: Or, let it be well pleaſing, and approved of; as ſincere prayer always is. In the ſame ſenſe the death of Chriſt is applied; *he loved us, and gave himſelf for us an offering and ſacrifice to God, for a ſweet ſmelling ſavour* ‡.

No ground is here laid, for the moſt unjuſt of all accuſations againſt this lawgiver, that he thought the divinity was corporeal. Moſes has taken ſo much care, when he uſes ſuch expreſſions, to purge them of groſs ideas, that we cannot, without the greateſt injuſtice, ſuſpect him of ignorance on this ſubject.

The expreſſion, however, ill underſtood, that *God ſmelled*, may have given occaſion to the notions which the heathens have formed of their Gods. Among them it was an opinion, that the Gods were pleaſed with baſking in the ſmoke of the incenſe which was offered to them in ſacrifice. Many of them, it is true, entertained nobler ideas: *The Gods*, ſays one, *have no need either of perfumes, or ſtatues; they regard only a willing and pure mind to ſerve them; and their meat is the doctrine of truth* §: Words not only wor-

* Levit. i. 9. † Pſal. cxli, 2. ‡ Ephes. v, 2. § Dion. Chryſ.

thy

thy of a pagan orator, but of the chriſtian divine of the ſame ſurname; nay, even of one of the prophets themſelves. Another aſſerts, that *there is no wiſe man who would wiſh to have it believed, that he could be gained by mere exhalations and vapors* *. But philoſophers of the firſt rank have not been followed by the crowd of their countrymen. The bodies of the Gods, it has been alledged, are nouriſhed by certain perfumations †. And a celebrated wit, to turn this opinion into ridicule, has ſaid, that *the gods left their* ORDINARY *of nectar and ambroſia, to taſte the fumes and the fat of ſacrifices.* ‡.

THE God whom we know, being a pure ſpirit, can reliſh, or be pleaſed with nothing, but what is ſpiritually good, the love and obedience of the ſoul. This is the only *ſmell* that is grateful to him.—The ſacrifice of our Redeemer, which is ſaid to be a ſweet ſavour, was his exhibition of ſubmiſſion, and actual obedience to the will and law of God; and the ſacrifices of Noah, and of the other patriarchs, and of the choſen people, were ſigns of the inward moral diſpoſitions of their hearts. A clean beaſt, or a clean fowl, brought to an altar, figuratively repreſented what the ſacrificer himſelf was, or wanted to be;—and our Lord, in the higheſt and moſt perfect degree, really was, and perfectly did, what *the offering up of himſelf* repreſented—ſpotleſs, acceptable, and efficacious.

To proceed: On the ſolemn occaſion of Noah's ſacrifice, and in conſequence of its ſweet ſmelling ſavour, *the Lord ſaid in his heart*—in language more

* Jamblichus. † Baron de Spanheim. ‡ Lucian de Sacrif.

ſuitable

suitable to his nature, he determined, resolved, or rather then declared his purpose, that he would *not again curse the ground any more for man's sake; for the imagination of man's heart is evil from his youth.* The sense and instruction of which words seem to be, that the Almighty would change his measures with men, so that they should have larger degrees of grace from him, both in regard to improvements and punishments; and seeing they were so inclined to wickedness, from the long and deep corruption of their natures and ways, which is the meaning of an *evil imagination from their youth*, God would not at least *smite other living creatures, as he had done*, with a flood, for man's sake; nor change the natural course of the world to scourge the sinners that dwell therein: *For*, said God, *while the earth remaineth, seed-time and harvest, cold and heat, summer and winter, and day and night, shall not cease.* This intimates that seed-time and harvest, and summer and winter had entirely ceased, without any distinction, at the time of the deluge; and so it is likely had day and night in a great measure also; and, therefore, made this part of the covenant, established with Noah, and with his seed after him, the more important.

Besides this, the Lord was also pleased to repeat to Noah and his sons the same blessing on the propagation of the human species, and the marks of dignity upon our natures, as he had given our first parents at their creation. A comparison of the blessings given to them *both* will evidently prove this to have been the case. To Adam and Eve God said, *Be fruitful, and*

*and multiply, and replenish the earth**: To Noah and his sons, he says, *Be fruitful, and multiply, and replenish the earth*: To our first parents it was said, *Have dominion over the fish of the sea, and over the fowl of the air, and over every living thing that moveth on the earth †*: To Noah and his sons it is said, *The fear of you, and the dread of you, shall be upon every beast of the earth, and upon every fowl of the air, and upon all that moveth upon the earth, and upon all fishes of the sea; into your hand are they delivered.*

THERE was likewise added, a grant of animal food; which seems clearly to settle the point that the use of it was not permitted before the deluge; though, by several learned men, this point is still contested. What they advance, however, when carefully collected and weighed, appears too weak to induce conviction against the received opinion, that the antediluvians did not eat flesh. Here the former comparison again takes place: To Adam and Eve was granted for food, *every herb bearing seed, and every tree, in the which is the fruit of a tree yielding seed ‡*: To Noah and his sons, the charter is enlarged, *every moving thing that liveth shall be meat for you, even as the green herb, have I given you all things.* The only restriction in this new privilege was, that *men should not eat the flesh of an animal in the life, that is, in the blood thereof*: Nor, consequently, should they eat any flesh cut off from any animal while it was alive; to prevent, we may well suppose, the inhuman maiming of cattle, and the putting any living creature to unnecessary pain and torture; as the practice can never fail of producing

* Genesis, i, 28. † Ibid. ‡ Genesis, i, 29.

many other pieces of cruelty and wickedness, even in social life.

In regard to the earth, the blessing upon it at the creation was, *Let the earth bring forth grass, and herb yielding seed, and the fruit tree yielding fruit after his kind, whose seed is in itself upon the earth*:* After the flood it is, *while the earth remaineth, seed time and harvest shall not cease. In the beginning, the lights in the firmament were appointed to divide the day from the night; and to be for seasons, and for days and years †:* The new blessing is, *cold and heat, and summer and winter, and day and night shall not cease.*

From these circumstances thus laid together, it has been ingeniously concluded ‡, that the old curse, denounced against the earth at the fall ||, was finished and compleated at the deluge. When the whole race of men, eight only excepted, were destroyed, the serpent having sufficiently bruised the heel of the woman's seed, the time came to relieve the world, with respect to this part of the curse so fully executed; and, therefore, a blessing was *once more* pronounced upon the earth; and a covenant of temporal prosperity confirmed to Noah, and by him to all mankind; making good the prophecy of his father at the time of his birth, *This same shall comfort us concerning our work and toil of our hands, because of the ground which the Lord hath cursed* §.

Objections to this theory have been raised in great abundance, particularly to this application of the

* Genesis, i, 2. † Genesis, i, 14. ‡ Dr. Sherlock, Disc. iv. on Prophecy. || Genesis, iii, 17, 18. § Genesis, v, 29.

words

words last quoted. It has been said, that when Lamech called his son's name Noah, which signifies *Rest*, he designed no more than to declare he should be *an husbandman*, and find out the use of wine. To this it has been answered, that though we are told, *Noah began to be an husbandman. and planted a vineyard*, he cannot yet, in reason, be supposed to have been the first *husbandman*, nor the first that invented wine; seeing his birth was one thousand and fifty-six years after the creation; and the earth was all that time offering its productions for supplies to men's necessity, who would not fail to improve their advantages as wants pressed upon them. And even supposing Noah was the first inventer of wine, how, it has been asked, does that invention take off the curse from the earth? or bring much consolation to mankind, under the labours of life? when only a very small number of those who toil in tilling the ground, are any way benefited by that discovery. The only rational interpretation of Lamech's speech on the birth of Noah is, therefore, thought to be this, that he, being a prophet, foresaw that God would, in his son's time, and out of a particular regard to his righteousness, remove the curse from the earth; and bestow all those blessings upon him, and his race, of which the world had been deprived since the fall *.

WHILE some have insisted, on the one hand, that the flood, by its effects, must necessarily have injured the fertility of the earth, and that the fruits of it could not be so nutritive as they had been, before the salt water of the sea had spoiled the soil; it has been ar-

* Revel. exam. Differt. xi, p. 134.

gued

gued by many, on the other hand, that, on the footing of the clearest hypothesis, the curse must have been taken off the earth, by the very nature of the flood itself. It is evident, say they, that this effect must have been necessarily produced, at that time, by the rich saturation of the earth with rain and salts, together with the constant supply of moisture from the clouds ever since. To these they also add, the infinite shoals of fish, all the carcases of animals, and the immense treasures of shells and marle that were opened up, and spread on the ground by the waters, which must have left a vast fund of fatness, on the heights, to be gradually washed down thence upon the lower lands, by every shower from heaven.

If this doctrine be admitted as probable or certain, the opinion of those must fall to the ground, who assert that it was in consequence of the injury done to the earth, by the universal desolation, and of its incapacity to produce as much nourishment as it did before, that the grant of animal food was made to man for his more comfortable subsistence. We must rather search for the reason of this indulgence in the wisdom and bounty of the great creator and Lord of all.

This gracious covenant being settled, as to all these articles, *a sign* or *token* of it was given, on the part of God, to insure its unchangeableness and perpetuity: *This is the token of the covenant, which I make between me and thee, and every living creature, for everlasting generations: I do set my* BOW *in the cloud; and it shall be for a token of a covenant between me and the earth; and I will look upon it, that I may remember the covenant*

covenant which I have established between me and all flesh. This is the manner of all the divine dispensations: Whenever any special manifestation from heaven has taken place, there has been always some memorial, or seal of ratification, annexed to it. Circumcision was a mark of the covenant made with Abraham; the passover commemorated deliverance from the Egyptian servitude; both serving as sacraments, or signs, of the *Jewish* covenant, as baptism and the Lord's supper do of the *Christian*; and the rain-bow was a token of the promise, *that the waters should no more become a flood to destroy all flesh, that was upon the earth.*

I DO *set my BOW in the cloud, that I may remember the covenant which I have established between me and all flesh,* is one of those expressions which may be easily qualified, by the notions which Moses gives us of the divinity, in other places of his writings. God stood in no need of this bow to be his remembrancer of the covenant, and, therefore, intended that its establishment in the cloud should serve to strengthen Noah's faith, and that of his descendants in all future ages.

IT has given great displeasure to some, that the imagination, there was never any rain-bow at all before the flood, should ever have been entertained. They say it is a mistake grounded on the grossest inattention; that the suppression of this phænomenon could not have been effected, without repeated miracles, and the constant interposition of the Almighty; seeing the rain-bow necessarily arises out of sun-shine and rain at the ſame time, and muſt be ſeen by every ſpectator ſtanding between the two objects, with his face turned towards the rain, and at ſuch a diſtance, as to let the ſun's reflected rays fall upon his eye, from an innumerable quantity of ſmall globular drops of falling water; which we cannot but ſuppoſe happened before the flood, and would, of courſe, form the rain-bow, the nature of which they thus more minutely deſcribe:

THE diſtinction of rain-bows is, the *interior* and *exterior*. The firſt is produced by the rays of the ſun, falling on an infinite number of drops of water, undergoing there two refractions, and a reflection between two, and from thence returning, coloured, to our eyes. The other is cauſed by the rays of the ſame orb, terminating on a vaſt collection of like drops, undergoing there two refractions and two reflections between two, and in the ſame manner returning to our eyes, coloured, as before. Of theſe facts, demonſtrations have been given, by very ſimple experiments, eſpecially by a torch, in a very dark night, and a watering-can, directly oppoſite, and at a certain diſtance, diſcharging a great quantity of water through its various perforations. The light of the former, oppoſed to the latter, paſſes through two reflections, and two refractions, and forms the exact appearance of the rain-bow.

HENCE, their concluſion is, that the rain-bow, a thing already in nature, was choſen for a ſign, a token or memorial of the covenant, which was then

made,

made between God and Noah; in the same manner as the Sabbath was declared to be the sign, or memorial of the covenant made between him and the sons of Jacob, on their deliverance from their bondage, though it had been appointed to be kept holy at the creation of the world, and in remembrance of that great work *.

This is the full force and extent of the argument; but as it hath nothing to support it in scripture, it's solidity may be justly suspected. The opinion of an eminent divine is, that the first curse was, in a great measure, executed by with-holding rain from the earth, during the whole period before the flood, or a considerable part of it, as well it might be, if the Almighty pleased †. In that case there could be no such phœnomenon, as has been represented. But admitting the existence of rain during that period, grounds in nature may still be enquired for, to support the foregoing reasoning; unless we assert the palpable untruth, that every disposition of the air, or every *garment*, or texture, of a cloud is adapted to produce a rain-bow. If other natural causes, with their motions and operations, depend upon the final, as the divine philosophy teaches us, they who acknowledge the scripture, have no room to think that either the clouds or the air had that peculiar quality and arrangement before the flood, which is requisite to the production of the rain-bow, and they now have; seeing this wonderful effect had no such use or

* M. Saurin, Disc. ix, p. 128.

† Revel. exam. Dissert. xi. p. 135.

 end

end then, as it hath had ever ſince. Having been appointed by God, to be a witneſs of his covenant with the new world; a meſſenger to ſecure mankind from deſtruction by deluges; if it had appeared before the flood, the ſight of it after would have been but a ſlender comfort to Noah and his trembling poſterity; whoſe fear, leſt the like inundation might happen again, was by much, too great to be removed by any common or uſual ſign. The ancient poets repreſented Iſis as the daughter of wonder, and ſent by Jupiter's peremptory command to Neptune, not to ſwell the waters, we may ſuppoſe, to annoy the world.

THE *bow ſhall be ſeen in the cloud*; not always, but often enough to remind men of the promiſe, and excite their belief of it, that the earth ſhall not be drowned again, though the clouds ſhould have thickened as if they threatened it. It is very remarkable that the rain-bow is a natural ſign that the clouds are beginning to diſperſe, and there will not be much rain after its appearance. For it is never formed in a thick, but in a thin, and almoſt pellucid cloud; ſo that glowing after ſhowers, which come from thick embodied clouds, it is a token that they are almoſt exhauſted. It is a token alſo that the great and good God of nature will never thicken them to ſuch a degree again, as to bring an univerſal flood upon the earth. Perhaps too, we may ſee in the mixed colours of the rain-bow, *the deſtruction of the old world by water, and the future conſumption of the preſent by fire*, whoſe flaming brightneſs prevails in the watery maſs *.

* Biſhop Patrick, in Loco.

WE

We ought, therefore, to incline to their side, who are of opinion, that there was no rain-bow before the flood, and that it is purely the effect of divine power on the disposition of the elements, to serve as the most striking signal, and everlasting memorial of the covenant God made with Noah, and all the succeeding generations of mankind. In this light its admirable form and composition force us to view it: *Look upon the rain-bow, and praise him that made it, very beautiful it is in the brightness thereof. It compasseth the heaven about with a glorious circle, and the hands of the most high hath bended it* *.

After this magnificent object, another point strikes us a few verses downward; *and surely your blood of your lives will I require; at the hand of every beast will I require it; and at the hand of every man, at the hand of every man's brother, will I require the life of man. Whoso sheddeth man's blood, by man shall his blood be shed.* That is to say, the beast that killeth a man shall be put to death; which is observed as a law, in these realms, to this day, in obedience to the *Noahic* statute, where ravenous beasts, brought from foreign parts, are first offered to the *King*, and, when refused, are put to death by the magistrate: And, in like manner, every human murderer, is put to death *by man*; a particular term in scripture for the judge, or civil officer. Here then courts of trial are divinely authorized; not only for the punishment of murder, but likewise, by parity of reason, of any other great offences, that may affect life, its possessi-

* Ecclus. Chap. xliii. ver. 11, 12.

ons,

ons, and enjoyments. And let those who are concerned, in raising rebellious against such a power, seriously consider if they be consulting the welfare of the state, whatever may be the limits and the claims of its jurisdiction, so long as the ends of religious and political government are pursued.

Here we have a rude draught of the institution of magistracy, of which, hitherto, we have not seen the smallest traces or intimations in the sacred history. On the contrary, it appears from the case of Cain, who was certainly a murderer, and of Lamech, in whose family there were the greatest disorders, that the most heinous of all crimes were left to be punished, as God, in his providence, should see fit.

Now, if murder, before the flood, was thus plainly exempted from punishment, judicially, much more would lesser instances of injury be, such as, probably, Lamech's was. And one of the reasons of this, no doubt, was, that there were no distinct states, nor regular governments among the antediluvians; who, spreading over the face of the earth, and removing farther from the place of public worship, had lost a sense of God, and lived in a disorderly manner, exercising rapine and outrage, as far as they had power, and were instigated by lust, avarice, and revenge, *till the* whole *earth was filled with violence.* An image, very instructive of distant provinces, which merely through their elongation from the mother country, attempt a revolt, and make a pretence of liberty a

cloak

cloak for all the licentiousness of which they are pleased to be guilty.

SUCH enormities and confusions, we cannot but be sensible, could not have passed unpunished under laws, and rulers, armed with power and authority. But without them, the old world must necessarily have been, as all States without policy are, and that of the Israelites is represented, *when there was no King in Israel, and every man did that which was right in his own eyes* *. The possibility of such a state we can conceive, and the shocking disorders that attend it.

IF it should be a question, what design the Almighty could propose, in leaving mankind, for some time after the world began, in this state of disunion and injustice; the answer may very freely be given, that it certainly was not to lead them into wickedness; but teach them, by experience, the necessity of laws and governors; and the reasonableness of submitting to them: Though even the contrary supposition, that magistracy, in some form or another, was instituted at the beginning, should be admitted; yet the licentiousness of the times had universally shaken off the yoke, and in no instance been obedient to it. And, therefore, the reason, that God did permanently establish it, after the flood, seems to be, that men would bear its restraint, when its utility and importance had fully demonstrated the want of it.

NOTHING more remains for remarks, within the compass of these chapters, except Noah's curse pro-

* See the book of Judges.

nounced

nounced upon Canaan, the ſon of Ham; who, in violation of all filial reverence and duty, had ſported with his aged grand-father's folly and wretchedneſs. Whether Noah had invented wine or not, which is purely problematical, it is certain, that either through ignorance of its ſtrength, or the infirmities of old age, he was *drunken* with it, *and uncovered within his tent.* And, from the circumſtances of the ſtory, it is more probable that Canaan ſaw him firſt, than his father Ham; who, nevertheleſs, inſtead of reproving his ſon for his levity, *told his two brothers without.* They, namely, Shem and Japhet, obviated farther diſgrace. Upon which *Noah awoke from his wine, and* knowing *what his younger*, or little *ſon*, or Canaan his grandſon, *had done unto him*, and his father had encouraged and propagated, *he ſaid, curſed be Canaan; a ſervant of ſervants ſhall he be unto his brethren.* The expreſſion is not to be conſidered as a malevolent wiſh, or imprecation, but ſimply as a prediction of the future abject condition of Ham's poſterity; much leſs is it to be underſtood as affecting any thing but their temporal and outward circumſtances; as appears from the whole of Noah's diſcourſe; who, being divinely inſpired, declared the Almighty's counſels; either in regard to the ſlaughter of the *thirty* kings, and moſt of the inhabitants of the land which bore Canaan's name, by the Iſraelites deſcended from Shem, whoſe *God and Lord Noah bleſſed*; or in regard to the Egyptians, the race of that impious patriarch, who have literally been *ſervants of ſervants* for upwards of two thouſand years: Not to mention the colour to which moſt of the Africans have been condemned either through this curſe, or the effects of the climate they have

have been obliged to undergo. The lighteſt of theſe tokens of the divine diſpleaſure, may be a ſufficient warning againſt all undutifulneſs in children towards their parents, for ever.

DISSERTA-

DISSERTATION XV.

Of the Tower of Babel; and Confusion of Tongues.

GENESIS XI.

THE waters of the deluge had made such an impression upon the minds of Noah and his posterity, that they confined themselves to the highest places, and the least accessible to inundations. The mountains of Armenia, where the ark rested, and their environs, continued to be their residence. But about two hundred years after, when their fears were dissipated, they descended into the vallies, and the low countries, and took possession of the plains of Chaldea, or Babylonia. Moses says, *as they journeyed from the east, they found a plain in the land of Shinar, and they dwelt there.* Now Shinar is Chaldea; where Babylon, according to the Septuagint, stood *. It is expressly said that the beginning of Nimrod's kingdom was Babel, in the land of

* Zech. v. 11. Sept. Ὀικοδομῆσαι αὐτῷ οἰκίαν ἐν γῇ Βαβυλῶνος. Heb. שנער

of Shinar*. And Daniel relates, that Nebuchadnezzar *king of Babylon came to Jerusalem, and carried part of the vessels of the house of God, into the land of Shinar* †. Shinar then is the country in which the city of Babylon was built, or, as is said, all those western territories which lie between the Tigris and the mountains of Armenia ‡.

The objections made to this account are; that the journeying of mankind from the place where the ark rested, to Shinaar, is said to be from the East; but a journey from the Gordian Hills to Shinaar, would be from the North; and that Xisuthrus, as the Chaldæans pronounce the word, or Fohi, according to the Chinese, was Noah; it must be more probable, that the first population, after the flood, was from the mountains near Bactria, which lie between Persia and the present dominions of the Great Mogul. To which the answers are; that Moses describes the situation of countries, from Arabia where he wrote; and the journey from Bactria to Shinaar is about 1200 miles, which it is not likely emigrants would travel, who might settle in better territories, nearer home.

Till this descent, from whatever place it was, the whole inhabitants of the earth were, undoubtedly, united in one compact body. For though in the chapter going before, Moses represents the posterity of Japheth as overspreading and possessing *the isles of the Gentiles*, that is, of Greece and Asia which lie in the Archipelago; the sons of Ham as going down into

* Gen. x, 10. † Daniel, i, 1, 2. ‡ Bocharti Phaleg. L. 1, Cap. v.

into Egypt, and the countries around, known to this day, in the learned languages, by ſeveral of their names; and the iſſue of Shem as occupying the Eaſt, or the lands of Meſopotamia and Padan-aram, the native ſoils, in future ages, of the renowned patriarchs; and ſays that *by theſe were the nations divided in the earth after the flood*; the whole of this account is to be underſtood of the genealogy of the nations after the diſperſion, of which we are now to treat, as appears undeniably from the words that follow, *every one after their tongues, and after their families*; for till this *journey from the Eaſt, into the plain in the land of Shinar, the whole earth was of one language, and of one ſpeech.* This circumſtance was neceſſary; ſeeing Noah and his ſons, had but one language at the flood, and were alive when this diſperſion of mankind over the face of the earth happened. And, indeed, how a diverſity of tongues could, in ſo ſhort a time after, take place, is not eaſily to be conceived.

This very difficulty occurring to Moſes, that the remoteſt generations might be acquainted with the circumſtances of ſo important an event, he inſerts the ſection in this chapter from the beginning to the tenth verſe, where he gives a full and ſatisfactory relation of the matter, with the cauſes and conſequences of it.

He informs us that the whole earth thus embodied, ſo to ſpeak, and uſing one language, moving together, we may ſuppoſe, by a general public act, or mutual conſent travelled towards the Weſt, and finding a ſpacious fruitful plain in the land of Shinar, determined to ſettle there, and to build a city and a

tower

tower, *reaching unto heaven.* The materials, he tells us, were *brick and mortar.* Of the exact dimensions of the tower, notwithstanding the disquisitions of learned men for their own amusement, the holy scripture says nothing. The greatest extravagance of thought has been indulged on this subject. With regard to the city itself, built by the sons of Noah, oriental authors say, that it was three hundred and thirteen fathoms in length, and one hundred and fifty one in breadth; that the walls of it were five thousand five hundred and thirty three fathoms high, and thirty three broad; and the tower ten thousand fathoms, or twelve miles high; dimensions the most disproportionate to each other, and the most needless that can be conceived. By the testimony of eye-witnesses, who examined the remains of the tower carefully, our belief is solicited that it was four miles high; but this not being sufficient to excite our wonder, a certain writer raises the height to no less than five thousand miles: Shameful extravagancies indeed. The only account we can depend upon, as to the dimensions of this tower, supposing it to be the same with that which stood in the midst of the temple of Belus, afterwards built round it by Nebuchadnezzar, must be taken from profane authors. Herodotus says, it was a furlong in length, and as much in breadth; and Strabo determines the height to have been a furlong, or the eighth part of a mile, or six hundred and sixty foot, which is itself prodigious; as thereby it appears to have exceeded the greatest of the Egyptian pyramids in height one hundred seventy nine foot, though it fell short of it at the base by thirty three. It consisted of eight square towers one above another, gradually decreasing in breadth; which,

which, with the winding of the ſtairs from the top to the bottom on the outſide, gave it the reſemblance of a pyramid. This antique form, joined to the extraordinary height of the ſtructure, eaſily induces us to believe it to be the ſame tower mentioned by Moſes; the forementioned monarch of Babylon finiſhing the deſign, which the ſons of Noah were obliged, by the confuſion of tongues, to leave unexecuted.

The ruins of this celebrated antiquity are now ſo, defaced, that the people of that very country are not certain of their ſituation; and this has occaſioned travellers to differ concerning it. Moſt of them, however, led by a tradition of the inhabitants, have judged a place about eight or nine miles to the weſt, or north-weſt of Baghdad, a city well known, to be the tower of Babel; where there is a building conſpicuous at a vaſt diſtance, ſtanding by itſelf in a wide plain between the Euphrates and Tigris, of ſun-burnt bricks, each a foot ſquare and ſix inches thick as ſome ſay; though there are great variations on this circumſtance, as alſo on the manner in which thoſe bricks are ranged *.

We may here, by way of apology for *ancient* oriental tales, obſerve, that in old times there ſeems to have been the profoundeſt ignorance of true philoſophy, which teaches us that the air, neceſſary to life, extends to no great diſtance above the ſurface of our globe, and falls infinitely ſhort of ſome of the extravagant altitudes aſcribed to that famous tower. Even Moſes himſelf, David, and other writers of the old

* Univ. Hiſt. Vol. 1, P. 322, text and notes.

teſtament,

testament, appear to have been in the same situation, in regard to the rain that fell from the clouds, concerning which; as it was invisibly prepared, they constantly speak, as if it was distilled from reservoirs, or fountains of water, treasured up above *. Nor is this any imperfection in the holy writings, which were never designed to instruct us in much more than what is intimately connected with our present duty and eternal welfare.

The top of the tower having been designed *to reach up to heaven*, is an expression plainly hyperbolical, and signifies no more than that the builders intended it should be a great height; as appears from many other passages of scripture, particularly from what is said of the cities of the *Anakims*, that *they were great and fenced up to heaven*; † and of the *waves of the sea, that they mount up to heaven* ‡; that is, rise and swell, by the violence of the tempest, till they mix, as it were, with the clouds, though their real elevation is very inconsiderable.

The intention of the builders was to make themselves *a name*, and to prevent their being *scattered abroad on the face of the whole earth*. The Hebrew word, here translated *a name*, may signify, figuratively, eminence and distinction; whence some have imagined, that the tower was designed as a mark, or sign, exposed to view, by which the inhabitants of the city were to direct themselves, by keeping it in sight when they were at a distance, lest they should wander away into uncultivated lands, from their own habitations. But

* Gen. i. Psalm cxlviii. † Deut. ix. 1. ‡ Ps. cvii. 26.

this

this is a childish conceit, as it is extremely easy for men, who have travelled any road a few times before, to resume and know it with great certainty again, without any such distant marks to assist them. It is, therefore, much more reasonable to suppose, that by *a name* *, the leaders of that people, of whom Nimrod was the chief, meant the same thing, that the word signifies in the other places of scripture †, a monument or token of superiority, to all succeeding generations, that they were the true original governors, to whom mankind owed subjection; and that other captains, who, it might be foreseen, should start up, and break the body, by erecting separate communities, were rebels and invaders. In short, that great building, and city about it, seems to have been a piece of state-policy, to keep the world together, perhaps under one head, at least under the successors of the present chiefs; and, by its strength, calculated to repulse bodies of foreigners that might attempt to break in upon them ‡.

To defeat their design, we are told *the Lord came down to see the city and the tower which the children of men builded: And said, behold, the people is one, and they have all one language; and this they begin to do: And now nothing will be restrained from them which they have ima-*

* Heb. שם † 2 Sam. vii. 23. viii. 13. 1 Kings v. 3.

‡ The Vulgate gives the fourth verse of the chapter a turn, which strongly favours the opinion, that the builders of Babel fell on that project, when they had reason, we know not from what cause, to apprehend that they would be scattered abroad: *Et dixerunt; Venite, faciamus nobis civitatem et turrim, cujus culmen pertingat ad cælum: et celebremus nomen nostrum* ANTEQUAM *dividamur in universas terras.* Vide Vulg. Edit.

gined

gined to do: Go to then, let us go down, and confound their language, that they may not underſtand one another's ſpeech. This repreſentation of the Almighty, however true in the purpoſe and conſequence of it, is, nevertheleſs, to be underſtood by way of accommodation to our conceptions; it teaches us that, by the effects, God made it appear, that he obſerved their motions, and knew their intentions. A manner of ſpeaking very common, and in our preſent embodied ſtate abſolutely neceſſary, to deſcribe the divine actions. And perhaps with reference to a myſterious doctrine, not to be expunged, Jehovah is introduced ſaying, *let us go down and confound their language*; though of the divine ſubſtance, and the influence of an inviſible agency on human actions, no account is given; nor could it be comprehended by us.

Of this council of God, mentioned on a variety of occaſions by the ſacred writers, it is our unqueſtionable duty to make the moſt devout and reſpectful uſe, till *that which is in part is done away, and that which is perfect is come*; when *we ſhall* no more *ſee as through a glaſs darkly, but face to face.**

When the project of the fooliſh builders was fruſtrated, into how many branches their language was divided, it is vain for us to enquire. The Greek fathers make the tongues formed at Babel, *ſeventy-two*†;

* 1 Cor. xiii. 12. † δύο καὶ ἑβδομήκοντα. Clemen. Alexand. Strom. L. 1. p. 338.

and the Latin fathers have followed them*. *Therefore is the name of the place called Babel, or Confusion, because the Lord did there confound the language of all the earth, and they were scattered abroad upon the face of all the earth, and left off to build the city.* The colonies, or nations, eſtabliſhed upon this diſperſion, are ſaid to have been the ſame in number, with the dialects that were immediately ſpoken †.

CONCERNING the firſt language there have been many enquiries and diſputes. St. Auguſtine, quoted below, in the eleventh chapter, of the ſixteenth book of his City of God, determines in favour of the Hebrew; and, by very ingenious arguments, makes his concluſion appear reaſonable. Stript of all additions, which it hath received in ſucceſſive ages, and had even in the days of Moſes, it bears undeniably evident marks of a very ancient language. And yet, whatever the number of languages might be after the confuſion, many of them, for ſome time, could not differ much from one another. For Abraham, an Hebrew, lived amongſt the Chaldeans, travelled amongſt the Canaanites, ſojourned with the Philiſtines, and lived ſome time in Egypt, during which peregrinations we do not find that he had any remarkable difficulty in converſing with them. Indeed after the ſtability of ſpeech was loſt, and language varied in time from itſelf, the tongues of different nations would, in a few ages, become vaſtly different, and unintelligible to one another. Thus, in the time of Joſeph, when

* Ex illis igitur tribus hominibus Noë filiis ſeptuaginta duæ linguæ.

† Totidemque gentes, quæ inſulas impleverunt. St. Aug. De Civ. Dei. L. xvi. p. 986.

when his brethren came to buy corn in Egypt, the Hebrew and Egyptian tongues were ſo unlike, that they uſed an interpreter in their converſation. Though many ancient languages, ſpoken by nations very remote from one another, retain ſtriking ſimilarities to each other, to this very day.

ANOTHER explanation has been given of this wonderful event. It has been imagined more natural and reaſonable to conceive, that the confuſion of tongues aroſe at firſt from ſmall beginnings, increaſed gradually, for many years, when the three families of the ſons of Shem, of Ham, and of Japhet lived together, and in time grew to ſuch an height, as to ſcatter mankind, of courſe, over the face of the earth. And the advice of the poet to the writers of his time, is given by this author to the readers even of the inſpired books, *never to let a God interfere, unleſs a difficulty worthy a god's unravelling ſhould happen**. But this thought ſeems not altogether to coincide with the Moſaic relation; and when the inſpired writer, in very pompous language, makes God interfere, we may ſafely believe that he did, and performed a miracle worthy of his wiſdom.

THE learned judge, mentioned in a foregoing diſſertation, calls this confuſion of languages, a diſmal cataſtrophe, and terrible convulſion. Here his Lordſhip is orthodox for once. But after a brief deſcription of it in the words of Moſes, what immediately follows? *By confounding the language of men, and ſcattering them abroad upon the face of all the earth, they were*

* Shuckford's Con. Vol. i. p. 146.

rendered savages. And without an immediate change of constitution, the builders of Babel could not possibly have subsisted in the burning region of Guinea, nor in the frozen region of Lapland. But who ever imagined that those dispersing communities, marched directly to the extremities of our continent? Elegant words have no weight in an argument, and impossibilities are incredible. It must have required ages to transport them so far, in which time, it is well known, the constitution of the body would be sufficiently fitted for the climate where they ultimately settled. The reason his Lordship gives, that mankind were thrown into a savage state by the confusion of tongues, is, that if it had not been so, *the colonies planted in America, the South Sea islands, and the Terra Australis-Incognita, must have been highly polished; because being at the greatest distance, they probably were the latest. And yet these and other remote people, the Mexicans and Peruvians excepted, remain to this day in the original savage state of hunting and fishing**. But will not his Lordship acknowledge; nay he does acknowledge, when he says, in the very same *sketch*, *men never desert their connections nor their country without necessity*, that it is always the poorest and most necessitous, and, therefore, in general, the most illiterate, that leave their *native soils*; consequently, that an estimate made of the perfection of the arts and sciences, by the original colonies of mankind, and always preserved, in a great measure, among them, from the condition of remote nations, must be as unfair, as to infer that *England* and the other kingdoms of *Europe* were in *a savage state*, when the vast swarms of ignorant *American* adventurers left them.

* Lord Kaims's Sketches of the History of Man. Sketch 1. passim.

WE

We shall now proceed to assign some reasons for such a singular interposition of providence. In the case of the building of Babel, and keeping mankind all together, we cannot but see how worthy it was of God, and necessary for the ends of his wisdom and goodness, to prevent the mischievous effects of the design. By this scheme of the builders a great part of the earth must, for a long time, have been uninhabited, uncultivated and over-run with briers and thorns, with woods and thickets, and wild beasts, which, according to ancient authors, did actually infest all neglected countries, and exercised the industry and valor of the primitive heroes to subdue, especially the latter. It was killing wild beasts, which early troubled the earth, and annoyed mankind, that gained Nimrod superiority and immortal renown in Asia, in the same manner as Hercules afterwards in Europe. *Nimrod*, says Moses, *was a mighty hunter before the Lord*, which Hebraism signifies the greatest and most eminent *hunter* that then was. Besides,

The bad effects which this project would have had upon the minds of men, and their morals and religion, was, probably, another reason, and the chief, why the Almighty strangely interposed to crush it as soon as it was formed. It would have enslaved, oppressed, and rendered wretched all mankind, except one, or a few, who exercised the tyranny over them. As to morals, though under any constitution, it cannot be denied, men may grow very wicked, and have been seen to do so under the best; yet it is absolutely certain, that tyranny and despotic power is the readiest and surest way, to deprive men of the use of understanding and and conscience; which opens a course for vice, superstition

perſtition and idolatry, eſpecially under violent and atheiſtical governors. Had the world, therefore, continued long in one body, under the uncontrouled dominion of ſuch, mankind muſt have fallen into the deepeſt corruptions, and the baſeſt ſervility, and ſtocked the earth again with a profane, and, at the ſame time, with a mean ſpirited race of mortals.

But when the deſign of the city and tower was baffled, by ſuch a confuſion of tongues, that the *men could not underſtand one another's ſpeech*, they were neceſſarily *ſcattered abroad*, *after their families*, *after their tongues*, *in their lands*, and, in ſucceſſion of time, through all *the nations of the earth*. Thus the contagion of wickedneſs had, for ſome generations at leaſt, new barriers placed againſt it; evil example was confined, and could not well ſtretch it's influence beyond the limits of one country, before commerce was eſtabliſhed; nor could wicked deſigns be any longer carried on with univerſal conſent, by a multitude of little colonies, ſeparated by the natural boundaries of mountains, rivers, deſerts, ſeas, and whoſe intercourſe was farther impeded every age by a variety of languages, growing ſtill more unintelligible to ſtrangers.

Thus did the wiſe and mighty ruler of the world oppoſe his ſcheme of providence to the folly and weakneſs of men, ſtill dealing with them like reaſonable creatures. It is probable, that when the confuſion of tongues, and the diviſion and removal of mankind into diſtant countries took place, their ſeveral deſtinations were fixed by God, and ſignified to them, at his command, by the mouth of Noah, who was ſtill alive, or of ſome other holy man among them, to prevent

vent ſtrife, and, perhaps, as was moſt ſuitable to their genius and diſpoſitions. That this was really the caſe, ſome have thought very clear from the words of Moſes * to the Iſraelites, to excite them to religious gratitude and ſervice; *Remember the days of old, conſider the years of many generations: Aſk thy father, and he will ſhew thee, thy elders, and they will tell thee. When the moſt high divided to the nations their inheritance, when he ſeparated the ſons of Adam, he ſet the bounds of the people according to the number of the children of Iſrael.* Others have thought that theſe words refer only to the ſubſequent diſtribution of *Canaan*; though the beſt commentators apply them to the diviſion of the earth among the ſons of *Noah*.

A MATTER quite oppoſite to that near the cloſe of the foregoing diſſertation, ſhall alſo bring us to the end of this. As one great cauſe of profaneſs in the earth before the flood, ſeems to have been the want of magiſtracy, ſo here again, after that period, we ſee men ſoon falling into the other extreme, and nearly as pernicious to virtue and human happineſs. We ſee a few aſſuming, and the many tamely ſubmitting to, an arbitrary juriſdiction, not only in the puniſhment of crimes, but likewiſe, we may well ſuppoſe, over men's perſons and wills, and all that they had; inſomuch that a divine interpoſition was neceſſary to diſappoint and fruſtrate it. Hence, if we may be permitted to judge, a regular government, *for a terror to evil-doers, and for encouraging* and rewarding *thoſe who do well*, muſt be the happy *medium* between anarchy and licentiouſneſs on the one hand, and deſpotiſm and

* Deut. xxii. 7.

ſlavery

ſlavery on the other. This, every ſtate ſo formed, and ſupported, demonſtrates; and, therefore, by all true friends of ſociety, while deſpotiſm and ſlavery are are to be hated and oppoſed, anarchy and licentiouſneſs ſhould never be abetted; but the dignity and authority of law and order regarded as inviolable. Righteous *powers are ordained of God: And whoever reſiſteth this ordinance, ſhall receive to themſelves damnation* *.

* Rom. xiii.

DISSERTATION XVI.

Of the first Colonies, or Nations, after the Flood.

GENESIS X. XI.

THE labours of the good Lord Bishop of *Bath and Wells*, of the learned Bishop of *Ely*, and of the critical *Mr. Pool*; on this subject, deserve the largest panegyric; and the commentaries of *M. Le Clerc*, and *Corn. a Lapide*, are far from being without use; and yet neither they, nor the rest of the celebrated writers, in the same tract, appear to have turned their attention sufficiently, to the difficulty arising from the genealogical lists contained in these two chapters. This difficulty results, chiefly, from the order in which the chapters are arrainged; the first being placed before the dispersion of mankind from the plain of Shinar, and in the next the descent of families added to the relation of that extraordinary occurrence.

INDEED it has been said, not without the shew of truth, that curiosity in this matter is needless and frivolous. But it ought to have been remembered, that,

that, without the knowledge of those descents from the sons of Noah, the fulfilment of the prophetic predictions and blessings concerning them could not be traced. How, for instance, could we know whether Japhet dwelt in the tents of Shem, or Canaan was a servant of servants *, what were the ships of Chittim †, or who Gog was ‡, if we remained ignorant where they were placed?

Now the solution of the difficulty seems to be this, that Moses in the tenth chapter, meant to describe the general diffusion of mankind over the earth, after they were scattered abroad, and, in the eleventh, to return again to the race of Shem, from whom he deduces the Hebrews. And this, by the way, may convince those who have indulged contrary thoughts, that, instead of writing the pedigree of his own nation, the sacred historian, till he comes down to a particular æra, has given a compleat and authentic account of all the families of the earth, from their common origin.

Upon this principle, therefore, we ground the following explanation of the passages under view. The sons of Japheth, of whom Moses first speaks, though he was the youngest of Noah's family, were, Gomer, mentioned by Ezekiel §, of whom, perhaps, came the Cimbrians, Josephus says, the Galatians ||: Of Magog, the Scythians: Of Madai, the Medes: Of Javan, the Greeks: Of Tubal, the Iberians: Of Mesech, the

* Gen. ix, 27. † Numb. xxiv, 24. ‡ Ezek. xxxix, 1.

§ Ezek. xxxviii, 6. See all the Prophets for the following account.

|| Joseph. Antiq. L. 1, cap. 7, whom also see.

Muscovites,

Muſcovites, or the Cappadocians: Of Tiras, the Thracians.

Of the ſons of Gomer, Aſhkenaz, and Riphath, and Togarmah, perhaps came the Germans, Paphlagonians, and Phrygians.

From the ſons of Javan, Eliſhah, and Tarſhiſh, Kittim, and Dodanim, it is ſaid came the Æolians, Cilicians, Cyprians, and the Epirotes.

By *theſe were the iſles of the Gentiles divided*, that is, not only ſuch places as were encompaſſed; but alſo to which they came, by ſea.

And the ſons of Ham, Cuſh, and Mizraim, and Phut, and Canaan. Hence came the Aſiatic Ethiopians, the Egyptians, Lybians, and Canaanites.

Cush begat the fathers of the Sabeans, and of the people who poſſeſſed Arabia, and the adjacent countries; and Nimrod mentioned before, *the beginning of* whoſe *kingdom was Babel, and Erech, and Accad, and Calneh, in the land of Shinar: And from that land he went forth into Aſſyria* *, *and builded Nineveh, and the city Rehoboth, and Calah, and Reſen.*

And *Mizraim begat Ludim, and Anamim, and Lehabim, and Naphtuhim*; denoting probably ſeveral nations in Africa; *and Pathruſim, and Caſluhim, and Caphtorim*, who carried the Philiſtines from the territories of Mizraim into the land of Canaan.

* So the Hebrew is to be read in this place.

And

AND *Canaan begat Sidon*, and the fathers of *the Hittites, of the Jebusites, the Emorites, and the Girgasites,* of *the Hivites, and the Arkites, and the Sinites, the Arvadites, and the Zemarites, and the Hamathites:* In short, of all the people from Sidon, on the side of Gerar and Gaza, westward, to Sodom, and Gomorrah, and Admah, and Zeboim, even to Lashah, on the east; and of *the families of the Canaanites that were afterwards spread abroad.*

THE *Children of* SHEM, were, Elam, from whom came the Elamites or Persians; Ashur, the Assyrians; Arphaxad, the Chaldees; Lud, the Lydians; and Aram, the Aramites, or Syrians.

THE children of Aram, were Uz, Job's country; and Hul, and Gether, and Mash, the seat of the Idumeans.

AND *Arphaxad begat Salah, and Salah begat Eber,* the father of the Hebrews, who had their name from him. Unto him was born Peleg, when the inhabitants of the earth were dispersed upon the confusion of languages, and his brother, whose name was Joktan. He was the father of thirteen who follow, whom Josephus places in the Indies, and from whose land, particularly that of Ophir, the ships of Solomon, that failed from Ezion-geber, brought gold. *Their dwelling* is said by Moses to be about *Sephar, a mount of the east.' These are the families of the sons of Noah, after their generations, in their nations; and by these were the nations divided in the earth after the flood.*

Now

Now these being their genealogies in the tenth chapter, the section at the end of the eleventh may be detached from the history of the dispersion, and supposed to contain the unbroken descent from Noah to Abraham, which appears to have been through ten generations, in like manner as ten had lived from Adam to Noah. Whence we see the life of man was much shortened after the flood, the time from that to the birth of Abraham being only about three hundred and seventy years, and from the creation to the flood, no less than one thousand six hundred and fifty-six *. The design plainly is to connect Terah, Abraham's father, with the line of SHEM, out of which was to spring the chosen family and people, and the messiah himself. This Terah, besides Abraham, was also the father of Nahor, and Haran, who begat Lot. *Haran died before his father, in the land of his nativity, in Ur of the Chaldees: And Abraham and Nahor took them wives: The name of Abraham's wife was Sarai*; who *had no child. And Terah took Abraham his son, and Lot the son of Haran his son's son, and Sarai his daughter in law, his son Abraham's wife, and went forth with them from Ur of the Chaldees, to go into the land of Canaan; and they came unto Haran, and dwelt there.*

* Indeed they married sooner.

DISSERTA-

DISSERTATION XVII.

Of Divine Appearances.

GENESIS XII.

THE next divine dispensation that was the most remarkable, after the deluge and the dispersion of mankind over the face of the earth, by the confusion of languages at Babel, is the calling of Abraham, distant from the first event four hundred and forty-five years, and from the second two hundred and five; as the chronology in a foregoing table shews. But before we proceed to consider the reason, the wisdom, and effects of this dispensation, it will be highly necessary and useful to review and explain those extraordinary appearances of God, so frequently mentioned in scripture, to good men, and whole bodies of them, when any new commands or revelations were delivered; that so readers, who either have not noticed them, or have not comprehended their meaning, may the better understand, and be duly affected by such singular occurrences.

It

It is true, we have often spoken of the *Schechinah*, a Rabbinical word used to signify glorious appearances, as in the cases of Adam, Cain, and Noah, with whom divine conferences, on different occasions, were held; but, besides the general narrative, there may be a more particular enquiry into several passages of scripture on this subject, and some instructions derived from hence, that may nearly concern us as christians.

Now, in the first verse of this chapter it is related that *the Lord had said unto Abraham*, or had appeared to him and said, *get thee out of thy country, and from thy kindred, and from thy father's house, unto a land that I will shew thee: And I will make of thee a great nation, and I will bless thee, and make thy name great; and in thee shall all the families of the earth be blessed. So Abraham departed, as the Lord had spoken unto him, and came into the land of Canaan. And the Lord appeared unto Abraham* there, *and said unto thy seed will I give this land: And he builded an altar unto the Lord, who appeared unto him.* This appearance in all probability, was in the same manner as that mentioned afterwards in the fifteenth chapter, of *the smoking furnace, and burning lamp*, which is only another expression for *the cloud and pillar of fire*, described, in other places, as signifying the divine presence. In a visible glory, perhaps, it likewise was; that *the Lord*, as it is in the seventeenth chapter, *appeared unto Abraham* again, *and said, I am the Almighty God; walk before me, and be thou perfect:* To Isaac also *, and certainly to Moses †, when in the wilderness of Midian, *he saw a bush as if it had been burning with fire, and the bush was not consumed.*

* Chap. xxvi. † Exod. iii.

These

These two emblems, for emblems of the divinity they only were, cloud and fire, usually accompanied each other, in those early religious administrations; or were separated, according as the circumstances of time and place rendered it necessary. We have an instance of this, with respect to the tabernacle, when it was set up in the wilderness of Sinai, where *the cloud of the Lord covered it, and the glory of the Lord filled it, and was within the tabernacle, on the mercy-seat* *, as the cloud was on the outside of it. And it is expressly said, that the appearance upon the tabernacle was, by day like a cloud; and like a fire, by night; suitable to the exigencies of the Israelites, who were to be guided and guarded by it.

So real and regular was the safe-guard and conduct, which this appearance afforded to the Israelites, that they never marched but when it moved, and where it led them. We are told that *when the cloud was taken up, from over the tabernacle, the children of Israel went onward in all their journeys: But if the cloud was not taken up, then they journeyed not till the day that it was taken up: For cloud and fire was on the tabernacle by day and night, in the sight of all the house of Israel, throughout all their journeys* †. And as the token of the divine presence thus directed them, *the Lord is said to go before them, and to lead them through the wilderness*, by this cloud ‡.

Not to mention the cloud and lightnings that covered the top of Sinai, when the law was promulgat-

* Exod. xiii, 21. Exod. xl, 34. Numb. x, 34. † Exod. xl, 36, 37, 38. Deut. viii, 15.

ed

ed, *out of which God answered Moses by a voice**, it is to be remarked, that from the glory of the Lord, or the bright shining within the tabernacle, which was always carried about, *the Lord spake unto Moses* every thing which he delivered to the children of Israel in the books of Exodus, Leviticus, and Numbers. *For when Moses went into the tabernacle of the congregation, to speak with God, then he heard the voice of one speaking unto him from off the mercy-seat, that was upon the ark of the testimony, from between the two cherubims; and he spake unto him* †; agreeable to the promise which God *had given him before, I will meet with thee, and I will commune with thee from above the mercy-seat, from between the two cherubims, which are upon the ark of the testimony, of all things which I will give thee in commandment, unto the children of Israel* ‡. *And when Moses and Aaron, Nadab and Abihu, and seventy of the elders of Israel went up unto the Lord, they saw the God of Israel, and there was under his feet, as it were a paved work of a sapphire stone, and as it were the body of heaven in its clearness* ||.

Likewise, when the kingdom of the chosen people was formed, many ages afterwards, the glory of the Lord, as upon a throne, had its residence in the holy place, in Solomon's Temple, after it had taken possession of the house at its consecration. The relation at full length, is thus given: *Then Solomon assembled the elders of Israel, and all the heads of the tribes, the chiefs of the fathers of the children of Israel, in Jerusalem, that they might bring up the ark of the covenant of the Lord, out of the city of David, which is Zion. And*

* Exod. xix, 19. † Numb. vii, 89. ‡ Exod. xxv, 22.
|| Exod. xxiv, 9, 10.

*all the men of Israel assembled themselves unto King Solomon, and all the elders of Israel came, and the Priests took up the ark. And they brought up the ark of the Lord, and the tabernacle of the congregation, and all the holy vessels that were in the tabernacle, unto his place, into the oracle of the house, to the most holy place, even under the wings of the cherubims. For the cherubims spread forth their wings over the place of the ark, and it came to pass when the priests came out of the holy place, that the cloud filled the house of the Lord: So that the priests could not stand to minister, because of the cloud: For the glory of the Lord had filled the house of the Lord.** For this reason, God is said in a multitude of passages, which all allude to this situation in the temple, *to dwell*, as the word Schechinah imports, or according to another translation, *to shine forth between the cherubims* †.

Isaiah saw this glory greatly increased by an host of angels, and heard the Lord speaking from a throne, high and lifted up, within the temple; as *Ezekiel* repeatedly did, with many awful circumstances, in the land of the Chaldees, during his ministry. After the Babylonish captivity, indeed, it is to be observed, that no where in the prophets, under the *second* temple, is there any mention made of the glory of the Lord in it, as there was in the first. The messengers then sent by God to his people received their commands in a different manner; and preparation was making, and men's desires were excited, for a new and more permanent dispensation.

* Kings viii, 1, &c. † Psal. lxxx, 1.

AND

And yet the new testament is not without affording us instances of such appearances. The glory of the Lord, or a bright cloud, *shone round about the shepherds in the fields of Bethlehem, and the angel of the Lord came upon them* *. *While Jesus spake to his disciples*, at the transfiguration, *behold, a bright cloud overshadowed them, and a voice came out of the cloud, which said, This is my beloved son, hear ye him* †. Saul saw the same appearance, when *suddenly there shined round about him a light from heaven* ‡. Peter also in the prison, who was raised up loaded with chains, *and the chains fell off from his hands* §. And St. John, in the plainest manner, and by the fullest manifestations, in many parts of his revelations.

Now were there no difficulties arising from the account itself of those appearances, we should have nothing more to do, than to believe and improve them. But, it will be asked, who, in such cases, was the person that appeared and spake? Was it that same existence whom we call, *God the father almighty, creator of heaven and earth*; or some other glorious being sent by him, and whose ministry led him to all those offices towards men? And what makes this question the more necessary is, that in several of the relations there is a seeming inconsistency and contradiction; especially where it is said, *The angel of the Lord appeared to Moses in a flame of fire out of the bush:* And yet it is said concerning the same person, *when the Lord saw that he turned aside to see that great sight, God called to him out of the midst of the bush; and said, I am the*

* St. Luke ii, 9. † St. Luke ix, 34, 35. ‡ Acts ix, 3. § Acts xii, 7.

God of thy father, the God of Abraham, of Isaac, and of Jacob; I AM, *that I* AM; *and thus shalt thou say unto the children of Israel; the Lord God of your fathers hath sent me unto you* *. Here it is plainly affirmed to have been an angel who appeared to Moses, and said, I am the Lord God; and yet it is certain that an angel of the Lord God is not the Lord God himself, whose angel he is. How then is this difficulty to be removed?

THAT it was not really God the father who thus manifested himself to the saints of old, is clear and incontestible from our Saviour's own words, who perfectly understood the whole affair of divine appearances. '*Ye have neither heard the voice of the father at any time, nor seen his shape* †. And again, *no man hath seen God at any time* ‡. And St. Paul says, *he is the invisible God, whom no man hath seen, or can see* ||. According to our Lord's rule then, when it is asserted, that the Lord, the most high God, appeared and spake to the Patriarchs and prophets, it is not to be understood, as if the appearance and voice, which they saw and heard, were, in fact, the form and shape, or voice of the Lord God himself; for *never, at any time, did they see his shape or hear his voice.*

AN eminent commentator ‡, indeed, thinks that the Greek word † translated, in some of those passages, *seen*, might as well be rendered *known*: But though this be a very good sense of it, and perfectly consistent with the doctrines of the gospel; yet it

* Exod. iii, 2. † St. John v, 37. ‡ St. John i, 18. || 1 Tim. vi, 16. § Grotius. † Εωρακε.

must

must fall far short of explaining all the phrases in the old and new testament, which represent God as absolutely *invisible*, *dwelling in light inaccessible*, *to which no mortal eye can approach*; and, therefore, the difficulty remains unobviated by this exposition.

One solution seems to be this; that in those divine splendors, or the Shechinah, God himself was present in some peculiar manner, attended with angels, as his ministers. Though by his immensity he is every where; yet by appearances stupendously glorious, he manifested his special approach to men, and held familiar intercourse with them by the mediation of his messengers, who spake in his name, and by his authority. Hence when they declared *I am the Lord God*; *I am the Almighty God*; I AM *that* I AM *; this was only true of God, who was present in the Schechinah, whom those blessed spirits personated, and in whose service they were employed.

In confirmation of this doctrine, let it be considered, that the scripture expressly says, it was an angel from the Lord who spake, when the Lord himself is said to speak. We read for instance, *the angel found Hagar, and said unto her, I will multiply thy seed exceedingly* †. *The Lord appeared to Abraham, and he lifted up his eyes, and lo! three men*, or angels in the shape of men, *stood by him*. When at Mount Moriah, he would have offered up his son in sacrifice, *the angel of the Lord called unto him out of heaven and said, By myself have I sworn, saith the Lord, that in blessing I will bless*

* Pentateuch, passim. ‡ Gen. xvi, 10. * Gen. xviii, 2.

thee

*thee**. And it is said *the Lord spake unto Joshua* †; and yet, from the context, it appears evidently that it was not the Lord himself who spake, but an angel, under the title of *the Captain of the Lord's host* ‡.

Let it be likewise considered, that, from repeated testimonies in the writings of St. Paul, it was not the Lord who immediately spake himself, either to Moses, or the people at the Holy Mount. *St. Stephen*, whose history was recorded by the directions of that apostle, *a man full of faith, and of the Holy Ghost*, informs us, *Moses was in the church in the wilderness with the angel who spake to him in Mount Sinai, and he received the law*, the constitutions he then published, *by the disposition of angels* ‖. And the same apostle positively declares, that *the law was ordained by angels* §; *and the word*, meaning the same law, *spoken by angels was stedfast* **. So that no doubt can remain about this matter in attentive and intelligent minds.

It is still, however, to be observed, that the law was given, and ordained by the Lord, the most high God, agreeably to the diction and injunctions of it. And all those appearances, now reviewed, being symbols of his presence, may, therefore, in this qualified sense, be said to be appearances of the Lord God himself.

In this very way, in fact, the people of God seem to have understood all such manifestations. When they saw a supernatural form, and heard a miraculous

* Gen. xxii, 17. † Joshua vi, 2. ‡ Joshua v, 15.
‖ Acts vii, 38. § Gal. iii, 19. * Heb. 1, 2.

voice,

voice, coming to them, and speaking as God himself, they knew, that it was only a messenger from him, speaking in his name. The angel of the Lord, as we have seen, appeared, and spake to Hagar, who knew instantly that it was the appearance of an angel, personating the most high: *She*, therefore, *called the name of the Lord, that spake unto her, thou God seest me* *. And *there wrestled a man with Jacob*, a man, a messenger from God, *and* yet *he called the name of the place peniel; because*, says he, *I have seen God face to face* †; that is, I have had a manifestation from him. The common token by which those manifestations were distinguished, was the glory which attended the messenger, who pronounced the words. And whenever that glory appeared, the Jews knew the message came from God, whoever it was that brought it.

It may be asked who this angel was that appeared and spake of old, in the name and stile of the Almighty? If it was always one, or more? The Messiah himself? Or any of the host of heaven? *who are all ministring spirits, sent forth to minister to them who shall be the heirs of salvation* ‡. This indeed is a very pressing difficulty; as angels are often denominated, in scripture, by their rank and ministry, but have seldom any personal names given to them. When Jacob said to the angel that *wrestled* with him, *tell me, I pray thee, thy name?* he replied, by way of check and prohibition of such idle curiosity, *wherefore is it that thou doest ask after my name* ||? Except Michael and Gabriel, whom we find frequently mentioned,

* Gen. xvi, 13. † Gen. xxxii, 30. ‡ Heb. i, 14.
|| Gen. xxxii. 29.

the

the one as an arch-angel and the other as an angel; there are not, perhaps, any other of these orders called by any particular names, within the compass of revelation. The Jews have supposed the first to have been their patron and guardian, from their emancipation till their entrance into the promised land. It is, however, the concurrent voice of antiquity, and of the most judicious Christians in these times, that our Lord Jesus Christ, before his incarnation, was the *Mediator* in the Schechinah, especially respecting the government and conduct of the Israelites: That it was he who brought them out of Egypt, and was their guide through the wilderness into Canaan in the form *of a cloud by day, and of a pillar of fire by night* *. For *said Jehovah to Moses, behold, I send an angel before thee to keep thee in the way, and to bring thee into the place which I have prepared. Beware of him, and obey his voice, provoke him not; for my name is in him* †. And by Isaiah he is called *the angel of God's presence, who in his love and in his pity redeemed his people, and bare them, and carried them all the days of old* ‡. This seems strongly to characterise the son of God, and therefore it is not unlikely, that under former dispensations of providence in the revelation of moral and religious truths, he was ordinarily, perhaps always, the divine messenger to men, in the same manner as angels have been often employed by himself in messages to the earth, in all periods of time, and even since his ascension into heaven, after his triumph over the cross and the grave.

* Exod. xiii, 21. † Exod. xxiii, 20, 21. ‡ Isaiah, lxiii, 9.

THE

THE doctrine, then, meant to be eſtabliſhed here is this; the ever bleſſed and divine Perſon, whom, ſince his incarnation, we diſtinguſh in the holy trinity by the name of JESUS CHRIST was the Lord God in the Schechinah, who ſpake in his own name, as the creator and proprietor of the univerſe, as the *father* of all the *ages* and œconomies; or was the ſpeaker to mankind from the Schechinah, where JEHOVAH, the Majeſty of God, was preſent.

NONE needs to object that this is an unworthy repreſentation of our Saviour, ſeeing it by no means reſpects his divine nature, nor makes him an angel, as angels really are; of an inferior, created, and dependent nature; but regards his office only, as the miniſter of God to man; which we ſee he afterwards conſented to be, in the moſt aſtoniſhing manner.

IF there be any difficulty apprehended in the atteſtation given at the holy baptiſm and transfiguration, it is carefully to be remarked, that, on both occaſions, it is only ſaid *a voice came from heaven* *, and *a voice came out of the cloud* †; which, inſtead of embarraſſing the foregoing doctrine, highly favours it.

BUT to bring this diſcourſe to a concluſion: It was certainly the peculiar honor and advantage of the Iſraelites, that they had ſuch a public viſible manifeſtation of the preſence and favour of God. *Who are Iſraelites?* ſays St. Paul, boaſting of the privilege, they *to whom pertaineth the adoption and the* GLORY ‡.

* St. Mat. iii, 17. † St. Mat. xvii, 5. ‡ Rom. ix. 4.

THIS

This was a dispensation well adapted to that age of the church, especially at its first institution under Moses, when men could not, by abstract reasoning, be so well acquainted with the nature and perfections of God; and, therefore, stood in need of some extraordinary visible token, to strike and affect their minds, with a sense of his presence, power and authority, favour and protection.

And in allusion to the Schechinah with which Moses conversed in the mount, it is to be observed, St. Paul tells the first believers, *we all*, that is all we Christians, *with open face, have the* GLORY *of the Lord*, reflected upon us, from the face of Jesus Christ, as from a mirror, *and are* in the dispositions of our minds, *changed into the same image* of goodness and excellence, and pass *from glory to glory*, or grow purer and brighter, *even as by the spirit of the Lord* *. *The word*, long unembodied, *was* at length *made flesh, and dwelt among us*; *and we* as well as the disciples, *behold the glory of* our Redeemer, *as of the only begotten of the father, full of grace and truth* †. By his living and conversing in the world, and teaching sinners fully and plainly the great truths relating to God's gracious purposes, our heavenly father, and his merciful regards to men, his presence in his church, and his power engaged in the defence of his children, and to bring them to the possession of everlasting rest, are more clearly and illustriously manifested in the gospel, than his favourable presence and protection were by the Schechinah in the wilderness, in the temple, or in any other place.

* 2 Cor. iii, 18. † St. John, i, 14.

WE,

We, who live under the dispensation of grace and truth, and are, or may be, so well acquainted with the nature and perfections of our maker and lawgiver, have no need of any extraordinary visible token of the divine presence. The glorious truths of the gospel, revealed by Jesus Christ, are our *schechinah*, shining from him on our minds, and filling them with comfort and joy, in the assured hope of his present care and blessing, and of the enjoyment of glory, honor and immortality, in the world to come.

DISSERTATION XVIII.

Of the Corruption of the World, preceding the calling of Abraham.

GENESIS XII.

Before we proceed to the exhibition of the grand ſcheme of providence, in the calling of Abraham, and the gracious purpoſes and effects of it; it may ſtill be neceſſary and uſeful to trace, as far as we can, the ſources from whence the idolatry and wickedneſs of the world ſo quickly followed after the general ſcourge, and rapidly increaſed in thoſe early ages.

Now, concerning this, it may be aſſerted with a high degree of probability, that the ſpreading of corruption ſo ſoon after the deluge, is not altogether to be imputed to ſimple irreligion, that is, to immediate and actual profanity, but, in a great meaſure, to religion itſelf, directed to wrong objects and purpoſes. While men retained *the knowledge* of the true God, they had not been careful *to glorify him as God*, by lives of of holineſs and obedience, nor to be *thankful** for his benefits, as St. Paul, on this very matter, plainly tells us. And through the pride and wantonneſs of human nature, indulging to idle conceits, and falſe reaſonings, they involved their own underſtandings, by degrees, and that of each other, in the thickeſt clouds of error and deluſion.

The heavenly bodies, perhaps, engaged much of their attention: The ſun, moon, and ſtars were probably conſidered as illuſtrious intelligences, which, by an eminent exaltation in the univerſe muſt have the higheſt intereſt in the favour of God, in the direction of human affairs, and the diſtribution of all temporal bleſſings; and, therefore, men would be led to ſuppoſe it ſufficient to all the purpoſes of religion, to ſecure their friendſhip, as mediators between God and them. That they did really carry their veneration for thoſe ſhining luminaries to an undue length, to a kind of worſhip and ſervice, we may clearly ſee from what is ſaid by Job, who is ſuppoſed to have lived cotemporary with Abraham, or in the age before him: Vindicating his own innocence, from a multitude of offences which his friends alledged againſt him, he uſes theſe words; *if I have beheld the ſun when he ſhined, or the moon walking in her brightneſs, and my heart hath been ſecretly enticed, or my mouth hath kiſſed my hand— then I ſhould have denied the God that is above* †; intimating, that thoſe who did ſuch things had forgotten the divine majeſty, ſupreme over all, whoſe miniſters only thoſe orbs, and all the hoſt of heaven, were. And when once men's conceptions were thus depraved, in

* Rom. i, 21.

† Job, xxxi, 26, 27, 28.

regard

regard to things which could neither hurt nor benefit them, the tranſition was eaſy, from reſpect and admiration, to homage and undue honor, by ſuch impious rites as were invented by the folly and ignorance of ſuch votaries. Thus it actually was: mankind were deceived, by the very religious profeſſion which they made, into the practice of all manner of lewdneſs and vice. For the attributes of thoſe ſuppoſed deities and benefactors of men, being feigned purely by human imagination, they would naturally be repreſented by thoſe who dreſſed up the theology, and had their own intereſts and luſts to ſerve, in ſuch a ſort as beſt ſuited their own corrupt taſtes and inclinations. At leaſt, if this was not the caſe at firſt, it may eaſily be conceived to have been ſo in proceſs of time, by after improvements on the original ſcheme of idolatry. And by this method men would be led to believe, that they might be religious, and gain health, long life, fruitful ſeaſons, plenty and proſperity, not only without the practice of holineſs and truth, but poſitively by lewd and wicked actions; and thus religion would be turned into an encouragement to vice, and the principles of reaſon and integrity extinguiſhed.

With reſpect to the progreſs of idolatry, the fact is certain, that the moſt odious idolatry came to be univerſally eſtabliſhed, which was ſucceeded, or rather attended, by abominable luſts and intemperance.

Then, either the wiſdom of the wiſeſt of men, would be loſt, or what was left of it would ſink into cunning, which would be exerciſed on the foibles of the reſt. Hence the notions of fate, deſtiny, fortune, chance,

chance, neceſſity, proceeding from the ſtars, and the nature of things, with many other deluſions, would be introduced. And it is well known that profeſſors of the vileſt arts aroſe, pretending to look into futurity, to gratify malicious deſires, to ſecure good, and prevent bad luck, to thoſe who conſulted them: *Diviners, obſervers of times, inchanters, witches, or ſuch as pretended to work on the mind and body, for evil purpoſes, by herbs or potions; charmers, conſulters with a pretended familiar ſpirit, wizards and necromancers**; and a long liſt of other ſuch impoſtors, many of whom were deceived wretches themſelves. And ſo far were they infatuated, that they made their ſons and daughters to paſs through the fire, at the peril of their lives, and many of them were conſumed, under the notion of ſacrifices to their idols, as we read in many parts of the ſcripture; probably that the former might gain their bleſſing, in ſtrength and fortune, in which the offerers expected their ſhare; and that the latter might be happy in their future favor. Thus their views, and conſequently their hope and truſt, were diverted from God, and his providence, to creatures of the imagination, and the baſeſt of men.

THUS did the neglect and abuſe of underſtanding, and the indulged irregular inclinations of the heart, prove principal ſprings and cauſes of this defection from God and his ſervice: But we may believe it was forwarded and completed by the ſugeſtions and inſtigations of *the devil and his angels, the prince of the power of the air, the ſpirit* whom *God* permits *to work in the children of diſobedience, and to deceive the nations* †. For

* Deut. xviii, 10. † Epheſ. ii. 2.

when

when men receive not the truth in the love of it, that they may be ſaved, God judicially ſends ſtrong deluſions, that they may believe a lie; that they may all be condemned who believe not the truth, but have pleaſure in unrighteouſneſs *

In this manner idolatry firſt began, and by theſe means it ſpread in the world; and would have prevailed univerſally, as the remaining uncorrupted few dropt off, and men of underſtanding were drawn in by various allurements, for wonderful is the influence of eſtabliſhed cuſtoms, and uncontroled general example,; inſomuch that the heart of Solomon the great and wiſe, was afterwards, through the love of pleaſure, ſo far turned away after idols, that he built high places and altars in honor of them, even in the city of Jeruſalem.

What now in ſuch circumſtances ſhall be done? The deluſions of idolatry are ſtrong, and the underſtanding weak, ſo that all nations were then running into it at once and alike. And ſuch was the infatuating and ſpreading nature of the infection, that there was no rational proſpect of the reformation of any one of them. Violence ſeldom works conviction; argument and reaſoning would have no effect, and the moſt dreadful judgments from heaven, were forgotten or diſregarded. The knowledge and worſhip of the one living and true God, the great principle of goodneſs, and of public and private happineſs, was now in danger of being totally loſt in the earth,

* 2 Theſſ. 11. 11. 12.

if

if the father and governor of men had not then, by a merciful ſcheme, prevented it.

And this ſcheme, under ſeveral variations and improvements, was to reach to the end of time; that idolatry might never again univerſally prevail; nor the ſenſe and ſervice of the living and true God periſh. The ſcheme was this; to chooſe and adopt one family, afterwards to be formed into a nation, inſtructed in religious knowledge by God himſelf, and favoured with ſuch extraordinary privileges and honors, above all other nations of the earth, as were in their own nature adapted to engage them, by the moſt rational motives, to adhere to God and his worſhip. At the ſame time, to prevent their being infected with the idolatries and vices of the reſt of the world, as they certainly would have been, had they mingled with them, they were to be diſtinguiſhed and ſeparated from all other people by their diet, their dreſs, and divers civil and religious rites and ceremonies; and more particularly circumciſion, by which they might be certainly known from all men. Thus they would be kept together in a body, and hindred from mixing with, and being corrupted by, their idolatrous neighbours, and in every reſpect fitted to be an example and inſtruction to them under the various diſpenſations with which they were to be viſited. And, further, their laws and religious inſtitutions being originally recorded in books, would more certainly be preſerved and known in all future ages and generations. Thus was there provided a ſtorehouſe of religious knowledge, concerning the being of God, his perfections, and providence;

a whole nation of priests, as they are expressly called, and a school of instruction and wisdom for all the world. Or the nation of the Israelites may be considered as a piece of leaven which, in process of time, was to leaven the whole lump or mass of mankind.

Abraham, a person of the most eminent piety and justice, was chosen to be the head and father of this nation; that as he would always be held in great veneration among them, he might always shine before their eyes as an illustrious pattern of godliness, and a preacher of faith and righteousness. This honorable testimony of Jehovah concerning him stands on record in these remarkable words, *I know him, that he will command his children and his houshold after him, and they shall keep the ways of the Lord, to do justice and judgment; that the Lord may accomplish unto Abraham, that which he hath spoken of him.*

It is greatly worth our while to observe more minutely the steps and methods by which God was pleased to discipline this notable patriarch, and to train him and his for the purpose in view. Abraham, as we heard in the beginning of the discourse, is required to cast himself wholly upon God's providence, by removing at the divine command, from his own kindred and country, to an unknown distant land, which God would shew him, assuring him of his presence and special blessing. Thus God took him under his immediate care and protection. In this strange land he wandered about as long as he lived, but God was with him every where. God appeared to him, and conversed with him frequently and familiarly

familiarly. By extraordinary interpositions, and express declarations from time to time God incouraged, directed, prospered, guarded and provided for him. He became very rich, great and honorable; but all was most visibly the gift and operation of God. God gave him repeated assurances, that he would make of him a great nation, give his posterity the whole land of *Canaan*, and that in his seed all the nations of the earth should be blessed. But the first fruit of this promise, *a son*, he was not to see, till the birth of that son was manifestly the miraculous effect of divine power, and insured all his hopes. What could be more engaging than all these circumstances? What more proper to excite in a man of Abraham's goodness, duty, affection, and confidence towards God? The same encouragements, blessings, and promises, are continued to his family, and repeated to *Isaac*, and afterwards to *Jacob*, and the same heavenly correspondence is kept up with them during their lives: Till at length *Joseph*, by a most wonderful series of events, settles his father and brethren, as had been likewise foretold, in *Egypt*, then a plentiful country of genius and learning, and the resort of the curious and inquisitive, to be a sort of nursery for them, till the time came that the *Amorites* were to be driven out of the promised land.

But we have rather anticipated the scripture history; and therefore shall conclude at present with observing, that the ground of this scheme, and of God's singular regard *to Abraham* and his posterity, was the *covenant of grace*, the *promise* or grant of favors and blessings to mankind in *Jesus Christ* our Lord; *who verily was fore-ordained before the foundation of the world*, *tho' not manifested till the last times**. This covenant or grant was first published to Adam immediately after his transgression; *Her seed*, meaning the woman's, *shall bruise thy head*, *O serpent*, *and thou shalt bruise his heel*. The same covenant, we may be well assured, was well known by all the ancient patriarchs; but much more clearly revealed to Abraham, as we see in the 12th, 17th, 18th, and 22d chapters of this book.

* 1 Pet. i, 20.

DISSERTA-

DISSERTATION XIX.

Of the Political, Religious, and Moral State of the Eastern Regions, about the Time Abraham was called.

GENESIS XIV, & XVIII, 20, 21.

As to the *political* ſtate of the world at that time, it plainly appears that mankind had formed themſelves into ſeparate communities, greater and ſmaller, as convenience and power determined, for their mutual ſafety and happineſs. The territories of ſome of the ſovereigns, we may be ſure were very confined, as the natural equality of men, in thoſe early ages, gave none of them any pretenſions to pre-eminence over others, and being all equally warlike, and equally jealous of their liberty, conqueſt would be no eaſy matter. Theſe facts appear evident from the account we have in the *fourteenth* chapter, of ſo many kings poſſeſſing provinces, which when joined together, would make no extenſive empire, like that of Babylon; nor is it unlikely that there were a great many more, within the bounds of Abraham's operations, whoſe names and actions are not recorded.

SUCH

Such petty governments were well calculated to promote internal juſtice and order, as the chief magiſtrate would be capable of attending to every branch of his office, with the greateſt eaſe: And yet intereſts being various, and ſometimes oppoſite, in the different ſtates, there would be many occaſions of injury, complaint and revenge; as formerly were in our own country, when it was divided into ſmall nations and kingdoms. Accordingly we here find *nine kings, four againſt five, joining battle in the vale of Siddim*, where, it ſeems, there was conſiderable carnage and plunder, occaſioned by incurſions which the king of *Elam*, and his confederates had made into the lands of thoſe kings who oppoſed them. It was at the concluſion of this battle, that *Abraham armed his trained ſervants, born in his own houſe, three hundred and eighteen, and purſued the conquerors unto Dan*, to reſcue Lot, his brother's ſon, who dwelt in Sodom; whom (when the king of that city had been killed) they had led away captive, with his houſhold, and *taken all his goods*. Returning victorious, the *new* king of Sodom went out, in a congratulatory and reſpectful manner, to meet Abraham; and likewiſe *Melchiſedec, king of Salem, who was the prieſt of the moſt high God, brought forth bread and wine*, to refreſh him and his ſervants, after the ſlaughter, and fatigue of their journey, *and* ſolemnly *bleſſed him*.

Having mentioned this royal-prieſt, we ſhall ſpeak at greater length of ſeveral perſons who were at that time, moſt eminent for their *piety, and ſervice of the true God*. This Melchiſedec was the moſt illuſtrious among them; and yet of his hiſtory ſtrange miſ-

conceptions

conceptions are entertained. It is clear that he was a worſhipper of the true God, a perſon of the moſt exemplary juſtice and ſincere devotion; remained abſolutely untainted amidſt the general corruption of the country in which he lived; and, for the greater promotion of true religion, was himſelf a *prieſt*, as well as a *king*, and performed the ſacred offices among his own people. From this diſtinguiſhed man, Abraham received a benediction in theſe remarkable words; *Bleſſed be Abraham of the moſt high God, poſſeſſor of heaven and earth; and bleſſed be the moſt high God, who hath delivered thine enemies into thy hand.* Thus Melchiſedec prayed for Abraham, and offered up humble praiſes and thankſgivings for the remarkable mercies of his late victory. And the patriarch on the other hand, paid his acknowledgements to the Almighty, by preſenting the tenth of what he had taken in the battle, to his prieſt, by whom he had been ſo devoutly bleſſed. Here then is a plain and ſtriking example of juſt ſentiments of God, of ſimple, but rational and hearty worſhip; and of grateful affections for his kind providence.

But what has been ſaid may not be ſufficient to ſatisfy the curioſity of every reader, concerning this ſingular perſonage; eſpecially as St. Paul has declared things of him*, which have greatly amuſed the unlearned; namely, that he was *without father, without mother, without deſcent. having neither beginning of days, nor end of life.* Now, in all this, no more was intended, than that his genealogy is not reckoned up in the ſame manner that the genealogies of ſeveral other

* Hebrews, vii Chapter.

perſons

persons and families are, particularly *in the house of Aaron*; nor yet his birth and death recorded in the history of the patriarchs. For who he was, the apostle precisely informs us; *this Melchisedec*, says he, *was king of Salem, and priest of the most high God* there, or of the place afterwards called *Jerusalem*; and, consequently, had both father and mother, and descent, and beginning of days, and end of life, as other men have, though the knowledge of those matters has not been transmitted to us. And the use made of his character, is, to convince the Jews, by an argument adapted to their own prejudices, that there was a priesthood distinct from, and prior to theirs, and of another order; *for this Melchisedec, is, by interpretation, king of righteousness, and after that also, king of Salem, that is king of peace*; and therefore his order was not, like the Jewish, ceremonial and temporary, but of an eternal, unchangeable, and universal nature, not limited to time or family; and so a fitter emblem of him, and of his priesthood, *who was to come*, concerning whom *God hath said, thou art a priest for ever* *, *and the sceptre of thy kingdom*, like that of Melchisedec's, *is a sceptre of righteousness* †.

But to return after this digression; it is probable that Abraham's neighbours and confederates, *Mamre, Eschol and Aner*, were likewise just and good men. For though they were Amorites, they might yet be uninfected with the vices and idolatries of their countrymen, seeing Abraham lived in friendship and alliance with them; and it was not till about four hundred years after this, that the sins of that nation were full.

* Heb. vii. 17. † Heb. 1, 8.

Nor

Nor can it be reaſonably ſuppoſed, that, in the patriarch's time, the principles of natural and traditional religion were totally extinguiſhed among the Amorites themſelves.

We are certain that Abraham himſelf was, in that age, an illuſtrious inſtance of the true knowledge and fear of God being preſerved in the earth, of righteouſneſs and wiſdom; of which, according to the divine teſtimony, he was a teacher *to his children and houſhold*, and, no doubt, to all others within the ſphere of his inſtruction and example. His hiſtory, from the firſt appearance of God to him, in the land of *Haran*, till his death in *Mamre*, where he was a ſtranger, is the moſt extraordinary, affecting and edifying imaginable; through which nothing breathes ſo much as love and reverence for the Almighty, and confidence in his truth and mercy: Eſpecially who muſt not be ſtruck with thoſe expreſſions of awful reſpect which he teſtified for his maker, when, in the benevolence of his heart, he interceeded for the preſervation of thoſe debauched and wicked cities, which were threatened with a ſignal and compleat deſtruction! *Oh*, ſays he, repeatedly, *let not the Lord be angry, that I have taken it upon me to ſpeak to him, who am but duſt and aſhes: And he drew near, and ſaid, wilt thou alſo deſtroy the righteous with the wicked: That be far from thee; ſhall not the* JUDGE *of* ALL THE EARTH *do right?*

Nor can we when ſpeaking of ſuch perſons, omit *juſt Lot*, Abraham's nephew, who lived in *Sodom*, when it's abominations were moſt atrocious; and yet, by an example incorruptible *reproved the filthy deeds*

of

the Sodomites, though to no effect, *their conversation* being incorrigible, and justly meriting the judgment to which they were reserved. He hath the honourable character, that *he was a righteous man, and his righteous soul was vexed with what he saw and heard of those among whom he lived** : For this *his life was saved* from their overthrow, and the angel, on that occasion, shewed him the condescending indulgence, *haste thee and escape, for I cannot do any thing till thou be come hither.*

Job likewise was, in the patriarchal age, a person of the most distinguished piety and devotion. The reality of his person, the eminence of his character, his fortitude and patience in very great afflictions, his preceding and subsequent felicity, are allowed by all who deserve any notice; and though various conjectures have been indulged about the time and place in which he lived, it is still generally concluded (and were the reasons to be repeated, they would appear very strong for such a conclusion †) that his existence was either co-temporary with that of Abraham, or, at most, not above an age after; as his book, in all probability written by himself, proves it, by a variety of marks, to be one of the oldest, as undoubtedly it is one of the noblest books in the world. His country was *Arabia*, demonstrable not only from local names, as Uz, Teman, and Shuhah, but (as the best critics acknowledge) from the many *Arabic* words which he mixes with his *Hebrew*. And for this very reason, admitting that Moses knew his case and writings, he might yet pass over him in the history of the primitive patriarchs, as he lived in another country

* 2. Peter, 11. 6, 7, 8, 9.
† Vide, Schultens in Jobum.

than

than Canaan, and was neither within the *Abrahamic* covenant, nor the *Jewish* peculiar.

WHAT the ſtate of religion, and it's principal doctrines were, we might here deſcribe, when writing on this period, but as they can be eaſily collected, from the above account of perſons that lived in it, we ſhall proceed to the *moral* ſtate of thoſe parts of the world, referred to in the title of this diſſertation, and ſuggeſted by the fatal cataſtrophe recorded in the *eighteenth* chapter.

THE caſe was this: Four cities, *Sodom*, *Gomorha*, *Admah and Zeboim*, which ſtood in a very extenſive, fruitful and pleaſant vale, and lying along the ſides of the river *Jordan*, were ſo infected with the idolatry ſpoken of before, and the vices uſually attending it, that the inhabitants of thoſe cities, enjoying plenty, and the moſt effeminating delights of their country, through eaſe, *pride*, *fulneſs of bread*, *and abundance of idledeſs* *, became, we have reaſon to believe, the moſt flagitious ſinners that were upon the earth, giving themſelves up to all ſorts of voluptuouſneſs and profanity; and at length, grew ſo debauched, that they indulged to the vileſt ſpecies of lewdneſs, which, from them, is called *Sodomy* to this day, *going after ſtrange fleſh*, *men with men working that which is unſeemly* †; inſomuch that God, infinitely holy and pure, beholding their enormous immoralities, and their in-

* Ezek. xvi, 49. † Rom. i, 27.

consiſtency

consistency with his government, resolved to consume such an abominable people quickly; and even destroy their country, with fire from heaven.

The Lord God therefore *said, because the cry of Sodom and Gomorha is great, and because their sin is very grievous, I will go down now, and see whether they have done altogether according to the cry of it, which is come up unto me; and if not I will know.* This representation of God, and of his counsels, every one will acknowledge, is not to be literally explained, any more than his going down to see the tower of Babel, and confound the language of the nations; as if he really had ears, like our organs of hearing, as if wickedness literally sent up a cry, or that God, who knows all things most minutely, on every occasion, could know them better on nearer and closer inspection; and, therefore, the whole is to be understood by way of accommodation to our conceptions, whose minds, in this embodied state, as was before observed, must be impressed with proceedings under the notion of our own; and plainly means this, that the crimes of the *Sodomites* and of the neighbouring towns were so multiplied and heinous as to exceed, *mount up above*, those of all other sinners in the world; and that the ruler of it, would, accordingly, attend, in a peculiar manner, to their iniquities, mark them out, and devote them to perdition.

BUT before the ruin of those execrated cities came upon them, the Almighty, in great condescension, announced the decree to Abraham, whose family was *then* selected from the rest of mankind; to be the receivers

ceivers and recorders of the divine will. That holy man, in his interceſſion, at the twenty third verſe, diſputed not the equity of the purpoſe; nor doubted the mercifulneſs of the moſt high; but only out of an ſtinctive ſympathy, which in good minds is always ſtrongeſt, pleaded for the wretched victims, over whom deſtruction impended, and that his kins-man and relations, who dwelt in Sodom, might be preſerved. And ſo great the goodneſs and compaſſion of God appeared to be, that, notwithſtanding the demerit of thoſe tranſgreſſors; ſo great his regard to thoſe that fear him, and his readineſs for their ſakes to beſtow bleſſings even upon the unworthy, he would have ſpared them all, if but ten truly ſober and righteous perſons could have been found in all thoſe cities of the plain; but they were univerſally and irrecoverably corrupted.

But the ſame grace which had preſerved *juſt Lot* from the contagion which reigned in Sodom, was likewiſe to protect him from that vengeance which was about to deſcend on it's ſinful citizens. For this purpoſe, the Almighty ſent to him two angels, who arrived at Sodom the day before it was to be deſtroyed. Thoſe angels he moſt complaiſantly invited, and hoſpitably entertained in his houſe, which excited the baſeneſs and brutality of the Sodomites to ſuch a degree, that nothing more, than their behaviour on that occaſion, needs to be adduced to ſhew what length they had carried principles of debauchery and profaneſs. *Where are the men that came in to thee this night? Bring them out unto us that we may* KNOW *them.* In obedience to the affectionate enquiry of the angels, about Lot's other relations in that wretched city, *he*

ſaid

ſaid to his ſons-in-law, who had married his two daughters, up, get ye out of this place; for the Lord will deſtroy this city; and no doubt, added many other things, concerning the execrableneſs of the inhabitants, to convince and alarm them: But ſo impious and depraved were they alſo, that all his warnings and ſolicitations were vain; *he ſeemed as one that mocked unto his ſons-in-law.* They ſaw, at that time, no appearance of their city, in a peaceable and flouriſhing condition, being deſtroyed ſo ſuddenly, by any means; and leaſt of all by fire from heaven; and, therefore, regarded their father's apprehenſions and advice as ridiculous and abſurd, the effect of a diſordered imagination, or of dotage; and ſo ſtaying in Sodom, received the juſt recompence of their incredulity.

At the dawn of the morning, *the angels took Lot by the hand, and led him out of the city with his wife, and two daughters; the Lord being merciful unto him*: And farther permitted him, at his own earneſt requeſt, *to flee to Zoar*, a town likewiſe deſtined to ruin, but not *overthrown* for his ſake.

Scarcely had Lot arrived at *that little city*, when *at the riſing of the ſun*, there was poured upon *Sodom and Gomorha, brimſtone and fire out of heaven.* The dreadful ſtorm *overthrew thoſe cities, and the other cities of the plain, and all the inhabitants of the cities*; and from it's being ſaid, *that all which grew upon the ground, was deſtroyed*, and other circumſtances beſides, it is not unlikely, that there was a terrible earthquake, which broke up the very ſoil of the earth; and a violent irruption of bituminous waters, which turned the

whole

whole valley into one heavy, fœtid and pestilential lake, called since *the dead*, or *salt sea*, about thirty miles long, and ten miles broad, and remains to this very day *: Thus the Almighty, for the wickedness of those who dwelt in them, overthrew those cities, that they should never be inhabited, nor dwelt in any more, from generation to generation.

THIS dreadful instance of divine vengeance, through the mercy of God, removed the bad examples of those daring sinners, had a natural fitness to awaken and reform the surviving, and was wisely intended to remain a perpetual monument of the wrath of God upon the wickedness of mankind.

ONE thing, on this subject, only remains to be considered; *Lot's wife looked from behind her, and she became a pillar of salt.* For the right use and understanding of this passage, it must be remembered, that the sulphureous storm did not begin to fall upon Sodom, till Lot had reached Zoar; but his wife looked back before he reached it; and on the way to that little city. At that time, therefore, Sodom, and the fine country around it, may be supposed to have appeared in the same pleasant and serene state as ever. Consequently it was a look of affection that she gave to the place, and of regret to leave it, and their goods that were in it, which, no doubt, were sumptuous, suitable to Lot's quality, and of great value. This shewed unbelief and distrust of what the angels had affirmed, that God would immediately destroy the

* See Mr. Maundrell, chaplain to the factory at Aleppo, p. 85.

country

country. She either did not believe, or did not regard their meſſage; left her huſband to proceed by himſelf, with his two daughters; and ſtopt by the way, and would go no farther, at ſuch a diſtance from *Zoar*, and ſo near to *Sodom* perhaps, as to be involved in the terrible ſhower, and thereby turned into a nitrous pillar. In no other way can the ſenſe and force of our Lord's admonition be underſtood; *remember Lot's wife* *. Let the judgment of God upon her, warn you, as if he had ſaid, of the folly and danger of lingering after, and being lothe to part with, ſmall and temporal things, when your life and happineſs, the greateſt and moſt laſting concerns, are at ſtake.

These and ſuch like monuments of the divine anger upon ſinners, were deſigned to inſtruct mankind in ſucceeding ages; and have as powerful and expreſſive a voice as any dictates whatever, either of experience or revelation; though, like all other awakening calls, they may be deſpiſed and forgotten. The inhabitants of Sodom and Gomorha had a recent inſtance of God's ſeverity, in the flood of Noah, which ſwept the offenders all away; but they let it ſlip out of their minds, and hardened their hearts, ſo as neither to apprehend or believe any ſuch danger awaiting themſelves, even when it was declared to them. We again have their deſtruction added to that of the Antediluvians, and in it a fit emblem of the univerſal conflagration, and of that puniſhment that will overtake all the ungodly. An apoſtle ſays, *the cities of Sodom and Gomorha ſuffered the vengeance of eternal fire* †; which is literally true in one ſenſe, as fire totally and

* St. Luke xvii, 32. † St. Jude.

for

for ever destroyed those cities never to be built again. Thus, in this dreadful catastrophe, *God revealed*, and gave a specimen of, *his* future *wrath from heaven against all ungodliness and unrighteousness of men* *. And tho' there should be no present appearances of it, we should not therefore be secure. For, as our Lord says, *the men of Sodom eat and drank, they bought and sold, they planted, they builded*; that is, were thoughtless and busy; *but the same day that Lot went out of Sodom, it rained fire and brimstone from heaven, and destroyed them all: Even thus*, says he, *shall it be in the day that the son of man is revealed* †.

* Rom. i, 18. † St. Luke xviii, 27.

DISSERTATION XX.

Of the Birth of ISAAC; and the Promises made to his Seed.

GENESIS XXI.

WHAT the Lord had ſpoken concerning Sarah, Abraham's wife, we have fully recorded in the ſeventeenth chapter of this book, at the ſixteenth verſe; *I will bleſs her*, ſaid God, *and will give thee a ſon alſo of her; yea, I will bleſs her, and ſhe ſhall be a mother of nations: Kings of people ſhall be of her.* This promiſe was again repeated, with farther aſſurance, ſoon after in the eighteenth chapter, in theſe words; *I will certainly return unto thee according to the time of life; and lô! Sarah thy wife ſhall have a ſon.* An event ſo much the more gracious, that, as appears from the hiſtory, Abraham was impatient and diſcontented at his going childleſs, and one not born in his own houſe was likely to be his heir; and ſo little to be expected, Abraham being now ninety-nine years old, and Sarah, as we gather from Abraham's account, eighty-nine, that no leſs than a miracle could bring it about; in-

insomuch that, though Abraham, conformable to his constant character, *believed in God*, respecting this matter, *and had it counted to him for righteousness* *, *Sarah laughed within herself, saying, after I am waxed old, shall I have pleasure, my lord being old also?* And received for her doubtfulness, bordering on unbelief, this just reprimand; *Is any thing too hard for the Lord?* Whose faithfulness did not fail through her unbelief; *For the Lord visited Sarah as he had said, and the Lord did unto Sarah as he had spoken.*

She conceived and bare Abraham a son, who called his name Isaac, as he had been commanded; and this is he whom the scriptures frequently denominate *the son of the promise* †, not so much for his being previously announced to the illustrious patriarch, when his hopes of a son were expired, as for the multitude of blessings, of which he was to be the instrument of conveyance from God to an innumerable people, through successive ages, then remote. *In Isaac*, said God, *shall thy seed be called*; *and bringing Abraham forth abroad*, perhaps to some of the mountains of Canaan, where he was a stranger, under a spacious extended sky, *said, look now toward heaven, and tell the stars, if thou be able to number them; for so shall thy seed be; even like the dust of the earth in number: and lift up now thine eyes, and look from the place where thou art, northward, and southward, and eastward, and westward: For all the land which thou seest, to thee will I give it, and to thy seed for ever.* In which gracious promise, on this occasion, the stipulations included are so obvious, that the

* Gen. xv, 6. Rom. iv, 9—22. Gal iii, 6.
† Acts, iii, 25. Rom. ix, 8. Gal iii, 29, and iv, 28.

plaineſt account, and briefeſt enumeration, will expreſs them; namely, an extraordinary regard, protection and favor; a wonderful multiplication of his race, even to the forming whole nations and kingdoms out of it; abundance of wordly honor and proſperity; the gift of all the land of Canaan, to a part of that prodigious increaſe of his ſeed; a part only it was; for Abraham's deſcendants by Hagar and Keturah, who were not of the promiſed ſeed, but of the branch of *Eſau*, which was ſeparated from it, had no ſhare in that inheritance of the holy nation; and, laſt of all, among theſe particulars, is comprehended the foundation and completion of all other promiſes through *Jeſus Chriſt, the ſon of David, the ſon of Abraham* *.

How aſtoniſhing is ſuch condeſcenſion on the part of the moſt high God, the maker and poſſeſſor of heaven and earth! to beſtow ſo much regard, and ſo many of his benefits, upon any one of his creatures, eſpecially ſo weak and undeſerving as man is! It is true, the ground of this indulgence towards Abraham, and his poſterity, was the covenant of grace, the promiſe or grant of favors and bleſſings to mankind in general in Chriſt Jeſus our Lord; for whoſe appearance all the diſpenſations of providence, from the earlieſt times were preparing: Yet though this was the main purpoſe, the methods of fulfilling it were ſuch as God uſually employs, and Abraham was honored as the *grantee* of ſuch bleſſings to the world, becauſe *he walked before the Almighty in his generation, and was perfect*; and conſtituted the head and father of a great and conſpicuous nation, becauſe the Lord

* St. Matthew, 1, 1.

knew

knew that he would command his children and his houshold after him, that they should keep the way of the Lord, to do justice and judgment. Therefore, every mark of distinction that attended him, and his progeny, may be considered as a temporal and immediate reward, for his eminent piety and righteousness; the divine goodness, in it's manifestations, being always singularly bountiful to every such excellent character.

NOR were these promises *to the father of the faithful*, more ample in their nature, than the accomplishment of every one of them was exact: For not to mention the numerous tribe of *Ishmael*, whom *Hagar* bare to him, and the families and states erected by *Keturah*, Abraham's second wife, who, as has been said, was never reckoned in the line of the chosen people, what incredible swarms issued from him through the channel of Isaac, whose birth we are now contemplating! in so much that in four hundred and thirty years after, that is, at the coming out of Egypt, where they had been as in a nursery, the *Israelites*, as reckoned by Moses and Aaron there, were *six hundred thousand and odds, from twenty years old and upwards, even all that were able to go forth to war*; which, by a common standard, when women and children are included, swells them to the enormous body of *two millions, carried as on eagles wings*, to the promised land, *and brought to God himself*: And what national blessings, above all people, his bounty shed down upon them, while they continued obedient, is well known, and an explanation here would only anticipate the history. Their population still increased; for in the days of King *David*, when he numbered the people of Israel and Judah, we see there were *thirteen hundred thousand men of war*; making

making the whole, according to the former calculation, no less than *five millions and two hundred thousand souls*, within the narrow limits of the realm of *Palæstine*. When the fulness of time was come, God sent forth his son among the people of the seed of Abraham, *according to the flesh*, and remembered the greatest of mercies, he had promised to him, and to his seed, *in whom all men were to be blessed.*

This ancient scheme, or gracious procedure of providence, is distinguished from others of a like nature, by the name of the covenant which God had made with Abraham, renewed with Isaac, and confirmed with Jacob; and, along with the *moral* law delivered at Sinai, the *ritual* of worship, and the statutes of *civil* obligation, was the ground and substance of that admirable œconomy, which obtained in the Jewish nation for *fifteen hundred years.*

And, in like manner, as all covenants, human and divine, have seals and ratifications, this had also it's sign or token. It is described in the seventeenth chapter of this book, slightly considered before; that *every male-child* among the posterity of Abraham was to be *circumcised*; to bear a secret mark in the flesh, as a testimony of their obedience, and of their belonging to the body of God's people: And so strict and unexceptionable was the command, and the blessings of the covenant were so dependant on the observance of this institution, that we read, at the fourteenth verse of this chapter; *And the uncircumcised man child, whose flesh of his foreskin is not circumcised, that soul shall be cut off from his people: He hath broken my covenant.* This was the obligation imposed with the promise; and, accordingly

accordingly, as he had done a year before to himself, and his son Ishmael, and to all the men of his house, *Abraham circumcised his son Isaac, being eight days old, as God had commanded him.* Here it is observable, that, as Abraham's name was changed at the institution of circumcision *, Isaac's was given to him, when he received the badge of initiation; signifying no doubt, that when God's covenant was entered into, there was a dedication of the person by name to his service, and a solemn enrollment among his people.

HENCE it is evident, that this covenant, whereof circumcision was the seal, was, like all other engagements, where two parties are concerned, reciprocal; and intended not only as a declaration and pledge of God's favor to the Jewish people, but likewise as a special obligation on all their posterity, to the same obedience and holiness, for which their progenitor had been so remarkable, even before he was called by God: For St. Paul says of him, that *he received the sign of circumcision as a seal of the righteousness of the faith which he had yet uncircumcised* †. And whereas the restraining men's carnal appetites, and *mortifying their members which are upon the earth* ‡, contain, in a manner, all good living, in as much as it destroys the chief temptations to the contrary; so the action and mark itself of circumcision imports, very significantly, the holy discipline, and severe morality, wherein they were to walk, who were thus admitted into covenant

* This circumstance was omitted in its proper place, because it was minute in the orthography; though in itself it is of great importance: As is also the name Sarah, changed from Sarai.

† Rom. iv, ii. ‡ Col. iii, 5.

with

with God. For it teaches directly, and forcibly admonishes, the duty of abating and limiting all looser desires; which, through the world, and especially in those eastern countries, proved a general source of all other injustice and irregularity; and, therefore, whatever symbolized and typified the due government of these, may, very properly, denote the suppressing likewise the rest of our inordinate affections, and preserving the purity and order of the whole man.

In fact, the rite was external, and the effect of it remained visible on one part of the flesh only, but the import was deep, and extensive through the mind and actions, as Moses, and the prophets explain and apply it; where they use the term *uncircumcised* to express whatever was improper, impure, or unholy. The legislator alledges his own inability of speech, in this stile, *O Lord, I am a man of uncircumcised lips* *; and concerning the fruit of new planted trees, which was reputed unclean, and forbidden to be eat of for three years, he says, *ye shall count the fruit thereof as uncircumcised.* Jeremiah thus complains of the Jews in his time, *to whom shall I speak and give warning, that they may hear? Behold their ear is uncircumcised, and they cannot hearken.* The grace and spirit of obedience is promised to them in these words, *The Lord thy God will circumcise thine heart, and the heart of thy seed to love the Lord thy God with all thine heart, and with all thy soul, that thou mayst live* †. And from these expressions, no doubt, St. Stephen, in the new testament, borrowed his stile, when he addressed the same people, *O ye stiff necked, and uncircumcised in heart and ears, as your fathers have been* ‡. Integrity of life then plainly ap-

* Exod. vi, 12. † Deut. xxx, 6. ‡ Acts vii, 51.

pears,

pears, from all these passages, to have been the first and great engagement laid on Abraham, and all his children by their circumcision.

A FEW reflections now remain to be made on this subject, that may be of practical use, and have a reference to the dispensation of the gospel, and its privileges, which succeeded the ancient covenant of the law, with its rites, and limitations. Under that covenant, it is well known, the people of the Jews received from God, according to his will and purpose, peculiar favor: *They were the people of his holiness* *, *and Israel was his son, even his first-born* †. The rest of the nations were comparatively, *strangers and foreigners*; nor had they any certain way to obtain the privileges, and assured hopes of God's people; to *become fellow-citizens with the saints, and of this houshold of God*, ‡ but by submitting to circumcision, and *keeping the whole law*, § of Moses. That the Apostle calls, *the middle wall of partition*, between Jew and Gentile; *even the law of commandments contained in ordinances*, and *to be broken down*, for the common benefit of the world ||; *that all the families of the earth might be blessed with faithful Abraham* **. And in him, and in his seed, whose prerogative *the* exclusive *adoption* once *was*, it is now the will of God, agreeable to his *fore knowledge and promise*, that, in *the adoption of sons* ††, not only the sons of Jacob and Joseph, but also all people, and nations, and languages, should be comprehended; and the glorious liberty, and the title of the children of God, made universal. The new institution of our

* Isaiah, lxiii, 18. † Jer. xi, 3. ‡ Eph. xi, 19. § Gal. v, iii. || Eph. xi, 14, 15. ** Gal. iii, 14. †† Gal. iv, 5.

Lord

Lord and Saviour, who *was before Abraham* *, and yet is his son, hath superseded the partiality and rigors of a carnal law, by the good-will and grace of a spiritual œconomy; and declared that, for the future, *there* should *be neither Jew nor Greek, neither circumcised nor uncircumcised* †, but one Lord and one shepherd. So that all good Christians throughout the earth, are as literally in covenant with God through Jesus Christ, and objects of his protection and blessings, as ever the Jews of old were, in right of their pedigree from Abraham, with whom their covenant was first established; which is the strict and literal meaning of a great many important passages in the New Testament.

The stipulation of the covenant of grace, NOW fully revealed, on God's part, is, instead of the increase of the Jewish race, a large accession of converts and kingdoms to the faith of the Messiah; salvation from the dominion of sin, and from the captivity of Satan and death, worse than that of Egypt; guidance through the wilderness of this polluted world; and an entrance, infinitely preferable to a temporal possession in Canaan, into the heavenly Jerusalem, and *an inheritance incorruptible and undefiled, and that fadeth not away* ‡; through Jesus the son of God, who excelled, beyond comparison, Abraham, and all other saints and saviours, in the dignity of his nature, which was divine, in his power with God, and also in the extensiveness and perpetuity of his institutions. On our part, we are bound, in obedience to God's authority and commands, to repent of all past offences,

* St. John, viii, 58. † Gal. iii, 28. ‡ 1 Pet. i, 4.

and to exercise faith in the doctrines, and merits of his son, for pardon and acceptance; under the equal and necessary pains of rejection and condemnation. And this is the Christian covenant, in its promises, conditions, and threatenings, through the glorious mediator of it.

Nor was it more necessary, that the people of God of old, should be entered solemnly into their covenant with the God of their fathers, Abraham, and Isaac, and Jacob, than it is under the gospel to be incorporated into the number of God's people: Nor yet that those who were circumcised should keep the law of Moses, than it is still among Christians, to observe and keep all that is required by the covenant; whereof *Jesus is the mediator*, lest they forfeit the privileges of that title; and indeed be cut off from among his people. The rite of our admission is known to be *baptism*; and our duty arising therefrom, it is hoped, is no less known; *Let every one, that nameth the name of Christ, depart from iniquity* *. To which may be only added, by way of information and instruction; that the signs of admission are altered with great propriety, from circumcision in the flesh, to sprinkling with water; to shew that we are the heirs and seed of Abraham, not by a carnal generation, but by a spiritual regeneration; by walking in the steps of his faith, *who is*, in that respect, *the father of us all*, if we be believers, and servants of God.

The last thing to be considered is, if the privilege of *children under the gospel*, can be fairly drawn, from the precedent *under the covenant made with Abraham?*

* 2 Tim. ii. 19.

ham? The answer is, by another question, that the promise of the new covenant being expresly said to *belong to us and to our children*, without any limitation of age, why should not they all without exception receive the sign of it, when they are called to partake of the promise itself? especially seeing the infants of the Jews were, by solemn sign, entered into their covenant; when they were as ignorant of the nature and condition of it, as those of Christians are: Nay, even the infants of proselytes to the Jews were, by that very same sign, and by immersion, or washing itself, admitted to the ancient privileges. Hence, supposing the apostles to imitate either of those examples, as they naturally would, unless they were forbidden, which they certainly were not; while they baptised whole families at once, which we know was the case; we cannot question, but they baptised, as the primitive Christians their successors, soon after did, *little children* among the rest; concerning whom our Saviour says, *of such is the kingdom of God*; And St. Paul says, that *they are holy*; which they cannot be reputed, without entering into the gospel covenant: And the only appointed way of entering into it is by *Baptism*; constantly represented by Christ and his apostles as necessary to salvation.

NOT that such converts in ancient times, as were put to death for their faith, before they could be baptised, lost their reward for want of it. Nor that such children of believers now, as die unbaptised by sudden illness, or unexpected accidents, or by neglect itself, which is not their fault, shall forfeit the advantages of baptism. Nay, of the persons themselves who designedly, through mistaken notions, either delay

lay their baptiſm, as the Anabaptiſts; or omit it intirely, as the Quakers; even of theſe it belongs to Chriſtian charity not to judge hardly, as if they muſt neceſſarily be excluded from the goſpel covenant, if they die unbaptiſed; but to leave them to the equitable judgment of God. Both of them, indeed, err; the firſt, through caprice and obſtinacy; and the latter eſpecially, through a ſtrange infatuation and blindneſs, ſeeing nothing is more plainly enjoined than baptiſing with water in the name of the Holy Trinity. But notwithſtanding, while they ſolemnly declare, that they believe in Chriſt, and deſire to obey his commands (the truth of which is open to God only) we can by no means conſider them in the ſame light with total unbelievers.

BUT calling *them people fooliſh and unwiſe* *, it muſt, at the ſame time, be declared that they are little better, who obſerve this ordinance only for form's ſake, or perhaps, acknowledging the ſolemn engagements into which they have entered by this ſacrament, live without care to fulfil them. For to no ſuch hypocriſy, or ſuperficial obedience, is God's favor, and eternal happineſs promiſed; ſeeing *he is not* a Chriſtian, to change St. Paul's words, *who is one outwardly*; *neither is that* baptiſm, *which is outward in the fleſh*; *but he is a Chriſtian who is one inwardly*; *and* baptiſm *is that of the heart in the ſpirit, and not in the letter*; *whoſe praiſe is not of men, but of God* †.

* Deut. xxxii, 6. † Rom. ii, 29.

DISSERTA-

DISSERTATION XXI.

Of Abraham's Sacrifice; and Sarah's Death.

GENESIS XXII and XXIII.

WE just now saw Abraham blessed, in the fulfilment of the promise that he should have a son in his old age, who should be the heir of his fortune and of his virtues, and whose posterity should become, in number, like the stars of heaven, and be the peculiar care and favourites of the most high: And now, in the twenty-fifth year of that son's age, before any of the great things spoken of were brought to pass, we see Abraham receiving this strange and alarming command from God, *Take now thy son, thine only son Isaac, whom thou lovest, and get thee into the land of Moriah; and offer him there for a burnt offering, upon one of the mountains which I will tell thee of.* A command indeed not more strange and severe, than seemingly destructive of the patriarch's expectations, which, he imagined, were founded on the divine faithfulness: And therefore some have denied that this direction could come from God; while others have thought that it was a trial rather of Abraham's discernment, than

than of his dutifulness; and many humble and devout minds feel great reluctance in their affections against this article of sacred history. Now the first opinion being directly levelled against the credit of the scriptures; the second inconsistent with them; and the weakness, and mere impulses of the human frame, giving rise to the scruples of the third sort; we might, agreeable to sound reason, and the word of revelation, which every where bestows unmixed commendations on Abraham's behaviour, shew, distinctly, the possibility of God's giving such an order; the evidence which Abraham had, and we may have now, of his actually giving it; the improbability, that the obedience paid to it should have any bad effect in after-times; and the good ends, that might be, and were, promoted by it. But as these heads have been, in the fullest and most ingenious manner, discussed by a late learned and pious prelate *, it is better to omit them here, than attempt any thoughts that might be new and more elaborate. And the Jewish fables, concerning this event, are not worth the relating.

The good reasons his grace had for examining those particulars, appear from the attacks that have been made on those several points. For instance, an infidel writer hath expressed himself thus; *The Jewish nation certainly, could never afterwards think it unlawful to kill an innocent child, seeing their progenitor would have sacrificed his only son* †. By such sneers, it is easy to distort, and turn into ridicule any matter whatever. And this he thinks he has a right to do

* Dr. Secker, Archbishop of Canterbury, vol. iv, ser. xvii.
† Toland. Voltaire, see Jewish Letters, *passim*.

in this place, as it is not said Abraham received the order with any sort of surprise; was reluctant to execute it; or expressed any joy, when a counter-command was signified to him. The unfairness of this way of arguing is evident to every one, who considers that a multitude of circumstances are omitted in all relations, whether they be written or spoken: And there is not the least doubt, that Abraham, as every man must, in the like situation, would be astonished at such a command; would necessarily feel the deepest sorrow; and the highest joy in return; though the sacred historian has drawn a veil over the agitations of his mind, too strong to be described.

A CERTAIN noble Lord has, likewise, censured Abraham severely, *for not expostulating with the Almighty on this occasion; when at another time*, says he, *he could be so importunate for the pardon of an inhospitable, murdering, impious and incestuous city*; meaning Sodom *. But was this philosopher really sure, that Abraham, in the utmost agony of paternal fondness, did not pray to God to preserve him from illusion and error; and that *if it were possible, this cup might pass from him?* And yet, when the will of God, so far as he was capable of judging, appeared to be otherwise, was it right or wrong to acquiesce, without farther expostulation? For Sodom, indeed, he did expostulate: But this was only a charitable plea for others; whereas the present affair nearly concerned himself. If Sodom was destroyed, all hope of repentance was cut off from a multitude of vile sinners; if Isaac suffered, it was not as a punishment to him; but as a

* Lord Bolingbroke.

trial

trial of his father's faith; which would surely be rewarded in both. And therefore, like the Saviour of the world, who earnestly solicited the salvation of others, Abraham, in the case of Sodom, interceeded; and as the same Saviour, like a meek and unresisting lamb, laid down his life, agreeable to the will of his heavenly father, Abraham, when required to sacrifice his son, obeyed, by the intent of his mind, till *the angel of the Lord called unto him out of heaven, and said, lay not thine hand upon the lad, neither do thou any thing unto him: For now, I know that thou fearest God, seeing thou hast not withheld thy son, thine only son from me.*

After the trial and triumph of Abraham's faith and zeal, in the case of his son Isaac, the death and burial of Sarah succeeded. She had been his wife, by a conjecture well supported by a series of facts recorded in their lives, about ninety years. Her whole age was an hundred and twenty-seven; of itself sufficient to account for her death, in a natural and necessary way, without having recourse to doubtful and fabulous relations. Several Jewish writers, however, who set no bounds to their fancy, when commenting on the books of scripture, say, that the devil, in revenge, for seeing Isaac, by an interposition of the Almighty, preserved to his father, told Sarah that he was actually slain; that, on hearing this, she instantly expired; and Abraham found her dead, at his return from Moriah *.

But instead of creating more prodigies than those related in the history of divine providence towards that family, we ought to confine ourselves to the annals of those great operations of that providence, the

* Pirké Eliez cap. xxxii.

knowledge of which God, in his wiſdom, has been pleaſed to tranſmit to us. As to Sarah, comparing the age at which ſhe bore Iſaac, his when he was going to be offered up, and the time of her death, we may certainly conclude, that ſhe lived twelve years after this ſingular inſtance of her huſband's obedience; and, in the company of ſo wiſe and devout a man, would ſpend that period of her days in repeated acts of grateful homage to her maker and benefactor for all his goodneſs; and not leſs for reſtoring her ſon from the ſacrificing knife, than for giving him to her at the firſt, when ſhe had deſpaired of any ſuch bleſſing. Fulneſs of years finiſhed her courſe at length, in expectation of future mercy.

When Sarah died, Abraham, whom God deſigned to be the proprietor of all the land of Canaan, poſſeſſed not ſo much ground in it as was ſufficient to be a place of interment. *Having not yet received the promiſe, he was only a ſtranger and foreigner among the men of Hebron.* In his conduct on this occaſion, we ſee how ancient the cuſtom is for every man to deſire and provide a *dormitory* for himſelf, and thoſe with whom he has been nearly connected. So ſtrong is natural ſympathy! and conſtant and univerſal the care of the mortal body itſelf, even after diſſolution.

DISSERTA-

DISSERTATION XXII.

Of Eliezer's Journey to Haran, and return with Rebecca.

GENESIS XXIV.

THE death of Sarah naturally turned Abraham's thoughts towards his own diſſolution. And, as was before obſerved, of all his temporal concerns his dear Iſaac, Sarah's ſon, and the ſon of the promiſe, occupied his mind moſt. This tender parent wiſhed to have him married to one, who might prove the ſincereſt conſolation to him, after the recent death of his mother, and divide with him the far greater conſternation and trouble, that would neceſſary follow on that of his father. Abraham muſt equally provide againſt Iſaac's return into Chaldæa, out of which God had brought him with his family; and againſt his marrying a Canaanitiſh woman. He therefore commanded Eliezer, whom he once thought would have been his heir, and whom Moſes ſtiles his eldeſt ſervant, either becauſe he was higheſt in dignity, or had been with him the greateſt number of years, to ſeek for his ſon, a wife in *Haran*, in *Meſopatamia*, in the family of Nahor, Iſaac's uncle, and Abraham's own brother.

It

It is true, that to take a wife out of this family was not altogether to avoid being allied with idolaters. But though it was not entirely clear of their impiety and corruption, it was not immersed so deep in either, as the other people of Chaldæa, or Canaan. This house, like many other, for a generation or two, where good principles have been inculcated, and an useful example set, had still in it seeds of pure faith, and religion. It cannot be doubted but the danger of idolatry was the principal motive which operated with Abraham in the several precautions he took, for hindering his son from marrying in any of the families of the Canaanites. And that the blood of Gods people should not be incorporated with that of unbelievers, was as unquestionably the cause of so many prohibitions afterwards repeated to the Patriarchs, on the same score. In short, it is not improbable, that the design of all those distinguishing precepts was, to preserve the list of the Messiah's ancestors entire, in the line of the promised seed, from Abraham, to whom the blessing was first intimated, down to his birth. And indeed this is the most reasonable account that can be given of the great exactness the Jews, soon after, observed in this matter, and were encouraged in so doing by the Almighty himself.

Abraham not fully satisfied with exacting a promise of Eliezer, demanded the confirmation of it with an oath; the form of which we have in the second and third verses; *put, I pray thee,* said the patriarch, *thy hand under my thigh; and I will make thee swear by the Lord, the God of heaven, and the God of the earth, that thou shalt not take a wife unto my son, of the daughters of the Canaanites among whom I dwell.* The manner of this

this oath, of which there is but one other example, in the forty-seventh chapter of this same book, hath occasioned many disputes among interpreters.

Some have believed that an engagement of this sort was never entered into, but by an inferior to his Lord, who hereby paid an act of homage to his master. While others have said, that it had a reference to the covenant of circumcision, by which the family and posterity of Abraham were allied to the true God; and that they forfeited all the blessings of that covenant, if ever they should prove perfidious in what they had sworn to observe. And there are not a few who have found deep mysteries in those sorts of oaths, and strong marks of the faith of the Patriarchs. *By the God of heaven and the God of the earth*, by whose name the oath was sanctified, many interpreters have understood the Messiah, who was to spring from the father of the faithful, according to the flesh, signified by putting the hand under the thigh.

We may well say of this, as of a thousand other passages in scripture, that if they had been more obscure, and at the same time, more useful and profitable, infinitely less pains would have been taken by commentators to render them clear and practical; as evidently appears in the huge volumes of their writings. And happy would it have been for the word of God, and multitudes of it's readers, if it had always been left to speak it's own sense, without the perverse glosses, which ignorant and partial men have put upon it! What does it avail us in these ages, that the reason of a custom, which obtained more than three thousand years ago, should be inexplorable, being so long exploded

exploded and obsolete? Can we not frankly own our ignorance of the matter, without endangering the reputation of our learning, and skill in the minutiæ of antiquity? Surely we may, without any injustice to ourselves or others, if we have but the modesty and self-denial to do it. And after all, according to a learned critic, the whole mystery of putting the hand under the thigh, and swearing in this posture, was the following declaration; *I submit to be pierced through with this weapon (a sword) if ever I shall violate what I now engage to perform.*

But to proceed in the story: Eliezer departed from Canaan with ten camels of his master's; after a solemn blessing, and a particular assurance given him, that God would send his angel before him, to prosper him in the way which he went. He arrived at Haran, in Mesopotamia, and standing without the city, prayed thus: *O Lord God of my master Abraham, I pray thee send me good speed this day, and shew kindness unto my master Abraham. Behold, I stand here by the well of water, and the daughters of the men of the city come out to draw water: Now therefore let it come to pass, that the damsel to whom I shall say, let down thy pitcher I pray thee, that I may drink; and she shall say, drink, and I will give thy camels drink also; let the same be she that thou hast appointed for thy servant Isaac; and thereby shall I know, that thou hast shewed kindness unto my master.* This prayer plainly shews the piety of those remote times, where the knowledge and fear of God were preserved; though it is confessed to be extremely singular in it's tenure, and must be interpreted by the peculiar dispensation the Almighty then followed with good men, in the first ages of the world. It be-

longs

longs not to any mortal to prescribe to providence any signal, by which we may have evidence before hand, whether our designs will be frustrated, or crowned with success. But yet God, and who can hinder him! shewed such condescension as this, before a written revelation of his will was vouchsafed, to his saints and people, when they were in the way of their duty, or engaged in any eminent services; of which the scriptures furnish us with sundry examples. Superstition, indeed, justly stiled the ghost of substantial religion departed, hath often imitated what hath been rationally practised. Nothing was more common among the Heathens than to require signs, as Eliezer here did, and to regulate their greatest enterprises by presages frequently as ambiguous, as they were imaginary; and therefore, most commonly, mere deceptions in the end. Thus the Philistines said they would know by the way which the ark took, if the calamity with which they had been afflicted, proceeded from the God of Israel, or from some other cause. Thus also Nebuchadnezzar, in suspense if he should wage war with the Ammonites, or the Jews, took two arrows, upon one of which he inscribed the name of Rabba, the metropolis of the children of Ammon; and on the other the name of Jerusalem, the capital of Judah, and having transposed and shuffled them again and again, he drew out one of them at a venture; which happened to have Jerusalem written upon it; and this determined the king of Babylon to make war against Judah. So trifling and uncertain, often, were the circumstances by which men, given up to a superstitious fancy, did, and still do, allow their resolutions to be fixed, and persuade themselves that they are divinely directed.

BUT

But this abuse of providence is no argument against it's superintendency in all cases, nor that it's operation is unworthy, when humbly implored, and, by a strong dependence, waited for. This was Eliezer's case: He had undertaken the present business at his master's command, of whose piety, and favor with the Almighty, he had seen many proofs before; and, therefore, entertained the fullest confidence, that prosecuting his purpose faithfully, and begging guidance and success from above, he would not fail in his design. And accordingly, the event justified his conduct and expectations: Before he had done speaking, that is, before he had finished the prayer repeated above, God heard him, and ordered it, that a damsel *very fair* and beautiful, should immediately come out of the city of Haran, carrying a pitcher upon her shoulder. This was, in fact, the daughter of Bethuel, the son of Nahor, Abraham's own brother. Her name was Rebecca; and this whole chapter gives such a favourable representation of her person, her benevolence, and other good dispositions, as prognosticates before hand how happy she would make the husband, for whom, by a sovereign appointment, she was manifestly designed; and how deserving she was of the honorable alliance with the chosen family of God.

When Rebecca met Eliezer, she was going to fetch water for the family, an occupation, together with keeping flocks and herds of cattle, which, to our astonishment, the simplicity of the first ages, assigned to women of the most distinguished quality; of which we have innumerable examples in sacred history itself, as well as profane; particularly in the case of the seven

ſeven daughters of *Ruel*, prince and prieſt of Midian, whom Moſes defended from the ſhepherds of the deſert, and aſſiſted in their rural toil. And could we, in theſe days of pride and effeminacy, diveſt ourſelves of prejudices in favor of our own way of living, we ſhould certainly love, and long after, the enchanting country ſcenes which the book of Geneſis, perhaps the oldeſt in the world, exhibits to us; ſo conducive to innocent pleaſures, good health, and that longevity for which thoſe ages were ſo remarkable. Eliezer now began to make trial, whether this blooming damſel who came out from the city firſt, was ſhe whom God had ordained for his maſter, by requeſting of her a little water, in that country extremely comfortable and precious, that her compliance or refuſal might ſerve as a ſign to him. He ſoon knew how it was to fare with him, by her humane and hoſpitable anſwer; *drink my Lord*, ſaid ſhe, *and I will draw water for thy camels alſo, until they have done drinking*. In gratitude for this amiable kindneſs, Abraham's ſervant preſented Rebecca with a gold ring, and two bracelets, of conſiderable weight and value. Here again our commentators, with great pains, enquire if this ring was really for the ear, as is here ſaid, or if it was a jewel for the forehead, after the eaſtern faſhion; and if Eliezer gave her any more than one. They have alſo induſtriouſly ſearched for the weight, value, and nature of the bracelets. Theſe things we barely mention on purpoſe, to ſhew readers, how ſome learned men have been employed in explaining the ſcripture.

Would not ſuch men bluſh, were they to ſwell their writings with a deſcription of the ornaments now in in ufe? And yet they fwell them with the exacteft defcriptions of thofe of the moft diftant ages.

This courteous damfel accepted Eliezer's prefent, and offered him lodging, and every fort of accommodation for his beafts, in the houfe of her father Bethuel. She ran thither before him, and related to her brother Laban every thing that had happened. As in the narrative, which is very long, and the incidents various, there is but once mention made of Bethuel, Rebecca's father, and as Laban appears to have directed every thing concerning the marriage of his fifter, it feems evident that their father was now in extreme old age. Jofephus, in the firft book of the Jewifh antiquities*, fays that he was dead, which is directly contrary to the account of Mofes, who hath exprefsly told us at the fiftieth verfe of this chapter, that Laban and Bethuel faid, *the thing proceedeth from the Lord.* Jofephus, to obferve it by the bye, is perhaps one of the moft unfaithful guides that can be followed, in fome paffages of the holy fcriptures, being fhamefully negligent, as would appear, in the ftudy of feveral parts of them, and very fanciful and partial in others. The apology offered for him is, that he had feen a copy of the Hebrew books, different from the prefent ones, and at leaft very near agreeing with the Septuagint †.

Laban having heard the relation of his fifter, and poffeffing fully her generofity and benevolence, went to meet Eliezer, and brought him to his own houfe, where his camels were put up, water provided for

* Cap. 16. † Shuckford's Con. B. 1. p. 60.

him

him and his attendants, and meat set before them for their refreshment. But this faithful servant, intent on the business entrusted to him, and which he considered as his chief duty at that time, would taste no provisions till he had set forth the design of his journey to Rebecca, and her family. It was easy to perceive by his recital as he went along, the direction of providence in the whole affair. Rebecca was consulted; and consented without difficulty, to a marriage which she could not but consider as the most happy event of her life; and instantly to follow a man charged with so important a negotiation. Eliezer then distributed in Rebecca's family the rich presents Abraham had sent; and the marriage was celebrated by festivity and rejoicing. He was pressed to spend some time in Mesopotamia, with this fair damsel, before he returned to his master for the connubial consummation. But he resisted the importunities, and forthwith departed with her, and her nurse, to deliver to Isaac the most precious gift of an accomplished spouse.

Rebecca and Eliezer arrived in the land of Canaan, between Kadesh and Bered, while Isaac was in the fields, at the even-tide, praying or meditating, near the well *Labai-roi*, which the angel had shewn to Hagar, when she was dying with thirst. Isaac knew Eliezer, who acquainted him who Rebecca was, and at the same time informed Rebecca that this was Isaac, his master's son. Then she lighted off the camel, prostrated herself before Isaac, and took a vail and covered herself; or a kind of mantle, after the manner of all the Arabian women on many occasions. And thus covering herself, she testified at once, according to the custom of her country, her modesty and submissi-

on,

on, two virtues most becoming the married state, into which she was just now going to enter.

Thus have we gone through the history of this chapter; and interspersed such remarks and reflections as the subject naturally suggested. And now, in conclusion, we ought certainly to renew the reflection, which, on like occasions, hath been often made, namely, that as the holy scriptures, in every part of them, have God for their author, and were intended for mens instruction and improvement in all ages, so do they most conspicuously contain the history of his providence in the management of human affairs, particularly such as concerned his own people, who were more immediately under his protection, and the objects of his care and blessing. No book in the world ascribes the chain of causes, and their ultimate effects, so uniformly to an overruling power, as this book does; in which we see the Almighty represented as the first mover, conducter, and finisher, of almost every transaction; thereby strongly impressing our minds with a sense, which we would otherwise be but too apt to lose, of our dependence on him for wisdom, direction, and a favorable issue in all our doings; who can with equal ease cross and defeat our purposes, and facilitate and bless the execution of them. Even in this marriage of Isaac, we visibly see a divine hand engaged; by which the whole train of it's circumstances seem to have been adjusted. And there is no doubt, though the operations of providence are not now so manifest as formerly, that it is equally active, and in the very same matters, when men prepare themselves for, and submit to it's agency. And therefore in the article of marriage itself, as well as in all other

other affairs of moment, every one entering on that ſtate, ought to have chiefly in their eye, with regard to their companion, ſuch principles and diſpoſitions as Rebecca had received from a regular and godly education; to implore wiſdom, diſcretion, and help of God, to fix on ſuch a perſon, and conciliate their affection, as will contribute to their happineſs, and be inſtrumental with them in promoting the divine glory in the world.

DISSERTA-

DISSERTATION XXIII.

Of the Death and Burial of ABRAHAM.

GENESIS XXV, 7, 8, 9, 10.

OF this great man, every part of whose life was so singularly venerable and instructive, this passage exhibits the dissolution and interment *Abraham gave up the ghost, and died, and was buried.* We may not, perhaps, be much affected at first with these expressions, seeing they only represent a condition to which he, in common with all mankind, by a penal unrepealable law of God, was obliged to submit. He died at the age of *an hundred and seventy-five.* His children, with filial piety, conveyed his body to the cave of Macpela, the only spot of ground that then belonged to him, as an inheritance, in the land of Canaan, and placed it close by Sarah's remains, there deposited eight and thirty years before; where, mingling together, they lie to this day, notwithstanding the ravages of time, and the devastations of invaders.

AND

And yet this event of Abraham's death, ſuggeſts very ſerious and important reflections. He, whoſe body was thus laid in the earth, and is now reduced to aſhes, was *the friend of God*; and had the promiſe from him, *I will be thy ſhield, and thy exceeding great reward.* This promiſe, it is true, was verified in part, in the conſtant protection afforded him, and the temporal proſperity with which he was bleſſed: And it is not denied, that worldly ſecurity and happineſs were, chiefly, the ſtipulated rewards of the covenant made with him. But can we poſſibly believe, that the land of Canaan, flowing as it was with milk and honey, was ALL included in this promiſe, made by the mouth of God himſelf, *to whom the earth and the fulneſs thereof belongs* *. In his ſight, of what value are a few bulls, and goats, and ſheep?—A few acres of land, or a whole kingdom? And ſhall a few years poſſeſſion exhauſt his liberality and munificence?

It is granted that Abraham was only a man; with all his excellent virtues, a ſinner; could claim no reward, properly ſpeaking, for his labours and ſufferings; nor exemption from death, the wages of iniquity, for the ſlighteſt inſtance. But he was the father of the faithful, an example of ſtrong belief and right action to ſucceeding ages. At the divine command, he abandoned his property, kindred and country, and believed incredible things. In obedience to the ſame command, though under the heavieſt anguiſh of heart, he built an altar, on which he was to ſlay his ſon, *his only ſon*, the ſource of his hope, his power and greatneſs; bound him with cords; took

* Pſalm xxiv, 1.

the knife; stretched forth his hand, and would have offered him in sacrifice, if the Almighty, when that of his mind was fully made, had not interposed. After this, is it possible, we may again ask, that temporary and terrestrial privileges, such as many of the most worthless men enjoy, should be all that was intended for this *good and faithful servant of God*? Or that he expected and wished for? God was certainly pleased with him, as he was with Enoch, translated immediately to heaven, and is, at all times, abundantly able and bountiful to make all the righteous happy for ever.

Besides, the very promise itself made to Abraham, of putting him into the possession of Canaan was not accomplished, if we understand it literally. He had indeed great riches; but his life was so full of great afflictions, that, in no period of it, can we find that promise, in any measure, fulfilled. *He sojourned only*, saith St. Paul, *in the land of promise, as in a strange country, dwelling in tents with Isaac and Jacob; the heirs with him of the same promise*; who thereby declared, that *they expected a better*, than that which had been promised to them on the earth, *even an heavenly*.

It is not to be doubted, that not only Abraham, but likewise all the religious men of his time, as well as of the preceding and subsequent ages, entertained the faith and hope of a future state. This has been the belief of all nations from time immemorial; and it is scarcely credible in the nature of things, that the greatest happiness of the present life, which might at any time, and would infallibly at length be totally destroyed, should ever become a solid principle of religion;

ligion; or be proposed by the Almighty as the sole reward of piety and goodness.

THESE, indeed, *were the days of the years of Abraham's life which he lived, an hundred threescore and ten years*; then *he gave up the ghost; and his son's, Isaac and Ishmael, buried him in the cave of Macpela.* Such circumstances of holy scripture we cannot too well remark. For the great promises made to Abraham, the conquests he should obtain; the country of which he was to be the sovereign; and the possession to be confirmed to him and to his posterity, all ended, with respect to him, in the grave. But are all the promises of God, under former dispensations, to be interpreted in this manner? In this manner were they all fulfilled? Or rather from such difficulties, are we not to draw convincing proofs of the immortality of the soul, and of the resurrection of the body? *I am the God of Abraham, of Isaac, and of Jacob* *, is a well-known declaration in the books of revelation. This must have a reference to a state beyond death, and the worms and putrefaction of a sepulchre. Our Lord's doctrine will, therefore, be one day verified, by the immortality of Abraham's soul, and the resurrection of his body, that *God is not the God of the dead, but of the living* †.

THOSE who allow the immortality of Abraham's soul necessary, upon the foregoing reasoning, will not perhaps, think the resurrection of his body an equally necessary consequence. It has been said, that the soul being the seat and sole residence of happiness, of which the body, in it's own nature, is incapable,

* St. Matthew xxii, 32. † ibid.

God might have fulfilled his promiſe to the utmoſt, in beſtowing on Abraham's ſoul, all the happineſs of which it was ſuſceptible, without raiſing his body out of the earth, which could contribute nothing to it.

THE objection plauſibly gains upon us, becauſe it aſſerts the real dignity of man; and teaches us, that the nobleſt and moſt ſublime part of our nature is not material fleſh, which conſtitutes a part of our being, but the ſoul, which raiſes us to a level with pure intelligences, not clothed with mortal bodies.

YET by an eſtabliſhed law, in regard to our natures, both ſeem to be neceſſary, in order to our happineſs. Men are compoſed of matter as well as of ſpirit; and he who made us hath ſo adjuſted thoſe two ſubſtances, that the one ſhould not have full enjoyment and ſatiſfaction, without the participation of the other. Hence we may preſume, that whatever happineſs we may enjoy, in the interval between death and the reſurrection, and how far ſoever this happineſs may exceed any that we can have on the earth, it will not be till after the union of the ſoul and body, that our happineſs will be completed. And on this account many paſſages of ſcripture refer our perfection to that period: *As for me*, ſays the pſalmiſt, *I ſhall be ſatisfied with thy likeneſs, when I awake*: And when Chriſt*, ſays St. Paul, *who is our life ſhall appear, then ſhall ye alſo appear with him in glory; and there is laid up for me a crown of righteouſneſs, which the Lord the righteous judge ſhall give me at that day:* And, finally, *beloved, it doth not yet appear what we ſhall be, but we know, that*

when

when he ſhall appear, we ſhall be like him, for we ſhall ſee him as he is. Happineſs, therefore, we may, and undoubtedly will enjoy, when body and ſoul are ſeparate, but not have it conſummated till after their reunion. Hence the promiſe of an *exceeding great reward* ſuitable to Abraham's compleat nature, equally ſuppoſes his ſoul to be immortal, and that his body ſhall be raiſed from the earth: The point here intended to be proved.

DISSERTATION XXIV.

Isaac deceived by *Rebecca* and *Jacob*, who obtains the Blessing.

GENESIS XXVII.

ISAAC, perceiving the end of his course approaching, having already lost the use of sight, wished to give the patriarchal benediction to his family. The benedictions of those extraordinary men ought not to be simply considered, as the effusions of an affectionate and good mind, which is filled with impotent wishes, and expresses rather what it desires should happen, than what is probable ever will. They were, in those days when the will of God was first unfolding, prophetic oracles, which marked out infallible events, and penetrated into the most distant futurity.

THE Patriarch on this important day, which was to decide the destiny of his children, paid too little attention to what had been formerly foretold concerning *Esau* and *Jacob*; perhaps indeed he had never rightly comprehended it. At the twenty-third verse of the twenty-fifth chapter, we are informed; *it was ſaid to Rebecca, before they were born, two manner of people and two nations ſhall be ſeparated from thy bowels; and the one people ſhall be ſtronger than the other people; and the elder ſhall ſerve the younger.* Following, in the act he was going to perform, no other guide than the emotions of his own heart, he purpoſed to give the eldeſt of his ſons, a token of that predilection which he had always entertained for him. It is much better to tax the Patriarch here, with want of attention and underſtanding, than with rebellion of heart, and an obſtinate reſiſtance of what had been before determined. However this was, we ſee he ordered *Eſau to bring him veniſon which his ſoul loved*, that having taken ſome ſuſtenance before a diſcourſe which he could not pronounce without a conflict, he might, with the more compoſure and deliberation, attend to the oracles he was going to declare.

But Rebecca, whom tenderneſs for Jacob rendered vigilant and induſtrious, informed him of the command that Eſau had received from his father. She repreſented to him the glorious conſequences of the benediction, which his rival-brother would derive, provided it was beſtowed on him; and in order to prevent it, inſtructed Jacob to preſent immediately to Iſaac the niceſt parts of two young kids of the goats, after dreſſing them in the beſt manner, to make them paſs, with the unſuſpecting old man, for veniſon. Jacob felt at firſt ſome reluctance to execute this device. He ſuggeſted to his mother, that if his father diſcovered the fraud, he would ſeverely puniſh him or her, who was the author of it, and denounce againſt them both maledictions, inſtead of bleſſings, which

they

they expected. Rebecca anſwered, that all the effects of that malediction, if any followed, ſhould fall upon herſelf. Jacob replied, that though his father had loſt all his delicacy of taſte, to diſtinguiſh the fleſh of a kid from that of ſome beaſt taken in the chaſe, yet at leaſt he could not miſtake when he touched his hands ſmooth and ſoft, in place of thoſe of Eſau his brother, which were all over *hairy*. Rebecca promiſed to remedy even this inconvenience, and, in fact, executed her promiſe, as ſoon as Jacob yielded to her ſolicitations. *She put on the hands of her younger ſon, ſkins of the goats, and on the ſmooth of his neck; and took the goodly raiment of the eldeſt, and clothed Jacob with it.* Here, ſays a certain author, the Rabbins have given the freeſt ſcope to their reveries. They aſſert that this goodly raiment was the ſame that God had given our firſt parents, immediately after the fall; that Nimrod, the firſt Emperor, had made it his royal apparel; that it had come down even to *Eſau*; and poſſeſſed the virtue of taming, and rendering tractable, the fierceſt beaſts.

BUT inſtead of ſuch extravagant and groundleſs fancies, it would be a great deal more pertinent to remark, how fertile in expedients the human mind is to ſurmount difficulties, when it is effectually engaged in the purſuit of favorite purpoſes; and particularly female imagination in the management of an intricate and curious affair; as this, and other inſtances, evidently prove.

IN effect, Rebecca's ſtratagem ſucceeded; and as Jacob's words to his father on this occaſion, muſt either exculpate him of falſhood, or fix the guilt on him

him; according to the different senses that are ascribed to them, they have been explained both ways, as interpreters have had less or more reluctance to charge the Patriarch with it, or to acquit him. The original is most literally translated, and signifies word for word, that Isaac having asked Jacob, *who art thou my son?* *Jacob said unto his father, I am Esau thy first-born; and have done according as thou badst me; sit and eat of my venison, that thou mayest bless me:* That Isaac having said, *how is it that thou hast found it so quickly my son; he said, the Lord thy God brought it to me:* That Isaac, having felt his hands, and found them hairy, *said, the hands indeed are the hands of Esau, but the voice is that of Jacob:* That he questioned Jacob a second time, *art thou my very son Esau? and Jacob said, I am.* Now, it is inconceivable, how any one examining these words, without any other design than to get the sense of them, can be in the least at a loss to see in all these speeches of Jacob a train of declarations opposite to the truth.

Some indeed paraphrase the first words in this account thus: *I am, he who brings thee venison to eat; Esau is thy eldest son**. Other interpreters understand them in this manner; *I am Esau*, that is to say, *I have taken his place, because he sold me his birth-right.* As also this sense has been put upon them; *I am Jacob to whom thou now speakest; but Esau is thy first-born.* One of the fathers adopts this reading; *I am Esau by right* †; and pretends that it is a figure, like that in the gospel, where *John the Baptist* is called *Elias.* Mental reservations have been recurred to, in this perplexing case of Ja-

* R. Jarchi in Genesis xxvii. † St. August. contra mendacium.

cob.

cob. But all these ways of justifying him only shew, how hard pressed interpreters have been in the attempt, and how strong and conclusive Moses's words are, which impute falshood to him. The fraud was impious! For what does not a wife owe to her husband, in so critical a situation! What does not a son owe to his aged parent! What does not one brother owe to another, in point of justice and affection. And we may frankly own that Rebecca was very criminal in seducing her son by such pernicious counsel; that Jacob was not less so in allowing himself to be practised on, in such an affair; that both seem to have imagined that a complication of frauds was necessary for the accomplishment of a divine decree. It, nevertheless, appears, that God, always less ready to punish than to manifest his favor, confirmed the paternal and patriarchal benediction of which Jacob's craft and extortion, in procuring it in this manner, rendered him unworthy.

If what has been said appears unsatisfactory in regard to so venerable a character as Jacob's, we may then be allowed to profess our ignorance about the matter; as well as about many other things; and it is certainly better to make this declaration once for all, than to give, for a clear and full solution, so many vain conjectures as interpreters have done, upon this and other puzzling passages of scripture.

But we return to the history. Isaac, deceived by his own sense of feeling, through the imposition put upon it, and by so many assurances made to him by Jacob, pronounced on the youngest of his two sons, the benediction he had reserved for the other. The

form

form of it is ſolemn: *Come near now, and kiſs me, my ſon: And God give thee of the dew of heaven, and the fatneſs of the earth, and plenty of corn and wine. Let people ſerve thee, and nations bow down to thee; be lord over thy brethren, and let thy mother's ſons bow down to thee: Curſed be every one that curſeth thee, and bleſſed be he that bleſſeth thee.* In this form, the Patriarch wiſhes, or rather as was ſaid, promiſes prophetically to Jacob, that rich and fructifying dew which fell ſo abundantly in Palæſtine, and ſupplied the defect of rain, which they ordinarily had but twice a year; in the month of April, when it was called the former rain, and October, when it was called the latter rain; of which we read in a great many places of the old teſtament. He promiſed him alſo a great abundance of the fruits, and other productions of the ground; which his poſterity had in that land almoſt beyond belief; and eſpecially the ſuperiority and pre-eminence of his brethren; the inhabitants of the nations ſurrounding Canaan.

AND *it came to paſs*, we are told at the thirteenth verſe, *as ſoon as Iſaac had made an end of bleſſing Jacob, and Jacob was yet ſcarce gone out from his preſence, that Eſau his brother came in from his hunting, and preſented veniſon to his father*; who exclaimed immediately for the deluſion that had been put upon him; and as Eſau preſſed him by words, ſighs and tears, to give him the bleſſing, Iſaac ſtill increaſed his anguiſh in telling him that he had already given it to his brother. Eſau then expoſtulated; *Haſt thou but one bleſſing, O my father?* It is ſurprizing that the Patriarch did not recall the bleſſing, and give it to him who was ſo dear, and for whom he had deſigned it. The Jews, it ſeems,

seems, entertain a notion that he saw Hell open before him; and that the frightfulness of the object hindred him from pronouncing predictions contrary to the purposes of heaven. The thought, in all likelihood, is chimerical; but we must at least suppose that some supernatural interposition regulated Isaac's mind. Some interpreters lay great stress on these words used by Moses, *Isaac trembled very exceedingly*; which they translate, *Isaac was absorbed in an extacy.*

However, to indemnify Esau in part, who to the full could not be indemnified, and to give him a large share of wealth and prosperity, though he could be no longer considered as his eldest son, Isaac gave him a blessing also. It is observable, that it is also expressed in a manner, which seems to contradict his refusal of granting him one of the same kind with that he had given Jacob; for he said to Esau, almost in the same stile that he had spoken to Jacob, *Behold, thy dwelling shall be the fatness of the earth, and of the dew of heaven from above.* Fact and experience not having confirmed this prophetic oracle, Esau having dwelt in Idumea, which is a dry and barren country, a learned critic, well known in Europe *, presumes that Isaac's words ought to be thus interpreted, *Thou shalt indeed be deprived of the fatness of the earth, and of the dew of heaven from above; but by thy sword shalt thou live, and thou shalt serve thy brother, and it shall come to pass, when thou shalt have the dominion, that thou shalt break his yoke from off thy neck.* But those who are of a different opinion pretend, that this

* M. Saurin.

first

first part of the oracle was sufficiently verified, even in the literal sense, by that abundance of worldly goods which Esau possessed. They add, that Isaac's refusal, at Esau's first coming in, respected only that part of the blessing which constituted Jacob superior to his brethren, and not the good things of another kind which were promised, and afterwards bestowed on him.

What the other part of the verse predicted to Esau, and his posterity, that they should be an enterprizing and warlike people, the event proved to be true; as we read in Josephus, and have several traces in the prophets, that the Idumeans, or Edomites, who were all the descendants of Esau, lived by the inroads they made on neighbouring territories, and by rapine, and extortions on those who travelled among them.

The verse last repeated deserves a remark and illustration; *Thou shalt serve thy brother; and it shall come to pass, when thou shalt break his yoke from off thy neck, &c.* This state of national affairs, when Jacob for some time should inslave Esau, and he in his turn free himself from the dominion of his brother, may be more clearly perceived among their descendants. For first we read that *David put garrisons in Edom; throughout all Edom put he garrisons; and all they of Edom became David's servants* *. And then again we see that those same Idumeans, who had been subjected by the Jews in the days of David, *revolted from them in*

* 2 Sam. viii, 14.

the

the reign of Joram *; and maintained their freedom eight hundred years, even till the famous *Hircam*, the conqueror of Samaria, and destroyer of the temple there, subdued them. They subdued the Jews in some sort, a second time in their turn. This was while Herod the Idumean reigned over them, and the posterity of that foreign prince held the sovereignty of Canaan during an age and an half. The truth is, if we stop at particular instances we shall find great difficulty in comprehending, wherein that pre-eminence and superiority, which was promised to Jacob over Esau, consisted, and therefore must own that it is only by giving the words a general signification, that we can find in them a meaning worthy of that infallible spirit from which they flowed, and dictated them to the dying patriarch.

Thus we have finished this famous piece of sacred history, in the Old Testament; and of which there is so much notice taken, and use made, by St. Paul, in the New. It lets us see, that amidst all the passions and designs of mortals, the purpose of God, according to his *will*, shall stand in the decrees and events of his providence. *The elder shall serve the younger; For Jacob have I loved, and Esau have I hated, when not being yet born, they had neither done any good or evil. What shall we say then? Is there unrighteousness with God! God forbid!* It is only in his appointments about the perishing distinctions and possessions of this world, that he acts in this sovereign manner, leaving every man free to improve himself, and the grace he

† 2 Kings, viii, 20.

receives,

receives, ſo as to ſecure his eternal happineſs in the world to come. *Let us all fear him, and his judgments, and endeavour, by all poſſible means, to pleaſe him, and keep ourſelves in his love.*

DISSERTATION XXV.

Of *Jacob's* Journey to Haran, and Servitude there.

GENESIS XXVIII, &c.

NOT reckoning it ſufficient to have beſtowed his bleſſing as in the foregoing chapter, on his beloved ſon Jacob, Iſaac added to it ſeveral advices and exhortations. He charged him eſpecially, not to defile himſelf by marrying a pagan woman, but to form an alliance with the houſe of Laban, his mother's brother, who dwelt at Haran in Meſopotamia: On this condition appears in a great meaſure to have reſted the fulfillment of the benedictions which he had pronounced. Jacob obeyed; and not expecting to receive the promiſes, without performing the condition to which they were annexed, he prepared himſelf immediately to execute his father's commands.

His departure for Haran, the viſion he had on the way, the incidents that befell him at his arrival, and during his ſtay in that place, together with his return to to his father in the land of Canaan; and the conflict he had with the angel, before he met his brother Esau, are all described in this, and the four following chapters, which we shall consider jointly, that we may abridge the history.

JACOB went out from Beersheba; and it is not a little surprising, that he who was Rebecca's favorite, the heir of a powerful family, and as it were already at the head of it, should undertake such a journey alone, and, as he says himself, in the thirty-second chapter, *with a staff in his hand.* It was, according to computation, four hundred and fifty miles; the dangers of which he encountered without the company of a single domestic. But the sacred historian seems to account for this strange circumstance: For after having related Isaac's commands, and the object of Jacob's peregrination, he adds, *Esau saw all these things*; and this would certainly suggest to him an apprehension, that his jealous and disappointed brother, might execute a design which he might have formed of killing him; and that secrecy and haste were prudent and necessary.

JACOB came as far as *Luz*, a pagan town, and afterwards one of the southern frontiers of the tribe of *Benjamin.* Instead of going into it, either because the inhabitants were idolaters, or he was doubtful of their hospitality, *he took of the stones of a certain place, upon which he lighted, after the sun was set, and put them for his pillows, and lay down to sleep.* Another striking picture, and undeniable proof, of the simplicity of the primitive ages. But a good man is never defenceless

or

or alone; in the ſilence of night, or the ſolitude of the leaſt frequented deſerts, any more than in the meridian ſplendors, or the moſt populous cities, having his God and maſter to accompany and protect him. Accordingly he had, in a dream, a miraculous communication from the Almighty, frequently vouchſafed to ancient believers, in the ſame manner. He ſaw the reſemblance of *a ladder, ſet upon the earth, and the top of it reached to heaven; and the angels of God aſcending and deſcending on it. And above it ſtood* the divine majeſty, repeating to his ſervant the promiſes formerly made to his grand-father *Abraham.*

By this image, it is evident, that God deſigned to aſſure Jacob of his protection, and that he ſhould have all the aſſiſtance he ſtood in need of in his preſent circumſtances. The Patriarch was alone in a wide waſte; dreading the reſentment of his brother; and laying the plan of a marriage: God ſhews him innumerable hoſts of heavenly beings, who ſurround and watch over him; and promiſes him a poſterity as the duſt of the earth in number, that ſhould ſpread abroad into all quarters of the world. That ladder then, and the intercourſe carried on by means of it, is to be conſidered as an expreſſive emblem, of a general providential direction over mankind; eſpecially of the particular care which God takes of his ſervants.

Some interpreters * have thought that it was a figurative repreſentation of our Lords incarnation, and of the gracious adminiſtration of human affairs now conducted by him: And a paſſage in one of the goſ-

* M. Saurin, p. 387.

pels

pels ſeems to encourage ſuch a thought, where our Saviour himſelf ſays, *hereafter you ſhall ſee heaven open, and the angels of God aſcending and deſcending upon the ſon of man* *, or by his will and orders; when things in heaven and earth ſhall be ſubject to his command, for the divine glory, and the benefit of mankind.

Jacob, deeply impreſſed, perhaps agitated, with the dream, awakening, cried, *ſurely the Lord is in this place! and I knew it not! How dreadful is this place! This is none other but the houſe of God, and this is the gate of heaven!* And he ſaid this, it is not unlikely, as the three diſciples did, when they ſaw our redeemer's transfiguration; *Lord, let us make here three tabernacles, not knowing what to ſay.* Of ſuch a diſtinguiſhed favor, however, he determined to leave a memorial, where he had received it. For this reaſon he changed the name of *Luz* into *Bethel*, that is, the houſe of God. He fixed in the earth the ſtone on which his head had lain, as a monument of this divine intercourſe; and anointed it with oil, in token of it's conſecration to that ſacred uſe; adding withal a vow, that *if God would be with him, and keep him in the way that he went, and give him bread to eat, and raiment to put on, ſo that he came again to his father's houſe in peace, then ſhould the Lord be his God; and of all that he gave him, he would ſurely devote the tenth to his ſervice* †.

Encouraged by ſo many promiſes, he continued his journey, and arrived ſafe in Laban's family. This man had two daughters, *Leah* and *Rachel*, whom the ſacred text deſcribes, and informs us that the lat-

* St. John, 1, 57.

† A certain *noble* author ſays, *this is an intereſted and craving vow*. But is it any more than a thankful acknowledgment for what Jacob had received; and of humble dependence for what he expected?

ter of them ſtrongly captivated Jacob's heart. But Laban, unfeeling and ſordid, far from embracing the opportunity of forming an alliance, of which virtue and affection would have been the bands, determined to make Jacob's inclinations towards his daughter ſubſervient to his own avarice. It was cuſtomary, indeed, among the ancients to demand of every man a certain dowry for his bride, or her relations. Laban exacted ſeven years ſervice; to which Jacob conſented; *and they ſeemed unto him a few days only, for the love he had to Rachel.*

THIS term being expired, he demanded his reward; and Laban carefully avoided every objection, that he might enſnare Jacob the more effectually. Gathering together all the people of his community, he made a marriage feaſt; but ſubſtituted Leah in Rachel's place. Such a piece of deceit could be eaſily practiſed in thoſe days, when the nuptial chamber was almoſt dark; and the bride cloſely vailed, when ſhe approached her huſband's bed. Every one, who underſtands Latin itſelf, knows, that the word *nubere* to marry, ſignified originally *to vail*: And Jacob's heart and imagination being wholly ſet upon Rachel, he was entirely unſuſpecting, and thought of nothing but her.

BUT in proportion to the groſsneſs of the impoſition put upon him, was the vehemence of his reſentment: Laban, in his own excuſe, pleaded propriety and cuſtom, which declared againſt the marriage of a younger daughter before an elder. And to convince Jacob that this was the ſole motive, Laban aſſured him that, for the ſame ſervice of other ſeven years, he ſhould

ſhould have Rachel alſo. Which was accordingly performed, and the prize beſtowed upon him.

To modern readers, it will, no doubt, ſound ſtrange that Jacob ſhould have had two wives at the ſame time, and thoſe wives ſiſters, who do not conſider, that, in the Patriarchal age and diſpenſation, God had not declared his will ſo fully, concerning either Polygamy, Concubinage, or the juſt degrees of conſanguinity, as he hath been pleaſed to do now; and yet, after that will has been declared, his authority, in all ſuch matters, is of equal force with any other poſitive law; or as if the law had been from the beginning.

In this country of Meſopotamia, were born, beſides Dinah, eleven ſons to Jacob, *ſix* by *Leah*, *two* by *Bilhab* one of the handmaids, *two* by *Zilpah* the other of them, and *one* by *Rachel*, namely *Joſeph*; for *Benjamin* was not born till after his father's return to Canaan. Thoſe men are generally diſtinguiſhed by the name of *the twelve Patriarchs*, from whom the whole Jewiſh nation, by a miraculous multiplication, agreeable to the promiſe of the moſt high, deſcended, and was in leſs than three hundred years afterward ſo exceedingly populous.

During all this period of ſervice, it would appear, that, beſides the two daughters, no other wages were allowed to Jacob, for his labour and fidelity in his father-in-law's family. Wherefore God, who proceeds not always, in ſuch acts, as a ſovereign ruler, but likewiſe as a righteous judge, communicated to Jacob, in a dream, the knowledge of an expedient, which ſhould amply indemnify his loſs, and make a large ſhare of Laban's wealth his own. The firſt thing to be done was to procure an agreement, that *all the ſpeckled and ſpotted cattle, and all the brown amongſt the ſheep, and all the ſpeckled and ſpotted among the goats, ſhould be his hire.* He was, next, *to take rods of green poplar, and of the hazel and cheſnut tree, and pill white ſtrakes in them, and ſet them before the flocks when they came to drink,* AND WERE CONCEIVING. The effect was, Jacob's flocks and herds increaſed exceedingly.

HERE two difficulties occur, and are often urged. One is, if Jacob's ſtratagem was lawful; and the other, whether thoſe flocks and herds became ſpotted by a natural proceſs, or an extraordinary and miraculous appointment. As to the firſt queſtion, there can be no doubt of the lawfulneſs of the Patriarch's conduct, ſeeing it was directed by God himſelf, who has *the property of cattle on a thouſand hills* *, and might, in this manner, correct Laban, for deceiving and injuring his ſon-in-law, as well as, by adverſe appointments in his providence, deſtroy thoſe cattle before his eyes. In regard to the other queſtion, we may aſſert that, in all probability, the phenomenon may be accounted for in an ordinary way: For if God had been pleaſed to work a miracle, it is hardly to be imagined that he would have inſtructed Jacob, for the accompliſhment of his purpoſe, in a natural experiment †. And both interpreters and philoſophers produce examples and proofs, beyond number, of the

* Pſalm l. 10. † Though in ſome inſtances miracles have been wrought when means have been employed; yet, for the moſt part, they have been performed, unaccompanied by any apparatus whatever.

power

power which the imagination of mothers has upon the *Fœtus*, immediately after it's production.

Be this as it may, Laban beheld Jacob's profperity with impatience. Aud his fons, far from endeavouring to reclaim their father from his injuftice and covetoufnefs, did all that they could to excite both: *This ftranger*, they faid, *was come to take away all their glory*, which, in the facred language, fignifies their *riches*. Jacob foon perceived that he had fallen into difgrace with Laban, and his family, and refolved to leave it by ftealth; as he was afraid to do it openly. He imparted to his wives the defign, and the motives of it, who readily acquiefced, and complained of their father in their turn. Under every difficulty he accordingly fled, with two wives, two concubines, twelve children, a great number of men, and of maid fervants, of flaves and cattle. But the feaft of fheep-fhearing, which Laban celebrated with his fons, at the diftance of three days journey, was favorable to them. Rachel, at her departure, ftole her father's gods. The word for them in the original is *Teraphim*, which fignifies refponfors or publifhers. The reafon of the name, the figure of the images, the manner of confulting them, and of receiving their anfwer, have opened a vaft field for the enquiries of the learned, without any advantage to mankind at this time *. Particulars of this fort, though within the compafs of the facred writings, can as little concern us, who are better inftructed in regard to the object of our worfhip, as the

* Thofe images had the figure of a man, and were the *penates* in thofe days. For a full account of them, fee Godwin's Aaron and Mofes, book iv. chap. ix.

notions

notions of an American Indian when he invokes *Yahoo*; or of the moſt ignorant Papiſts when they pay their *congees* to the niched images of a Romiſh temple. Laban being addicted to idolatry, which is the offſpring of ignorance and fancy, he might, on different occaſions, and as his purpoſe required, uſe his *Teraphim* as he pleaſed. There are many commentators, who imagine Rachel ſtole them only for the value of their compoſition, viz. Gold, adorned, perhaps, with precious ſtones. Therefore,

We find, as might be expected, Laban had no ſooner learned that Jacob had left his ſervice, with all the wealth he had lately acquired in it, than he purſued him, under all the emotions of a covetous and avaritious man, deſpoiled of his treaſure. *But when a man's ways pleaſe the Lord, he maketh even his enemies to be at peace with him*, ſays Solomon *. Accordingly he appeared in a dream to Laban, and gave him a charge concerning Jacob, to do him and his family no harm. And the conſequence was, after ſome altercation, that though the one had it in his power to uſe violence, and the other good cauſe of diſſatisfaction and complaint, they both *made a covenant before the Lord, by erecting an heap of ſtones, and eating thereon*, a mark of reconciliation and friendſhip, *that they ſhould never paſs that heap to do one another any injury. And early next morning, Laban kiſſed his daughters, and their ſons, and bleſſed them, and departed, and returned unto his place.* Thus was Jacob happily delivered from his preſent fears.

* Prov. xvi. 7.

But

But, as has been often remarked, though the Patriarchs were the most tender objects of the Almighty's love, they were not free from troublesome and cross incidents in life. God thereby designed to elevate their minds above terrestial things, and their expectations to heaven, where all his magnificent promises were to be fulfilled. Hence it was, that Jacob had no sooner escaped from one formidable enemy, than he saw himself threatened by another, still more powerful and unrelenting. No length of time, it is often found, proscribes hatred and revenge; though it dissolve marble and rocks, it often leaves a vindictive heart unpenetrated. Indeed it was not to be expected that even fifteen or sixteen years, which Jacob had passed in Mesopotamia, could extinguish Esau's wrath against him; they could only suspend it.

Such reflections were revolving in Jacob's mind, when *the angels of God met him like an host*, confirming the saying of an holy man, seven or eight hundred years after this apparition; *The angel of the Lord encampeth round about them that fear him, and delivereth them* *. The same God who shewed Jacob, when he was going into Mesopotamia, angels ascending and descending upon a ladder, to assure him of their protection and assistance in his journey, made those same spiritual beings appear, to support him, by their presence, against what he had to fear at his return. And thus was fulfilled the promise made to him at Bethel, *Behold I will be with thee, and keep thee in all places whither thou goest, and bring thee again into this land.*

* Psalm xxxiv. 7.

When the best disposition of his family and substance was made for meeting Esau, to procure his favor, and to save, if possible, Rachel and Joseph, Jacob's dearest pledges, night came on; and the Patriarch being left alone, *there wrestled an angel with him in the form of a man, until the breaking of the day.* Whether this wrestling was real, or only a simple vision in a dream, as the ladder was, cannot positively be determined; though many have ventured to affirm both ways. Either of them we may safely chuse; for in either we will find the design answered; which was to comfort Jacob, and assure him of the blessing the Almighty had in reserve for him. *And he called the name of that place Peniel, for, said he, I have seen God face to face.*

In this sketch of the Patriarch's history, during the term mentioned, every reader must have perceived affecting and edifying events; this lesson, especially, is obvious, that a divine providence presides over the minutest affairs of life; and that much more ought to be ascribed to it's agency, than we, in these days, seem to imagine or believe: Good men of old reduced every occurrence to it's operations; and their pious example ought always to be imitated.

DISSERTATION XXVI.

Of *Jacob's* Love for *Joseph*; and his Brethren's Hatred.

GENESIS XXVIII, &c.

BY way of preparation for the following discourse, nothing more is necessary, than to inform, or rather remind readers of what they already know; that while Jacob was on the road to Hebron, and not far from his father, *Rachel*, from the beginning the sovereign mistress of his heart, *travelled, and had hard labour, and as soon as she was delivered of Benjamin, died* *.

THUS is ascertained, with an historical exactness, the birth of the twelve Patriarchs, whose names and descents are so often mentioned in the books of the old testament.

THE first thing to be observed in this chapter is, that *Jacob settled in the land wherein his father was a*

* Gen. xxxv, 16.

stranger,

ſtranger, in the land of Canaan. Here *Iſrael*, for into this name had Jacob's been changed, educated his family, and made them his aſſiſtants in huſbandry. Joſeph, Rachel's ſon, had the largeſt ſhare of his affection. Among other reaſons, this ought to be one, for marrying the object of our pureſt and beſt founded love, that the children may have that love reflected on them to the laſt. And, as Moſes obſerves, Joſeph being the ſon of Jacob's old age, he would naturally draw his father's fondneſs on him; as all mankind deſire to be, as it were, renewed in their offſpring, when they are about to leave the world themſelves. Though, by this rule, it may be thought Benjamin, the youngeſt of all, would have preſſed harder on the old man's heart, we are yet to conſider that affection may be often pre-engaged; and Joſeph might have anticipated that power in the Patriarch's mind, as he was the firſt born after his deſpair of Rachel's fruitfulneſs. There is no neceſſity for ſuppoſing, as ſome interpreters have done, that Joſeph was wiſer, or more wonderfully attracting, than all his other brethren were; though, from the figure he afterwards made in life, it is not in the leaſt improbable.

At the ſame time that we muſt acknowledge, the predilection of a parent for one child more than another, is often inaccountable; yet whatever may be the cauſe of it, and however juſt and intenſe the paſſion; we ought, nevertheleſs, to caution every one carefully to conceal it from the reſt; leſt jealouſy, the moſt dangerous poiſon poſſible, ſhould infect the whole family. Jacob, ſagacious and experienced as he was, had not this command over himſelf. Not only was his heart always open for Joſeph, but he outwardly teſtified

testified his ascendancy by every distinguishing mark. *He made him a coat of many colours*; or, as some interpreters describe it, a long robe or mantle, to denote the sovereignty and dominion he should have over his brethren. Perhaps the Patriarch had no respect to this, when he clothed his son agreeable to his own fancy.

SUCH marks of preference could not but inflame the hatred of his more advanced, discerning and ambitious brethren. And he became so much the more odious to them, that *he brought unto his father their evil report*. The indeterminateness of the expression leaves us at liberty to suppose, that this report was either of some profane words, or some wicked action of which they had been guilty.

THEIR jealousy, their contemptuous speeches, and revengeful projects were, accordingly, every day redoubled; while the most significant presages were, at the same time, given of his elevation above them all. He had two visions, as we may call them, on his bed in the night, which he could not conceal, and related them to Jacob in presence of the whole family. He dreamed that *he, and his brethren were binding sheaves in the field, and that his sheaf arose, and stood upright, and received the obeysance*, the homage *of the rest*. He dreamed also, that *the sun, and the moon, and the eleven stars did obeysance to him*. Those dreams, it is not to be doubted, came from God, and prognosticated that astonishing greatness to which he afterwards rose. This application of them we may make with the greater certainty, as it seems to have been the will of God to establish such methods of prediction, under former

dispensations,

dispensations, to give some foreknowledge of his future designs.

Indeed, if all the principal images in this last dream must have had some literal correspondence, before we can thus apply them; while Jacob, who seems to have been represented by the sun, and his eleven brethren by the same number of stars, prostrate themselves before Joseph, and put themselves under his protection, as they actually did in Egypt; we cannot well comprehend who answers to the moon, seeing Rachel was dead, not only at the time his brethren bowed to him, but also when this very dream happened.

But, be it observed, that to verify a dream, it is not necessary, that every constituent object, presented to the imagination, should correspond to some particular event. It is sufficient, as in a parable, if all the scattered ideas are so collected as to terminate in one general reality. This actually happened in the case before us. Nothing could more aptly prefigure to a man his future power and dignity, than the sun, the moon, and the stars humbling themselves at his feet. And several commentators are of opinion, that after Rachel's death, Leah, or some other of Jacob's wives, discharged the office of a mother to Joseph, and is here described by the moon, who, together with the rest of a numerous family, should fall down and worship him. But whatever truth there may be in the assertion, that Joseph's loss of his mother was affectionately supplied, we find Moses, who gives us a list of the persons that went down into Egypt with Jacob, makes no mention of any of his wives: They had probably all died in the

the land of Canaan, before the memorable famine had commenced, which occasioned their removal from it.

JACOB, perhaps, perfectly understood that those dreams had a divine origin; but perceiving likewise the bad effect they might have upon his other children, he rebuked Joseph when he related them; and said, as we may paraphrase his expostulation, what! shall I, who am an hundred years old, thy own mother who is dead, or thy step-mother so kind and indulgent, and thy brethren, so averse to thy promotion, come and reverently solicite thy patronage!

BUT however seasonable this rebuke was, the design of it was frustrated. Repeated notices of superiority, produced such malice in his brethren, that his life could only appease them; and they were never satisfied till they had an opportunity of indulging that malice to the full.

THE Patriarch commanding Joseph to go and *see whether it was well with his brethren, and well with the flocks*, after wandering a long time in the wilderness, he came up to them in *Dothan*. Another strong image of those primitive times, when such a scope of country was occupied by innumerable flocks and herds, which were watched by ten sons of an eminent and potent prince; who thought of no other employments in a land, where every ones wealth and greatness consisted solely in cattle and corn; and not in titles, and places of preferment, with which we are now acquainted. No sooner did those men see their helpless and unsuspecting brother, coming to visit them, than they formed the bloody project of taking away his life. Reuben was ſhocked at the propoſal; either becauſe the violent expedition of two of his brethren among the *Shechemites*, in the affair of *Dinah*, and which had brought ſo much diſgrace upon their houſe, had ſufficiently diſguſted him at blood; or, being the eldeſt of the family, he conſidered himſelf more immediately anſwerable to his father for their conduct. He, therefore, oppoſed his brethren's cruel deſign: And if he did not ſucceed in diverting their fury altogether, he at leaſt diminiſhed it, by turning it into another channel. He adviſed them to caſt him into one of the pits of the wilderneſs, like thoſe pools or wells, of which we read in the eighty-fourth pſalm, purpoſely dug for receiving and preſerving the rain, uſed inſtead of ſprings in hot and ſandy countries; and out of which he intended to draw Joſeph, at a convenient time, without the knowledge of the reſt. The overture was hearkened to, and followed: And thoſe barbarous men, *took a younger brother*, who had no defence but tears and cries, feeble and unavailing when oppoſed to hatred and revenge, *and threw him into the pit*.

After they had executed this atrocious deed, they ſaw *a company*, or caravan, *of Iſmaelitiſh merchants, who were going down to Egypt, with their camels, bearing ſpicery and balm, and myrrh*, to be uſed in preſerving dead bodies from putrefaction, for which Egypt was then ſo famous. Thoſe merchants always travelled in large bodies, as they do in many places at this day, for their greater ſecurity againſt robbers, and againſt wild beaſts. Judah ſuggeſting to his brethren that they might ſell Joſeph to that company, they agreed; and their deſign in this criminal traffic, being leſs

from

from avarice, than to get rid of a brother whom they abhorred and dreaded, they rated him lower than the ordinary price at which ſlaves were afterwards ſold; and actually gave him up for *twenty pieces of ſilver*. Though moſt interpreters underſtand by this ſum, ſo many *ſhekels* *, which, in our currency, amount only to two pound ten ſhillings; there are ſome, who make them only *Gerahs*, in all half a crown †.

Reuben was not preſent when this ſtep was taken. He ſtill hoped to accompliſh the humane and juſt deſign he had formed, of delivering him to his father again. His ſurpriſe and grief were, accordingly, exceſſive when he ſaw his hopes fruſtrated; and perhaps thought Joſeph was dead. He rent his cloaths, and, returning to his brethren, ſaid, *The child is not! and I, whither ſhall I go?—And Joſeph's brethren took his coat, the coat of many colours, and having dipt it in the blood of a kid, they ſent it to their father*; preſuming he would inſtantly believe that an *evil beaſt* ‡ had deſtroyed him. Jacob, incapable of imagining that his ſons could be acceſſary to the death or baniſhment of their brother, or ſo wicked as to put any impoſition on him in a matter of ſuch dreadful conſequence, was caught in the ſnare; and the thorough perſuaſion of Joſeph's death, coſt him as much ſorrow and affliction, as if he had been really murdered or devoured. *Joſeph*, ſaid he, *is without doubt rent in pieces!* and immediately manifeſted every mark of diſtreſs, that a tender parent may be allowed to feel, when he loſes a ſon, whoſe value is heightened to him, by the love which he has conſtantly beſtowed on him. *Jacob rent his cloaths, and*

* B. Patrick. † Siclis, Vide Polum. ‡ So *wild beaſts* are called in ſcripture.

put

put ſackcloth upon his loins, and mourned for his ſon many days. And all his ſons and his daughters roſe up to comfort him; but he refuſed to be comforted; and ſaid, I will go down into the grave unto my ſon mourning. And he wept for him. And from this affliction and ſorrow of his, the reflection obviouſly forces itſelf upon us, that Jacob's ſons, knowing his affection for Joſeph, and foreſeeing how he would receive the news of his death, and ſpend the remainder of his days in miſery, were as impious and criminal in this reſpect, as in the act of ſelling their brother, whoſe future honor was poſſible, while their father's peace and happineſs were torn by their ſacrilegious hands for ever from him. What a dreadful curſe, without repentance and extraordinary grace, muſt all children guilty of ſuch wickedneſs, in the juſt judgments of God neceſſarily incur!

MEAN while, the *Iſmaelitiſh* merchants, whom Moſes likewiſe calls *Midianites*, probably becauſe that company was a mixture of thoſe two neighbouring nations, carried Joſeph into Egypt, and ſold him with the reſt of their merchandiſe. *Potiphar an officer of Pharoah's, and captain of the guard*, purchaſed him. Much criticiſm has been beſtowed upon the two deſignations given here of this great man, hardly worth relating, and without making the matter any clearer in the end. Concerning Joſeph himſelf, the hero of the whole relation, we are expreſsly told, at the beginning of the thirty-ninth chapter, that *the Lord was with him, and he was a proſperous man. And Joſeph found grace in* Potiphar's *ſight, for he made him overſeer over his houſe, and put all that he had into his hand; ſo that he knew not ought he had, ſave the bread which he did eat;* till his wife caſt her eyes wantonly on Joſeph, *who*

was

was a goodly person, and well favored. The consequence of this affair, through the artifice and resentment of a disappointed woman, and the thirst of revenge in a jealous husband, was Joseph's unjust confinement in a prison; where, in a strange land, and obnoxious to one of the King's favorite servants, we might have reasonably expected his sudden death; or rather in the most public and dreadful manner. But this is anticipating the history, which, hereafter, will be more fully considered.

Thus, we have, briefly, seen an innocent youth, first sold by his brethren, for the love his father bore to him, and the information he gave of their faults, and again by the Midianites, to be the slave of a man who soon cast him into prison for righteousness sake. And all this came to pass by a singular providence; that by the same interposition, which only could provide and direct all the means leading to it, he might afterwards be raised almost to regal honor and authority. The whole dispensation was preparatory to that more complicated and extensive one, by which a whole nation of his own kindred and descendants were to be formed in Egypt, and whom God Almighty, the wise ruler of the world, designed to be the keepers of his sacred will, and lights to the whole earth, till the last days, when he should send forth his own son in human flesh.

Between Christ the son of the eternal father, and him whose history we have been contemplating, it may be proper barely to observe, that divines, of good sense and sound judgment, have often drawn a long and striking parallel: And it is certain, that an enlightened and pious mind, may find ſtrong and uſeful ſimilitudes on this ſubject, though it is not convenient to be over-exact in the application of many circumſtances.

We may aptly conclude with the words of the hundred and fifth pſalm, where the tranſactions we have been viewing are dſtinctly commemorated; *O give thanks unto the Lord; call upon his name; make known his deeds among the people; talk ye of all his wonderous works; for how terrible is he in his doings towards the children of men.*

DISSERTATION XXVII.

Continuation of *Joseph's* History, till the arrival of the ten Patriarchs in Egypt.

GENESIS XXXIX, &c.

WHILE Jacob, at a greatly advanced age, and under other trials and difficulties, was every day remembering and lamenting his beloved ſon's tragical end, and aſtoniſhed, beyond meaſure, what could poſſibly be the meaning of thoſe dreams, and in what manner they might be fulfilled, which had brought envy and ruin upon that innocent youth; for when he related them, we are told his father obſerved them; while Jacob, I ſay, was thus exerciſed at home, Joſeph, by a wonderful providence, was paving the way for his father's and brethren's preſervation, in a future ſeaſon of diſtreſs, and for the commencement of that grand diſpenſation, the forming out of a few perſons an illuſtrious multitude of people, who ſhould be the guardians of the laws of God in the promiſed land, till

the

the coming of the Messiah, who should establish a covenant with the whole earth.

INDEED, with *the blessings that rested on the head of him who was separated from his brethren*, there was, for a short time, a severe affliction mingled. The secret appointment of God, as well as the workings of human passions, produced, we may be certain, the cross accident. This being slightly touched in the foregoing dissertation, must necessarily have a larger place here. The case was this: While Potiphar availed himself of the prosperity that attended Joseph's conduct and designs, his wife, influenced by the immodesty and unchastity which highly prevailed among the Egyptian women, viewed Joseph's person, and was captivated by his charms. And as almost the whole sex, when once they have exceeded the first limits of shame, easily disregard all otheir restraints, this licentious woman, not being able, either with the blandishments or threatenings, which *Josephus* *, mentions, to persuade this righteous youth to sin against God, resolved to compel him. The same historian relates some fine speeches, which Joseph employed, on this occasion, in order to check and defeat the purposes of his mistress. But the most eloquent and pathetic speech possible, at such a juncture, could not have been so expressive of his abhorrence of such an act, nor so effectual a guard to his innocence, as what he immediately did, without speaking a word, at least so far as we know from the sacred relation: Moses, who, on a former occasion, hath recorded Joseph's expostulations, only says at this last attack, that *he left his garment in her hand, and fled, and got him out.*

* Antiquit. Judaic. Lib. 11.

The

The *adulteress will hunt for the precious life,** is an observation by wise Solomon; which, no doubt, signifies that when she is despised, she will proceed to the last extremity, till she has revenged herself for the contempt of her favor, and the disappointment of her lust. Potiphar's wife, accordingly, accused Joseph of the crime of which she herself only was guilty, in her polluted imagination and desires. Her husband perhaps saw through the affair: But as the slightest suspicions of a woman's infidelity, reflect upon the man against whom it has been designed, Potiphar condemned Joseph, to save his own honor; and yet at the same time, to satisfy his conscience, he carried his resentment no higher than imprisonment; though he might have had his servant's life, for the offence of which he was impeached. And even for this loss of liberty, some compensation, by the direction of an invisible judge and ruler, was made to Joseph. Instead of experiencing in confinement, the pains and miseries of a captive, or the disgrace of an atrocious detested criminal, he enjoyed, in some measure, the condition of a free man, and was treated with a distinguishing respect. He had maintained and asserted his innocence, and heaven had given weight to his words, by the remarkable successes which had accompanied all his negotiations. This, and his constantly mild and exemplary demeanor, *in the place where the king's prisoners were bound*, soon gained him the same ascendancy over the jailor's mind, that he had lately had in the house and affections of Potiphar.

In the same prison, we are told, were two of Pharoah's officers of considerable quality, for some offence

* Proverbs vi. 26.

they

they had committed againſt their lord the king. The one was butler, or cup-bearer, the other baker; and tho' theſe names may ſuggeſt to us very mean ideas at firſt, we are yet to conſider that this ſcene is laid in Egypt, where, inſtead of ſlaves, and the lower claſſes of people, being admitted to the moſt menial offices, none but perſons illuſtrious by their rank and birth, were ſuffered to hold them, or to have any employment in the houſes of their kings.

Now each of thoſe ſtate priſoners had a dream; the one dreamed *that he ſaw a vine having three branches, which firſt budded, then bloſſomed, and laſtly brought forth ripe grapes*; and that having Pharoah's cup in his hand he preſſed the grapes into it, and gave the cup to Pharoah. The other dreamed *that he had three white baſkets, with all manner of baked-meats for Pharoah on his head, and the birds came and did eat them.* Joſeph told the butler that *in three days he would be reſtored to his dignity and office*; *and the baker, that in the ſame ſpace of time he would be hanged, and his fleſh devoured by the birds of the air.*

Both interpretations were fully juſtified by the reſpective events. The baker was condemned to die, as Joſeph had foretold; and the cup-bearer obtained favor. But tho' a man ſo extraordinary, as Joſeph muſt have ſeemed to be, had feelingly ſolicited his intereſt to bring him out of the dungeon, and told him that *he was ſtolen out of the land of the Hebrews*, and had done nothing in Egypt for which they ſhould put him *in ward*, the butler, on his own re-eſtabliſhment, immediately forgot him. Ingratitude, indeed, is ſaid to be the vice of courtiers; and, of ſome excellent

panegyrics

panegyrics and ſermons, the celebrated author obſerves, that, for the moſt part, thoſe who riſe from diſgrace or meanneſs, to high degrees of glory, and to diſtinguiſhed fortunes, forget and deſpiſe thoſe who have been the companions and witneſſes of their paſt indigence; and remove, from their ſight and remembrance, every object that can renew the image and mortifying reflection of their former diſtreſſes *. This writer had, perhaps, ſeen his own ſenſible remarks many times verified.

And it came to paſs at the end of two years, either from Joſeph's impriſonment, or the butler's promotion, *that Pharoah* himſelf *had dreams which mightily troubled him, and made him ſend in the morning, for all the magicians of Egypt, and for all the wiſe men thereof*; but to no purpoſe. Then it was that the chief-butler, to procure relief and ſatisfaction for the anxious monarch, mentioned Joſeph, who was in the priſon with him, and commended his knowledge and wiſdom. The Hebrew interpreter was, inſtantly, brought before the king; who informed him, that *he had ſeen in a dream*, on the banks of the Nile, *ſeven cows, fat-fleſhed, and well-favored; and they were fed in a meadow. And quickly there appeared ſeven other cows, poor, and very ill favored, ſuch as had never been ſeen in all the land of Egypt; and theſe laſt eat up the firſt, without fattening them.* In like manner, he ſaw, in another dream, *ſeven ears of corn, on one ſtalk, full and good; and ſeven ears thin, and withered, and blaſted with the eaſt wind, ſpring up after them; and theſe thin ears alſo devoured the ſeven good ears:* And the king concluded, with declaring the

* Flechier, Evêque de Nîmes, part. II.

ignorance

ignorance of his own *magicians*, and demanded Joseph's explanation.

Joseph, first of all, refreshed the monarch's memory concerning a maxim established, we are told, among the Egyptians, that the art of divination was not an human acquisition, but the gift of heaven*. *It is not in me*, says he, *but God shall give Pharoah an answer of peace*: And having thus confessed the revealer of secrets, for the assistance he was about to receive, the dreams were interpreted. He informed Pharoah that both of them signified the same thing; and the doubling of the vision shewed that the event was decreed by God, who would shortly bring his purpose to pass. *The seven fat cows, and the seven good ears of corn, represented seven years of plenty*, which were just commencing; *and the seven lean cows, and seven blasted ears of corn, denoted seven years of famine*, which should immediately succeed them. How natural the types! *Ears of corn* were exceedingly expressive of the condition of Egypt, in regard to it's plenty or want; and *cattle* not less. An ox was the hieroglyphic for the earth, agriculture and all sorts of food. And the *Nile*, on the banks of which Pharoah saw those objects, was the most universal cause of the poverty or riches of that country. *Egypt*, Pliny tells us †, was visited with famine, when that river rose no higher than twelve cubits; with scarcity, when only thirteen, when it rose fourteen, the people rejoiced; fifteen, they promised themselves all kinds of necessaries; and sixteen, innumerable pleasures and delights. That river was, therefore, worshipped as a God ‡. And hearing

* Herodot. Lib. II.

† Plin. Hist. Nat. Lib. v. Cap. ix.

‡ Voss. de idol. Lib. II.

that *Greece* was only watered and fructified by rains, and not by rivers, as their country was, the *Egyptians*, humorously said, that it might, on certain occasions, be defrauded of it's treasure by some surly god, and reduced to very hard cheer *.

PURSUING the history, we find that Joseph did more than foretel what was to happen: He proposed measures of which Pharoah might avail himself, and make the seven first years of plenty, mitigate the rigors of the other years of scarcity and want: He advised the king to appoint officers for collecting the fifth part of all the produce of the land of *Egypt*, during the years of plenty; that when the famine came, the inhabitants might not utterly perish.

THIS important view of things, and the wise counsel, in consequence, offered, induced Pharoah, not only to give Joseph his liberty, but likewise promote him immediately to the highest station in the kingdom. He commanded him to be acknowledged by all his subjects, as *the deliverer of Egypt*, owned himself the superiority of his wisdom, and that *the spirit of God* was *in him*. Besides conferring on Joseph the superintendence of the royal family, the king made him also lord of the whole land, and ordered all the people to obey him.

HAVING thus communicated to him a real and effectual power, Pharoah, moreover, adorned Joseph with all the exterior symbols and marks of it. *He arrayed him in vestures of fine linen*, for which Egypt was the wonder of the world, *put a gold chain about his*

* Herdot. Lib. II. Cap. xiii.

neck,

neck, and a ring on his hand, taken from his own: An act common in the eastern nations, to denote high exaltation, and great delegated power.

EQUIPPED in this manner, Joseph was shewn to the people in a royal chariot, preceded by officers, who made proclamation, accompanied with the most pompous and solemn apparatus, that the king's pleasure was, they should *bow the knee*. The translation of the word *bow the knee*, is attended with some difficulty. In Hebrew, the first syllable signifies *father*; and the second, in Syriac, *king* *. Whence some learned interpreters have thought that the compound expressed the father of the king. But, notwithstanding the countenance given this interpretation, by what Joseph himself said to his brethren, that *God had made him a father to Pharoah*, a certain critic †, well skilled in those languages, by the smallest change in the spelling, supports the common version, *bow the knee*.

A WELL known custom among the people of the east, was to give new names, from particular circumstances, to such persons as they adopted into their service. Sundry instances of this we have had already by divine authority, in the names of *Abraham*, *Sarah*, and *Israel*; and more occur in the course of the scriptures. Thus Pharoah, on Joseph's advancement, called him *Zaphnath-paaneah*; which some have rendered *the saviour of the people*, but the far greater part of the ancients, *revealer of secrets*.

THE king, moreover, formed for Joseph a powerful alliance, by marrying him to *Asenath*, the daugh-

* Heb. אברך. † Ainsworth on Genesis xli.

ter

ter of *Potipherah*, prieſt and prince *of On*, or *Heliopolis in Egypt*, famous for the worſhip of the ſun, and where was annually celebrated, with infinite magnificence, a feaſt in honour of that luminary. From this marriage with *Aſenath*, who ſome ſay, immediately renounced idolatry, and acknowledged the true God, ſprung two ſons; *the firſt was Manaſſeh, for*, ſaid Joſeph, *God hath made me forget all my toil, and all my father's houſe*; the ſecond *Ephraim, for*, ſaid he again, *God hath made me to be fruitful in the land of my affliction.*

Thus, though the prophet's expreſſion be ſtill true, that *God hideth himſelf* *, there ſometimes are unfoldings of the clouds, with which he frequently covers himſelf, and ſuch affecting ſtrokes of providence as ſhew that he never abandons the government of the univerſe. In this hiſtory of Joſeph we have ſeen innocence oppreſſed by calumny, and groaning in a priſon, among malefactors But, in his elevation, we have alſo ſeen, the ſame innocence breaking forth in all it's ſplendor, and univerſally acknowledged. Examples of this kind are evidences that *the Lord reigneth* †, and give us confidence in his equity and wiſdom.

* Iſaiah xlv. 15. † Pſalm xcvii. 1.

DISSERTA-

DISSERTATION XXVIII.

Of JOSEPH's behaviour to his brethren; and their return to CANAAN.

GENESIS XLII.

THE famine foretold by Joseph at length commenced. It may appear ſomewhat ſtrange, that preparations for it, during ſo many years in Egypt, and a ſtill longer ſpace before, ſhould never have conveyed to Jacob, any account of ſo extraordinary a man in that country; nor the circumſtances of his name, his nation, and high promotion from ſlavery, appear to raiſe ſtrong conjectures in his mind, and make him apply Joſeph's dreams, which, having preſaged ſuch ſingular fortune, had incurred the envy of his brethren. The difficulty will vaniſh when we reflect, that, beſides the perſuaſion, reaſonably entertained by Jacob, that Joſeph was devoured by a wild beaſt, which prevented all ſearch for him, and deſtroyed the fondeſt expectations; poſts and couriers, like thoſe we now have, were then altogether unknown; and intelligence between nations much leſs remote,

remote, by no means regularly carried on, ſo far as certain hiſtory inſtructs us, till the reign of Cyrus the great, who eſtabliſhed thoſe methods of intercourſe. And yet the report, that there was corn in Egypt, is perfectly conſiſtent and natural, when ſevere hunger, and the fear of a lingering death, would forcibly engage the enquiries of every family, and make men of every condition ſeek for relief.

In this kingdom, therefore, Jacob's ten ſons arrived, and appeared before Joſeph; whom the forementioned ſpace, and foreign ſumptuous apparel had ſo diſguiſed, that not the leaſt ground for ſuſpecting him to be their brother could poſſibly remain: While their dreſs, language and aſpect, made him inſtantly know them. Emotions, too various to be encountered at once, then roſe in his mind; and, in part, produced that ſingular conduct towards them, which, perhaps, in every act, cannot be fully juſtified; though the whole, taken together, teſtified the greateſt wiſdom, and tended to the diſcovery of his ſecret deſign. This was to know whether Jacob and Benjamin were ſtill alive; but neceſſity required him to behave in ſuch a manner, as to leave himſelf at liberty to conceal the truth from his brethren, or to make the diſcovery as he ſhould think fit. His ſtern accuſation, that they were enterpriſing ſpies, who had come into the land to explore the weakneſs of it's fortifications, and the defects of its government *, of which they might take advantage, a learned geographer of the ancient territories † obſerves, was the more reaſonable, as thoſe men had come from a quarter where Egypt could eaſily be attacked and invaded by an enemy.

* This is M. Le Clerc's gloſs. † Herodot. Lib. iii. Cap. v.

enemy. The vaſt deſerts of Cyrene, Lybia, and Ethiopia, which bounded it on the weſt and ſouth, were its impregnable barriers there.

In their reply, they defended themſelves with the ſimplicity which always accompanies truth and innocence. *Thy ſervants*, ſaid they to Joſeph, *are ten brethren the ſons of one man in the land of Canaan*; who would hardly expoſe themſelves to the common dangers of ſuch a bold deſign, eſpecially when their father had loſt a ſon already by a fatal accident, and only one left with him of the whole family.

By this ſtratagem Joſeph learned that Jacob and Benjamin were ſtill alive; but in order to obtain farther information, he made the weakneſs of their evidence a farther argument of his ſuſpicions; and told them that nothing could deliver them from the harſh treatment of which they might perhaps complain, but the moſt ſatisfactory exculpation of themſelves. *Let one of you*, ſaid he, *go into Canaan, and bring down thither that young brother whom ye ſay is there:* Your innocence ſhall be proved by your chearfulneſs to comply with this command; otherwiſe, *by the life of Pharaoh, ye are ſurely ſpies.* The notion which ſome interpreters have entertained, that by this form of affirmation Joſeph ſwore religiouſly, and impiouſly aſcribed to the monarch of Egypt the perfections of the ſupreme God, is without any foundation; as is alſo the remark of ſome ſevere moraliſts, that he had contracted the habit of ſwearing profanely in an abandoned court. The expreſſion is the ſame in ſubſtance with that uſed by *Abigail* to *David*, when ſhe ſaid, *as thy*

ſoul

ſoul liveth *, which is only a ſtrong aſſertion, in regard to the convictions or intentions which a perſon may have conceived. In the ſame manner the firſt chriſtians, who were always ſo ſcrupulous about every appearance of idolatry, always proteſted and ſwore by the life of the emperors, while they conſtantly refuſed to appeal to the genii and falſe gods †.

To convince them, by the ſeverity of his conduct, that his ſuſpicions were not feigned, Joſeph ordered his brethren to be ſeiſed, and ſhut up in priſon, where they remained three whole days; and then had the condition of their liberty and lives again repeated, with this relaxation that, inſtead of nine being kept as hoſtages for their fidelity, they might go to their native country with proviſions, and only one ſhould be detained till they returned with Benjamin.

The various incidents in the whole affecting relation are all equally intereſting and new; but the limits of this work will not allow us to unfold them all, in an hiſtory larger than the text, which every one poſſeſſes. There we ſee deſcribed the anguiſh of the patriarchs' hearts in Joſeph's preſence, and his inexpreſſibly tender feelings touched; Simeon bound with the greateſt rigor, perhaps for his general violence and injuſtice, and as having been the principal adviſer to ſell Joſeph to the merchant-men; the return of the nine with corn, and their ſurpriſe and fear when every one found the money in his ſack which he had paid to Joſeph's commiſſary in Zoan. We have

* 1. Sam. xxv. 26. † Juramus ſicut non per genios Cæſarum, ità per ſalutem eorum quæ eſt auguſtior omnibus geniis. Tertull. Apologet. Cap. xxxii.

repreſented

represented in the Mosaic account, their arrival at their own habitations, and their father's house, where they told all the strange things that had befallen them; Jacob's affliction when he heard of Simeon's captivity, whom he considered as lost for ever, and Reuben's declaration of the farther demand which the Lord of Egypt had made of Benjamin, without whom they were never to see his face again, nor expect to have Simeon released: *But*, said he, *slay my two sons, if I bring him not to thee; deliver him into my hand, and I will bring him to thee again:* Who received the indignant answer; *Ah! wherefore did ye deal so ill with me, as to tell the man that you had another brother! Me have ye bereaved of my children! Joseph is not! and Simeon is not! and ye will take Benjamin away! all these things are against me! My son shall not go down with you; for his brother is dead, and he alone is left*, the single pledge of my love for Rachel; *and if mischief befal him in the way in which ye go, then shall ye bring down my grey hairs with sorrow to the grave.*

But seeing the grain consumed, and himself and family surrounded with all the horrors of famine, Jacob's paternal love and tenderness were conquered, and he at last consented that Benjamin should go with his brethren. He gave them his best advice; presents for the governor of Egypt; the money which had been put into their sacks, perhaps inadvertently; and his blessing in these solemn words, equally expressive of his piety and affection; *God Almighty give you mercy before the man, that he may send away your other brother, and Benjamin*; *yet*, mark his resolution mixed with the bitterest sorrow, *if I am bereaved of my children, let me be bereaved.*

In

In the multitude of their thoughts within them, and with which they would perplex one another, his sons arrived in Egypt the second time, and were introduced to Joseph, who immediately asked the important question; *is your father well, the old man of whom ye spake? is he yet alive? and seeing his brother Benjamin, his mother's son, he said, God be gracious to thee my son.* So full and overwhelmed was his soul with joy and sympathy, he could add no more at this time.

Next, Moses describes a feast suitable to the bounty and magnificence of a prince, with all the peculiar arrangements, which his dignity, and a difference in religion, demanded. At this feast, Joseph distinguished Benjamin, by appointing for him five times as much as for any of his brethren; agreeable to an ancient custom, recorded by Eusebius, in the ninth book of his Evangelical Preparation, from Alexand. Polyhistor. After this indulgent hospitality, the ruler of Joseph's houshold was privately commanded to fill the sacks of his brethren with corn; to put the price of it in them as before, which they had, most ingenuously, and with the greatest amazement, acknowledged to have found on their way; and to inclose, besides, his silver cup in Benjamin's. Thus innocently involved in apparent circumstances of complicated guilt, they were not long departed, when by Joseph's instructions, they were stopt by the same officer, and severely reproached with baseness and ingratitude, in stealing the cup in which his master *used to divine.* Commentators have multiplied opinions beyond number, concerning this expression. The word in old times was, very probably, of an indifferent signi-

 fication;

fication *; and, therefore, some have translated, *is not this the cup in which my lord drinks, and consequently would soon call for* †? and others, *is not this the cup in which my lord drinks, and by which he hath proved you,* and found that you are worthless men ‡? The latter explanation has been followed by a great many interpreters both ancient and modern §. Others translate literally, especially the Jews, who believe that Joseph was a magician.

THIS character, originally, had nothing bad in it: It only expressed great wisdom and knowledge, till it was afterwards perverted, and became as deservedly hateful, as it was vain and ridiculous. Indeed as many ‖ have given descriptions of the various methods of *divination by cups* in Egypt, and in other countries, Joseph, at the same time that he derided such methods, might, nevertheless, so far carry on the disguise, as to make his brethren believe, in their ignorance, that he was skilled in that art.

HOWEVER that was, they were astonished at the charge; protested their innocence, and devoted the guilty person to death, and themselves to slavery. But how much greater was their astonishment and dread, when the cup was found with Benjamin, which obliged them to return to Joseph's house, and expose themselves to his resentment!

* Bishop Patrick in loco. † Targum of Onkelos. ‡ Arabic Version. § Vatable in loco. ‖ Voyez Bodin des sorciers. Liv. II. Vide Cornel. Agrip. de occulta philosophia. Lib. I. Wierus de magis infamibus. Cap. xii. &c. &c. who have largely described those methods. But Bishop Patrick says, we do not know now what they were.

THE

The concluding ſcenes where Joſeph makes himſelf known to his brethren, and receives his father, ſhall be the ſubject of the following diſſertation.

DISSERTATION XXIX.

Of JOSEPH's making himself known to his Brethren; and JACOB's descent into EGYPT.

GENESIS XLV, &c.

BEFORE we proceed to the matter of this dissertation, we shall dwell a little longer, on what was just hinted before; namely, the probable reasons that determined Joseph to pursue his course of behaviour towards his brethren; which seems to have something so singular and extraordinary in it, that it is impossible to forbear such questions as these: What could induce him to postpone, to an uncertain hereafter, the joy of a good father, which the knowledge of his beloved son's safety, and high honor, must necessarily give him? Instead of making him happy instantly with the news, why should he invent fresh causes of sorrow and sufferings? Why was not his first care, when Canaan groaned under the severe scourge of famine, to provide an ample and lasting subsistence for

his

his family? Could he, whose authority and influence were unbounded in Egypt, apprehend any bad consequence from a discovery of his birth and nation, which his language, and his own confession, had already fixed? And even if this should have been the case, ought he not to have surmounted the apprehension, performed his duty, and left the event to Providence?

In his contrary conduct there is apparently something difficult, and crossing the dictates of religion and nature: And yet, Joseph's character being so amiable and compleat, that few, if any, equal it in other respects, we may rest assured that he had solid and wise reasons for this conduct; some of which, perhaps arising out of peculiar circumstances, we cannot now suggest; while a few may be given that are perfectly plain and natural. Perhaps his affection for Benjamin made him afraid of exposing him to the farther envy of his brethren, and wish to have him in safe possession. Perhaps he was unwilling, for a while, to reveal the guilt of his brethren in regard to himself. Perhaps also, prudence made him decline risking any thing in point of fortune, at a time when his father's house required his aid so much; till a convenient season should occur, when he might make them ample compensation for a few severe acts, without hazarding his own interest. At least, as he was so remarkably blessed and prospered by heaven, we may be satisfied that the grounds of his procedure were good.

These reflections being premised, the present passage now comes to be considered. Judah's affecting

ing speech to Joseph, we have related in the foregoing chapter, which an Hebrew commentator paraphrases thus: When we appeared the first time before thee, O my Lord, we answered simply all the questions thou wast pleased to ask, touching our family. We told thee that we had a father, stooping under years, and the weight of continual fatigues and adversities. We said that we had a brother extremely dear to him, having been the only son left of his mother, after his brother had come to a tragical end. Him my Lord, with grievous threatenings, which sounded in our ears all the way, thou commandedst to be brought. We related what had happened to our father. He refused to send his child, till the force of famine, and confidence in my tenderness and promises, prevailed over his paternal fondness. Then he let him go, and lo! he stands before my Lord! For him I am responsible, and on his life my father's depends. Have compassion, I beseech thee, and let the misery of the old man, if this child is not restored to him, and whom he parted with against his will, move thy soul. If a sacrifice must be made, accept of me: On me pronounce sentence, and inflict the pains he hath incurred. With all my heart I consent to be one of your slaves, on the condition that my brother is set at liberty. And let pity for his youth, let pity for my misfortune, affect my Lord less, than for the absent, fond, old father. Suffer not that mighty hand of thine to crush us, under which, as an hallowed altar, we have taken refuge, and looked for protection from our calamities. Feel for an old man, who, during a series of many years, hath pursued the paths, and improved himself in the practice of probity; and is highly esteemed among the

Syrians,

Syrians, though he professes a religion different from theirs, and follows another sort of life *

This paraphrase, so full and conformable to the account Moses gives of the matter, must be pleasing to every reader, and aptly introduces the motives, and the manner of Joseph's making himself known to his brethren. First of all, the emotions of his own heart, so heightened by the workings of pure nature, could no longer be controled; then his brethren's affliction; the thoughts of Jacob's grief, if he saw not Benjamin return, and heard that he was in bondage; and the desire of seeing his father soon; together with the assurance he now had of the anxiety of the Patriarchs about their father's happiness; of their relentings, and bitter remorse, for having sold himself; and their kind usage of his brother; those feelings and reflections prevailed at last, over all the maxims of human prudence and policy; and forced him instantly to disembarrass and comfort them, and discover the strange conclusion to which those mysterious scenes were to come. He commanded the Egyptians, who were waiting, to withdraw. Distraction or restraint are highly painful, in the swelled effusions of love and tenderness; and we are naturally unwilling to lay open the heart, in the presence of such as cannot enter into our feelings, and in some measure partake of them with us.

When Joseph and his brethren were alone, he poured forth a flood of tears, accompanied with this declaration, in tremulous and broken accents; *I am Joseph; doth my father yet live?* And as *his brethren were troubled*, and could not answer him, he imme-

* Philo Judæus, *de Josepho*, pag. 558.

diately

diately administered all the relief in his power; he said, *come near to me, I pray you; and they came near*; when he farther said, *I am Joseph your brother, whom ye sold into Egypt. But be not grieved, nor angry with yourselves that ye sold me hither; for God did send me before you to preserve life. These two years hath the famine been in the land; and yet there are five years, in the which there shall be neither earing nor harvest. And God sent me before you, to preserve you a posterity in the earth, and to save your lives by a great deliverance. So now it was not you that sent me hither, but God, and he hath made me a father to Pharaoh, and lord of all his house, and ruler throughout all the land of Egypt.*

In this manner did Joseph make himself known to his brethren; whom, instead of condemning for their cruelty towards him, he in some measure, justifies, by representing the over-ruling hand of God as conducting the whole affair; and deducing so many great and important consequences from it. At this most delicate crisis, he hath given a surprising evidence of the superiority of his understanding, of his wisdom, and piety at once. And when his brethren could hardly believe what they had yet heard and seen to be true, he descended, still farther, to the most intimate familiarity, and said again, *behold your eyes see, and the eyes of my brother Benjamin, that it is my mouth that speaketh unto you.* Having thus convinced them, almost against the testimony of their senses, Joseph pressed them to depart for Canaan; to inform his father that he was still alive; of all his glory which they had seen in Egypt; and to beseech him to come down into that kingdom without delay. Lest the Patriarch's infirmities, and the length of the way, should prevent him from undertaking the journey, his son

proposed

proposed to settle him in *Goshen*, which was a division of the *lower Egypt*, on the east of the Nile, bordering on Arabia, and the frontiers of Palæstine. Near this stood the city in which the kings of Egypt then resided, where Joseph himself staid with Pharaoh; called *Zoan* in the seventy eight psalm; and by some profane authors *Tanis*, as also by the Septuagint *. This proximity Joseph alledged to his brethren, as a reasonable motive which should determine Jacob to remove to a place, where, with the greatest ease, he might have intercourse with his son. Pursuing the history, in the following verses of the chapter, we find, he, finally, said, *haste you; and go up to my father, and say unto him; thus saith thy son Joseph, God hath made me lord of all Egypt; come down unto me, tarry not. And thou shalt dwell in the land of Egypt; and thou shalt be near unto me, thou, and thy children, and thy children's children, and thy flocks, and thy herds, and all that thou hast.*

Thus Joseph disposed of a province of Egypt, without the knowledge of Pharaoh, and, no doubt, knew he might, without abusing his authority; which shews us the dignity and power to which he had advanced himself, and the confidence that was reposed in his justice. The prince himself was no sooner apprised of the arrival of the sons of Jacob, than he confirmed every thing which Joseph had done. He conversed with them himself; urged them to depart; and come back quickly, with all they had, into his dominions. He ordered all sorts of carriages to be prepared for them; and all sorts of provisions which might be necessary in their journey. And lest the transporting their furniture, should retard their

* In loco.

return,

return, and Joseph's felicity, the king bade them, not regret what they might lose, or leave behind, as it should be largely repaid in Egypt.

JOSEPH, officially, executed Pharaoh's commands, and was the willing minister of that prince's liberality and magnificence. He supplied his brethren with all kinds of provisions and chariots, and loaded them with rich presents for Jacob. To all of them he gave, each man, changes of raiment; in which consisted a great part of the riches of the ancients. In the book of Judges* we see *Samson* promises thirty change of garments to any one that should interpret his riddle; and demands the same number if they could not. *Naaman the Syrian* brought ten changes of raiment, from his master to the King of Israel †, with many other things, for his good offices with the prophet Elisha, that Naaman might be cured. In the times of the *first Roman Emperors*, this species of luxury had risen to such a degree, that, as *Plutarch* relates ‡, *Lucullus the Prætor* had two hundred changes of raiment; and *Horace* makes them five thousand §. To this custom, very probably, *St. James* refers, when he says, *weep ye rich men, for the miseries that shall come upon you; for your riches are corrupted, and your garments are moth-eaten* ‖.

As, in this distribution, Benjamin was distinguished far above the rest; *for Joseph gave him three hundred pieces of silver, and five changes of raiment*, and such an evident partiality might excite their jealousy, and Jo-

* Judges xiv, 12, 13. † II Kings v, 5. ‡ Tom. I; in vita Luculli. § —— Tibi millia quinque esse domi chlamydum —— Horat. L. I, Ep. vi, 44. ‖ St. James v, 1.

seph's

seph's promotion occasion disputes among his brethren, he, therefore, exhorted them, above all things, to preserve unity and concord among themselves.

THOSE sons of Jacob, thus departing from *Zoan*, performed their journey, and arrived in *Canaan*, where they related to their father all the strange things they had seen in Egypt. When they told him, that *Joseph was yet alive*, and governor of all that land, the Patriarch's raptures were so excessive that they affected the animal frame, and threw him into a *lipothymy*, or fainting-fit; the usual and natural effect of a sudden surprise; and the more agreeable, it is the more powerful. Jacob had no expectation that Joseph was alive; and his elevation to such honors as they mentioned besides, could not but overwhelm the Patriarch with joy. To all gladness of heart, and even comfort, he had been a stranger since Joseph's supposed death; and now the whole tide of it, to compensate for all his sorrows, rushing on him at once, was too much for him to resist. But recovering from the extacy, *when he saw the ten he asses laden with the things of Egypt, and ten she asses laden with corn and bread, and meat for him by the way, and the wagons and chariots, which Joseph had sent to carry him*; knowing them to be beyond the power of fiction, and what the ability of none under the affluence and greatness of a prince could supply; *the spirit of Jacob revived in him*; and he was convinced their relation was true. And fully transported with the hope of beholding Joseph, he breathed out, abruptly, these expressive words; *it is enough*; *Joseph my son is yet alive*; *I will go and see him before I die.*

AFTER

After Jacob had left Hebron, where he had long dwelt, God appeared to him in the same place, which his grandfather Abraham's piety had already rendered famous, namely *Beer-sheba*, in the most *southerly* parts of Canaan, and near that wilderness through which his posterity went, when they came from Egypt. He promised to be with him in his journey; to make him see his son; and that *Joseph should put his hands upon his eyes.* An expression full of signification: This being one of the last acts of tenderness to the dying, Jacob was hereby shewn that his exit should be peaceable in Egypt, and among his own dutiful and affectionate children. Penelope in *Homer*, speaking to Ulysses of Telemachus, prays to the Gods, that *the same son of theirs might close both their eyes.* And *Ovid's* paraphrase of the Greek is, *may the gods, when the will of the fates is fulfilled, grant thy eyes and mine he may shut.* Profane historians themselves furnishing us with many examples of this phrase, it must have been very ancient, and universally understood.

When Jacob approached Egypt, he sent Judah before him, to procure directions for *Goshen* *. Joseph

* Hanc regionem invenire labor haud levis est: Nam in Septuaginta derivari videtur vox a גשם, *pluvia.* Et Hieronymus *in traditionibus Hebraicis*, de hac voce sic loquitur; *Si ut in nostris codicibus est, per extremum* m *scribitur gosem, quod mihi nequaquam placet, Terram significat complutam*; גשן. *In imbrem vertitur: Ac si diceretur, in terra irrigua.* Sed tamen insuperabilis non est, quum illi senes, qui in Ægypto scripturas transtulerunt, aiunt, Γεσεμ Ἀραβιας. Ex his apparet, venerandos hos interpretes, atque Ægypti locorum probe gnaros, *Goschenis* nomine ea loca intellexisse quæ Palestinæ & Arabiæ proxima sunt. Et constat, porro, ex strabone, Lib. xvii. aliisque authoribus, Heroum urbem fuisse prope sinum Elaniticum rubri maris. Spicil. Jamesonii Cap. 1.

dispatched

dispatched guides; made ready his own chariot; and went up thence to meet *Israel* his father. Presenting himself before him, in expressive silence *he fell on his neck, and wept on his neck a good while.* When, like all other passions, after long and violent exertions, joy, love, tenderness had subsided, *Israel said unto Joseph, now let me die since I have seen thy face, because thou art yet alive.*

THUS have we come again, in the course of this work, to another great period in the history of divine providence, which requires to be connected with the other periods that have gone before it, since the destruction of the old world. From the deluge to the calling of Abraham, four hundred and forty-five years may be reckoned, within which time the particular events have been described. And from the calling of Abraham, till Jacob and his family went down into Egypt, two hundred and fifteen years. Hence six hundred and sixty years is the age of the world, at this time, since it's restoration from water. New measures, therefore, notwithstanding that general scourge, by which the Almighty severely punished the whole earth for it's corruption, appear to have been necessary to instruct mankind, and keep alive the knowledge of the true God among them. For this purpose we have heard so much, during a large portion of the sacred history, of one particular man, whose various fortunes were not on his own account, but had respect to a vast body politic, and the world in general. For this, also, were seventy souls afterwards brought from a far country, to reside, with the consent of the whole nation, in *Goshen*, the richest province in Egypt. Here their situation, manners, and way

way of living, kept them ſeparate from their idolatrous neighbours, and ſafe from hoſtilities, to which they muſt have been expoſed, as they grew numerous in their enemies country of Palæſtine. Thus God, by a ſurpriſing train of events, planted the family of Abraham in a nurſery, where they were to grow up a great and mighty people, *in whom all the families of the earth were to be bleſſed.*

DISSERTATION XXX.

Of *Jacob's prophetic* Benedictions; and Death.

GENESIS XLVIII. XLIX.

ISRAEL, after his introduction to Pharaoh himself, with five of his sons, having lived in the country of Goshen, for seventeen years, where *he had possessions, and grew and multiplied exceedingly*, and seen Joseph's greatness and virtues, approached the end of his pilgrimage, at the age of an hundred and forty-seven years. Before his death he desired to bestow on his family the prophetic and patriarchal benediction. Hearing that Joseph, whom he had invited from *Zoan* * the capital, was come, he was refreshed with the news; and, collecting all his strength, sat upon the bed and pronounced a few brief emblematical sentences.

* Urbs antiquissima, regia, & videtur ea fuisse illius *Pharaonis* regia, in quem Deus decem illas horrendas plagas effudit. Spicil. Jamesonii.

VARIOUS

Various were the methods, by which the Almighty communicated to men in old times, the knowledge of his immediate pleaſure, and of his remote appointments. Beſides the *Schechinah*, already deſcribed, viſions, voices and dreams, were frequently employed for this purpoſe, in the patriarchal ages; and, under the Jewiſh œconomy, the urim and thummin on the high prieſt's breaſt-plate. But of all other methods, the moſt regular and certain, and then ſubſiſting, more or leſs, according to men's circumſtances, was direct *inſpiration*; whereby God, without the intervention of any of the ſenſes, tranſacted immediately with the underſtandings of men; while they were awake, their powers active, and their minds calm and undiſturbed. This, as indeed it was, the choſen people called *revelation* by the illumination of the Holy Ghoſt; and appears to have been the illuſtrious mode purſued at the opening of the goſpel-kingdom; when the apoſtles of our Lord were enabled, by divine illapſes, to apprehend clearly the truths delivered to them, and foretel what ſhould afterwards come to paſs.

In this way was Jacob inſtructed, what he ſhould utter on this important occaſion, by the father of ſpirits, whoſe foreſight reaches from the beginning to the end of things.

The ſolemn ſcene begins with the introduction of Joſeph's two ſons to the dying patriarch, who embraced and kiſſed them, and, from the overflowings of an affectionate and grateful heart, ſaid to their father, *I never thought to ſee thy face, and lo! God hath even ſhewed me thy children*; and immediately adopted them.

them. Their equality of rank, and title of inheritance, are thus signified; *Ephraim and Manasseh are mine, as Reuben and Simeon*; Jacob's two eldest and most legitimate sons by Leah; *they shall be mine.* The connection of the following words may not instantly appear; *for when I came from Padan, Rachel died with me by the way.* But, besides the necessity he was under *to speak*, as Balaam said, *that which the Lord had put in his mouth*, these words very probably express the human motive which determined Jacob to raise Joseph's sons to the same dignity with his own; namely, because they were the grand children of Rachel, that beloved consort, whose death had been so dolorous to him, and whose dear idea he could not banish from his mind.

The first example on record in the world, of *the imposition of hands*, is given in this passage, where we read that *Israel stretched out his right hand, and laid it upon Ephraim's head, who was the younger, and his left hand upon Manasseh's head, who was the first-born.* Joseph, supposing that the order of his father's hands was the effect of his infirmities, endeavoured to correct it; but *Jacob said, I know it my son, I know it; Manasseh shall also become a people, and he shall also be great; but truly Ephraim shall be greater than he, and his seed shall become a multitude of nations.* This declares the circumstance to have been directed by God, who had decreed the *wordly* superiority of the younger over the elder. In two hundred years afterwards we, accordingly, find the prediction was fully verified, by a general muster of the Israelites in the wilderness, when in the tribe of Ephraim there were forty thousand and five hundred men able to bear

 arms,

arms, and in that of Manasseh only thirty two thousand and two hundred. And though in some instances the case was otherwise, the prophecy cannot be affected, as the tribe of Ephraim, for a succession of ages, was vastly more considerable than the other; produced the famous Joshuah; was the chief tribe in *Israel* after the schism under *Rehoboam*; and often the name of the whole kingdom. For this preference no other reason can be assigned, than the mere will of God, who distributes honors, and all kinds of advantages as he pleases. Shem also, though younger, was set above Japhet; Isaac above Ishmael; Jacob above Esau; Judah and Joseph above Reuben; Moses above Aaron; and David above all the other sons of Jesse.

The imposition of Jacob's hands was accompanied with a blessing on Ephraim and Manasseh, whose prosperity was to be so great, that, in all future ages, when the highest felicity was wished to an Israelite, they should say, *God make thee as Ephraim and Manasseh.* This form, in fact, the Jews observe, in blessing the men, in all countries, at this day; and, in blessing the women, God *make you as Sarah and Rebecca**.

Blessings on Joseph were repeated and multiplied. Besides the province, in the promised land, bestowed on his posterity, Jacob said to him, *I have, moreover, given thee one portion above thy brethren, which I took out of the hand of the Amorite, with my sword and with my bow.* Whether these words have a metaphorical or a literal meaning, it is not easily determined. They are supposed to refer, to that piece of land he

* Grotius in Gen. xlviii.

had

had bought of Hamor the father of Shechem; and from which he was afterwards obliged to drive the *Amorites*, who had invaded it, by force. Some diſtinction, like a birth-right, was certainly conveyed; perhaps all that Jacob could then actually leave. And Joſeph's interment in that place fixes the point, that this was the paternal inheritance.

THE ſeveral bleſſings which Jacob's ſons received, from this laſt will of their father, are contained in the forty-ninth chapter. According to the eaſtern ſtile, remarkably adorned with deſcriptions, it abounds, throughout, with the boldeſt figures, and the moſt ſtriking imagery, which, of all other paſſages in the old teſtament, render it the moſt difficult to explain. The various fortunes of his ſons depending on very remote periods, it was not fit that Jacob ſhould deſcribe every article diſtinctly: And, for this very reaſon, the divine inſpirer might throw ambiguity into many parts of this ſolemn benediction. We may aſſert, however, in general, that this laſt teſtament, contains reflections upon the paſt lives of the twelve Patriarchs, agreeable to their ſeveral tempers, their actions and fates; and fixes the borders of their habitations, their advantages and neceſſities, after their children entered Canaan, with an admirable accuracy; as is evident from the latter hiſtories of that people.

INSTEAD of pretending to explain and apply every thing which the Patriarch then pronounced, we ſhall only, in general, remark, that Jacob, at the beginning of his diſcourſe, related the divine appearance and promiſe made to him, in his youth, at Luz or Bethel, and on which he had always reſted his faith and dependence. The promise, there, contained a grant to his seed after him, of the land of Canaan, *for an everlasting* possession. This land, by the direction of the spirit of God, without any positive divisions, is, accordingly, parcelled out, and significantly described, in the passage before us. But, the term *everlasting*, when applied to the Jewish dispensation, must be, and in the clearest manner is, limited in most places in the old testament. In the tenth verse of this chapter, there is a most evident restriction of it to a definitive time.

In the *common* blessing of Judah, at the eighth verse, Jacob says, *Judah, thou art he whom thy brethren shall praise*, in allusion to his name, which comes from a root that signifies praise and acknowledgment; and afterwards foretels the victories and conquests, as the prince and governor of his father's children, which he should obtain over his most formidable enemies; and were signally accomplished on a variety of occasions. But this pre-eminence and power, this prosperity and success, were to last only for a certain time, and till another scheme commenced. *The sceptre shall not depart from Judah, nor a lawgiver from between his feet, till Shiloh come, and unto him shall the gathering of the people be.*

Here men's fancies, prejudices, and interests, have applied these words to the most foreign purposes; while, taken in connection, and consistently with the analogy of the old and new testament, they appear easy, pertinent and conclusive. The word translated *sceptre* literally signifies that badge of royalty, or a shepherd's crook; which perfectly corresponds

to

to the idea of government, particularly among the *Jews*, whose supreme king and ruler was, by a peculiar phrase, called *the shepherd of Israel* *. The term *lawgiver* hath nothing equivocal in it: And both prerogatives were to be inherent in the tribe of Judah, till Shiloh came. *Shiloh* hath had significations put upon it beyond number †; but seems plainly to be derived from the Hebrew verb *Shalah*, to be in tranquillity and rest, or from the noun, peace-maker ‡.

But who this Shiloh is, who should deprive Judah of the sceptre, and assume it himself, as the gathering of the nations to him imports, we have yet to resolve. Without the smallest degree of probability, some have proposed Moses, Saul, David, and Jeroboam; and others Nebuchadnezzar, and Vespasian, who finally destroyed the city and temple of Jerusalem, and every vestige of an independent government in Palæstine. The ancient Jewish divines were, unanimously, of opinion, that Shiloh was the *Messiah*, whose kingdom should be universal, and reign endless. And indeed, notwithstanding the many interruptions of the royal descent, and heavy chastisements for their rebellions, with which the people of God were visited; it was not till the days of Herod the *Idumean*, as was before mentioned, who filled their throne at our Saviour's birth; or rather of Titus and his father, about forty years after the ascension; that the sceptre was totally wrested from the hand of every Israelite; and hath never, on any occasion, been swayed in Canaan, or any where else, by any of the Jewish race.

* In multis locis. † Rabbi Bechai in Gen. xlix. 10. ‡ Aben-Ezra, in loco.

THIS

This circumſtance, joined with a thouſand other evidences, clearly demonſtrates that the adorable perſon, whom we worſhip, is the Shiloh, the peace-maker, who was to be *ſent*, as the name likewiſe imports; and whoſe coming ſhould be the greateſt glory and bleſſing of Judah, and of all Iſrael, though he ſhould put an end to their temporal diſtinctions, and lay the foundations of another polity, on which the union of many nations, in the ſame moral and holy ſubjection, was to be raiſed.

Many zealous modern Jews have been ſo hard preſſed by this circumſtance, that they have believed the moſt extravagant of all fables ever invented, to prove that the ſceptre was ſtill in the tribe of Judah, and would continue till the coming of their expected Meſſiah. They have been told, that there is a large province, between Perſia and India, where there is a great multitude of Jews, governed by their own prince, deſcended from the tribe of Judah; ſome ſay, ſurrounded by a ſabbatic river, others, by a wall of fire; and enjoy the greateſt proſperity and plenty. This fiction is, evidently, propagated to evade the force of the prophecy now under our view. But that colony, and the Jewiſh ſceptre, ſhould have been placed in the moon, like the paradiſe before deſcribed, beyond the limits of our knowledge; as the beſt authorities convince us, that no ſuch region exiſts on the face of our globe.

This is what Iſrael ſpake unto the twelve tribes; and when he had made an end of commanding his ſons, he gathered up his feet into the bed, and yielded up the ghoſt. Forty days were obſerved, in embalming his body with aromantick aromantic drugs, and thirty in hardening it with salt and nitre, during which his family, after the Egyptian manner, mourned; and then proceeded for the land of his nativity, and the land of promise, with the most magnificent retinue of which we read, in any records of such remote antiquity.

If the faith of true believers in God, the assurance of inquisitive christians that their Saviour is the promised *Shiloh*, and the filial duty of children be strengthened and confirmed by the present instructions, the labour of explaining these pages will not have been in vain.

DISSERTATION XXXI.

Of the State and Policy of Egypt after the Death of *Jacob*; and the Birth of *Moses*.

EXODUS I. and II.

THE illustrious founders of the Jewish nation, *Joseph, and all his brethren, and all that generation*, in the space of sixty years after the death of Jacob, *died*. But the promises made to Abraham, and renewed to Isaac and Jacob, were still remembered, and faithfully accomplished, by their blessed author, in a manner suitable to his own divine majesty. *Seventy souls*, as Moses reckons, or as it is in the Septuagint, which *St. Stephen* follows, *threescore and fifteen*, was the whole number of the seed of Jacob, at his descent into Egypt. The difference between the two copies will be reconciled, when we reflect, that, agreeable to the genealogical lists in the chronicles*, Ephraim and Manasseh had sons born to them in that kingdom;

* 1. Chron. vii. 14. & 20.

five,

five, probably, before that event, whom the Septuagint take into the account, though the Hebrew leaves them out. From that ſmall number, in two hundred and fifteen years, ſprung ſix hundred thouſand men able to bear arms, beſides women and children *. If the rule was ſo early obſerved, that none ſhould be called forth to war under twenty years of age, nor above ſixty, reckoning all the reſt, with all the women and old men, there could not be fewer than fifteen hundred thouſand perſons, or, agreeable to the former calculation, there might be two millions. Whether polygamy, winked at by the ruler of the world, or for the hardneſs of men's hearts, and the general corruption of their manners, tolerated, if any will inſiſt it was, before the law; whether the prolification among women in Egypt; or any ſupernatural force at that time applied, were the cauſes of this extraordinary multiplication; it concerns us very little to enquire. It is ſufficient that we ſee in this event, the truth of the divine promiſe to Abraham; *I will multiply thee exceedingly: Look now toward heaven, and tell the ſtars, if thou be able to number them; for ſo ſhall thy ſeed be.* Moſes has only ſaid, *that the children of Iſrael were fruitful, and increaſed abundantly, and multiplied, and waxed exceeding mighty, and the land was filled with them.* The ſeveral words here uſed for the ſame thing, ſhew the extraordinary fecundity of the *Iſraelitiſh* women in Egypt; and a celebrated Rabbi †, hath expatiated largely upon all of them, and with the greateſt propriety. The very ingenious remark ſome of his nation make upon the ſecond word, which has been obſerved by one of our beſt commentators ‡, ought not to be unnoticed here. They think that

* Exodus xii. 37. † Abarbanel, in loco. ‡ Bp. Patrick.

the

the Hebrew * expreſſes the vaſt increaſe among fiſhes; and the ſame term is, in fact, employed in the bleſſing God pronounced upon them, at the twentieth verſe of the firſt chapter of Geneſis. It has been interpreted by a very learned and moſt laborious man, the Iſraelites *were born in multitudes* †. From the example of a wife of a certain citizen, who had *two and fifty children*, and never brought leſs than three at a birth ‡; and it's having been ſaid that the *Egyptian* women themſelves were ſo fruitful, that ſome of them at four births brought *twenty* children §; the notion has been indulged that the *Iſraelites* brought *ſix* at a time, by the extraordinary bleſſing of God upon them.

However this was, and notwithſtanding the advantages the kingdom might have derived from their population of it, the proſperity of this people ſoon became the ſubject of the ſtrongeſt jealouſy, and of the moſt alarming apprehenſions in the minds of the Egyptians. Their habitations were not confined to *Goſhen*, which grew too narrow for them. *All Egypt* was overſpread with *Iſraelites*. They were now in a condition to determine the fate of the country; and, by joining with foreign enemies, to ſubdue their maſters. This ſeems to have been the reaſon, or rather the plauſible pretext, for the ſeverities which they immediately experienced.

Moses, indeed, ſays, *there roſe up a new king over Egypt, who knew not Joſeph.* This phraſe has been variouſly underſtood: That this king had neither

* Heb. וישרצו † Benedictus Arias Montanus: Produxerunt ſe; nati ſunt in multitudine. ‡ Gaſpar Schottus. § Ariſtot. Hiſtor. Animal. Lib. vii.

known

known him, nor his father, nor any of his brethren; or, according to others, was indifferent about his hiſtory, and unmoved by the motives which had determined the conduct of his predeceſſors. The term *new* has inclined many interpreters to think, that Moſes ſpeaks of a foreign prince who had then conquered Egypt, and was ignorant of the remarkable occurrences in it's annals. It is true, after that kingdom had been governed for many ages, from the days of *Mizraim*, one of the ſons of Ham, by princes born in the country, and of lineal deſcent, ſtrangers from *Arabia and Phenicia* invaded it; and poſſeſſing themſelves of *lower Egypt*, and *Memphis*, eſtabliſhed a ſucceſſion called *ſhepherd-kings*; who yet never penetrated into *upper Egypt*, nor affected the kingdom of *Thebes*. But this invaſion was before the days of Abraham; who had his wife taken from him by one of that race; and the uſurpation terminated under *Thethmoſis*, who baniſhed the *ſhepherd-kings*, and reigned over all Egypt, long before Joſeph was carried down into that country, by the merchant-men. Hence a *new king*, in this paſſage, can only mean what has been above expreſſed; or, at moſt, one of another family, and a remote heir of that monarch, who had ſo kindly treated Joſeph, and his father's houſe *. *Ramſes-miamum* is ſaid to have been the name of that prince; who is known in ſcripture by that of *Pharaoh*, common to all the kings of Egypt †. He reigned ſixty-ſix years, and made the Iſraelites undergo the vaſt hardſhips which Moſes relates. *Behold*, ſaid he to the Egyptians, *the people of the children of Iſrael are more and migh-*

* Hiſtoire des Egyptiens, par Rollin. † Archiepiſc. Uſſerius. For the origin of it, quod iis commune erat, uſque ad Babylon. Imper. Temp. ſee Spicileg: Jameſonii. Cap. 1. p. 3.

tier

tier than we. Come on, let us deal wisely with them, lest they multiply, and it come to pass that when there falleth out any war, they join themselves to our enemies, and fight against us, and so get them up out of the land. Therefore they set over them task-masters——and made their lives bitter with hard bondage, in mortar and in brick, and in all manner of service in the field.

It well deserves to be remarked, that the fear of the Egyptians, *lest the Israelites should get them up out of the land*, must have arisen from what they had frequently heard, that their design was not to stay always in Egypt; that their fathers had only come down as sojourners; and had received a promise that their seed, after a certain period, should possess Canaan. And the nearer that period approached, the more, no doubt, they would be speaking of it.

Josephus * informs us, that his nation was employed by the Egptians in cutting, and filling, many canals, with the waters of the *Nile*, in building mounds and ramparts to restrain the force of that river when it swelled, in erecting some of those monuments of madness, the Pyramids, in learning all sorts of arts, and in inuring themselves to the hardest labour. And Moses says, *they built for Pharaoh treasure-cities, Pithom and Raamses:* The former now thought to be *Pelusium*, the most ancient fortified place in Egypt, is called by Ezekiel †, *the strength of Egypt*; and by Suidas the monk, who knew the state of that country distinctly, in the reign of Alexius Comnenius, *the key of Egypt*, as it was the entrance from Syria: The latter gave name to the whole region where the Israelites dwelt, and probably was a frontier town

* Josephus, Lib. ii. Cap. v. † Chap. xxx. 15.

likewise,

likewise, on the side of Arabia. In those cities were corn and oyl, wine and other riches of Egypt, laid up, agreeable to the regulations which Joseph, during the years of plenty, had wisely introduced.

But the more they afflicted them, the more they multiplied and grew: or, in the Hebrew Idiom, which the vulgate* has preserved, *as they afflicted them*, by how much the more they oppressed them, by so much the more they grew, *so they multiplied*. The Jewish historian† piously observes, on this occasion, that none can resist the will of God, whatever arts they devise. His power, evidently, supported that people in their deepest distresses, and blasted the schemes of their enemies, which they had barbarously contrived for their destruction. Not only their vast fruitfulness, threatening commotions within the state, alarmed and offended Pharaoh and his people; but we are likewise told, that one of the Egyptian teachers, called by the name of *scribe of the holy things*, and who passed among them for a great prophet, declared to the king that there would be born, at that time, an Hebrew child, whose virtue would be admired by all the world, who would exalt the glory of his own nation, humble Egypt, and possess immortal renown ‡. To prevent this, as the same historian thinks, Ramesesmiamum, like bloody Herod at the birth of Christ, formed the design of murdering, as soon as it was born, every male-child among the Israelites; expecting thereby to defeat the prediction, and finally crush the whole seed. The mid-wives were to be his executioners. When they performed their office to the

* Quantoque opprimebant eos tanto magis multiplicabantur, et crescebant. † Josephus, Lib. ii. Cap. v. ‡ Josephus, Lib. ii. Cap. v.

Hebrew

Hebrew women, they were commanded *to kill every ſon, and leave every daughter alive.*

But the mid-wives feared God; and the ſanguinary mandate filled them with horror. The Egyptians of that profeſſion would feel the ſentiments of humanity; and regard for their nation, and a ſenſe of religion, would reſtrain the Iſraelites. All of them diſobeyed the king, and covered their pious rebellion with an innocent artifice. They ſaid that the Hebrew women were *lively*, eaſy in parturition, or ſkilful themſelves like mid-wives, as the original inſinuates *, and delivered before they could come to them. Whether this was a fact, as ſome have preſumed, or an official falſhood, it is not eaſy to aſcertain. There is, however, the cleareſt evidence, that God, in rewarding them for their conduct, approved of it: *He made them houſes*: This, though one divine eminent at the Reformation †, and ſome others, are of a contrary opinion, muſt ſignify, that God either proſpered them in riches and affluence, or, becauſe they had ſaved the lives of the Hebrew children, increaſed the number of theirs. Which of theſe ways it was, or whether they told the whole truth, or ſuppreſſed a part of it, in ſome caſes lawful, and even commendable, none have any right to condemn them, ſeeing God did not.

UNDER the operation of this barbarous order, Moſes, by whom God was ſoon to manifeſt his power, and give effect to his promiſes, was born. His father and mother, Amram and Jochebed, were not only of the ſame tribe and family, but their conſanguinity was ſo cloſe, that interpreters have been greatly troubled

* Heb. כי חיות חנה

† Calvinus, in loco.

in

in explaining, how a *nephew* could ever lawfully marry his *aunt*. For the historian plainly tells us, that *Amram took him Jochebed, his father's sister to wife**. But, without taking the benefit of other similar examples in scripture, there is nothing very extraordinary in this match. To cut off all ground of cavilling from the profane querist, or infidel reader of the sacred books, we ought frankly to acknowledge, what has been before asserted, that the prohibitions concerning the degrees of affinity in marriage, are not so much founded on the original law of nature, as on a positive command from God. It is utterly impossible that he should ever have laid any of his creatures under the necessity of violating original obligations. But in the first ages, particularly near the creation, it was absolutely necessary, that not only relations of this proximity should marry one another, but that even brother and sister should enter into those bands. It must, therefore, have only been in after times, for certain reasons which we may plainly see, and others perhaps we do not, that the degrees of kindred were prescribed. Hence good men need not be alarmed when they read of such marriages; nor unbelievers triumph because they are recorded; a positive law of God being of equal force with any of an eternal nature.

Of this marriage, Moses was the fruit. But to be born under such miserable circumstances, was only to die prematurely. For the king betrayed by the midwives, changed his measures, and charged all his people, especially his officers, *saying, every son that is born ye shall cast into the river, and every daughter ye shall save*

* Exodus vi. 20.

alive.

alive. Amram and Jochebed, to preserve the innocent victim, *who*, according to St. Stephen, *was exceeding fair*, and some of the Jewish doctors say, *had an angelic form*, from the fury of his persecutors, contrived all possible means; and actually hid him *three months.* But Pharaoh's diligence, and that of his emissaries, could not be long eluded. The parents, accordingly, resolve to resign Moses, and commit him entirely to the care of providence. Of the rushes of the Nile, with which it's banks were planted, they constructed a cradle, to which they perhaps gave the form of those little boats, with which that river was continually covered; and, *daubed with pitch and slime*, the precious deposite was laid among the reeds, by the river's brink. Here the tender mother, the fond father, the affectionate sister, the humane heart, may indulge all their feelings, and curse that cruelty which authorized such a decree. Nor was Miriam, the sister of this wretched babe, unaffected on this occasion. She fixed her eyes closely on the place where her brother lay; and, while employed in this sorrowful office, believing, every moment, that he would immediately fall into the hands of his executioners, *Pharaoh's daughter*, either according to the rites of the Egyptian religion, or the custom of the great, *came down to the river to wash herself*, and was made signally subservient to the providential design.

This princess has been called *Thermutis* *; and, said to have been married to a petty king of Egypt †; to have had no child; and, as a consolation for her barrenness, adopted the infant; whom she called *Mo-*

* Josephus Lib. ii. Cap. v. † Euseb. Præpar, Lib. ix. Cap. xxvii.

ses;

ses; from two Egyptian words which signify, *drawn out of the water*; and *instructed him in all the wisdom* *, in all the arts and learning that flourished in that kingdom.

The heart of princes is in the hand of the Lord, as the rivers of water: And he turneth it whithersoever he will †. And, inspiring Pharaoh's daughter with tender feelings for this exposed infant, she, accordingly, no sooner saw the cradle than she ordered it to be brought to her; and, opening it, was struck with the child's beauty, and softened by it's tears. The princess easily knew, that he was an Hebrew infant, by the deplorable situation in which she found him, and the sacrament of circumcision which he had received. Miriam's offer, to find a nurse, was accepted, without delay. Like a dutiful child and sister, she related to Jochebed what had happened, who immediately run, and undertook with transports, which nature only knows, and words cannot express, the commission which *Thermutis* gave her, of nursing this out-cast for her.

In the manner now represented did the Israelites fall into slavery in Egypt, and under the severest oppression and sufferings. But by these was the power of God rendered the more conspicuous, in their preservation and deliverance. The more cruelly they were treated, they increased the more, till they were numerous enough to be formed into a nation. Then Moses was born, strangely preserved, royally educated, and raised up to be their saviour. And shortly after his investiture with the divine commission, we

* Acts vii. 22. † Proverbs xxi. 1.

ſhall ſee the vials of divine wrath poured forth, one one after another, upon the land of *Ham*: When *God made bare his arm*, or gave the moſt ſignal and ſtriking demonſtrations of his being and power, infinitely ſuperior, not only to all human ſtrength, but alſo to all the pretended deities, in which the Egyptians truſted.

DISSERTATION XXXII.

Sketches of the Life of *Moſes*, for eighty Years.

EXODUS II. and III.

THE hiſtory of that great man's life, though written by himſelf, ſeems to be very defective, from his birth till God appeared to him in the wilderneſs of Sinai, which comprehends a period of eighty years. We are only told, that *when the child grew, his mother brought him unto Pharaoh's daughter, and he became her ſon*, by adoption. There can, however, be no doubt that he was employed, during ſeveral years of his youth, in the acquiſition of knowledge, becoming his diſtinguiſhed condition, in a country ſo improved as Egypt was. Some authors give a detail of the ſciences in which he was profoundly ſkilful; ſuch as arithmetic and geometry, harmony, and the ratio of numbers one to another, medicine and muſick. They tell us that he likewiſe underſtood ſymbolical philoſophy, and was deeply inſtructed in practical

 aſtronomy:

astronomy: That he had for his masters the most famous among the Egyptians, Chaldeans and Greeks*. His skill in poetry is manifest from his majestic and beautiful compositions, suited to almost every occasion. Of his abilities as an orator and historian, we have also sufficient evidence in the writings that bear his name.

But, from what St. Stephen says, that *he was mighty in deed*, it, moreover, appears, that a part of the forty years which Moses staid in Egypt, was spent in more hardy and renowned exercises than study alone: And some of his exploits, which gave proofs of his courage and prudence, are actually recorded. Josephus himself says that he was, by the decision of an oracle, appointed general of the Egyptian army, which was sent to oppose that of Ethiopia †. And Philo Judæus affirms, that he not only recovered the cities which the former had lost, but likewise conquered the latter, led his troops into the heart of the country, and took the capital ‡. That Moses himself does not mention those transactions, supposing them to be true, either in the writings which he might compose during his residence in Midian, or did set forth after he became the Jewish captain and lawgiver; we will not wonder when we consider, that this would have been writing his own history only, without any connection

* Clemen. Alexand. Strom. Lib. 1. p. 343. where the curious reader will find a fragment of a Jewish tragedy on this subject. But the good father was certainly misinformed in regard to the Greeks, among whom all science seems to have been unknown at this early period; and till Orpheus the Thracian, and Cadmus the Phenician, carried it among them. The latter lived co-temporary with *Joshua*. † Antiquit. Judaic. Lib. ii. ‡ In Vitá Mosis.

with

with the plan of God's providence, which it is the united ſcope of ſcripture to repreſent, in an unbroken ſeries; particularly in regard to the ſtate of religion and virtue in all ages: And nothing more.

The brilliant actions, and growing merit of this hero, and adopted ſon of the princeſs, would have procured for him the chief honors of the court of Egypt, if nobler deſigns had not obliged him to reject them. The high rank which he held in the houſe of Pharaoh, never once obliterated from his mind the humiliating circumſtances in which he was born. Though raiſed to the moſt active and honorable poſts which the government had to beſtow, he ſtill remembered that he was an *Hebrew*, and that his nation was in ſubjection. His own generous nature, and impreſſions from God on his mind, determined him to leave the palace, to viſit his brethren in Rameſes, to be an eye-witneſs of *the rigor with which they were made to ſerve*, and inſtantly give a preſage of what God would one day work for them by his hands.

After his arrival, the firſt thing he ſaw was an Egyptian ſmiting an Iſraelite. It is highly probable, that the oppreſſor was one of thoſe taſk-maſters, whom Pharaoh had appointed over the Jewiſh people; and who, under the pretence of fidelity to their prince, indulged their own cruelty and reſentment by the ſufferings of poor ſlaves. Moſes ſhuddered at the ſight, and, in a tranſport of indignation and rage, ſlew the Egyptian. The next day, when two of his countrymen were ſtriving together, he endeavoured to reconcile them by ſuggeſting that they were *brethren*,

ren, and in their circumſtances inteſtine broils and diſſentions, would inevitably weaken their intereſts, and obſtruct their future proſperity. But this truly patriotic champion, while he hoped they would immediately comply with the friendly purpoſe, and jointly accept of his advice and propoſal, ſhared the common fate of almoſt all who attempt either to ſuccour the injured, or reconcile the contentious and unruly parts of mankind. *Who made thee a prince and a judge over us? Intendeſt thou to kill me, as thou killedſt the Egyptian?* was the inſolent and haughty challenge which he received. Finding the *thing was known*, that the paſſions of his brethren might, even unwarily, bring puniſhment upon him, and Pharaoh himſelf, notwithſtanding his diſtinction and ſervices, proceeding againſt him, for the capital offence of the death of one of his natural ſubjects; Moſes fled to *Arabia Petræa*, on the other ſide of the red-ſea; and about an hundred and twenty miles from *Zoan.*

THE circumſtances in his journey, his conduct on the occaſion related, and the reward he received for it, beſides being ſimple, natural and credible, as every one will ſee in the account given of them by himſelf at large; are, likewiſe, ſo ſimilar to the other hiſtories of the patriarchal ages, eſpecially in the book of Geneſis, we ſhall not enter on deſcription in this place. The great ſcarcity of water, in all thoſe countries of the eaſt, where the moſt important ſcenes were acted, in which the moſt eminent inſtruments of God's providence were employed, produced, in a great meaſure, at this time, by the appointment of God, the connection between Moſes and Jethro,

whoſe

whose daughters he had assisted in watering their flocks.

THIS man, by the title given him, seems to have been *prince* and *priest* of that place; or the supreme head and conductor of civil and religious affairs; in the same manner as the caliphs, after the death of Mahomet, were among the Saracens, in the same country; as the emperors of Japan, till very lately; and some of the Bishops of Germany are to this day.

JETHRO *gave Moses, who was content to dwell with him, Zipporah his daughter*, for a wife; by whom he had a son called *Gershom*, which signifies *a desolate stranger*. Whether this priest and prince was a worshipper of the true God; or of false deities, adored in Midian, and all the neighbouring countries; and whether he may be classed with those religious men described in the nineteenth dissertation; we can draw nothing, with certainty, from the opinions that have been given. Perhaps the contentment Moses had in dwelling with him, his acceptance of his daughter, and the account of his behaviour, after the Israelites had crossed the Red-sea, may favor the conclusion, that he had resisted the contagion of idolatry, which almost universally prevailed. This, at least, is clear, that Moses lived with Jethro for the space of forty years in the wilderness of Midian, where he followed the only occupation practicable in that country, at least that has been common till the present time. And, according to some learned men, he employed the leisure he had, in his profession, in composing some of those admirable books, particularly Genesis, with

with which the world is now blessed, and which, we hope, will be preserved, as they have heretofore been, by a wonderful providence, till time shall be no more.*

While Moses enjoyed this solitude, the sufferings of the Israelites increased, and their cries went up incessantly to heaven. Egypt had changed its king, during this period; but the sons of Jacob had only changed one tyrant for another, and were laid under a heavier yoke. *God heard their groaning, and looked upon them, and had respect unto them*; and, as was said already, raised up Moses to be their deliverer. His commission, for this purpose, was given him in a manner altogether majestic and divine. Feeding Jethro's flocks, he had one day led them to Horeb, which, probably, by way of anticipation, is called *the mountain of God*, because the law was afterwards to be published on Sinai, another top of the same ridge of rocks of which Horeb is a part. Here seeing a bush burning, without being consumed, he was astonished at the sight; and, approaching to take a nearer view of it, heard a voice coming from thence, which said; *Moses, Moses, draw not nigh hither; put off thy shoes from off thy feet, for the place whereon thou standest is holy ground.*

The design of such phenomena, and the person who spake from them, having been discoursed of at

* M. Huetii Demonst. Evangel, prop. iv. cap. iii. The book of Job, thought by some to have been composed by Moses, is, probably, of an older date, and was written by the sufferer himself. This matter, however, is uncertain; though the history is, undoubtedly, real. See Differt. xix, p. 298.

great

great length already †, nothing more remains to be considered, in this place, but the circumſtances of the appearance here related. Theſe were purely ſymbolical: The buſh repreſented the Iſraelites; the flames, which ſurrounded it, expreſſed the tribulations in which they were involved; and fire, of an unconſuming quality, beſides proclaiming the divine preſence, and diſtinguiſhing the viſion from all the works of fancy, and the arts of impoſture, ſignified, finally, that they ſhould not, in the leaſt degree, be waſted by their ſufferings.

MOSES was commanded to *put off his ſhoes from off his feet*, in token of that reſpect with which every worſhipper ought to be filled, and of the purity to be ſtudied, when the Creator is ſolemnly approached. To this command, perhaps, the cuſtom of eaſtern and ſouthern nations, in ſubſequent ages, and of which there are ſtrong veſtiges to this day, may be referred, of putting off the ſhoes at the door of churches and moſques. Though the cuſtom, by God's ſpecial command, may have been eſtabliſhed before the days of Moſes, and what he did was only in obedience to it, this is a certain evidence that he knew it was God with whom he was now converſing.

THAT converſation, on certain principles, admits ſtrictures, and requires an explanation; but the bounds of this performance exclude them. We ſhall, therefore, for want of room, not of ſufficient matter, proceed, from this part of the hiſtory, to the appear-

† See Diſſertation xvii.

ance

ance of Moses, and Aaron who was joined with him in the commission, before the King of Egypt, *where they shewed wonders, in the sight of all his people.*

DISSERTATION XXXIII.

Moses and Aaron appear before Pharaoh; and bring Plagues upon Egypt.

EXODUS, V, &c.

AT the burning buſh the Lord had ſaid to Moſes, *I have ſurely ſeen the affliction of my people which are in Egypt, and have heard their cry, by reaſon of their taſk-maſters; and I am come down to deliver them out of the hand of the Egyptians, and to bring them out of that land, unto a good land and a large, unto a land flowing with milk and honey. Come now, therefore, and I will ſend thee unto Pharaoh, that thou mayeſt bring forth my people the children of Iſrael out of Egypt.* He had declared himſelf to be *the God of their fathers*; proclaimed his nature and perfections in thoſe remarkable words, I AM THAT I AM, which have been highly reſpected for their majeſty, by Jews, Pagans, and Chriſtians; and commanded Moſes to make him known, by that moſt abſolutely perfect name and appellation of God, *to the*

the people. To obviate their unbelief, and convince Pharaoh himſelf that the demand to releaſe the Iſraelites was made by divine authority, God had armed Moſes with the power of working miracles: The inſtant converſion of *his rod into a ſerpent*, and inſtant reſtoration; *his hand* immediately *becoming leprous*, or white, *as ſnow*, and changing *again as his other fleſh*, were ſpecimens only of what he ſhould perform.

Furnished with this commiſſion, Moſes prepared himſelf to leave Jethro's houſe, and to approach Egypt, where *all the men were dead who ſought his life*; at the ſame time he was aſſured by God, that Pharaoh would diſregard his meſſage. Aaron, who was an eloquent man, and to *be inſtead of a mouth to* Moſes, in this arduous undertaking, met him, by divine inſtruction, very near Midian, *in the mount of God*, that they might have the more time to deliberate on the commiſſion, before they entered Egypt. On their arrival there, *they aſſembled the elders of Iſrael, and* Moſes *did the ſigns in the ſight of the people; who bowed their heads and worſhipped, becauſe the Lord had looked on their affliction, and had viſited them.* Then, addreſſing the king, they told him, *Thus ſaith the Lord God of Iſrael, let my people go, that they may hold a feaſt to me in the wilderneſs.*

Instead of provoking him, by demanding abruptly the liberty of that people, it is obſervable that thoſe holy men took the method which prudence ſuggeſted, to ſoften the Prince into compliance with their requeſt. They only begged permiſſion to carry out the Iſraelites three days journey into the wilderneſs, where they might offer ſacrifices to their God, which

which might be displeasing to the Egyptians, in their own land. And if they failed to pay him that homage, they represented that he might visit them with plagues, which might prove fatal to the whole kingdom. Of this conduct we have many examples in other passages of scripture; particularly where we see Samuel, agreeable to the command of God, going to Bethlehem; and telling the elders of the town, who trembled at his coming, that he was come to sacrifice to the Lord; which was only a part of his design, the main purpose being to anoint that son of Jesse, of whom the Lord should signify his choice, in the room of Saul, who was rejected for his disobedience *. Our blessed Saviour himself used the greatest caution and circumspection, in his dealings with obstinate and unworthy men. This seems to be a principle of the soundest wisdom, as it is the safest and most effectual method of proceeding, in enterprises that cross men's affections, their passions, and wordly interests. And so far as the relation goes, there is not the least violation of truth.

But Pharaoh's answer, suitable to his character, was; *who is the Lord, that I should obey his voice, to let Israel go? I know not the Lord, neither will I let Israel go.* From this speech, impious as it is, we are not to infer, that Pharaoh, though he was an idolater, disbelieved the existence of an eternal and supreme being. Atheism was not the system in Egypt, nor ever established in any kingdom on earth. All nations have had their Gods, though frequently they have been *vanities* and *lies*. But having, like the rest of mankind at that time, adopted tutelary deities founded on fiction,

* 1 Samuel, chap. xvi.

and

and formed to their own fancies, the God of the Hebrews, the living and true God, was UNKNOWN to the Egyptians. And besides that the rites of his religion were not established by law within Pharaoh's dominions, the wretched condition of those who ascribed to him supreme honors, would inspire that haughty prince with no high idea of his majesty and power; especially as the prosperity and adversity of the votaries, fixed in men's imagination, at that time, the greatness and might, or the impotence and weakness of the several divinities which they adored.

RESISTING so powerful an argument as that of religion, and urged, by Moses and Aaron, in such a becoming and dutiful manner, we need not wonder if Pharaoh should add to his impiety the most cruel oppression. Instead of diminishing the sufferings of such a vast number of unhappy men, he, accordingly, increased the weight of that yoke under which they had so long groaned. The laziness of the people, he alledged, made them fond of celebrating festivals, and that, in order to rouse them, their tasks must be doubled. For this purpose, the straw which they had mixed in their bricks, or with which they had covered them from the sun, was no longer to be supplied, and yet the same quantity to be made, and in the same manner. In vain did the sons of Jacob represent the impossibility of fulfilling an order so severe! In vain did they complain of this tyranny! The tears which their miseries extorted from them served only to augment the stream; their very sighs were construed crimes. Their bodies, worn out with this barbarous service, were galled with the scourge of a merciless superintendant. They must sink under the weight

of

of their work, or the severity of their punishment, if they were not able to perform it.

At this critical period, as the case has been often, instead of recurring for consolation and deliverance to God, when there was all the reason in the world to despair of either from their earthly masters, the Israelites reproached his servants, and ascribed their growing sorrows to their folly and misconduct. Moses himself, as well as on other similar occasions, cannot be fully excused, for such bold addresses to the Almighty; *O Lord, wherefore hast thou so evil intreated this people? Wherefore is it that thou hast sent me?*

Now, when reasonings, and proper conclusions from them, were rejected and overlooked, by subjects enslaved, as well as by their oppressive prince; and the patience and compassion of God to be equally exercised, towards his murmuring people, and his distrustful ministers; miracles were necessary, and such as should greatly terrify the one, and establish the other in their faith. But, before they were displayed, *the Lord*, in undeserved and peculiar condescension, *said unto Moses, Now shalt thou see what I will do to Pharaoh: For with a strong hand shall he let* the people *go, and with a strong hand shall he drive them out of his land: I am the* Lord*: And I appeared unto Abraham, unto Isaac, and unto Jacob, by the name of God Almighty, but by my name* Jehovah *was I not known to them.* This cannot signify that those patriarchs were ignorant of this name of God, which expresses not only his eternal existence and immutable truth, but also his omnipotent power; for the whole book of Genesis, in Hebrew, testifies the contrary; and, therefore, must mean,

mean, that though he was known to them as Jehovah when they *received* his promiſes, he had not yet been known by that name, in *giving* thoſe promiſes effect; but would now employ him (i. e. Moſes) for that purpoſe, and manifeſt his power, *by ſigns and wonders*, to ſhew that his providence and faithfulneſs were ſtill the ſame.

By *ſigns* and *wonders*, in holy writ, are meant all ſuch operations, as it is above the ſkill of man to contrive, above the power of any thing in nature, any thing but the God of nature himſelf, or ſome agent by him ſpecially commiſſioned, and impowered, to perform. Theſe things, being intended to *ſignify* who are appointed by God, as the meſſengers of his will to men, are, on that account, fitly termed *ſigns*; they are *wonders* alſo, as they are out of the ordinary phenomena, and ſurpaſs the abilities of mortals: And of *theſe* the holy ſcripture every where ſpeaks, as the moſt proper and full evidence of a divine miſſion and authority.

What the common ſenſe and reaſoning of mankind has been on this head, will appear from this ſingle reflection; that all religions, whether true or falſe, not only thoſe of Moſes and Chriſt, but even the heatheniſh ſuperſtitions of every kind, have, at their firſt appearance, given countenance to themſelves, by real, or pretended, miracles. Numa, at Rome, Amida and Brama, in the eaſt, and Mango-Copal in Peru, did, as hiſtorians inform us, thus endeavour to perſuade their followers into a belief of thoſe *religious*, and civil opinions, which they introduced, and into the practice of their ſeveral ſacred rites and ceremonies:

Even

Even *Mahomet* himſelf is ſaid to have made ſome faint attempts this way, though, when he miſſed of ſucceſs, he retreated to the great and ſtanding miracle of the *Koran*, which was, he ſaid, ſent immediately from heaven to him by the angel *Gabriel**.—So that miracles have been ſecretly and unanimouſly agreed upon by all men, as the proper medium of proving any religion to be of divine appointment; elſe, the founders of all religions would not thus indifferently have appealed to them; nor would they, who embraced thoſe religions, have ſo univerſally ſurrendered themſelves up to their authority.—The objection, againſt this argument, which the enemies of revelation have made uſe of, That ſince *all* religions have, at their firſt riſe, equally pretended to miracles, this way of proof, which hath ſo often deceived men, can never, with any certainty, be relied on, we pretend not to anſwer here; as the work is deſigned for another claſs of readers, and matters more important are ſtill before us †.

Signs and *wonders* were, accordingly, made to Pharaoh demonſtrations that the commiſſion, by which Moſes and Aaron acted, was divine. With that rod, the virtue of which had originally conquered the obſtinacy of the former, and convinced the latter, and all Iſrael, that he was ſent, by the God of their fathers, for their deliverance from bondage, they made the king of Egypt feel the weakneſs of his own ſceptre. Of it's figure, and the inſcriptions on it, certain Rabbins have told ridiculous ſtories; and ſome heathen

* See the Koran, by Geo. Sale gent. vol. i. p. 19. 175.

† But ſee Dr. Atterbury, the Bp. of Rocheſter's ſermon, on this ſubject; whence the foregoing reaſoning has been extracted; with alterations.

 writers

writers have related, that it was placed in the temple of *Isis*, where the Egyptians paid it religious honors. However this was, we may draw the conclusion from this circumstance, that it's operation was known by the Gentiles; and see that *profane history* supports the records of the *sacred*. When those two messengers of the most high, venerable by their years, the one fourscore, and the other fourscore and three, and still more to be feared for the consequences of their commission to him, which they now repeated, to give the Jewish people their liberty, and put an end to a cruel slavery which they had long endured, came into Pharaoh's presence the second time; he, agreeable to the common sense of mankind, demanded of them *a miracle*, which might equally prove that the God who sent them claimed his submission, and that they were really his servants: *And Aaron casting his rod before* him, *and before his servants*, *it* immediately *became a serpent*.

PHARAOH, who was well accustomed to see the works of magic, was yet very little concerned, and, to confront them with Moses and Aaron, only sent for the practitioners in that art, with whom Egypt abounded. In this he followed the established rule of the ancients, who always determined any dispute among enchanters by the nature of the miracles they performed. According to the Pagan system, the greatest miracles were wrought by the greatest genii and gods *.

* Vide Gaulmyn, de vitâ Mosis, page 241.

THOSE

Those magicians, the chief of whom might be *Jannes and Jambres* *, neither refused, nor seem to have been afraid, to enter the lists with such competitors, whom, it is said, they told, that to bring enchantments into Egypt was like carrying water to the sea. *They cast down every man his rod, and they became serpents.* The only superiority which Aaron had over them, at this time, was, that *his rod swallowed up theirs*; and thus deprived them of the symbols and instruments of their power. The like success those magicians had, *in turning the waters of the Nile into blood*, which stank, and killed the fish; and in *the bringing up frogs upon the land*; but, at the fourth miracle, wrought by Moses and Aaron, they *said to Pharaoh, This is the finger of God*; and, after the seventh, *could* no longer stand *before those holy men, because of the boyl*, which *was upon the magicians*, as well as *upon all the Egyptians*

Here, we must confess it to be the most difficult task, to account for that amazing power of working miracles, at least things very wonderful to us, in men who were confessedly the followers of false gods. In regard to this, the learned may be divided into two classes; those who think that what the magicians did were mere prestiges, illusions, or tricks, performed by dexterity and slight of hand, and believed to be real only through the weakness and prepossession of men's

* 2. Tim. iii. 8. An old fragment said, that Jannes and Jambres, were the scribes of holy things among the Egyptians——flourished at the time the Jews left Egypt——were equal to any in the secrets of magic——and unanimously chosen to oppose Moses, the captain of that people, whose prayers were powerful with God. Euseb. Præpar Lib. ix.

 minds

minds; and those who ascribe such works to secrets in the art of magic, and the concurrence of demons.

In opposition to the first class, it has been alledged, that the relation of Moses leaves no room to doubt, that the operations abovementioned were effects of the magical art, and of some diabolical interposition. He hath used no other terms, indeed, than those he would have done, though his intention had been to signify, that those rods which the enchanters brought with them were really turned into serpents. But it is to be considered, that the language of scripture is frequently accommodated to the received opinions of former ages; that it appears to adopt the very prejudices of men; and seldom is employed in philosophical disquisitions. Of this we have a remarkable instance in the book of Joshua*, where the *sun and moon* are said, expressly, to have *stood still*. We may, therefore, still suppose that those who are here called *wise men and sorcerers*, were only jugglers, who pretended real miracles. Indeed the words by which they are denominated in the original scriptures, and used by the best translators of those scriptures, strongly countenance this opinion.

As a farther confirmation of this, and in opposition to those who ascribe the works of the magicians to secrets in the art of magic, and the concurrence of evil spirits; it has, with great probability, been said, that the power of working miracles is the prerogative of the Almighty alone, and when they are performed by any of his servants, as instruments in his hand, they are incontestible evidences of his presence and

* Chap. x.

pleasure.

pleaſure. A real miracle being the interruption, inverſion, or total change of the eſtabliſhed courſe of nature, it is, beyond all queſtion, moſt reaſonable to believe that nothing in the univerſe can effect either, but *the finger* of him who is the creator of it.

But it will be aſked, what reſpect is due to hiſtory *, which gives us accounts of enchantments and prodigies, whether real or imaginary, in all ages. Certain teſtimonies from thence, ſome men will regard as ſuperior to all argumental oppoſition; while, with others, the very beſt teſtimonies will have as little weight, at preſent, to convince them that ever there were ſuch things, as the ſtrongeſt aſſurances would have had, in former ages, to convince the ſuperſtitious part of mankind, that all the exhibitions of ſorcery, which they beheld, were the effects of impoſture and credulity. To avoid ſcepticiſm and error, we may, then, adopt this ſober ſentiment, that men exquiſitely ſkilled in arts, which they had long practiſed, availed themſelves of the ignorance of the people; and becauſe their knowledge, though perhaps not very extenſive, far exceeded that of the rude multitude, they pretended, and were believed, that it was ſupernatural. Of this many inſtances, even in modern times, might be given, after all the improvements which natural proceſſes, and the human underſtanding, have received. The fanciful figures, and uncouth incantations, uſed in all ſuch practices, are ſufficient to diſparage and confute them.

As to what is ſaid of the magicians in Egypt, it may be juſtly doubted whether their rods were converted

* In this argument, Oracles are not concerned.

into

into real ſerpents, as they appear to have been quite inert, when the rod of the Hebrew prophet moved towards them, *and ſwallowed them up*. It is equally doubtful whether they had any influence over the waters, *which Moſes* had previouſly *turned into blood*, ſeeing they could give no aſſiſtance to Pharaoh, in reſtoring thoſe waters to their former ſtate; or any ſhare in the *bringing up of the frogs*, which they could not remove from *the houſes, and bed-chambers, and beds of Pharaoh, and his ſervants, and of the people*, as the king ſeems to expect they would have done, when *he called for Moſes*, and beſought him to *intreat the Lord, that he* might *take them away*. And very ſoon after, when other miracles were introduced, and various operations in the clouds and the air, toward which no concurrent natural cauſes, in the power of a mere man, could poſſibly be applied, they relinquiſhed their own pretences, and acknowledged *the finger of God* *.

While, therefore, thoſe magicians only juggled, and exerciſed their fictitious art to it's utmoſt extent, Moſes and Aaron were the miniſters of Jehovah, who ſhewed his matchleſs power in the waters, on man and beaſt, and in the firmament above, that he might ſpare, and not deſtroy, Pharaoh and his people, and work obedience in the heart of that proud and obſtinate prince, which he himſelf, and not God, had hardened

* If any ſhould think that Pharaoh could not poſſibly be deceived, and that the magicians wrought real miracles, they muſt yet acknowledge that thoſe men, having no power of their own, muſt have been aſſiſted by God, who in the end ſhewed them their folly.

dened*. The annihilation of *their rods*, the *corruption of the water*, in *all the ſtreams, rivers, ponds, and pools* of it, the miraculous multiplication of odious reptiles, and their direction to unfrequented places, from which they could not, by art, be baniſhed, might have convinced the magicians that their power was vain; and, in effect, they confeſſed it was. But till the moſt *noiſome vermin, ſwarms of flies, the murrain* and *death of cattle* of all kinds, together with ſores and diſeaſes on themſelves, were brought forth and inflicted, thoſe deſigning and ſelf-intereſted men never deſerted their poſt. Then *the Lord God of the Hebrews commanded* his ſervant *Moſes to ſtand before Pharaoh, and ſay, if thou wilt not let my people go, that they may ſerve me, I will at this time ſend all my plagues upon thine heart, and upon thy ſervants, and upon thy people*; or, thou ſhalt feel my power in the ſevereſt manner; *that thou mayeſt know that there is none like me in all the earth.* While *the peſtilence* raged, after a day's notice, that he might *ſend*, and ſave all his *cattle, and all that* he had *in the field*, the Lord *cauſed it to rain a very grievous hail*, attended with *thunder, and fire mingled with the hail, ſuch as hath not been known in Egypt, ſince the foundation thereof. The locuſts*, which covered *the face of the earth* ſo *that one* could not *ſee the earth*, followed; *and eat the reſidue of that which remained from the hail*, and every tree *which grew out of the field. They* alſo *filled the houſes of Pharaoh, and the houſes of all his ſervants, and the houſes of all the Egyptians. Before them there were no ſuch locuſts,*

* It is aſtoniſhing to every attentive reader of the ſcriptures, how the expreſſion, *God hardened Pharaoh's heart*, ſhould ever have been miſunderſtood, and ſo erroneouſly applied—Indeed our common tranſlation of it is very arbitrary.

neither

neither after them shall there be such. *Thick darkness, for three days,* ensued over *all the land of Egypt*; while *the children of Israel,* in Goshen, and in all other places, *had light in their dwellings*; in like manner as the other plagues had never reached them.

When Pharaoh's heart was so far *softened,* that he would have *let the people go with their little ones,* if they would *let* their *flocks and* their *herds stay,* as hostages for their return, or a recompence for his loss of them, only one miracle, or *plague,* more was necessary. It had been *said to Pharaoh,* at the beginning, *thus saith the Lord, Israel is my son, even my first born.* *Let my son,* therefore, *go that he may serve me: And if thou refuse to let him go, behold, I will slay thy son, even thy first born**. Now was the time for the execution of this threatening. *The first born in the land of Egypt, both of man and of beast were,* accordingly, *slain,* while the Israelites remained, as before, in peace and safety.

An angel was the awful executioner; whether a good or bad is equally uninteresting to us, and difficult to be known. That it was the latter, a passage in the psalms, where *evil angels* are mentioned, seems to make the opinion probable. But instead of *evil angels,* almost every commentator has observed, that, without any violence to the original, the words may be as well rendered *messengers of evil.* That angel, who executed the divine judgments upon Egypt, appeared, perhaps, in a visible form, the more effectually to inspire the tyrants, with a sacred dread of the God who declared himself in favour of the Jewish people. Moses and Aaron, by stretching out their arms, as signals for the miracles that went before, had

* Chap. iv. 22. 23.

conferred,

conferred, as it were, new powers upon nature: But when the laſt, and moſt terrible, of all the plagues was to be inflicted upon the devoted people, God himſelf was more immediately the executioner. *The firſt born of Egypt* were to be the victims; and the ſcourge was general. Neither the maſters, nor the ſlaves, the prince, nor the ſubject, men nor beaſts were excepted. For ſays the ſacred text, *there was not a houſe where there was not one dead.* Whether by the general expreſſion, we are to underſtand all the *firſt born*, in every caſe and denomination, ſo that fathers and mothers, as well as the firſt ſon or daughter, might be the objects of this decree, or only the firſt born in each houſe, the interpreters of ſcripture are not agreed. Though it were carried to it's utmoſt extent, the doctrine would be juſtified by it's analogy to the Hebrew ritual, which *conſecrated to the Lord all that firſt opened the womb, both of man and of cattle*, in commemoration of this deliverance.

UNDER ſuch a ſudden and dreadful calamity, the Egyptians would immediately invoke their gods, and expect aſſiſtance from them. But their gods alſo were involved in it, and their idols overthrown. *And againſt all the gods of Egypt I will execute judgment; I am the Lord.* We afterwards read, that *the Egyptians buried all their firſt-born, which the Lord had ſmitten among them* *. Hence it is probable, that thoſe beaſts which were their principal deities, Apis, Mnevis, and ſuch like, no doubt the firſt-born of cattle, or idols repreſenting them, were likewiſe deſtroyed. Some of their own ancient writers confeſs, that, in one night, all theſe were thrown down, and broken in pieces.

* Numbers xxxiii. 4.

And,

And, in after times, the same threatenings were denounced; *behold the Lord rideth upon a swift cloud, and shall come into Egypt; and the idols of Egypt shall be moved at his presence, and the heart of Pharaoh shall melt in the midst of it* *. *I will kindle a fire in the house of the gods of Egypt, and Nebuchadnezzar shall burn them, and carry them away captives: He shall break also the images of Beth-shemish*, or the statues of *Heliopolis*, the city of the sun; *and the houses of the gods of the Egyptians shall he burn with fire* †. And, insulting the false divinities, it is said, *declare ye among the nations, publish, and set up a standard, publish and conceal not; say, Babylon is taken, Bel is confounded, Merodach is broken in pieces* ‡. *Dagon* also *fell down before the ark of the Lord of Hosts, and had his hands and his feet broken off from the trunk* §. Let the enlightened mind, and the generous heart here drop a tear, that ever human nature should have fallen so low, as to trust in those gods that are no saviours, and can neither support nor protect themselves!

THIS fatal catastrophe was still heightened by the season in which the Almighty appointed it to happen. *At mid-night I will smite all the first-born in the land of Egypt, from the first-born of Pharaoh that sits on the throne, unto the first-born of the captive that is in the dungeon; and all the first-born of the cattle.* Darkness, which covers all pleasing objects, and clothes every thing in the most gloomy colours, increased the terror, which tumult and confusion had excited. Pharaoh, and his court, heard the alarm, and saw their misery and danger: When the King *sent for Moses and Aaron, and said unto them, rise up, and get you forth from among*

* Isaiah xix. 1. † Jer. xliii. 12. 13. ‡ Jer. l. 1.
§ Sam. v. iii.

my

my people, both you and the children of Iſrael; and go, and ſerve the Lord as ye have ſaid. And leſt the deſtroying angel ſhould ſtill proceed in the bloody vengeance, he farther added, *Take alſo your flocks, and your herds, and be gone; and bleſs me alſo.*

THUS, *by a ſtrong hand*, were the Iſraelites brought out of ſlavery, with which they had been oppreſſed, during the long reign of Rameſſes-Miamum, and a part of that of his eldeſt ſon Amenophis, who, according to ſome *, was the Pharaoh who was drowned in the Red-ſea; or, according to others †, during the reign of Seſoſtris, whoſe vaſt improvements in Egypt hiſtory deſcribes ‡, in which he employed ſtrangers, and a part of the reign of his ſon Phero, ſo like the name we have in the ſcriptures. The character given of this laſt prince by Herodotus, makes it very probable that it was he, with his army, who was overthrown in the purſuit after the Iſraelites §. That hiſtorian informs us of one action, which ſhews how far he had degenerated from the magnanimity of his father, the greateſt prince of Antiquity. At an extraordinary overflow of the Nile, when it roſe above eighteen cubits, Phero was ſo enraged, that he threw a javelin into the river for its correction.

THOSE two periods fixed on, make no great difference in chronology; as in the general liſt of the kings of Egypt, from the foundation of the empire, we find, that Rameſſes-Miamum, Amenophis, Seſoſtris, and Phero ſtand next to each other *. But there is

* Uſſerii Chron. Sacr. † Le pere Tournemine. ‡ Diodor. Sicul. § Voyez Hiſt. Ancienne des Egyptiens, par. M. Rollin. p. 103. * Vide, Herodot.

the fulleſt evidence, that it was the laſt of thoſe monarchs who periſhed on the impious march. His acceſſion to the throne of his father is placed in the two thouſand five hundred and forty-ſeventh year of the world *, and the departure from Egypt, according to ſcripture chronology, was two thouſand five hundred and fifty-ſix years after the creation. Hence that event falls into the ninth year of Phero's reign.

* Voyez. Rollin Hiſt. Egyp. who follows Herodotus.

DISSERTATION XXXIV.

Of the Inſtitution of the PASS-OVER; and the Iſraelites borrowing of their Neighbours the Egyptians.

EXODUS, XI, and XII.

FROM the circumſtances of this hiſtory, it appears, that ſome days, a week or more, elapſed, between the revelation to Moſes, that all the firſt-born of Egypt ſhould be ſlain, and the execution of that terrible judgment. For, after the threatening had been denounced, we read, that he and Aaron were commanded to *ſpeak unto all the congregation of Iſrael, ſaying, in the tenth day of this month they ſhall take to them every man a lamb, from the ſheep or the goats, according to the houſe of their fathers, a lamb from an houſe—it is the Lord's Paſsover.* This they were *to kill, and with the blood of it* mark *the two ſide-poſts, and the upper door-poſt of their houſes,* that *the blood* might *be a token where* they were, and *the plague* ſhould not come, when the deſtroying

deſtroying angel ſmote *the land of Egypt*. And this may ſignify to us who are chriſtians, the neceſſity and efficacy of the blood of that *lamb* who was, in the purpoſe of God, *ſlain from the foundation of the world* *, and *without the ſhedding* of which *there is no remiſſion* †. By a figure, very uſual in ſcripture, not only the feaſt, but the lamb itſelf, was called the paſs-over, from an Hebrew, or rather a Chaldaic word, which ſtrictly ſignifies to overlook or paſs-by, in alluſion to the mercy and protection which the ſight of the blood brought them, from the avenger.

On the night of the fifteenth of *Abib* this feaſt was to be celebrated; a night of terror and death to the deſcendants of *Ham*; between whom and Iſrael *the Lord put a difference, that he might multiply his wonders in the land of Egypt.* In another paſſage ‡, it is true, the fourteenth day is mentioned: But the reaſon of this is, the lamb was then killed, to be ready againſt the evening, which, at ſix o'clock, was the beginning of a new day with the Iſraelites. The meaning of the word *Abib*, notwithſtanding much enquiry about it, is not yet diſtinctly known. This month has alſo been called *Niſan*, which, a learned critic § tells us, ſignifies *banner*, becauſe at that ſeaſon of the year armies were wont to take the field. On this account, no doubt, the heathens called it *Mars*, after that fabulous deity, who, they believed, excited and preſided over wars. We, borrowing the name from them, call it *March*. This month, ever after, continued to be the firſt of the *eccleſiaſtical* year among the Jews, as *Tiſri*, or *September*, was that of the *civil*. Four

* Revel. xiii. 8. † Heb. ix. 22. ‡ Levit. xxiii. 5.
§ Bocharti Hieroz. pars. 1. lib. ii.

other

other divisions of time, seldom referred to in scripture, need not be mentioned here.

The lamb to be sacrificed, of which the flesh was to be eaten, was at least to be *eight days* old, and not above *a year*; provided on the tenth day of the month, and the intermediate space employed in examining its soundness and purity; for it was to be *without blemish*.——Twelve blemishes are enumerated in the law of God * which rendered this lamb, or any other beast, unworthy of acceptance. In this part of the institution there is great moral significance; namely, that every thing his creatures have, in the utmost perfection, ought to be devoted to God, as every thing is from his bounty, and depends upon his power. Our view is, likewise, directed to the great redeemer of mankind, and the glorious antitype, who is called *the lamb without spot and blemish* †, whose oblation was sufficiently meritorious to reconcile heaven and earth, and supersede all future sacrifices.

The flesh of this lamb was to be roasted with fire, which, like most of the other circumstances, is supposed, and by men of profound erudition ‡ almost demonstrated, to have been appointed in opposition to the practices of idolaters, and their enormous superstitions and profanities. The Egyptians, we are informed, constantly boiled, and never roasted, the animal offerings which they presented to the Horæ, or hours, by them regarded as goddesses.

It was not to be *eaten raw*; that is, as a Jewish interpreter § understands it, agreeable to the *Jerusalem*

* Levit. xxii. † i. Peter i. 19. ‡ Spen. de leg. Heb.
§ Maimonides.

version,

version, *half roasted*, when some of the blood still remained in the flesh; but to be thoroughly dressed, in opposition to the feasts of *Bacchus*, where women and old men, intoxicated with wine, tore, amidst streams of blood, the throbbing flesh of victims offered to that god, whom, on that account, they sometimes called *the god that feeds on raw flesh* *. And since those feasts of Bacchus had their origin in Egypt †, the opinion seems to have a very strong foundation.

The whole sacrifice was, likewise, to be eaten at once, at least none of it preserved till another day: An ordinance not peculiar in the case of the Passover; it extended to all solemn oblations, except those of *free-will*, some part of which might be kept till the day after, and if not eaten then, it was on the third day to be burnt with fire ‡. This law might be, also, directed against that superstitious practice of the heathens, of keeping fragments of their sacrifices in their houses, under a belief that they would bring them great advantages §.

Neither shall ye break a bone thereof, was another command of God, concerning this sacrifice; perhaps to condemn the votaries of the aforementioned deity,

* Illic inter ebrias puellas, & vinolentos senes, cùm scelerum pompa præcederet, alter nigro amictu teter, alter ostenso anguine terribilis, alter cruentus ore, dum viva pecoris membra discerpit, &c. Vide Jul. Firm. de Error. profan. relig. p. 10. Castellan. de Festis Græc. p. 83. Et Spencer. de lege paschatis, lib ii. cap. iv. p. 265.——Reges gentiles ita solebant facere—— Accipiebant animal, & abscindebant illi membrum aliquod, ac postea comedebant illud. Maim. Mor. Nevoch. pars. iii. cap. xlviii. p. 496. † Herodot. lib. ii. cap. 49. ‡ Levit. vii. 16. 17. § Casaub. lib. iii.

who,

who, in the celebration of their myſteries, exhibited every mark of brutality and diſtraction. They crowned themſelves with ſerpents; gave way to the moſt frightful agitations, that they might appear more ſtrongly influenced by the god; eat the raw fleſh of the beaſts they offered; and brake all their bones. Thus, as the illuſtrious author *, already cited, has laboured to ſhew, may the rites of the Paſs-over be oppoſed to the ſuperſtitions of the Pagans; and the inſtitution be conſidered, a deliverance from idolatry, as well as from bondage †. At the ſame time it ought not to be overlooked, that the prohibition of *breaking the bones* of the paſchal lamb, typified and prefigured one circumſtance attending the death of our bleſſed Saviour, ſeeing an apoſtle ‡ has expreſsly remarked it.

After all theſe requiſites were obſerved, the worſhippers at the firſt Paſs-over were to eat the ſacrifice with *their loins girded, their ſhoes on their feet, and their ſtaff in their hands*; becauſe they were *in haſte*, and diſpatch was neceſſary in their difficult and perilous ſituation. They were, moreover, to join with it *unleavened bread, and bitter herbs*, partly to remind them of their hardſhips in Egypt, and partly to commemorate ſuch an unexpectd reſcue from captivity, that they had not time to prepare ſweeter and more ſavory proviſions. And for *ſeven days* after this feaſt, no *bread* but *unleavened* was to be found in their houſes.

In Egyyt the Iſraelites killed the paſchal-lamb in their own houſes; out of which none of the fleſh was

* Spencerus de Rit. Heb. Tom. i. lib. ii. cap. iv. ſect. ii. p. 264. † See the *paraphraſe* of *Jonathan*, in loco. ‡ St. John xix. 36.

to be carried: But, if one family was too ſmall to conſume it, another next to that was joined, and the company, making a fit number of ſouls, eat it altogether. The tradition among the Jews is, that it was neceſſary ten at leaſt, and not more than twenty, ſhould partake in one place.

EVERY perſon circumciſed, whether a natural Jew, or a ſtranger, a free-man or a ſlave, muſt obſerve this rite. Whether women, who had not undergone the initiating operation, were likewiſe obliged, cannot be determined by the law itſelf. At the great feaſts, they were not required to go up to Jeruſalem in after ages; that command reſpected only the males. It is certain that they were indiſpenſibly obliged, during the days preſcribed, to abſtain from leavened bread, to eat bitter herbs, and ſuſpend all ſorts of work. Nor is it at all improbable, that many of the women, though they were not expreſsly commanded, went to Jeruſalem, at the celebration of the Paſs-over, and even eat of the lamb; as of the other ſacrifices, evidently of the *heave-offerings*, and the *wave-offerings* of their own gifts, the daughters of Iſrael, as well as the ſons, not in a ſtate of uncleanneſs, were partakers *. While the tabernacle was in Shiloh, *Hannah*, with her huſband, went yearly thither †, and offered ſacrifice, and, there is little doubt, ſhared of the feaſt, which might be that in the mouth of *Abib*. *David, when he had made an end of offering burnt-offerings, and peace-offerings, dealt among all the people, as well to the women as men, to every one a cake of bread, and a good piece of fleſh, and a flagon of wine* ‡; the very offerings which he had laſt made.

* See Numbers xviii. 2. † 1 Sam. 1. 4. ‡ 2 Sam. vi. 19.

CONCERNING

Concerning children, nothing has been prescribed; and the Jews have, accordingly, disputed this point with one another. Some of them have said, that seven years qualified the circumcised, for the participation of this sacrifice; ten have been the term of others; and twenty the last standard which has been set up *.

All Israel, therefore, who were circumcised, clean from legal defilements, and could come to the place of sacrifise, were indispensibly required to observe this ordinance, at the time appointed, *according to all the rites, and the ceremonies of it.* But because *there were certain men*, when it was observed the second time, *who were defiled by the dead body of a man, that they could not keep the Pass-over on that day*; *the Lord*, therefore, *spake unto Moses, saying, if any of you, or of your posterity, shall be unclean, by reason of a dead body, or be in a journey afar off; he shall yet keep the Pass-over unto the Lord; but it shall be on the fourteenth day of the second month at even, according to all the ordinances of the Pass-over* †. The divine lawgiver, in great wisdom and compassion, fixed those terms; and none but he could alter them. With regard to another institution, it was ranked among the crimes of *Jeroboam*, the first king of Israel, that *he ordained a feast in the eighth month, on the fifteenth day of the month, like unto the feast that was in Judah*, on the fifteenth day of the seventh month, which was that of tabernacles; *and offered upon the altar, which he had made in Bethel, and burnt incense, even in the mouth which he had devised of his own heart* ‡. If *Hezekiah's* sacrifice be made an objection §, it ought to be remembered, that the profanations of

* Menoch. de rep. Hebr. lib. iii. p. 259. † Numb. ix. 6. &c. ‡ 1 Kings xii. 32, 33. § 2 Chron. xxix.

Ahaz his father having unhallowed the temple, the good prince, of his own free will and accord, as soon as the house of God was cleansed and repaired, to avert the divine displeasure from him and his people, entered into covenant with him. And the same has been done by others on similar occasions.

Nor were the Jews more strictly confined to certain seasons, than they were careful to watch their approach; especially the time of the Pass-over, after they were settled in the holy land. Their Sanhedrim usually sent two men, to the western borders of Judæa, who announced, with the utmost speed, the appearance of the new moon, which regulated all their months. And since their last and great dispersion, when the temple was destroyed, they yearly print a calendar, which shews the changes of that luminary, the four seasons of the year, and every other period in which their religion is concerned *.

The Paschal-lamb, as has been said, was, at first, slain, and eaten in the common houses of the Israelites in Egypt, who had not, nor would they have used, the privileges of the temples, in that country, for public religious service. In the same manner our blessed Lord celebrated its holy succedaneum, his own supper, in an upper room, without any regard to the splendor of those buildings which are reared at the common charge. This victim, as well as all others, was, afterwards, sacrificed in the *tabernacle*, the established residence of the Almighty with his people. And when the *temple* was finished, that was the place where all sacrifices were to be offered.

* M. Saurin. Disc. xlviii. M. Basnage, Histoire de Juifs.

Crowds

Crowds innumerable, accordingly, assembled at the holy city, on all solemn occasions, particularly at the Pass-over, for the reason before assigned. With a view to convince Nero of the strength of the Jewish nation, which he affected much to despise, we are told, that Cestius begged the priests to contrive a method of finding out the number of people that might be at Jerusalem itself, at a time. For this purpose, they chose that of the Pass-over, when they reckoned the lambs, which amounted to two hundred and fifty thousand, and six hundred; consequently, each of them having been, by the law, appointed for ten persons, and frequently there were more, the total must have been two millions five hundred and fifty-six thousand souls at least; all males.

HAVING thus described this holy rite, which was one of the Jewish sacraments, with all the particulars in the original institution, and the future observance of it; we shall now consider the conduct of the Israelites towards the Egyptians, on the days preceding the Pass-over, and the manner in which they left them. Those, as they were commanded, *borrowed* of these people, *jewels of silver, and jewels of gold, and raiment: And the Lord gave the people favour in the sight of the Egyptians, so that they lent unto them such things as they required; and they spoiled the Egyptians.* This, by some, has been reckoned an horrid crime; a disparagement of the legislator's morals to persuade his people to such a piece of villainy; and of his sense to relate the command. But, notwithstanding the affected zeal of infidels, to support what they call truth and rectitude, nothing will be found in their arguments, on this fact, but chicane and buffoonery.

Happily

Happily for the world, those men prove wretched reaſoners, and appear leſs than half-learned, when they vilify revelation, which diſplays God's ſovereignty over the world, in the righteous and uncontrolable exerciſe of his own glorious perfections. For,

INSTEAD of *they borrowed*, the word may as well be tranſlated *they aſked* *; and inſtead of *they lent unto them*, it would be a juſter verſion, *they let them have* †. And the fact itſelf juſtifies this interpretation. The Egyptians had been thoroughly terrified at what had happened among them, by the miniſtry of Moſes; eſpecially at the laſt dreadful plague upon all their *firſt-born*. They were, therefore, willing to grant the Hebrews every thing that they demanded, and even to bribe them for their own future ſafety; for, ſaid they, *we are all dead men*.

BESIDES, the Almighty had an incontrovertible right to transfer that property from one people to another; and none can reverently bar his title, to whom the whole earth belongs. Nor was this diſpenſing with the laws either of nature or nations; the procedure was adapted to the nature of the caſe. The Iſraelites, without divine authority, could not have indemnified themſelves with juſtice, for the injuries they had received, and the ſervices they had performed, during, at leaſt, an hundred years ſevere ſervitude, under four kings; and from the uncle of the laſt, named Buſiris, of whom hiſtory gives the

* The Hebrew word certainly ſignifies, *petant, poſtulaverunt*.
† *Commodaverunt eis.*

very

very worst character, had, in the absence of Sesostris, experienced all the rigors of a most tyrannical government *. In taking from them what the Egyptians were willing to give, there could be neither fraud nor theft. But when the command of their maker was interposed, it was the duty of the Israelites to take and keep what was so given them, as their own.

As to their going out of Egypt at all, let it be, likewise, observed, that God had the same right to deliver them out of Pharaoh's hand, that he had to settle Canaan upon them, the distinguishing inheritance long before promised to their fathers. That he could do both, for the purposes of his own glory, and the good of mankind in general, none can be so madly impious as to deny. And after he had made this design known, as he frequently had, by many and signal miracles, it was a direct defiance of heaven to detain that people longer, to claim their service, or expect a restitution of what they had received. It is frenzy to dispute, whether the king of Egypt, or the King of Heaven and Earth, ought to be obeyed.

Finally, no ill use, the thing greatly apprehended by unbelievers, can possibly be made of such a precedent as this, by any honest man in his senses. If any man, or any nation, shall, at any time, shew such a commission for acting as the Jews did, we shall then chearfully acknowledge their claim ; but not otherwise. If no such commission be ever pro-

* Voyez Rollin Hist. des Egypt. imprimê a Amster. p. 112.

duced, let none ridiculously think, that their behaviour is a precedent for other things which bear no resemblance to it.

DISSERTA-

DISSERTATION XXXV.

Of the Departure of the ISRAELITES from Egypt; and PASSAGE through the RED-SEA.

EXODUS, XII, XIII, XIV, and XV.

IT has been said by unbelievers, who shall be nameless, that the Israelites, long before their departure, were formidable to those who held them in captivity, and, joined to a foreign enemy, could have made a conquest of the land, in which they were strangers; for which reason, *the Egyptians drove them out.* We shall, therefore, obviate this plea; and then proceed to the history.

ONE of the kings of Egypt indeed, perhaps Amenophis, or his predecessor on the throne, had *said to his people, if there falleth out any war, they may join themselves unto our enemies, and fight against us, and so get them up out of the land.* This, it must be confessed, shews a dread on the part of the Egyptians, for their hard usage of those whom their fore-fathers had hospitably received into their country; but no design on the part of the Israelites. Their hostile neighbours were the Arabians and Ethiopians; the one on the east, and the other on the south; for, on the north

and

and weſt, Egypt, as has been ſaid, was bounded by the Mediterranean, and the deſert and burning ſands of Lybia and Cyrene. From the former, there could be little danger, as the Iſraelites had built a chief-town, and a fortreſs of the ſame name, by the king's orders, as well, we may ſuppoſe, to ſecure their own ſubjection, and prevent their flight, as to defend the kingdom on that quarter; and againſt the latter, we have been told, Moſes went, and brought trophies and territories to the country that had given him birth. The fear of the Egyptians muſt, therefore, be aſcribed to their own ſeverity, and the knowledge they had of the divine promiſes; and, inſtead of *driving out the Iſraelites*, the plagues inflicted on themſelves obliged them to reſign the *favoured* people to the care of the Almighty, whoſe arm had been ſo ſignally ſtretched out to deliver, and receive them. Though, as in all other diſpenſations of this ſort, preparation has, for the moſt part, been made, that people, it cannot be denied, were, by their numbers, in a capacity to encounter many difficulties, and atchieve great things. Miracles are never wrought without abſolute neceſſity; and when that neceſſity ceaſes, they are not to be expected, till other extraordinary occaſions call for them.

The hiſtory, therefore, informs us, that Moſes drew out ſix hundred thouſand men of war, beſides women, old men, and young people under twenty years of age; and *a mixed multitude* with them, either proſyletes, contractors in marriage, or perſons who were willing to undergo all the dangers of a deſert, for every delight under tyranny and oppreſſion. Of all thoſe

those classes, perhaps there were many among them. And the whole might amount to above three millions.

The place of rendezvous were the plains of *Rameses*. These were in Goshen, at the extremity of Egypt, which lay nearest to Canaan. Here Jacob, and his sons, had their first settlement; and, notwithstanding the dispersion through the other provinces, their posterity had formed a large Hebrew colony; equal in numbers to some little kingdoms.

From thence, in a short time, Moses might have conducted them to the promised land: From the one kingdom to the other, there was only about three days journey. But fierce and war-like tribes of people lying on the way, men, accustomed to slavery, and emerging, as it were, from under Pharaoh's rod, could not be sufficiently courageous to oppose them; especially the vigorous efforts of the Canaanites, whom they openly professed to expel from their own land: And miracles were no oftner to be wrought for them, than difficulties occurred, which their own ingenuity and strength were unable to surmount. In their present circumstances, they could neither form, nor execute, the heroic design of resisting regular troops, or attacking places of defence. Besides, though this army should have had the courage, it is highly probable that they wanted arms for the enterprize. For the word *harnessed*, by which some have thought the Israelites were fully equipped for their expedition, is yet so doubtful in the original, and the attempts of erudition * to fix it's true meaning so

* Calmet in Exod. xiii. 18. p. 140.

fruitless,

fruitless, that if evidence be insisted on for what we believe, we must still remain ignorant of this matter, after all our researches. As they extorted nothing from their oppressors, there is a strong presumption that they were not armed: And to have put them in a condition to act either offensively or defensively, would have been inconsistent with the policy of the kingdom. Indeed, as the dead bodies of the Egyptians, who were swallowed up by the red-sea, were cast a-shore, it is very likely that their arms were conveyed there also: With these the Israelites might, afterwards, accoutre themselves, in a better manner than they were before.

THAT the courage necessary for the chosen people might be then formed, before they were put to the last proof of it, against that country which was destined for their possession; or, at least, that they might force a passage through their enemies by the way, and transmit a war-like spirit to their descendants; the Almighty, instead of leading them from the south, the situation of Egypt, towards the north, where Palæstine lay, ordered, therefore, a movement to the east, where there was a vast and inhospitable desert, forming the frontiers of Egypt on the side of Arabia-petræa, and affording many occasions for the display of his power. In their route, they came, first, to Succoth, which signifies *the city of tents* *, though the reason is unknown. They travelled next to Etham, the last town in ancient Egypt, and the situation of which has been examined lately, by a person of great learning †. Here they described several windings in their course, and came at last, to an opening in a chain of mountains,

* M. Saurin, Disc. xlix. p. 94. † Dr. Shaw.

tains, called *Pi-hahiroth*, that is, *the mouth*, or clift, of the mountains of *Hiroth*. Here, it is to be observed, that, all the names in this part of the journey being Hebrew, the Israelites were, undoubtedly, the authors of them, without any regard to those by which the places had been called before. But those names are of such significance, from a faculty in the ancient languages, some of which still exist, that we have the situation and quality of the place represented in the very name given to it.

A MIRACULOUS phenomenon, dark on the one side, and luminous on the other; or different in substance as well as appearance; in the form of a column, was the guide of this *peculiar people*. When it was day, it directed them where they should go, and sheltered them from the intense heat of the sun; and shewed them their tract by night, when their march was necessary and proper. It obstructed, moreover, the view of their enemies; and was as the throne of God from whence they looked for counsel and protection. Moses says, *the angel of the Lord, who went before the camp of Israel, removed and went behind them*, when Pharaoh, and his army, approached; *and the pillar of the cloud went from before their face, and stood behind them*: Or, in other words, as the angel moved, so did the cloud; the one being subservient to the other. Some Rabbins, who have followed all the extravagant flights of human fancy, and many others who have imitated them, have said, that this angel, or wall of fire between the Israelites and Egyptians, was Michael. While others, in all ages, who have attended more closely to the various dispensations of grace from heaven, have been of opinion, that the *Schechinah*, or bright

bright ſhining light, mentioned particularly in early periods, was the ſon of God *, to whom the government of the world was ſpecially committed. From this appearance, which was the ſymbol of the divine majeſty, God is ſaid to have converſed with Moſes; and given him every neceſſary direction in this ſingular expedition.

MEANWHILE, the impreſſion, which the late plagues had made on Pharaoh's mind, began to be fainter. By this time, he, and his ſervants knew, that the Iſraelites had undertaken their march with another view than that of celebrating a feaſt, in the wilderneſs: For when they let them go, they impoſed on themſelves by this notion †. They now reflected on the loſs which the country muſt ſuſtain, by ſuch a diminution of it's inhabitants; and, perhaps, might ſtill flatter themſelves, that the power of the God of Iſrael, extenſive as it had appeared to be, was yet limited, like that of the falſe deities.—The heathen theology, of which the Egyptians were believers and followers, aſſigned a diſtrict of operation to every one of their divinities: Some were thought to preſide over the hills, and ſome over the vallies; as we ſee in the advice which the ſervants of the king of Syria gave him ‡.

DELUDED in ſome ſuch manner as this, or merely to rectify his own miſtake, *Pharaoh took ſix hundred choſen chariots, and all the chariots of Egypt, and captains over every one of them, and purſued after the children of Iſrael,*

* See, again, Diſſertation xvii. † If fraud, on the part of Moſes and Aaron, ſhould be urged in this matter, it may be anſwered, that, in telling only a part of the truth, they were guilty of no falſhood: See 1. Sam. xvi. 2. 5. ‡ 1 Kings xx. 23.

and

and overtook them, encamping by the sea, beside Pi-ha-hiroth, over against Baal-zephon. On the nineteenth day of *Nisan* probably, when the three days mentioned were expired, Pharaoh left Zoan for this pursuit, and came within sight of the Israelites on the twentieth, towards evening. The distance from Succoth, where the latter had first stopt, to Etham, was only *eight* miles, and from thence to Pi-ha-hiroth, *sixteen*. Pharaoh's army, Josephus * says, consisted of seven hundred chariots, fifty thousand horse, and two hundred thousand foot, with shields. The sacred text itself, besides the account given above, informs us farther, that the *Egyptians pursued after the Israelites, with all the horses and chariots of Pharaoh, and his horsemen, and his army.* In such a situation, how great must the embarrassment of the fugitives have been! On the west, a chain of mountains! On the east and north, the sea! And Pharaoh's army, on the south! What part shall they chuse!—Cross the mountains!—they are inaccessible! —Pass over the sea!—they have neither mariners nor vessels!—Fight!—they want instruments of war, and skill to use them!—Let them turn their face, then, towards that cloud where their great leader resides, and put themselves under the shadow of his wings till this calamity is past. Let them call to their aid that invincible arm, which had hitherto supported them, *and doth ever valiantly* †.

This they neglected, and acted quite contrary. As *Pharaoh* would naturally *say, the wilderness hath shut them in,* when they were surrounded by the sea, and craggy mountains, which it was impossible to pass, and be thereby encouraged to attack them; the Israelites

* Antiquit. judaic. lib. ii. cap. vi.

† Psalm cxviii. 15. 16.

elites

elites themselves condemned their captain for bringing them into such distresses. They murmured against Moses, and, in the most sarcastical and reproachful language, or rather full of discontent and rage, said, *because there were no graves in Egypt, hast thou taken us away to die in the wilderness? Wherefore hast thou dealt thus with us?*

In the meekness of his soul, and the fullest expectation of assistance on this critical occasion, the man of God cried unto the Lord, who had directed him to take this course, instead of going from Etham round the Cape of the Red-sea; and received power and commandment to extricate his people from their present difficulties. *Lift up thy rod*, said Jehovah, *and stretch out thine hand over the sea, and divide it; and the children of Israel shall go on dry ground through the mids of the sea: And I will get me honour upon Pharaoh, and upon all his host, upon his chariots, and upon his horsemen.*

God had brought the Israelites to a place, where, it strongly appeared, they were to fall victims to the highly incensed monarch of Egypt; but it was only to magnify his own power and justice in the destruction of Pharaoh, and the great men of his kingdom. All the former judgments upon their cattle, their corn, their bodies, and their children, were just chastisements for the wrongs which they had done to his people, and keeping them in undeserved bondage. But he had not yet called them to an exact account, for destroying so many male-infants of the Hebrews, as they had drowned in the river. For that innocent blood he reckons with them now, and made them

them the executioners of his vengeance upon them-selves, by giving them up to their own proud pre-sumptions of success, in pursuing those whom they lately besought to depart out of their land*. Infa-tuated resolution! Cruel oppressors, take warning! *Be wise, O ye kings: Be instructed, ye judges of the earth* †.

THAT Moses had the fullest expectation of assist-ance, appears from what he *said to the people*; *fear ye not, stand still, and see the salvation of the Lord, which he will shew you to-day: For the Egyptians whom ye have seen to-day, ye shall see them again no more for ever.* And having declared this revelation to them, he stilled their clamours, and banished their fears. Over the sea ‡, he, then, stretched out his rod, to which every thing was become obedient; and the waters were instantly parted asunder. *And*, accordingly, *the chil-dren of Israel went into the midst of the sea upon the dry ground; and the waters were a wall unto them, on their right hand, and on their left.*

THIS, indeed, may be thought hyperbolical, like the same expressions in the next chapter, where Moses, in his song, says, *the waters were gathered toge-ther, the floods stood upright as an heap, and the deeps*

* Bp. Patrick, in loco. † Psalm 11, 10.

‡ Why this famous gulf is called the *Red-Sea*, the learned have laboured much to find out; but are not yet agreed. For the epithet *red*, the Hebrew word is *Suph*, which signifies a large rush, or flag; and, perhaps, this sea was thus distinguished, from those water plants, which grew in such abundance on its banks. From some other circumstance, therefore, it has been denomi-nated *red*.—Perhaps, coral of that colour reflected from the bot-tom.

were congealed in the heart of the sea. Such descriptions, it has been said, are very allowable in poetry, as they magnify the power of God, who can do such wonders; though, in sober language, there is no necessity for supposing any other thing here, than an instantaneous revulsion of the waters into the Ocean, or caverns of the earth, at the divine command; when, the channel being left bare, hardened, and rendered solid by a strong east-wind, the Israelites might safely march over it for several leagues, to the opposite shore*. But, however prudent and philosophical this thought may be, to obviate the multiplication of miracles, it is not poetry alone, that we depend on, for this extraordinary march of the Israelites through the Red-Sea; but *sober history*, antecedent to that song, which informs us, *the waters were a wall unto them, on their right hand, and on their left:* And when a miracle is wrought at all, we need not wonder at the greatness of it. Without insisting on circumstances, with which we are, in a great measure, unacquainted, the heaven-protected people, under the guidance of the pillar of light, arrived on the other side of the gulf, before the rising of the sun: When the other part of the promise was, likewise, fulfilled.

PHARAOH, and his army, hot in pursuit, either, furiously, ventured on evident perils, or, blindfold, entered the watry domain, and were swallowed up by its returning waves. Moses, after the manner of human speech, says, *in the morning watch, the Lord looked*, with a frown of disdain, *unto the host of the Egyptians, through the pillar of fire, and of the cloud, and troubled the host of the Egyptians, and took off their cha-*

* M. Saurin Disc. XLIX. p. 99.

riot-

riot wheels, that they drove them heavily; to give them a proper sense of their iniquity, and season for repentance; and they, accordingly, *said, let us flee from the face of Israel, for the Lord fighteth for them against the Egyptians.* But Moses stretching *forth his hand over the sea*, it *returned to* its *strength when the morning appeared, and the Egyptians fled against it*; but *the waters covered the chariots, and the horsemen, and all the host of Pharaoh that came into the sea after* the Israelites: *There remained not so much as one of them.*

THUS was proud Phero, and his mighty host, overthrown, by one of the greatest miracles that God ever wrought in favour of his chosen people. Perhaps it is the greatness of the miracle, that hath made some men be at such pains to sully the splendor, and lessen the dignity of it, by suggesting, artfully, the following objections.

THAT arising from the strength of the Israelites, has been answered at the beginning of the discourse: But the shortness of the time, in which all this is said to have happened, is thought to lay the foundation of an insuperable argument against it. Moses, it is true, allows no more than from the evening till the morning, which at the *Equinox*, when this transaction was, makes twelve hours. Perhaps, on due consideration, that space will be found sufficient for the march, even of the unwieldy body of Israel, over nine or ten miles of ground, especially if what is alledged by several Jewish writers be true, that they were divided into *twelve* parallel columns, according to the number of their tribes; which is, by no means, unlikely, as this division was observ[ed] on almost every other occaſion: Or only into *five*, as the word *harnaſſed*, when they left Egypt, ſeems to ſignify in the original *.

The paſſage through the Red-ſea has been compared with ſundry events recorded in profane hiſtory; particularly with what happened to Alexander, at the head of his Macedonians at the ſea of Pamphylia, when he marched againſt the Perſians; to Scipio at Carthage; to Lucullus at the river Euphrates; and to ſome others in later times. In regard to which, the poet's rule, never to introduce a god, unleſs ſomething worthy of his power is to be effected, might ſerve as a ſufficient anſwer, and diſcredits entirely the deſign of all ſuch undertakings, by which no other purpoſe appears to have been ſerved, but the gratification of unbounded ambition, and the extenſion of worldly empire. We ſhall, however, repreſent thoſe events, in the order of time in which they happened, that the very nature of them may render any ſerious conſideration needleſs.

The Jewiſh hiſtorian himſelf lays the ground for the firſt compariſon, where, after deſcribing the paſſage over the Red-ſea, he ſays, I have thus related what I find written in our ſacred books: And none ought to think it impoſſible, that men who lived in the innocence and ſimplicity of the firſt ages, ſhould have found out, for their own ſafety, a paſſage through the ſea; whether it might have *opened of itſelf*, or been divided by the will of God; ſince the ſame thing happened long after to the Macedonians, under the command of Alexander, when God was pleaſed to make uſe of that nation in deſtroying the Perſians.

* Heb. חמשים. Sep. πεμπ[illegible] ſc. γενεα. Vulg. Armati.

Thus.

Thus all the historians, who have written of that prince, report; and I leave it to every one to judge as they please *.

SCIPIO, *Livy* says, at the conquest of Carthage, was told by some fishermen, that he might, with ease, carry his army, at low water, to the foot of the city walls. He took the hint; and about the middle of the day, the waters following their natural course, and a north wind, which sprung up at the same, driving them with the greater rapidity, the marsh, or bay, was so fordable, that the waters scarce went to the men's girdle, and only to the knees of some of them. But what wisdom and prudence thus effected, he endeavoured to make the people regard as a prodigy †.

PLUTARCH's account of Lucullus is very similar. When, by long uninterrupted marches, he had arrived at the banks of the Euphrates, the winter rains and snow had so exceedingly swelled the stream, that the river was amazingly rapid and impetuous. This gave him great uneasiness; for he knew it would require much time to procure boats, and provide a bridge for the passage of his forces. But, towards the evening, the flood began to abate, and sunk so considerably that night, that the next morning he found the river, not only confined within it's original channel, but shallower than usual; insomuch that the people of the country, when they discovered several heads of land, like little islands rising above the waters, which seemed to stagnate round them, considered Lucullus as

* Josephus, Antiquit. judaic. lib. ii. cap. vii. † Vide Tit. Liv. lib. xxvi. cap. xlv.

some

ſome deity, who had wrought a miracle, and forced the river to ſubmit, and yield him a ſafe and expeditious paſſage *.

In the ſame liſt is placed what hiſtory relates of an event, which fell out an hundred and five years ago. The combined fleets of England and France, conſiſting of an hundred ſail, threatened the coaſts of Holland, and actually meditated a deſcent at the *Texel.* Forty-ſeven ſhips of war, twelve frigates, and twenty fire ſhips, under the command of Admiral *Ruyter*, were, humanly ſpeaking, very inadequate to ſuch a formidable armament againſt them. But the deſign of their enemies, ſays the hiſtorian, failed in a way moſt extraordinary. On the night when the attack was to have been made, the *ebb* laſted *twelve whole hours*, which the ſailors conſidered as a miracle. This extraordinary reflux was, likewiſe, followed by a violent tempeſt, which totally diſconcerted the enemy's fleet, and obliged thoſe, who came hoſtilely againſt Holland, reſpectfully to leave coaſts which providence defended in ſuch a miraculous manner †.

Such are the arguments, uſed by ingenious and unbelieving men, for diſparageing this greateſt of all miracles, becauſe it was the moſt public, and the leaſt liable to the charge of illuſion. The bounds preſcribed for this work preclude a minute examination of thoſe facts, when we might retrench what love for the marvellous hath added to the truth.

Of Alexander's expedition, whatever Joſephus may have thought of it, Plutarch ſpeaks very ſoberly.

* Plutarch. in vitâ Luculli. † Vie de l'amiral Ruiter, Liv. xii. Et auſſi M. Saur. Diſc. xlix. p. 108.

He

He says, his passage through Pamphylia has been very pompously described by historians, and represented, in the highest degree, marvellous and astonishing; as though, by some divine power, the waves which used to roll impetuously from the main, and hardly ever left the beach, under the steep broken cliffs, uncovered, had retired to afford him a passage. But Alexander, in his epistles, mentions no such extraordinary event, but only says, that in his march from Phaselis he went through the passage called Climax *. And Strabo's account is this: Near the city of Phaselis, between Lycia and Pamphylia, *there is a passage* by the sea-side, through which Alexander marched his army. This passage is very narrow, and lies between the shore and the mountain Climax, which overlooks the Pamphylian Sea. It is dry at low water, so that *travellers pass through it with safety*; but when the sea is high it is all covered over. It was then the winter season, and Alexander, who depended much on his good fortune, was resolved to set out without staying till the floods were abated, so that his men were forced to march up to the middle in water †. So fanciful a writer as Quintus Curtius, who embellishes all his narrations with circumstances partly true, and partly miraculous, deserves very little consideration; and yet even he allows, that, after a north wind had driven the waters into the capacious bed of the ocean, Alexander and his army went through *the shallows* of the Pamphylian gulf, under mount Climax, with the water almost to their middle ‡.

Livy's account of Scipio's approach to the walls of Carthage is equally rational; as it plainly shews us, that

* Plutarch in vitâ Alexandri. † Strabo lib. xiv. ‡ Quint. Curt. lib. ii. p. 138. Edit. Hag. Comit. 1727.

the

course of the tide, and the situation of the sands about that city, were well known to the fishermen who had frequented the coast; and that the historian charges the conqueror with *a pious fraud*, with which he worked on the minds of the credulous *.

In the passage of Lucullus over the Euphrates, Plutarch, also, is so far from insinuating a miracle, that he ascribes it to natural causes; and says the people of the country only considered him as some deity, who had forced the river to submit.

The affair in Holland, however providential for the states, has nothing in it extraordinary: At the *Texel*, where the water is shallow, the tide is, often, seen not to return for *nine hours* †, when the wind is strong in a certain direction; and nothing is more common than violent storms on that coast. It was, nevertheless, pious in the *Dutch*, to celebrate with songs of praise to the Almighty, their seasonable deliverance; if flattering notions, that the favour of heaven was peculiarly confined to themselves, were not unreasonable, nor made them violate the dictates of universal justice.

But admitting all those relations to be true, in all their circumstances, there is not one of the events to be compared with the passage through the Red-sea, as we have it described. Besides, the prediction of Moses that it would happen, the rod he employed, the

* Hoc, cura ac ratione compertum, in prodigium ac deos vertens Scipio, qui ad transitum Romanis mare verterent et stagno auferrent, viasque ante nunquam initas humano vestigio aperirent; Neptunum jubebat ducem itineris sequi, ac medio stagno evadere ad mœnia. † Note on the margin of Saurin's Disc.

facility

facility and quickness of the passage, the rashness of the enemy, and their tragical end, all concur in placing the event above every parallel; and nothing but an immoderate desire to depreciate the miracles recorded in the sacred history, could ever have raised any doubts concerning it. It's wonderfulness needs to be no objection: All the events which happened to that nation, whose history we are now writing, from the time the promises were made to Abraham, till they were all fulfilled, demonstrate that they were under a sovereign direction. There runs through the old testament, which contains the annals of the *Jews*, an indissoluble chain of facts, for fifteen hundred years, harmoniously framed, and forming a whole, of which no part can be wanted, while each supports and explains another.

Before we conclude, let one objection more be considered; though it is as contemptible, as its author * was bitter against all religion whatever. He says that Moses had a passage through the Red-sea in a way perfectly natural, by the help of second causes; for we read, in the account given by Moses himself, that *a strong east wind blew all that night, and made the sea dry land.* No doubt, by allowing that the event did really fall out, the infidel, by the circumstance which he introduces, meant to destroy the miracle, by comparing it with the other events which we have just now examined. But had he ever considered, that the most natural things become miraculous, when they obey at the times fixed, the voice of a man, whose doctrine depends upon their concurrence? That winds should blow, and make waters retire; that the sun, likewise,

* Spinosa, Tract. Theolog. Polit. cap. vi.

should

should one hour glare, by his beams, around us, and another be covered with clouds, are things perfectly natural: But, notwithstanding, if any one should make those winds blow at his command, and the sun shine, or hide himself, would, not this prove, of itself, that what was natural at one time, was purely miraculous at another? Would it not be still more so, if it had *been foretold*, and at a time when it could be least *foreseen*, without a special revelation from the God of nature? *The passage*, under our view, *was facilitated by a wind*; and Moses *had foretold* that the Jewish people should pass over the Red-sea in safety: But how could he *foresee* that a wind would rise to harden the sands? God only, *whose word the stormy wind fulfills* *, could make *the east wind* blow *on the earth* †, at his pleasure. This wind, I say, only facilitated the passage, by drying, and giving consistence to the muddy channel; it was not so much as the instrumental cause, to make the waters remove out of their ancient place; for these *were divided, and the children of Israel went into the midst of the sea; and the waters were a wall unto them on their right hand, and on their left*; contrary to the course of nature, and the action of all winds that ever blew. And, as a farther confirmation of the miracle, as soon as *Moses*, at God's command, *stretched forth his hand over the sea, the sea returned to it's strength, and overthrew the Egyptians, and Israel saw them dead upon the sea-shore*; when they sung the inimitably sublime canticle in the chapter following.

Nor, of this amazing catastrophe, are we destitute of many testimonies, which strangely corroborate the account Moses himself has given, though much of the

* Psalm cxlviii. 8. † Job. xxxviii. 24.

fabulous

fabulous is connected with true history. *Strabo*, depending on ancient histories from which he copied, says, there happened on the coast between Tyre and Ptolemais, one of the most wonderful things, and rarely seen at any other time. While the people of Ptolemais were engaged in battle with Sarpedon, the sea came upon them; and though they fled, with the utmost precipitation, the waters, by a violent influx of the waves, overwhelmed and destroyed them, in a variety of ways, and their bodies were found mixed with dead fishes *. Here the scholiast, on this place, observes, that what happened in the Idumean sea, is transferred to the Tyrian, and interpolated with many false circumstances. Sarpedon, he says, is ignorantly mistaken for a proper name; but, in Hebrew, *Sharphaddon* signifies the captain of deliverance, a character well agreeing with that of Moses †.

ATHENÆUS relates almost the same history; still fictitious and deformed. I know, says he, that Posidonius the stoic has spoken of a multitude of fishes, when Tryphon Apamensis fought against Sarpedon, the general of Demetrius, at the city of Ptolemais. Sarpedon, shut up by the Mediterranean, retreated with his forces; while Tryphon's army, who had conquered him, directing their course by the sea-side, were instantly overtaken by a huge wave which rose aloft, and rushed upon the land, and every one drowned. The wave retiring, an immense heap of fishes was left with their dead bodies. Then Sarpedon's soldiers, hearing of the calamity, came to the place, and, sparing the corps of their vanquished enemies, carried

* Strabo, lib. xvi. † Spicil. Jam. p. 208.

away

away a great quantity of the fishes, and erected a trophy to Neptune in the suburbs of the city *. These little stories of Strabo and Athenæus, the scholiast again remarks, do not altogether agree, as is evidently seen; and yet it is certain, that their relations are grounded on nothing else but the passage of the Israelites through the Red-sea; though it is basely and wickedly disguised †. Indeed had it been truly represented, and firmly believed, there would have been no such idolatry as was established in the most civilized nations; and where it was established, if the power of the supreme God had been acknowledged, Neptune, and every other creature of the imagination, would have been robbed of their offerings.

Last of all, Diodorus gives a similar relation, less corrupted, in this manner. Among the Ichthyophagi, that is to say, those who fed on fishes, and lived by the western coast of the Red-sea, there was a tradition, preserved through many generations of their ancestors, that the sea formerly opened by a violent reflux; that it's very bottom appeared dry, and covered with verdure; that the waters divided themselves into two parts; but returned again with great fury, and united as before, in their natural state ‡. Here, certainly, we see the passage of the Israelites, not obscurely described, even by a profane historian. The event is said to have happened in the Arabian gulf itself, and many ages before the remembrance of those who reported it to Diodorus.

* Athen. lib. viii. cap. 2. † Spicil. Jam. ibid. ‡ Diodor. Sicul. lib. iii.

Here,

HERE, then, is a miracle, which, all muſt confeſs, was wrought by the Almighty, in favour of his choſen people! This, in connection with others, almoſt equally great and conſpicuous, performed by the miniſtry of Moſes, demonſtrate, beyond gainſaying, the miſſion and authority of that legiſlator to have been divine. Let unbelief, therefore, bluſh, *and all iniquity ſtop it's mouth.*

DISSERTATION XXXVI.

Of the ISRAELITES wanting Water in the Wilderneſs of *Shur*; that of MARAH made ſweet; QUAILS and MANNA cover their Camp.

EXODUS, XV, and XVI.

A CERTAIN writer * hath obſerved, that, in a great many inſtances, we muſt endeavour, in the beſt manner poſſible, to ſupply defects in the chronology of the ſcriptures. No term, ſays he, can be more ambiguous, than that which is uſed by the ſacred hiſtorians, when they ſay, *And it came to paſs*, or, *After theſe things*. This, he adds, is almoſt equally employed by them, to denote an inſtant, an hour, a day, a year, ſometimes a whole age. The truth of the remark muſt be confeſſed, which the excellent author was far from deſigning as a cenſure; and every one will allow, that a few days make a very inconſiderable difference in the annals of the world. In profane hiſtorians, of ancient times, there is the ſame omiſſion of dates.

* M. Saurin, Diſc. L. p. 126.

BUT

But the difficulty here is not great. About a week may be ſuppoſed to have paſſed, from the departure of the Iſraelites out of Egypt, till their arrival on the oppoſite ſhore of the Red-ſea; *they came into the wilderneſs of Sin, on the fifteenth day of the ſecond month*; *and on the firſt day of the third month, they came into the wilderneſs of Sinai.* Hence the particular incidents, now delineated, fall within the compaſs of thirty eight days; that is from the twenty-third of *Niſan*, till the firſt of *Sivan*, incluſive; *Ijar* having but twenty-nine days.

Marching from the ſea, the Iſraelites travelled three days in the wilderneſs of *Shur*, or, as it is called in the book of Numbers*, the wilderneſs of *Etham*; which was the name of the whole country, that lies round the head, and the ſouth and north ſides of the Red-ſea. This perfectly obviates the difficulty in the account, that *they encamped in Etham, in the edge of the wilderneſs*, the day before they came to the ſea, and were ſtill in that wilderneſs after their paſſage through it; which has induced ſome to think, that the Iſraelites did not go quite a-croſs the gulf; but, after forming a ſemicircle, came out at the ſame ſide, on which they entered it: A conceit, which, beſides being injurious to the miracle, is grounded on ignorance, that the vaſt deſert mentioned encloſed the Red-ſea on all ſides, as well towards Arabia as Egypt. In this part of the wilderneſs, they were ſeverely ſcorched by the ſun, and had almoſt periſhed for want of water. The hiſtorian makes their next encampment to have been at *Marah*, which afforded them a ſupply of that element; but they could not drink of it, for it's bitter-

* Numb. xxxiii. 8.

neſs; occaſioned, perhaps, by its running through rich beds of nitre, very common in thoſe countries, and giving the water a very offenſive ſmell and taſte. The ſituation of this place cannot be geographically aſcertained; as the name was accidentally given it by the Iſraelites, on account of the circumſtance now mentioned; but is ſuppoſed to have been near that, where Hagar, with her ſon Iſhmael, was in the ſame diſtreſs for water, that they had been before they came to Marah. Like her, they ought to have *wept*, in ſupplications for relief, from him in whoſe hand is the life and breath of man, and that he would quench their thirſt, with a wholeſome and refreſhing ſtream in thoſe ſultry regions. But, inſtead of recurring to an omnipotent and gracious providence, *the people murmured againſt Moſes*, who *cried unto the Lord*; and, though their diſtruſt might have provoked the divine reſentment, his prayers were effectual on the preſſing occaſion. *The Lord ſhewed him a tree, which, when he had caſt into the waters, the waters were made ſweet.*

Here ſome difficulties occur. What this tree was, we are not told. The *Jews* ſay, it was of a bitter taſte, which might be the caſe, to heighten the miracle. Others are of opinion, that it had in it a natural quality to ſweeten the waters; as *Pliny*, in ſome inſtances, ſhews. The firſt inſiſt, that the effect was produced by the power of God alone; and the ſecond think, that the divine interpoſition went no farther, than directing Moſes, immediately, to the tree which could produce it. The ſide muſt now be taken, to which we chuſe to incline. Pliny's teſtimony, in many natural experiments, is acknowledged to have little credit with the learned; and trees, plants and minerals,

minerals, which he might have discovered, possessing the virtue of changing the taste of a small vessel of water, can never be reasonably supposed to have sweetened a stream, at which many thousands quenched their thirst. Nor can the act of *Elisha*, who purified the springs at Jericho, by casting into them a cruise of salt *, be urged on this occasion. Though he used that expedient, at the time specified, it could never have preserved those springs sweet for any long space of time, as we find it did; much less removed barrenness from the soil, and prevented death by it's unhealthfulness, an effect likewise ascribed to this act: And the prophet's command, to *bring a new cruise, and salt therein*, was, evidently, designed to shew the men of the city, that the *cure* was miraculously performed by the power of God, and not by that of the small portion of salt which he then applied. When a divine agency is concerned, the simplest means are sufficient. The *spittle and clay*, which our blessed Lord applied to the eyes of a blind man, could not possibly have a more natural tendency to restore the strength and perfection of the optic nerve, than any other substance of the most indifferent kind. The waters of *Marah* were, therefore, sweetened by that power alone which commands all nature; and sometimes pursues methods, for his own purposes, which appear to us the most unfit and repugnant.

THE first covenant which God made with his people, after he had redeemed them from the power of their enemies, was at this place. Such a sensible miracle performed in their sight, added to that of their passage through the Red-sea, was an evident proof of

* ii Kings ii. 21.

the Almighty's care and protection; and an engagement, on the part of the Israelites, to fidelity and obedience. Here it is, accordingly, said, God *proved them*, or tried the ingenuity and sincerity of their hearts; and required by *a statute and an ordinance*, that, in remembrance of what he had done, they should *diligently hearken to the voice of the Lord their God, and do that which was right in his sight, and keep his commandments.*

Some commentators* are of opinion, that, for their more regular government, God now gave that people a few rules to be observed for the present, till he should more fully declare his will to them from Mount Sinai. The Jews, depending upon a very ancient tradition, reduce them to two in number; of which a certain Rabbi gives this account: It appears, says he, from the scripture, and quotes Jeremiah †, and from the Cabbala also, that the first precept which God gave us, after we came out of Egypt, was not concerning burnt-offerings and sacrifices; but it was that given us at Marah, *If thou wilt diligently hearken to the voice of the Lord thy God*; where he gave us a statute and a judgment. And it is a certain tradition, that *the statute* was the Sabbath; and *the judgement* was the taking away all iniquity ‡. That is to say, to do justice;

* Bp. Patrick, in loco. † Jeremiah v. 12. v. 19. ‡ Constat ex scriptura & ex cabbala simul, quod principium præceptorum nobis datorum non sint verba de Holocaustis & Sacrificiis. Nec enim opus est, ut ullo modo defatiges intellectum tuum in Paschate Ægypti; illa autem, de quibus hic agitur, fuerunt præcepta post exitum ex Ægypto. Primum nunc præceptum, quod post exitum datum est, fuit illud, quod in Mara accepimus. *Ibi*

justice; and, especially, as some explain it, to honour parents.

From Marah the Israelites marched to *Elim*, *where were twelve wells of water; and threescore and ten palm-trees, and they encamped there by the waters.* This movement, made by the direction of a kind providence, or by mere human wisdom, together with the circumstances of the place where they now pitched their tents, several of the Jews have represented and applied very fancifully. They have said, that the twelve wells of water were designed to correspond to the number of the twelve tribes; the seventy palm-trees to that of the elders of Israel; that each tribe, accordingly, pitched their tents round one of those fountains; and the seventy elders sat under the shadow of the trees; and that a marvellous strange bird, as big as an eagle, of various colours, and a most sweet voice, appeared to them on this occasion *. But this is all the work of the imagination; and there is, probably, an error in the computation of time: For there is little reason to think, that the high court of the elders was yet constituted; and, besides, a celebrated critic is of opinion, that the Hebrew text may be read, *the children of Israel came to the forests* †. The name, which signifies *Rams*, intimates that there was good

Ibi posuit ei Statutum & Judicium. Statutum itaque, cujus ibi mentio fit, est *Sabbathum*; *Praeceptum* vero, sunt *judicia*, sublatio nempe omnis iniquitatis. Volo dicere, fides opinionum verarum, ut novitatis mundi, &c. Deinde praeter fidem hanc opinionum verarum; sublatio iniquitatis inter homines. Maimon. More. Nevoch. par. iii. cap. xxxii. p. 436.

* Hierus. Targ. Paraph. Jonath. Ezek. Trag. † Bocharti Hieroz. pars. i. lib. ii. cap. xviii.

pasture there; and likewise plenty of water, which nourished and moistened the grass.

Those, again, who are fond of allegory, will find in the writings of the fathers the fullest satisfaction on this, and similar passages of the scriptures. Some of them alledge, that the wood which sweetened the waters at Marah was an emblem of the cross of Christ, which sweetens the bitter ingredients of human life; that the twelve fountains of water at Elim were figures of his apostles; and that the threescore and ten palm-trees represented the seventy disciples, who were sent out to preach the gospel among the *Jews* *. After this sort, have men of false taste, in all ages, wrested the plainest passages of the word of God, to serve purposes which were never intended. For their use this work is not calculated.

After their departure from Elim, there is a defect here in the history; which may, however, be supplied from a passage in the book of Numbers †, where we are told, that *the children of Israel removed from Elim, and encamped by the red-sea*; that is, near an arm, or bay of it; where it shot eastward, and fell in on the land, whither their course was directed. The reason why Moses omits this station may be, that nothing remarkable happened at it. Some have thought they now went backwards, as they came to the Red-sea again; but this was by no means the case: Though, it must be confessed, they might have gone a nearer way to Horeb, than by turning so far to the south: And yet some important purposes may

* Tert. adver. Judæos, cap. xiii. † Numb. xxxiii, 10.

have

have been ſerved by this meaſure: Another ſight, particularly of the Red-ſea, might impreſs on their minds a deeper ſenſe of their late wonderful deliverance. Several things might be inſerted here from the Rabbins, but they are no farther uſed in this work, than they illuſtrate the ſcriptures: And *Talmudical* fables are utterly rejected.

FROM this ſtation, wherever it was, *the* whole *congregation of the children of Iſrael came, on the fifteenth day of the ſecond month, after their departing out of the land of Egypt, unto the wilderneſs of Sin.* Conſequently, at the laſt place they did not ſtay long. This wilderneſs is not to be confounded with that, where *Miriam*, the propheteſs, died. *In both the Engliſh and Hebrew Bibles* *, *the ſpelling is different.* The latter appears, moreover, to have been near *Kadeſh* †, and not far from the *Salt Sea* ‡, or the *dead-ſea*, by ſome authors called the *aſphaltite lake.*

THE ingratitude and diſtruſt of the Iſraelites returned at this place, as ſoon as they were expoſed to a new trial. Seeing the proviſions, which they had carried with them out of their captivity, almoſt conſumed, they regretted their departure from Egypt, as if it had been the moſt indulgent and delightful country to them. Though led immediately by the hand of the almighty, and many a time reſcued and refreſhed in a ſupernatural manner, that rebellious people then wiſhed, that they had ſpent the remainder of their life under Pharaoh's oppreſſive *Iron* Sceptre. *Would to God*, ſaid they, *we had died by the hand of the Lord*

* Exod. xvi, 1, thus צן. Numb. xx, 1, סין † Numb. xx, 1.
‡ Numb. xxxiv, 3.

in the land of Egypt, when we sat by the flesh-pots, and did eat bread to the full: For ye, meaning Moses and Aaron, *have brought us forth to this wilderness, to kill this whole assembly with hunger.* There might be a few pious men among them, but they could scarcely be discerned amidst the multitude, who magnified their former condition, that their present might appear the more miserable; though there was no danger of their perishing instantly when they had large flocks of cattle to feed them.

To excite their thankfulness once more, by removing this calamity, the Lord promised, not only to satisfy their wants, but their lusts also, at least for a certain time; and to furnish them constantly afterwards with what might be necessary for their support. Thus *will I prove this people, whether they will walk in my law, or no.* Moses and Aaron, the messengers of the divine will, accordingly informed them, that they should immediately see the Lord, or the bright cloud, which, it is probable, had removed to a greater distance from them than usual, because of their murmurings; but was now to approach their camp, and about to break forth in a glorious manner; and that in the very *evening of the same day, they should have flesh to eat, and in the morning, bread to the full.*

While Aaron was yet speaking, *the whole congregation of the children of Israel looked toward the wilderness, and behold, the glory of the Lord appeared in the cloud;* and from thence was repeated to Moses, what he had before delivered, perhaps in the audience of all the people; *At even ye shall eat flesh, and in the morning ye shall be filled with bread.*

The

The divine promise was fulfilled: *At even their camp was covered* with creatures, distinguished by a word of an exceedingly difficult and ambiguous signification in the original*. The Septuagint, the Vulgate, and all the modern editors of the scriptures in every language, translate it *quails*; which are birds of game; and were vastly numerous in those parts of the world, as Josephus informs us†. But among all the Jews, he is the only person who has rendered the Hebrew word *quails*. The rest of them either retain the original term, or make it stand for another thing than that kind of fowl. None of their descriptions, however, agree with the account which Moses gives in the book of Numbers ‡, nor with any winged animal that we know, except a kind of *locusts*; very different from those which annoyed Egypt; and with which the Arabic and Persian gulfs abounded §. When we come forward to the passage in that book, where the phenomenon is most minutely represented, this subject may be treated at greater length.

Here it will be said, that, of whatever kind those creatures were, there could be no miracle, as they are confessed to have been so plenty, and as it were peculiar to those regions. But it would be just as fair to alledge, that there was no divine interposition, when the great draught of fishes was taken, by casting the net as *Jesus* commanded, because the sea is their proper element, and contains them in shoals; or when *St. Peter* found a piece of money in the mouth of a fish, because it might have picked it up with it's food.

* Heb. השלו † Josephus, lib. iii. cap. 1. ‡ Numb. xi. 31. § Vide job. Ludolp. Differt. *de locustis*.

For

For in all ſuch caſes, as has been ſaid already, the miracle lies in adapting any thing inſtantaneouſly to the intended purpoſe and exigency.

Besides, though thoſe regions be ſuppoſed to have been the chief reſort of ſuch creatures as the Iſraelites fed on, the production of ſuch an infinite number of them muſt have been truly miraculous. They were not, indeed, ſupplied with them conſtantly, during their ſojourning forty years in the wilderneſs; but in all caſes of neceſſity they were ſent to them; and at *Taberah, the ſix hundred thouſand men of war, and the whole mixt multitude that was among them, lived on them for a month at a time.* And though we read in the ſeventy-eighth pſalm, that when God ſent them to their camp, *he cauſed an eaſt wind to blow in the heavens, and by his power brought in the ſouth-wind, that he might rain fleſh upon them as duſt, and feathered fowls like as the ſand of the ſea*, this is not to be underſtood as a diminution or denial of the miracle, but an eſtabliſhment of it in the moſt triumphant manner: This ſhews us clearly, that the powers of nature were employed in giving the miracle it's full effect, by driving thoſe creatures from their receſſes, and making them fall in the midſt of the camp of Iſrael, and round about their habitations. It is impoſſible to think otherwiſe, if we believe what is recorded in the afore-cited paſſage. When that vaſt army murmured and wept for fleſh, after an interruption in the falling of the *quails*, *Moſes ſaid unto the Lord, ſhall the flocks and the herds be ſlain for them, to ſuffice them. Or ſhall all the fiſh of the ſea be gathered together for them, to ſuffice them?* Then *the Lord, whoſe hand is never ſhortened, brought quails again from*

from the ſea, and let them fall by the camp, as it were a day's journey on this ſide, and as it were a day's journey on the other ſide, round about the camp, and as it were two cubits high upon the face of the earth. But thoſe particulars ſhall all be examined in another place.

We ſhall now proceed to conſider the *Manna*, that miraculous bread which fed the choſen people for full forty years of their pilgrimage, without ever failing them. The following is the account Moſes gives of it: *In the morning the dew lay round about the hoſt. And when the dew that lay was gone up, behold, upon the face of the wilderneſs, there lay a ſmall round thing, as ſmall as the hoar-froſt on the ground. And when the children of Iſrael ſaw it, they ſaid one to another, it is Manna; for they wiſt not what it was.*

From this account two queſtions have been raiſed: The one reſpects the name given to this bread from heaven, and the other it's nature. On the former, the moſt ingenious efforts of criticiſm have been employed *, where there ſeems to be little neceſſity, and with as little ſucceſs. Nothing can be plainer than the words themſelves, and the connection makes their ſenſe, if poſſible, ſtill more obvious. Moſes had promiſed that, in the morning, the Iſraelites ſhould have bread to the full; but from what quarter, or of what quality, he had not informed them. *When the dew that lay round the hoſt was gone up*; that is, partly melted to moiſten the earth, and partly exhaled by the heat of the ſun; they ſaw ſomething entirely new, and, looking at one another, ſaid, *What is this? for they wiſt not what it was*; or were as much at a loſs to know, if this was the proviſion they had expected, as

* Vide Salmas. *de manna*. Critic. Sacr. M. Le Clerc.

how

how to judge of its quality. *And Moses said unto them: This is the bread which the Lord hath given you to eat.* These facts and circumstances appear simple and natural. As for the name, which is made up of two words thus, *Man-hua*, the first Egyptian, and the second Hebrew, it evidently signifies, *What is this*, as by far the greatest part of the learned acknowledge. And by that name, or, as we spell it, *Manna*, the Jews ever afterwards called *this gift* from heaven; as one celebrated critic * hath thought the word likewise signified. And the Rabbins read, *This is the thing which the Lord hath prepared* †. But such interpretations are not warranted by the Hebrew text.

THE *Manna* was in small grains, *like coriander seed, and the colour thereof, like the colour of Bdellium*, a transparent pearl. It fell in the night with the dew, and the Israelites were obliged to gather it early in the morning, before the heat increased. An *omer*, containing between five and six pound weight ‡, or something less than half a peck of our measure §, was the *portion* of each man. When covered from the sun, it appeared hard and solid, *was grond in mills, beat in mortars, baked in pans, and made into cakes; and the taste of it was as the taste of fresh oyl.* The quantity has been thought too great for each man's consumption. But it has been ingeniously observed, that the manna, as described by Moses, being of a globular figure, must needs have many empty spaces between every *three* or *four grains*, and those vacuities may be very reasonably estimated a *third* part of the vessels capacity. Being *a*

* M. Le Clerc in Exod. xvi. 31. † Vide Critic. Sacr. Pol. Synop. Critic. in loco. ‡ M. Saurin, Disc. L. § Bp. Patrick, in loco. Bp. Cumber. Scrip. W. and M.

light

light food, it muſt likewiſe be porous, and of a ſpungy contexture of parts. Beſides, it would be waſted, in dreſſing, by the fire. Conſequently three *quarts*, *the tenth of an Ephah*, might, probably, be reduced to three *pints* of an oily liquid ſubſtance; a quantity no way extraordinary in an hungry deſert. And, if this reaſoning be not concluſive, and we muſt allow that they had too much, we may ſee the deſign of this abundance was to unite them all together, by a proper ſenſe of their mutual wants and neceſſities. When they were ſick, and unable to gather for themſelves, they depended on the health and beneficence of others. St. Paul, evidently, alludes to this very caſe, when he exhorts the Corinthians to charity; *let your abundance be a ſupply for the wants of others, that their abundance alſo may be a ſupply for your want, that there may be equality. As it is written, he that had gathered much, had nothing over; and he that had gathered little, had no lack**. Children would receive from their parents, the weak from the ſtrong, and the robuſt and induſtrious would have the more for their labour, by gathering an *omer* for every perſon in the camp.

THAT the production of this bread was miraculous we can no more doubt, than with reſpect to that of the *quails*. Common manna, by ſome ignorantly confounded with this, every one knows, is a gum, produced from two different trees, but which are of the ſame genus, being both varieties of the *aſh*; and that the fineſt manna of all is that which oozes naturally out of the leaves in *Auguſt* †. But from the na-

* ii. Corinth. viii. 14. 15. † Johnſon. Hill. Ornus: Fraxinus rotundiore folio, et fraxinus humilior minore et tenuiore folio. Lewis.

ture

ture, circumstances and properties of this manna, every particular related of that which fed the Israelites, is different. For instead of exuding from trees, the manna, in the wilderness, fell, immediately after the dew, out of the air, where it had been *prepared*, as some of the Rabbins very properly observe, and in such innumerable globules as were sufficient for the sustenance of that vast multitude which marched to Canaan. Instead of adhering to the fingers in handling it, as common manna does, in its most solid form, this became an hard body, and required the greatest force to break it. Instead of continuing fresh for a great number of years, the property of the other, the manna in the desert soon grew putrid, and a receptacle for worms. Instead of having a physical quality, it had the power of giving nourishment and strength. Instead of being found mature and fit for use, during one or two months of the year *only*, as is said to be the case with common manna, that of which we are now speaking, was fresh, good and plenty every day of the year, except the *seventh* of every week; but on the *sixth* there was a double portion; which is truly another miracle of itself. Hence, without difficulty, we may pronounce the manna given to the Israelites altogether miraculous and supernatural; as it was altogether different from any thing ever known, before or since, in that, or any other part of the world. Indeed so sensible were they of this themselves who saw it, and their posterity after them, that, we are told, they anathematized all who were of a contrary opinion. And, that there might be always in the Jewish republic an authentic monument of this miraculous food, *Moses commanded an omer of manna to be put into a pot, a pot, and laid up before the Lord; that is, before the testimony, to be kept for all generations.*

Thus were the sons of Jacob provided with flesh, by an heavenly direction, and a sky prepared bread, for forty years, in their way to the land of promise. For we read, *when the children of Israel encamped in Gilgal*, at the end of forty years, *and kept the Pass-over on the fourteenth day of the month at even, in the plains of Jericho*; that *they did eat of the old corn of the land on the morrow after the Pass-over, unleavened cakes, and parched corn in the self-same day. And the manna ceased on the morrow after they had eaten of the old corn of the land, neither had the children of Israel manna any more, but they did eat of the fruit of the land of Canaan that year* *. This, however, does not mean that they tasted no flesh of cattle, or bread of corn, during that space of time; for when they offered sacrifices, and celebrated feasts, they partook of certain portions of the beasts and of the cakes which were used; especially at the Pass-over; as we see in several passages of the following books. But all this, in the immediate service and worship of God, was so inconsiderable, as to be but a small part of their constant subsistence. We may, therefore, say that their whole dependence, for meat and drink, was upon a continual miracle which the Almighty performed for them.

Of such a miracle, indeed, we have no similar instance in the history of Providence. That wrought for Elijah is, by no means, equal to it. And yet, if we maturely consider the ends to be answered by this dispensation, our wonder will be lessened; or rather,

* Joshua, v, 10.

considering

confidering the daily courfe of Providence, in other refpects, it may be greatly raifed. For what but inceffant exertions of divine power, wifdom and liberality, afford the protection which every moment we receive, and the gifts, from unfeen fources, which render our lives comfortable and happy, through the wildernefs of this world, to *the reft remaining for the people of God?* Though things are produced by a natural procefs, and we know fome of the laws by which they are perpetually governed, the firft eftablifhment of thofe laws was, neverthelefs, as great a miracle, as if we fhould fee flefh for hourly nourifhment, and *our daily bread*, falling out of the clouds before us. In both cafes, it is equally the operation of the hand that formed us, and *preferves our foul in life**. *God caufeth the grafs to grow for cattle, and herb for the fervice of man; that he may bring forth food out of the ground: And wine that maketh glad the heart of man, and oyl to make his face to fhine, and bread which ftrengtheneth man's heart.* †.

* Pfalm lxvi, 9. † Pfalm civ, 14, 15.

DISSERTA-

DISSERTATION XXXVII.

Of the murmuring for Water at REPHIDIM; war with AMALEK; and the salutation and counsel of JETHRO.

EXODUS, XVII, and XVIII.

MOSES, having fully related what passed at Sin, carries us next to Rephidim, and omits here two encampments which he mentions in the book of Numbers *, the one in Dophkah, and the other in Alush. We cannot but observe, that the historian's design in that book, is very different from what he proposes in this of Exodus. Here, his intention was, briefly, to collect all the great events which fell out to the Israelites in their journey in general; whereas, in the book of Numbers, he hath given a compleat description of their whole course. Hence it is, that in Exodus notice is taken of about *fifteen* of their stations only, and so many as *forty-two* are marked out afterwards.

THE encampment at Rephidim was distinguished by two memorable occurrences. The first was the murmuring of the Israelites for want of water, in the same manner as they had found none in the wilderness of Shur, and the miracle God again wrought to supply this want. He commanded Moses to take the

* Numb. xxxiii, 12, 13.

same

ſame rod with which he had ſmitten the river of Egypt, and turned it into blood, or the Red-ſea as ſome underſtand it, and ſtrike the rock of Horeb, and immediately a freſh and copious ſtream iſſued forth *in the ſight of the elders of Iſrael.* The ſecond was the war with the Amalekites, in which that people was defeated. Of the firſt miracle we ſhall ſay nothing more in this place, having every where preſented to us the murmurings of the Jewiſh people, and God's mercies to them; and ſhall have alike inſtance to examine in the book of Numbers, when both together may be conſidered more ſucceſsfully in conjunction, than taken ſeparately. To the ſecond, therefore, we ſhall immediately proceed.

If we had an exact ancient map of that part of the wilderneſs which is called Rephidim, and had better information of the territories of Amalek, reflections on this paſſage of the ſacred hiſtory might be more particular and ſatisfactory. But ſo far from being able to give perfect memoirs on this occaſion, we do not ſo much as know, whether Amalek was only ſome eminent *perſon*, like the head of a numerous tribe, or houſhold; or a kingdom conſiderably extenſive and powerful, containing many petty princes, and their dependants, under one great and ſovereign head. We are inclined to think the boundaries, under that name, were not narrow, nor the people within them unwarlike, or few. See what interpreters have collected, and is moſt generally received among them, on this ſubject.

In the book of Geneſis we find an Amalek, the ſon of Eliphaz, and of a concubine called Timna, the

the grand-son of Edom, or Esau *. We may, therefore, with the greatest reason, suppose, that he was the chief, and founder of the kingdom of the Amalekites. It is true, we hear of this name as early as the days of Abraham, long before Eliphaz himself was born †. But it is no uncommon thing in holy writ, to give names to places by which they were known only in future periods.

The country of the Amalekites was, between the southern frontiers of Idumea, and the coasts of the Red-sea. They have sometimes been called Phenicians, because they lay on the borders of their country, to the west or north-west of Arabia Petræa. This was the first people the Israelites found on their journey. As they were descended from Esau, they might possibly retain some of the hatred which he had borne toward his brother Jacob, and have the same aversion to the Israelites that the Idumeans had, from whom we must distinguish them. The Jewish doctors were of this opinion: *When*, say they, *our people had passed the Red-sea, they were attacked by wicked Amalek, who hated them, because of the birth-right which Jacob had taken from Esau* ‡.

To stop the Israelites in their march, was the design which the Amalekites had formed. Having watched their route, and suffered the advanced guard to pass them, they fell upon *the hindmost of* them, *and smote all that were feeble*, and *faint and weary* §. This partial attack soon brought on a general engagement. And as the Amalekites, by opposing the Jewish peo-

* Genesis, xxxvi, 10, 11, 12. † Genesis, xiv, 7. ‡ Targ. Hierosol. in Cant. Canticor. II, 15. § Deut. xxv, 17, 18.

ple, opposed God himself who was their leader, they very soon experienced the truth of what, perhaps, had been before written *, *who hath hardened himself against him, and prospered?* They came against Israel with a formidable army; the rabbins say † provided with enchantments, and employed against Moses the same art which they thought that legislator had so successfully used in Egypt, and might make him triumph again in the fields of Rephidim. But *there is no enchantment against Jacob, neither is there any divination against Israel: According to this time*, as on all other occasions, *it shall be said of Jacob, and of Israel, what hath God wrought* ‡!

Against this enemy Moses employed two things, action and prayer. The direction of the war he committed to Joshua the son of Nun, whose future victories were so great, that they acquired for him the name, which signifies *deliverer*. He took on himself the duty of prayer, with two other men whom he engaged in the pious office. One of them was Aaron his brother, and the other Hur, whose genealogy the history has omitted. The common opinion is, that he was the son of Caleb, husband of Miriam the sister of Aaron and Moses, father of Uri, and grandfather of the famous Bezaleel, of whom we read in the first book of Chronicles §. But some interpreters, who have admitted that the Hur of whom we are now speaking, might be the husband of Miriam, have yet doubted if he was the Hur mentioned in the last named book, for reasons which it is of no importance to relate. It is most certain, that he was a person of

* Job, ix, 4. † Jarchi in Exod. xvii, 8, 2. ‡ Numb. xxiii, 23. § 1 Chron. II, 19, 20.

great

great eminence for wiſdom and piety, as Moſes made him his companion at this time, and afterwards left him with Aaron to judge the people, when he himſelf went up to Mount Sinai to receive laws from God *.

THOUGH it was indiſpenſible in Moſes to join the maxims of human policy with religious duties, as it is from the union of theſe two things alone that we can promiſe ourſelves ſucceſs in our undertakings, God, however, ſo ordered it on this occaſion, that the event of the battle ſhould depend upon his prayers, and not on his prudence or authority. From the top of the hill, where he was with thoſe two holy men, he could ſee the order of the army, the proweſs and ſkill of the commanders, and inſtruct them, by ſignals, where to charge with the greateſt proſpect of advantage. On the other hand, the people could ſee Moſes, and animated by that marvellous rod which he held in his hand, and which had already wrought ſuch great wonders, they would fight with intrepidity, and promiſe themſelves an infallible victory.

BUT however powerful the efforts of Iſrael were, they prevailed only ſo long as Moſes held up his hands to heaven; when they were let down, Amalek turned the battle. The conflict continuing, and *the fleſh weak when the ſpirit was* very *willing*, *Aaron and Hur*, therefore, to aſſiſt infirmities, *ſtayed up his hands*, and kept them *ſteady until the going down of the ſun:* When, by this concurrence of prayer and de-

* Exod. xxiv, 14.

 pendence

pendence, of faith and action, Israel conquered, and Amalek was put to flight.

Instructive lesson to all mankind! Example worthy of imitation! To pray with effect, we must pray with perseverance. Sometimes, indeed, God prevents our requests, agreeable to his own promise; *before my people call, I will answer, and whiles they are yet speaking, I will hear* *. But sometimes, also, he hides himself, to increase the value of his favours, and proportion them to our capacity, who are too apt to despise what we acquire with ease, and esteem nothing, as we ought, till it has cost us much pain. But how difficult is it to keep the mind, for a long time, so stretched and intent as prayer requires! The hands of Moses were supported by Hur and Aaron! Nor is the soul of man without it's supports when devotion is ready to languish. Sometimes the hope of obtaining; sometimes the fear of losing; now the expectation of renewed grace; then gratitude for favours already received; these passions and affections, alternately rising, excite and animate the believer, and keep him from being *weary or faint in his mind.*

Such reflections as these seem to be more just, as well as more useful, than those which many of the mystics have deduced, from this example of the man of God. They have enquired in what position he held his hands, whether joined, or cross-wise, and been very positive in their applications of this sort †. And a certain Jew hath not been more happy in allegorizing this subject. He pretends that God designed to

* Isaiah lxv. 24. † Tertul. cont. marc. lib. iii. cap. xviii. Just. Martyr. cum. Tryp.

signify

signify by this circumstance, that the Amalekites had their inheritance upon the earth, but the Israelites sought theirs in heaven; and that as heaven is superior to the earth, the Israelites were to be the conquerors of their enemies *.

God commanded Moses to keep a faithful register of the victory which he had now obtained, and to rehearse it to Joshua, who was to be his successor, and enjoin him to *blot out the name of Amalek from under heaven* †. This command was afterwards repeated, and finally executed to the utmost extent, in the reigns of Saul and David ‡. After their time no more mention is made of the Amalekites: If any of them remained, they were mixed, either with the Idumeans, or with other contiguous nations. Thus did *the parable of Balaam, which he took up when he looked on Amalek*, prove an important prediction; *Amalek was the first of the nations, but his latter end shall be that he perish for ever* §.

Nor is the hatred of the Jews against the Amalekites yet extinct. One of their canons declares, that they were commanded to destroy the very traces of that people, and to remember always their wicked and perfidious hostilities, which they had waged, with the utmost malice and force, against Israel ||. And it is elsewhere said, that when the Messiah comes, the seed of Esau, and of Amalek, shall be utterly destroyed by the power of the Jews, which shall highly prevail over them **.

* Philo de vitâ Mosis, lib. i. † Deut. xxv. 19. ‡ 1 Sam. xv. 8. 1 Chron. iv. 43. § Numb. xxiv. 20. || R. Maimon. in Mischna. ** R. Menach. in Exod. xvii. 14.

Moses

Moses built an altar to ſerve as a memorial of this victory. He does not ſay that he offered ſacrifices on it, as *Joſephus* in his third book has advanced. Of altars built, to perpetuate the remembrance of extraordidinary occurrences, we have inſtances in the book of *Joſhua*, and of the firſt and ſecond *Samuel*.

The inſcription on that which Moſes erected, on this occaſion, was Jehovah-niſſi; or the Lord is my banner. Hence it hath been ingeniouſly conjectured, that the heathens gave Bacchus the appellation of *Niſius*; and by ſubſtituting the name *Dio*, for *Jehovah*, they called him *Dioniſius* *; from *Jehovah-niſſi*, the inſcription of which we are now ſpeaking.

The hiſtorian likewiſe informs us that he ſaid, in connection with this inſcription, *Becauſe the Lord hath ſworn that the Lord will have war with Amalek from generation to generation.* Theſe words, thus tranſlated, have no difficulty in them. But they are not agreeable to the original. The reading there, word for word, is, *Becauſe the hand upon the throne of God, war of God againſt Amalek from generation to generation.* And more obſcure than the text itſelf is the tranſlation by the Septuagint, *Becauſe God fights with an hidden hand againſt Amalek from age to age.* In the vulgate the words are thus rendered, *Becauſe the hand of the throne of God, and the war of the Lord, ſhall be againſt Amalek, from generation to generation.*

Various elucidations of this paſſage of holy writ have been attempted by learned and ingenious men.

* Bocharti Phaleg. lib. i. cap. xviii. Vide Diod. Sicul. in Biblioth. lib. iv. de origine Verbi Dioniſii.

Becauſe

Because JAH, and not JEHOVAH, follows *Kes*, which signifies *throne*, a very celebrated critic * supposes that the two words ought to be joined together; and says they would then express the last day of the month, on which this battle was fought, in the manner following; *This pillar was set up on the last day of the second month, to declare irreconcileable war with Amalek for ever.* But this has been thought too bold a conceit, and solidly confuted †. It is a more plausible conjecture, which is to be found in several authors, that *laying the hand on the throne*, was a form of swearing; as *touching the altar* was among some nations; or, as among ourselves, *laying the hand on the bible*; an outward character of inward sincerity, and of a solemn oath. Whence the poet ‡ says, *Atheists touch the altars boldly without trembling*. There is, however, nothing in scripture to warrant this; and other interpretations appear more eligible.

THE most learned and laborious bishop of *Ely* adopts this reading, *Because the hand of Amalek is against the throne of the Lord*, that is, against God himself, *therefore the Lord will have war with Amalek from generation to generation* §. This, indeed, is perfectly easy and natural, and consistent with the history. Because Amalek had affronted the divine majesty, in coming out and opposing God's design, who, in a visible, and most glorious manner, not unknown to the neighbouring nations, conducted the *Israelites* to the land which he had promised to give them, that king-

* Jos. Scalig. lib. iii. De Emend. Temp. † Theod. Hackspan, in difficil. loc. SS. Scrip. ‡ Intrepidos altaria tangere. Juv. Satyr. xiii. § Patrick in loco.

dom

dom should be prosecuted by the effects of his displeasure, till it was totally destroyed.

ANOTHER learned commentator * hath offered an explanation, differing very little, in regard to the connection and propriety, from the former. Substituting one letter for another, he reads *Nes* instead of *Kes*, and, consequently, translates *ensign* or *banner* in place of *throne*. Then the sense will be this; *Because the hand of Amalek is lifted against the Lord who is my banner*, and to whom I have built an altar with this very inscription, *there shall be war perpetually between Israel and Amalek.*

BUT it is now time to proceed to the salutation and counsel of Jethro. His daughter Moses had married during his sojourning in Midian, and carried with him out of that land, and his two sons by her, when he returned to Egypt: But, perhaps, at her own desire, *he had sent her back* to her father, at what period of time we cannot be certain; though, probably, it might either be, when both of them saw the troubles which were likely to arise in that country; before the Israelites could obtain their freedom; or immediately after his son's circumcision in the inn by the way.

HAVING *heard of all that God had done for Moses, and for Israel his people, Jethro took Zipporah, and Gershom and Eliezer, and came into the wilderness, where he encamped at the mount of God.* This was *Horeb*, called *the mount of God*, from the divine appearances that were on it; and not far from Midian, as *Moses, when he kept the flocks of his father-in-law, led them to that*

* M. Le Clerc. in loco.

mountain.

mountain. And, by messengers, informing the law-giver, that *he was come to him, with his wife, and his two sons*, Moses *went out to meet* Jethro, *and did obeisance, and kissed him; and they asked each other of their welfare: And they came into the tent.*

THEIR future discourse accurately examined, and some other circumstances considered, may assist us in ascertaining a point, about which commentators have been strangely divided. It has been a subject of debate, at what time Jethro came from Midian, with his family; whether immediately after the war with Amalek, or some time after, when the affairs of the Israelites were better regulated. Two great men *, and many others, have been of opinion, that this visit was after the giving of the law on Sinai; though they are far from being agreed about the precise period, if it was near the end of the *first* year, or some time in the *second*. And another very learned man says, that the account is no other way to be received, than of a thing that happened after the promulgation of the decalogue †.

Now, can one reasonably suppose, that Jethro would not take the first opportunity to visit Moses, and to bring him and his nearest relations together, after he had heard of the departure from Egypt, and the passage through the Red-sea; the news of which could not but have reached him, who was a borderer upon this wilderness? What else could induce Moses to insert the circumstances of the visit, which was certainly made at one time or another, in this part of his

* Usserius A. M. 2514. Dr. Lightfoot in loco. † Seld. lib. ii. de Syned.

general

general hiſtory, if that viſit was not made in the order of time in which he relates it? Joſephus cloſely follows him, without diſcovering the leaſt doubt about the chronology. And what are the inſuperable objections againſt our believing, that the event really happened at the ſeaſon which ſeems here to be clearly fixed?.

It has been argued, that this piece of ſacred hiſtory ought to be inſerted after the tenth verſe of the tenth chapter of *Numbers*, becauſe, at the twenty ninth verſe, we read, after a deſcription of the march from Sinai, that Moſes requeſted *Hobab, the ſon of Raguel* * *the Midianite, Moſes' father-in-law*, to accompany the choſen people through the wilderneſs, to the promiſed land: And this march began *on the twentieth day of the ſecond month, in the ſecond year*. And Moſes, moreover, in the firſt chapter of *Deuteronomy*, where he recapitulates paſt tranſactions, declares his appointment of the judges, whom Jethro adviſed him to conſtitute, to have been after the Lord had ordered them to depart from *Horeb*.

But all this certainly will have little weight, when we conſider, that *Hobab* might viſit Moſes, at a place ſo near his own reſidence, ſeveral times after his father had returned home. And though we are informed, that Moſes did follow Jethro's counſel, in regard to thoſe judges, we are not told at what time he appointed them. It is by no means probable that he could do it, in the ſhort ſpace which intervened, between the

* Some have thought, that the prieſt of Midian had three names, *Reuel, Jethro*, and *Raguel*: But it is more probable, that *Reuel* was the father of *Jethro*, who was alſo called *Raguel*.

time

time when that counsel was given, and the publication of the law. What is alledged from the sixteenth verse of this chapter, where Moses acquaints his father-in-law, that he made the people, who came to him for justice in any matter, *know the statutes of God and his laws*; cannot deserve our regard, however seriously urged; as referring to the *statutes* and *laws* at Sinai; where we may be assured, if human prudence had not already pointed out the method, the Almighty would have given his servant proper directions about the administration of public justice, in the same manner as about every thing else. The *statutes* and *laws*, therefore, mentioned in this place, we may presume, were nothing more than wise decisions by Moses, agreeable to *natural* justice, and, consequently, to the will and law of God.

In short, whoever considers the material parts of the conversation, between Moses and Jethro, with attention, must be of opinion, that the interview was in the order of time, as it is here set down. For, at this meeting, Moses only relates what God had done to *Pharaoh*, and to the *Egyptians*; how the Lord had *delivered them*; and *all the travel that came upon them by the way*: Which comprehends the plagues of Egypt, the passage through the Red-Sea, the scarcity of water and bread, and the battle with Amalek: Or all that had yet befallen the Israelites; and of which we read in the foregoing chapters. But if it had been subsequent to the publication of the covenant at *Sinai*, is it not very probable, nay absolutely certain, that he would have spoken of the most remarkable circumstances of all, God's glorious appearance to them on that

that *mount*, and the law, in it's vast extent, including all the parts of it, which he had delivered to them?

JETHRO *rejoiced for all the goodness which the Lord had done to Israel*; and, *blessing the Lord*, confessed that he was *greater than all God's*. Being a priest, he also *took a burnt-offering, and sacrifices, for God*; that is, to be offered to God; and having wholly consumed the former on the altar, no body ever partaking of it, *Aaron, and all the elders of Israel, came to eat bread with Moses father-in-law before God*: In the most solemn manner, they feasted on the *peace-offerings* which had been presented, of which all the worshippers at the *sacrifice* had, usually, their share *.

EITHER observing, or being informed, what insupportable pains Moses took in *judging the people*, this sagacious man, with the greatest modesty, gave him the most salutary *counsel*, and assured him, that it would receive the divine approbation, by the good success that should attend it. The wise institutions which he here recommends, are so plain in themselves, that we need not at present enlarge on them; especially as they will occur again, in places where the administration of *civil* justice, among the Jews, will require to be more minutely considered.

And Moses let his father-in-law depart; and he went his way into his own land.

* See Dissertation xxxiv. page 450.

DISSERTA-

DISSERTATION. XXXVIII.

Of the encampment at SINAI; and the SANCTIFICATION of the Israelites, previous to the giving of the LAW.

EXODUS, XIX.

THE Israelites, immediately upon their murmuring for want of water, had moved from *Rephidim*, toward that part of the wilderness where *Horeb* stood; and yet seem to have returned thither again to fight with *Amalek*; and, afterward, to have been led, by the glorious cloud, to the other side of the mountain, which is called *Sinai*, where that bright appearance, the emblem of the divine majesty, rested.

THIS was *on the first day of the third month*, after *the children of Israel were gone forth out of the land of Egypt*; or forty-five days. Five more were spent in receiving messages, and preparing themselves *to meet with God*, before the Law was delivered. The Jews, therefore, ever since, observe *Pentecost*, as a memorial of that dispensation, *fifty days* after their Pass-over. Here, then, is a rule by which we may judge of the length of the months, mentioned in the writings of Moses. For, on the fifteenth day of March the Israelites departed from Egypt, and on the first day of the third month they came into *the wilderness of Sinai*; which makes it manifest, that their calculation of time almost corresponded with our own.

IN

In relation to Palæſtine this deſert lay eaſtward, and was denominated from a chain of mountains which interſected it. St. Paul plainly tells us, that *Sinai is a mountain in Arabia* *, whereof Horeb was one top, and a third conical rock, on one of the ſides of it, another. The two former are now called, by the people of that country, Tur; and the latter, by modern geographers and travellers, St. Catherines †, where ſtands a building, poſſeſſed by Chriſtian monks, for devotion, and the reception of Pilgrims.

On Sinai, Moſes was ſeveral times with God, who, *the firſt day*, commanded him to remind the Iſraelites of the favours which they had received from him, and of the great wonders which he had done in their behalf. He commanded him, likewiſe, to urge thoſe miracles of grace and power, as motives of ſubmiſſion to his laws; and, moreover, to inform them, that this obedience was the condition of his Almighty protection and guidance in future, and of the continuance and increaſe of their felicity.

That Moſes might have the moſt ſtriking apprehenſions, of the importance and juſtice of the covenant about to be propoſed, the preſent ſituation was choſen by divine wiſdom. He was now ſtanding on a very lofty mountain, from whence he might view the courſe by which the Almighty had brought them out of Egypt, after many ſigns and wonders; the Red-ſea, through which he had led them, by an unknown path; the deſert, where he had ſuſtained them, by a conſtant miracle; and the way to the land of promiſe,

* Galat. iv, 25. † Thevenot, *Voyage du Levant*. Dr. Shaw's Travels, &c.

the

the object of their desire and hope, into which he engaged to conduct them, *by a strong hand, and an outstretched arm.* The words, at the fourth verse, with which Moses was to begin the solemn transaction with the people, are full of significance and sublimity: *Ye have seen*, said he, from the mouth of God, *ye have seen what I did unto the Egyptians, and how I bare you on Eagles wings, and brought you unto myself. Now, therefore, if ye will obey my voice indeed, and keep my covenant, then ye shall be a peculiar treasure unto me above all people; though all the earth be mine. And ye shall be unto me a kingdom of priests, and an holy nation.*

THIS allusion to the strength, and wonderful affection, of that fowl to its young *, *I have carried you as on eagles wings*, is descriptive of the kind and safe protection which God had given to his people: In the same manner, *my peculiar treasure*, signifies, that they were as dear to the Almighty as things which are preserved with the greatest vigilance and care: And, finally, the promise, that they should be *unto* him *a kingdom of priests and an holy nation*, was calculated to excite in the Jews an exalted idea of the privileges which they should enjoy. For royalty, with which priests were antiently invested, implied, not only exemption from servitude, but also power; and, in all probability, there is a reference here to the custom established in Egypt, from whence the Israelites had immediately come; where the rights of the priests were permanent and inviolable, by a common law of the state, passed in the time of the famine, when Joseph pur-

* Vide, Bocharti Hieroz. p. 11, lib. 11, cap. v.

chased

chaſed lands from all the reſt of the Egyptians, and left the ſacred inheritances untouched*.

THEIR obedience, as has been ſaid, was the term of this favour; and, notwithſtanding their rebellions, and the calumnies of an enemy, equally bitter againſt Judaiſm and Chriſtianity †, a father of the church ‡ has proved, that this favour was, moſt effectually and extenſively, ſhewn to the Jewiſh people, in the ſalutary and profitable laws given to them; by which they were early taught to know the true God, to believe the immortality of the ſoul, and the rewards and puniſhments in the life to come, and to contemn *divination*, with which mankind had been univerſally abuſed; together with a great many other things of the utmoſt importance.

MOSES *now* deſcended from the mountain, and, having aſſembled the chiefs of families, and the elders of the people, or the principal men among them, diſcloſed his meſſage; when, as of one man, the voice was unanimous; *All that the Lord hath ſpoken*, WE WILL DO. Thus was Moſes plainly, as St. Paul teaches us, *the Mediator* §, in this covenant.

THE *next day* he went up again to the mount, and, after reporting this anſwer of the people, received aſſurances, that the divinity of his miſſion ſhould be eſtabliſhed, among that very people who had the beſt opportunities of examining it. And herein lies the diſtinguiſhing difference between true prophets, and others who have impoſed their pretences on vulgar

* M. Saurin, Diſc. LII. † Celſus Philoſophus, Epicuri Sectæ, in Lib. cont. Chriſt. ‡ Origen. § Galat. iii, 19

belief.

belief. Impostors, founding new religions in the world, have, for the most part, affected converse with some deity; and, to conciliate respect to the laws they delivered, declared that they received them from heaven itself. In this manner acted Zoroaster, Lycurgus, Numa Pompilius, and Seleucus *; Mahomet also, and several others. And the legislation of Moses, in modern times, being treated with no higher respect, by undiscerning infidels; the very people who were, at first, to submit themselves to it, might have suspected its authority, after the knowledge they had of imposture in those early ages, if its blessed author had not provided some *criterions*, by which it might appear to come undeniably from himself. The Lord, therefore, told Moses, that a voice should be directed to him with such distinct words, and in the presence and hearing of so great a multitude, that not one of them should ever have room to doubt, that he was appointed by him to be his messenger to them. *A thick cloud*, it was likewise declared, should be the vehicle of the divine Majesty, that the people should not see the God of Israel, but might *hear when* he *spake with* Moses, *and believe* him *for ever.* This method was, accordingly, so efficacious, in all succeeding ages, to convince them of their prophet's integrity, that, in the very last periods of their constitution, we find the Jews acknowledging that they *knew God spake by Moses* †. And, on many occasions, voices from heaven were addressed to our blessed Saviour, for the same purpose, that his mission, in every other respect superior to that of Moses, might not be behind it in this very important circumstance ‡.

* Plutarch, in eorum vitis. † St. John, ix, 29. ‡ St. Matthew, iii, 17, xvii, 5. St. John, xii, 28, &c.

PREVIOUS to the grand design, *The Lord said unto Moses, the third* time he had been with him *, *Go unto the people, and sanctify them to-day and to-morrow, and let them wash their clothes, and be ready against the third day: For the third day the Lord will come down in the sight of all the people, upon Mount Sinai.* This descent was to be from heaven, in a darker cloud than that which had hitherto conducted them, and from which some rays of a glorious majesty that was in it, were to break forth upon them, to strike them with greater awe. To prepare themselves for this appearance, the whole assembly was required to observe, with the greatest exactness, certain rites of abstinence and purification, that they might behold, without profanation, the august symbols of Jehovah's presence among them.

THE ceremonies ordained and practised, on this occasion, passed into standing laws among both the Jews and Gentiles, and were religiously observed by them ever after, when they were about to approach any divinity †. Washing clothes, cleansing the body carefully with water, fasting and devotion, and refraining from the most lawful things, when they might pollute or distract the mind, are acts of which history furnishes us with the longest train of examples.

MOSES was, likewise, commanded to place barriers round the sacred mount, the very extremities of which no man was to approach, that they might have a juster reverence for God. Transgression here was to be expiated by death. *Whosoever toucheth the Mount, whe-*

* See verse 9. † Maimon. Mor. Nevoch. P. iii, Cap. xxxiii, Seld. de Syn. L. I.

ther

ther it be beast or man, he shall surely be stoned or shot through with a dart, he shall not live. The signal for leaving their camp, and coming to the foot of the mount, where they might more plainly hear the voice of God, was to be the protracted, or drawn-out sound of the trumpet, which would be less terrible, than when the blasts were shorter and broken. *And Moses came down from the Mount unto the people*; and made them ready, agreeable to these instructions, against the third day.

DISSERTATION XXXIX.

Of the giving of the LAW on SINAI.

EXODUS, XIX, and XX.

NOW the important day was come, and which is rendered for ever memorable, by the most pompous and terrible sights and sounds that ever affected the senses of mortals. God was exalted as on his throne, and had *thousands and thousands of angels* *, to be the ready ministers of his grace or vengeance, about him. *The earth shook, the heavens also dropped at the presence of God, Sinai was moved at the presence of the God of Israel* †. Fear penetrated all the powers of a vast army; and Moses himself, who had been well accustomed to divine appearances, lost his fortitude, at the descent and summons of the divine Majesty.

BUT the circumstances of the *apparatus*, which accompanied the promulgation of the LAW, demand the minutest examination. *On the third day*, in the morning, after the command had been given to sanctify the people, *there were thunders and lightnings*,

* Psalm lxviii, 17. † Psalm lxviii, 8.

and

and a thick cloud; from which *flaming fire* presently burst, so that the mountain could not be seen *; *and the voice of a trumpet exceeding loud*; or the heavenly ministers, who were attendants upon the *Schechinah*, made a sound like that of a trumpet, beyond what the force of human breath could produce. All these were tokens that God was approaching; irresistible incitements of the people's attention; and called them, authoritatively, to come and appear before him, and receive his commandments. Accordingly, when their *trembling* was abated, by the remission, we may suppose, of the tremendous sound, *Moses brought forth the people out of the camp, and they stood at the nether part of the mount*; that is, near the foot of it, but at a respectful distance, as they had been strictly enjoined.

NOTHING could be seen on Sinai but *smoke*, mixed with flame, resembling *a furnace, which burnt unto the midst of heaven* †, or above all the lower regions of the air. But though *smoke and fire*, arising from gross materials, be, for the most part, inseparable, yet their concomitancy here is to be no otherwise understood, than that such appearances then affected the eyes of the Israelites. For, what is called *smoke* was, no doubt, the *thick cloud*, in which it appears, at the ninth and sixteenth verses, the *Schechinah* descended, and was entirely concealed; and the shining *host of angels*, was the appearance which they saw of *fire*, to which they are compared in the psalms ‡. And Moses himself expounds it in this manner; *He came with thousands of his holy ones, and from his hand went a fiery law for them* §.

* See verse 18. † Deut. iv. ii. ‡ Psalm civ. 4.
§ Deut. xxxii. 2.

UNDER

UNDER this *exceeding weight* of awful *glory*, *the whole mount quaked greatly*. The Almighty *looked on the earth, and it trembled**. *And when the voice of the trumpet founded long, and waxed louder and louder*; by fudden blafts, tranfcending thofe that went before; not only *the people trembled*, but now it grew fo very terrible, that *Mofes* himfelf *fpake*, and faid, *I exceedingly fear and quake †*.

GOD then *anfwered him by a voice*; probably, by the voice of the trumpet, which might be made articulate, with the organs of fpeech, by the divine power; and bidding him not to be afraid, but prepare himfelf to came up to *Sinai*, when he received notice. *And the Lord came down upon the mount*: It was faid before that *he defcended on it*: The meaning, therefore, in this place, muft be, that the *Schechinah* now fettled *on the top of the mount*, or the higheft part of it; that there might be the greateft diftance between him and the people, who ftood at the foot of it, when he fpake to them. *Mofes*, who ftood below, though not fo low as the people, was immediately *called up*, while darknefs, fplendors, thunderings and the trumpet, were in their full ftrength, to the prefence of God; and, confequently, entered into the *fire* and *fmoke*; or, into the *cloud*, and *glittering company* of the heavenly

* Pfalm civ. 32. † Nufquam in vetere teftamento legitur quid fit locutus: Sed Apoftolus ad Hebræos xii. 21. id exprimit, dicens, adeò fuiffe terribile vifum quod appareret, ut mofche diceret, expavefactus fum et tremebundus. *Vel adeo formidabile —— expavefco et contremifco*. Tremell. & Jun. nota in loco. *vifum*, one fenfe fubftituted for another; very common in fcripture. *And all the people* SAW —— *the thunderings*, and *the noife of the trumpet*. Exodus xx. 18.

inhabitants,

inhabitants, with which the mountain was ſurrounded, upon God's appearance there*.

In ſuch circumſtances, and, independant of menaces, the limits of themſelves were ſo venerable, there could not poſſibly be an Iſraelite, one would think, ſo preſumptuous as to paſs the preſcribed bounds. Some of the people, however, when Moſes diſappeared, had either ſhewn ſome inclination to approach nearer, out of curioſity; or God, who knew their thoughts, anticipated their purpoſe. *And the Lord ſaid unto Moſes, go down, and charge the people, leſt they break through unto the Lord to gaze, and many of them periſh. And let the prieſts alſo, which come near unto the Lord, ſanctify themſelves, leſt the Lord break forth upon them.* Though God be infinitely *gracious*, and *fury is not in him* †; though he loves, and *pities* his creatures, *as a father pitieth his children*, yet he requires that they ſhall *fear him* ‡. He *is greatly to be feared in the aſſembly of the ſaints; and to be had in reverence of all them that are about him* §. Who the prieſts were, of whoſe ſanctification nothing was formerly mentioned, has been a matter of diſpute among the learned; As Aaron and his ſons were not yet conſecrated. The moſt probable opinion is, that *they were the prime and moſt honorable perſons in the ſeveral tribes*, who had alſo a ſhare in the adminiſtration under Moſes; and not the firſt born, by any ſpecial right which they had to the office **. They alſo were to be *clean* and *holy*, leſt, otherwiſe, when they *came near* to ſacrifice, the Lord ſhould be offended;

* The ſtory which the Perſians tell of their *Zoroaſter*, is certainly taken from this very paſſage of ſacred writ. Vide Huet. Demon. Evang. † Iſaiah xxvii. 4. ‡ Pſalm ciii. 13. § Pſalm lxxxix. 7. ** Conrad. Pellican.

which

whlch ſuppoſes that they might approach *nearer* than the people.

Moses thought this precaution needleſs, having given *all* a ſolemn charge, and *ſet bounds about the mount*, which he calls *ſanctifying it*. *But the Lord ſaid unto him, Away, get thee down, and thou ſhalt come up, thou, and Aaron with thee: But let not the prieſts and the people break through, to come up unto the Lord, leſt he break forth upon them. So Moſes went down unto the people*, and delivered the meſſage to them, and to the prieſts, as he had been directed; and, with Aaron his brother, returned to the mount, but not to the top of it; where he was before, as will appear in the proper place.

When every thing was ſettled for the great object in view, and during this ſcene of *terrible majeſty*, except the ſound of the trumpet perhaps, a voice, ſo great that all the people, who were amazingly numerous, diſtinctly heard it, came out of the midſt of *the thick darkneſs and the fire* *;——*And God ſpake all theſe words, ſaying*,——

I am the Lord thy God, which have brought thee out of the land of Egypt, out of the houſe of bondage.

I. Thou ſhalt have no other Gods before me.

II. Thou ſhalt not make unto thee any graven image, or any likeneſs of any thing, that is in heaven above, or that is in the earth beneath, or that is in the water under the earth: Thou ſhalt not bow down thy-ſelf

* Compare Exodus xx. 21. with Deuteronomy iv. 12. 33.

ſelf to them, nor ſerve them: For I the Lord thy God am a jealous God, viſiting the iniquity of the father's upon the children unto the third and fourth generation of them that hate me: And ſhewing mercy unto thouſands of them that love me, and keep my commandments.

III. Thou ſhalt not take the name of the Lord thy God in vain: For the Lord will not hold him guiltleſs that taketh his name in vain.

IV. Remember the ſabbath day to keep it holy. Six days ſhalt thou labour, and do all thy work. But the ſeventh-day is the ſabbath of the Lord thy God: In it thou ſhalt not do any work, thou, nor thy ſon, nor thy daughter, thy man-ſervant, nor thy maid-ſervant, nor thy cattle, nor the ſtranger that is within thy gates. For in ſix days the Lord made heaven and earth, the ſea, and all that in them is, and reſted the ſeventh-day: Wherefore the Lord bleſſed the ſabbath-day, and hallowed it.

V. Honour thy father and thy mother: That thy days may be long upon the land which the Lord thy God giveth thee.

VI. Thou ſhalt not kill.

VII. Thou ſhalt not commit adultery.

VIII. Thou ſhalt not ſteal.

IX. Thou ſhalt not bear falſe witneſs againſt thy neighbour.

X. Thou

X. Thou shalt not covet thy neighbour's house, thou shalt not covet thy neighbour's wife, nor his man-servant, nor his maid-servant, nor his ox, nor his ass, nor any thing that is thy neighbours.

The *thunderings, and the lightnings, and the noise of the trumpet, and the smoke of the mountain*, being continued, *the people*, as soon as the law was given, instantly *removed, and stood afar off*: From thence, *they sent the heads of their tribes, and their elders** to Moses, who *came near him*, on the side of the mountain, which was his place, at the time of the foregoing revelation; and intreated him to *speak with* them for the future, and promised to *hear* him; but that God would *not speak with* them any more, *lest* they *died*. By the mouth of those messengers, he answered the people, that their lives were in no danger; that God only intended by this dreadful appearance *to prove* them; that they might have an awful sense of him in their minds, by having continually before them, the glory of his majesty, which had lately so much affected them; and that their only fear might be the offending him, by disobeying his commandments. But, agreeable to their own request, as he reminds them, in the recapitulation of those transactions †, *the Lord*, in great condescension, *heard the voice of your words, which ye spake unto me; and the Lord said unto me, I have heard the voice of the words of the people, which they have spoken unto thee: They have well said all that they have spoken. O that there were such an heart in them, that they would fear me, and keep all my commandments always, that it might be well with them, and with their children for ever! Go say to them, get you into your tents*

* Deuter. v. 23. † Deuter. v. 28. &c.

again.

again. But as for thee, ſtand thou here by me, and I will ſpeak unto thee all the commandments, and the ſtatutes, and the judgments which thou ſhalt teach them, that they may do them in the land which I give them to poſſeſs.—And Moſes drew near unto the thick darkneſs, where God was.—

Many of thoſe *commandments, and ſtatutes, and judgments*, were delivered at this very time, and are recorded in this, and the three following chapters. The reſt, in his legation, were communicated during his *forty days* reſidence on the mount. Before that period commenced, he *came and told the people all the words of the Lord*, which he had then received; *and all the people anſwered with one voice, and ſaid, All the words which the Lord hath ſaid, will we do. And Moſes wrote all the words of the Lord* *: Which come not under our conſideration here.

In this covenant, Moſes was ſtill the *mediator*, or rather repreſented the Almighty; and Aaron, Nadab, and Abihu, his two ſons, and ſeventy of the elders, that is, of the principal men among the *Iſraelites*, perſonated the vaſt aſſembly. Thoſe men were ordered to go up to the mount with Moſes. This contract, therefore, was eſtabliſhed on the ſide of the hill; and all the ceremonies anciently accompanying covenants, were duly obſerved. At the ſolemnization of fœderal engagements, in times of old, monuments of the promiſes were erected; ſacrifices offered; declarations, by this act, virtually made, that the party violating ſubmitted to death; and, laſtly, there were feaſts on the fleſh of the victims †. At Sinai all theſe rites were performed. Moſes *ſet up twelve ſtones*, which

* Exodus, xxiv. 3. 4. † Vide, Tit. Liv. L. 1. cap. xxiv.

repreſented

represented the twelve sons, or tribes, of Jacob; *built an altar*, upon which, those who were appointed for the holy service, devoted *burnt-offerings*, and presented *peace-offerings before the Lord*; *took blood and sprinkled part of it on the altar*, which was instead of the throne of God, *and part of it on the people*, or their representatives; *the book* also, wherein were a few laws, *he sprinkled, and said, Behold, the blood of the covenant, which the Lord hath made with you, concerning all these words*; and concluded the solemnity by *eating and drinking*, on the declivity of the mountain. And, besides these pactional rites, that it might appear, in the most illustrious manner, the Almighty was concerned in the treaty, he vouchsafed a sensible token of his presence. *Aaron, Nadab, Abihu, and the seventy elders, saw*, as well as Moses, *as it were the foot of a throne, composed of Sapphire stones, resembling the body of heaven in it's brightness*; or the wide expanse of blue æther, bespangled with shining stars.

DISSERTATION XL.

REFLECTIONS on the foregoing DISSERTATION.

AFTER what we have now seen, and circumstantially considered, we are, as it were, forced to acknowledge, that the commission, by which Moses acted, was truly and evidently from God; and to declare unbelief, in this matter, to be blindness and infatuation. His first account of the great design, at his arrival in Egypt from Midian, and that he was appointed to be their deliverer and lawgiver, might, perhaps, be suspected by the Israelites, when he made the discovery; and doubtful to this day, without other testimonies than his own word. To convince every one, success itself in the enterprize might not have been sufficient; as this might, possibly, have been the effect of wisdom, power, and perseverance. But all following events in connection with the command and promise at the *burning bush*, concur to confirm our faith: *The plagues* in Egypt; *the passage* through the Red-sea; *the overthrow* of Pharaoh, and his host, the waters of *Marah* made sweet; the *quails*, and the *manna*; and the crystal fountains of *Horeb*, opened with the touch of a rod; all those facts and certainties banish hesitation from the mind. In very few, if in any, of those instances, could collusion with others,

or

or perſonal deceit, be of any avail: The whole relation, manifeſtly, ſuppoſes a power and ſuperintendency beyond the privilege of any created being, uninveſted with a ſpecial miſſion and authority from God. In ſhort, when Moſes is ſaid, *to have done all thoſe wonders in the ſight of Pharaoh, and in the ſight of all Iſrael*, that God himſelf did them by him, is the ſenſe in which all ſuch ſayings are literally to be underſtood.

But let us ſtill add, to all thoſe ſtupendous acts, the giving of the *law* on Sinai. The ſcene is pompous, majeſtic and terrible; exceeds the deſcription and imagination, as far as it exceeds the contrivance and exhibition of mankind; and could only proceed from the eternal ſplendours, and divine magnificence of the Almighty, who is the King of Glory, and the Lord of Hosts. All natural operations are excluded from the *cloud, the lightnings, the thunderings, and the voices*, which covered, and came from the *holy mount*. Moſes was an aſtoniſhed ſpectator, and heard, with *exceeding fear*, God ſpeaking *out of the midſt of the fire*, when he *ſtood between the Lord and the people*. And when he was called up to the mount, to receive the law on *tables*, he was commanded to take with him ſome of the *Nobles*, the great men, and of the beſt quality in Iſrael, that they might be witneſſes of his entering into the place where the divine majeſty appeared; and might alſo have ſome ſight of it themſelves.

Him, that people could not, poſſibly, but regard with awe, as *the ſervant of God*, and honour with the readieſt and moſt grateful obedience, who had been appointed

appointed by JEHOVAH to be their earthly *mediator*, and to conduct them to their *resting-place*. This they, accordingly, did, and their posterity after them, through all the periods of the Jewish church and commonwealth; and wherever *the sons of Jacob* are settled at this day, they, who have had the best opportunities of being convinced of his integrity, declare their belief, in the most public and resolute manner, that Moses was the prophet of God, to their nation. And while the record before us exists, the authenticity of which cannot be questioned, the law, and the circumstances of its delivery at Sinai, will stand in place of a thousand miracles, to prove that he had a divine commission, with considerate men, from one generation to another.

THE simplicity, excellence, and extent together with the reasonableness and utility of the MORAL LAW *in the ten commandments*, it is neither proper nor necessary to set forth here: And this has been, often, diligently done by pious and learned men, for the benefit of the word, and not without success. One thing may be suggested, that the laws of those commandments bind every reasonable creature in the world, as they contain no more, in substance, than what was originally written on the consciences of all men; or delivered to our first parents in conferences with God; and ought to be explained and recommended to christians under the gospel, accompanied with other motives, and *established on better promises, under a better covenant* *.

FORMING a comparison between the two great dispensations represented in the scriptures, we will

* Heb. viii, 6.

find

find it obvious, that when the law was given by God, or by Moſes to the people, the imagination was ſtruck before the underſtanding was enlightened; the eyes and ears of men had terror preſented to them, before their hearts were touched; and effects in their conſcience, followed the moſt dreadful impreſſions made on their whole corporal frame: And, on the contrary, when the goſpel-kingdom was opened, we find, that ſpiritual glory and power, ſo to ſpeak, were diſplayed in the higheſt perfection; the bleſſed meſſenger of it deriving greatneſs and majeſty from the divinity of his own perſon; the purity of his life; the excellence of his precepts and doctrines; the mildneſs of his invitations; the dignity and beneficence of his miracles; and the efficacy of his death; and which are all calculated to work on the minds of men, and improve them, without alarming or engaging the external ſenſes. This difference is the ground of the following noble words, in the twelfth of the Hebrews; *Ye are not come unto the mount that might not be touched, and that burned with fire, nor unto blackneſs and darkneſs, and tempeſt, and the ſound of a trumpet, and the voice of words, which voice they that heard, intreated that the word ſhould not be ſpoken to them any more. But ye are come unto Mount Zion, and unto the city of the living God, the heavenly Jeruſalem, and to an innumerable company of angels, to the general aſſembly and church of the firſt-born which are written in heaven, and to God the judge of all, and to the ſpirits of juſt men made perfect, and to Jeſus the mediator of the new covenant, and to the blood of ſprinkling, that ſpeaketh better things than that of Abel.* That *cried*, for vengeance, *from the ground* *; this *was ſhed for remiſſion*, and *obtained eternal redemption* for us †. And,

* Gen. iv, 10. † Heb. ix, 12.

curſed

cursed is every one that continueth not in all the things which are written in the book of the law to do them. But the righteousness which is of faith speaketh on this wise, If thou shalt confess with thy mouth the Lord Jesus, and shalt believe in thine heart, that God raised him from the dead *, *depart*, accordingly, *from all iniquity* † *and look*, and, by *living soberly, righteously, and godly in this present world*, prepare *for that blessed hope, and the glorious appearing of the great God, and our Saviour Jesus Christ* ‡ *thou shalt be saved.* And may every sinner count *this a faithful saying, and worthy of all acceptation* ||.

Before we conclude, there are certain expressions, both in the old and new testament, which may be reviewed in this place, and adjusted to one another. *The law*, an evangelist says, *was given by Moses, but grace and truth came by Jesus Christ* §. St. Stephen asserts, that *the law was received by the disposition of angels* **. An apostle teaches, that *it was ordained*, delivered and confirmed, *by angels, in the hands of a mediator* ††; and that the gospel was introduced into the world, by the ministry of the son of God: And on this doctrine rests the strength of his argument; *If the word spoken by angels was stedfast, and every transgression and disobedience*, of the law, *received a just recompence of reward; how shall we escape if we neglect so great salvation, which at first began to be spoken by the Lord, and was confirmed unto us by them that heard him* ‡‡.

* Rom. x, 6, 9. † ii Tim. ii, 19. ‡ Titus, ii, 12, 13. || i Tim. i, 15. § St. John, i, 17. ** Acts vii, 53. †† Gal. iii, 19. ‡‡ Heb. ii, 2, 3.

Now in all this, when things are ſettled, and conſidered ſoundly, there is no ſort of difficulty. For Moſes was plainly, as we have ſeen, the mediator and manager of that law which proceeded from Sinai; and in no other ſenſe has any one ever alledged or underſtood, that it was *given by* him. With regard to its promulgation *by the diſpoſition of angels*, we know, that *God ſpake all the words of it*, from the midſt of their hoſt, who were *all miniſtring* to him, at that auguſt ceremony. The law was, likewiſe, *ordained*, perhaps uttered after God, *by angels*; or, by the earthquake, the tempeſt, the lightning, and the thunder, they might render it more venerable; as the plagues that were in Egypt, though God ſent them, are aſcribed to their agency. From this circumſtance, therefore, St. Paul's reaſoning derives its force; that, inſtead of employing angels, or men, ſuch as Moſes and the prophets, who, in a certain ſenſe, were angels alſo, that is, meſſengers, ambaſſadors, or ſervants, as he formerly did, in communicating and propagating his will to mankind, for the purpoſes of truth, righteouſneſs, and piety; God hath now, more *openly* than ever, and literally *face to face*, ſpoken to them, under the goſpel, in the very perſon of his own eternal and ever bleſſed ſon, whom, *whoſoever hath ſeen, hath ſeen the father alſo* *, who hid himſelf, from the people at Sinai, in the cloud and fire on the Mount.

This ſenſe of thoſe text is perfectly conſiſtent with every other paſſage of ſcripture, and with the analogy of faith, and ought to excite in Chriſtians the greateſt care to *honour the ſon, even as they honour the father* †. For, if, after having deſpiſed all his other

* St. John, xiv, 9. † St. John, v, 23.

ſervants

ſervants and meſſengers, we deſpiſe the ſon alſo, what can we expect from the Lord of the vineyard, but his heavieſt wrath, and that our portion ſhall be with unbelievers *?

* St. Matthew, xxi, 33.

END OF THE FIRST VOLUME.

Lightning Source UK Ltd.
Milton Keynes UK
UKHW020602120219
337137UK00005B/802/P

9 780483 845800